Regional Satraps and the Battle for India's Foreign Policy

Regional Satraps and the Battle for India's Foreign Policy

Kalyani Shankar

Vij Books India Pvt Ltd
New Delhi (India)

Indian Council of World Affairs
Sapru House, New Delhi

Published by

Vij Books India Pvt Ltd
(Publishers, Distributors & Importers)
2/19, Ansari Road
Delhi – 110 002
Phones: 91-11-43596460, 91-11-47340674
Fax: 91-11-47340674
e-mail: vijbooks@rediffmail.com
web : www.vijbooks.com

ISBN: 978-93-86457-33-2 (Hardback)

ISBN: 978-93-86457-34-9 (ebook)

Contents

Preface

This book is different from others on India's foreign policy in two ways. First it focuses on the influence and manoeuvrings of the regional satraps on the directions of foreign policy taken by the Union Government. It investigates whether and why the State chieftains are getting more assertive and whether their influence is growing. It also illustrates how India's "Neighbours First" policy clashes with the vote bank policy of the Provincial chieftains. I have tried to project the domestic side of India's foreign policy with particular reference to Sri Lanka, Bangladesh and Nepal.

The second, I have tackled the subject as a journalist and not as an academician. For four decades I have followed and covered the developments in the Provinces mentioned in the book. I have excluded the two big neighbours – China and Pakistan – as they deserve individual treatment.

A number of people have helped in conducting my study and I wish to thank each one of them. I owe my special thanks to External Affairs Minister Sushma Swaraj who found time to give me her perspective. I particularly wish to thank the Indian envoys in Sri Lanka Yash Sinha and Pankaj Saran in Bangladesh and their staff for helping me meet the important leaders. It was fascinating to interact with the Bangladesh leaders like Gen Ershad, Begum Khaleda Zia, Dipu Moni, Gowher Rizvi, Asaduzzaman Noor, Farooq Sobhan, Rehman Sobhan and H.T. Imam who had been players in Bangladesh's foreign policy. The Daily Star editor Mahfuz Anam needs a special mention. Equally fascinating was to interact in Sri Lanka with Sri Lankan Prime Minister Ranil Wickremesinghe, President Chandrika Kumaratunga, Gen. Sarath Fonseka, Gotabhaya Rajapakse, Sampanthan, Karuna, Wigneswaran and other Sri Lankan leaders as well as the insight given by Panruti Ramachandran, Elangovan, Nedumaran and Col. Hariharan from Tamil Nadu. Prof S. D. Muni, NCP leader D.P. Tripathi and the Nepal Prime Minister Prachanda provided an insight on Nepal. I also wish to acknowledge the help rendered by the Assam Chief Minister Tarun Gogoi, Union minister Gen. V.K. Singh, Former ministers Yashwant Sinha, K. Natwar Singh, Saugata Roy, former Speaker of Lok Sabha Somnath Chatterji, former Foreign Secretaries Muchkund Dubey, Shyam Saran, Lalit Mansingh, Kanwal Sibal, Nirupama Rao and Shiv Shankar Menon. My thanks are also due to D.R. Kartikeyan, Jayant Prasad, Shiv Shankar Mukherji and A.S. Bhasin. New York University Prof. Ralph Buultjens has provided valuable inputs. I wish to acknowledge the help rendered by my daughter Shylashri Shankar.

The importance of the book lies in the information obtained from the primary sources. Thanks to the ICWA's support, I had also visited Sri Lanka and Bangladesh and met with the top leadership involved in their foreign policy. The conclusions are based on inputs from all these sources. Almost all the interviews are recorded. Needless to add that the analysis and the conclusions in this book are mine, and cannot be attributed to the ICWA.

The ICWA has given me all the help required in completing this book and my sincere thanks to the Director General Nalin Surie and his predecessor Rajiv Bhatia. Though this is not an academic book in view of the fact that it is based on information from the primary sources, it may be of interest to researchers on the domestic dimensions of India's foreign policy. The analysis in this book pertains to the influence of the regional satraps and the Centre's response till December 2015.

Chapter 1

Introduction

Independent India is a unique State where religious, ethnic and cultural entities are clubbed together by an overarching nationalism and growing economic networks. The glue is indeed the Union Government. Virtually right from the beginning some hostile forces and rival external powers have tried to unglue India by attacking and weakening the Union Government. This was attempted in various ways - by conflict, by diplomacy, by clandestine and other means.

The Central Government has been able to resist all these and defend the States to keep the Union going largely because it had full control and the wherewithal of how to respond to the external challenges. Its grip on the foreign policy was total. The three provisions of the Indian Constitution give the Union Government full powers to conduct foreign affairs. The first is that the Parliament has power to make any law for the whole or any part of the territory of India, for implementing any Treaty, agreement or convention with any country (Art 253). The second is that the Union Government has full executive powers for the implementation of its laws, treaties and agreements (Art 73). The third is to prevent the States from obstructing the administration of laws by the Union Government, the executive powers of the States are to be so exercised as not to impede or prejudice the exercise of the executive power of the Union (Article 257).

The Context

It is time to look back and assess whether there was a national consensus on the government's foreign policy making and also its evolution. Was any attempt made to involve all stake-holders on foreign policy issues? Are the States right in asserting for a bigger role in the making of foreign policy, particularly the Border States with the neighbouring countries in the changing scenario? Has the Centre taken note of the gradual and growing linkage between foreign policy and domestic policy as both impinge on each other? It is indeed a two-way channel, where domestic policies get reflected into foreign policy and in the reverse foreign policy agenda is also used to bolster up domestic policy.

There is no doubt that the State satraps are insisting on a bigger say. Why has it happened? How seriously is it affecting the making of India's foreign policy and constricting freedom of the Union Government? Is it a temporary phenomenon or will it continue in the future? Will the Centre have to continuously negotiate its policy with these States and will the latter have a veto of sorts on Centre's foreign policy? These are the questions that need to be probed.

The Hypothesis

1. **The Centre is likely to take unilateral foreign policy decisions even though at times it affected the States in a negative way when it is strong.** Prime Minister Jawaharlal Nehru was able to steer his foreign policy the way he wanted, just informing the State chieftains after the decisions were taken.

2. **When the interests of the regional satraps and the Centre converge, they are likely to be on the same page.**

   This applies to Tamil Nadu, West Bengal and the North East as well as Bordering States of Nepal. Of course there are variations depending upon the issues and the context. Sometimes the regional satrap supports the Centre and at other times the same leaders oppose it. This was what happened in the case of West Bengal chief minister Mamata Banerjee who supported the Land Boundary Agreement after being persuaded by the Centre but opposes the Teesta treaty till today.

3. **The States are likely to get their way when the Centre is weak.** This has been proved in the past three and more decades, in

the coalition era. This was more so in the last decade when Prime Minister Manmohan Singh had to bow to the wishes of the Dravidian parties on the Sri Lanka policy and West Bengal chief minister Mamata Banerjee on the Teesta treaty.

The study will also go into when the regional satraps are powerful enough to influence the national foreign policy and when they are not. It is clear that there are at least three areas of concern for the State Chieftains. **Most of the disputes with the neighbouring countries have been on water sharing, land and security, which impinge on the States.** Water sharing is a dispute with almost all the neighbours. Security on the border also more or less concerns all Border States and so is land. Immigration from the neighbouring countries also causes problems. The point to note is that while the States may not have direct control over India's foreign policy, three important subjects – water, land and law and order fall under the purview of the States.

I would like to study under what conditions these regional satraps play their role in supporting or opposing the national policy. The study also investigates whether the role of the regional satraps in the making of India's foreign policy has not only increased but also will continue to grow. Political pulls and pressures, demands and influences particularly from the States, which border on the neighbouring countries, constrict the Centre's authority in the making of India's foreign policy over the decades. A look at India's map shows that barring Karnataka, Madhya Pradesh, Chhattisgarh, Jharkhand and Haryana, almost all Indian States have borders with a foreign country or share international waters.

It is also due to the advent of coalition politics in the past three decades since the regional parties had become partners not only at the Centre but also in some States. **The Centre had come under the grip of the powerful regional satraps (most of whom have founded their own parties) playing a consistent role limiting the freedom and flexibility of the Centre in dealing with the neighbours. Will their number increase because of the splintering of the polity, as the national parties are not able to meet the aspirations of the people?**

Will they come together and form a pressure group? The study will also go into these aspects.

It should also be noted that the regional chieftains are strong in their own right because of their electoral strength. The present Modi government has emerged with a single party majority after 30 years but it is too early to predict whether coalition politics has ended. The next elections may again throw up a coalition government. The spectacular performance of the Aam Admi Party (AAP) in the 2015 Delhi Assembly elections proves that even after a stellar performance in the 2014 Lok Sabha polls the Bharatiya Janata Party could be routed. The downslide has continued for the BJP in the 2015 November Bihar elections where it lost miserably to the Janata Dal (United), the Rashtriya Janata Dal (RJD) and the Congress Party combine.

Has the Union Government understood the importance of the growing influence of the Provincial Chieftains while formulating the foreign policy? To a certain extent it has. This was evident in the present National Democratic Alliance (NDA) government taking the West Bengal Chief Minister Mamata Banerjee on board to sign the long pending Land Boundary Agreement (LBA) with Bangladesh in June 2015. This could develop into a new long- term element in the making of the neighbourhood policy of the Centre.

In the Indian federal setup, States play a key role in implementing the economic reforms and social schemes while the Centre makes the broad policies. Since the opening up of the Indian economy in the nineties, many States are vying with each other to attract Foreign Direct Investment (FDI). States benefit from foreign aided projects in socio economic sectors. They can use the money for development of their respective States.

If one looks at India's neighbourhood, two main challenges are clear. One is with its big neighbouring adversaries – Pakistan and China - as both are major countries with nuclear weapons with large standing armies and have had major wars with India. Both support each other and have strong international allies inside and outside the region. In dealing with the Pakistan - China challenges, New Delhi still had complete authority in making and executing foreign policy.

The second is that India's neighbours perceive it as selfish and overbearing. They resent what they perceive as India's 'big brother' or some even call it a 'big bully' attitude towards its smaller neighbours. However, remarkable changes have recently taken place in the second area of concern in the neighbourhood particularly with regard to engagement with countries bordering India- Sri Lanka, Bangladesh, Myanmar, Bhutan, Maldives and Nepal.

Ambassador Satish Chandra, Dean, Centre for National Security and Strategic Centre points out that most of our neighbours suffer from a deep sense of neglect due to the absence of sustained linkages particularly at the political level. Exchange of high level visits between India and its neighbours on a frequent and regular basis related to the entire gamut of national activity would help alleviate this feeling of neglect and also foster closer understanding and cooperation. It would, in addition, minimise misperceptions about India and promotes mutual trust. He suggests that in its exchanges with each of its neighbours India must not hesitate in spelling out its expectations and laying down red lines that should never be crossed in relation to its core interests. In this context, while India could be relatively relaxed about the linkages developed by its neighbours with other regional or extra regional powers it should certainly frown upon such linkages being used against its interest.

Moreover proactive steps need to be taken to resolve at the earliest long-standing political and economic disputes with each of India's neighbours. "Joint management of waters, connectivity, energy grids, easier movement of peoples etc. could all form part of this exercise. India's implementation record in fulfilment of political and economic understandings solemnly undertaken leaves much to be desired. Time bound fulfilment of its promises is essential if India is to command respect."[1]

The Northeast is a particularly a sensitive region of India. These States called 'Seven Sisters' have international borders and have a special significance for India's security, connectivity and prosperity. They have huge stakes on India's relations with the neighbouring

---

1 Satishchandra, 'India's-neighbourhood-policy.'   www.   Vifindia.org/ article/2012/june27

countries. Northeast is also a key element of the India's "Look East" policy, which involves relations with the 10-member Association of Southeast Asian Nations (ASEAN). Indian Prime Minister Narendra Modi is now talking of "Act East" policy, an improvement on the "Look East" policy. An increase in the connectivity between ASEAN, Bangladesh, Myanmar, China and the Northeast has the potential of transforming the region fundamentally.

The Role of Union Government

The Indian Constitution clearly defines the powers to the Centre and the States and also some concurrent powers. Unlike the United States of America all the residuary powers are vested with the Centre and not with the States. Despite all these, they are extremely important and are gradually beginning to take more assertive role. "For example Washington overruled Hudson Harmon's argument absolute sovereignty over natural resources in conceding Mexico's claims for compensation on the Rio Grande and Ottawa has deftly managed Quebec's unceasing efforts to tilt the country towards the Francophone by categorically asserting its right to Treaty making powers," former Foreign Secretary Krishnan Srinivasan points out.[2]

It is pertinent to note that no formal structure exists in India, where the States can interact with the Ministry of External Affairs. Further, they are not allowed to have direct dealings with foreign countries nor are they allowed to establish offices abroad, as is the practice in some countries like Canada and Australia. The States have been involved only at the implementation level. It is the Union Government, which has the powers of Treaty making. Article 253 of the Constitution excludes the States as well as the Parliament from the exercise of Treaty making. The Parliament comes into the picture only in case a law is required for the implementation of a Treaty, while the States are totally excluded.

Border States and Provincial Leaders

In the past three decades regional parties have been increasingly trying to exercise some influence over foreign policy especially with regard

---

2   Krishnan Srinivasan, 'The Centre cannot hold', The Telegraph, Calcutta, India, February 25, 2013.

to India's neighbouring countries. In certain cases, they have even intervened on issues what previously would have been considered the exclusive domain of the Union Government. This is mainly because of the increasing clout of the regional parties and the fracturing of the polity as well as the weakening of the Centre.

In recent times the States as well as Parliament are also becoming assertive claiming some influence in the power of Treaty making. The classic example was how the Left parties, which were national in character supporting the United Progressive Alliance 1 (UPA) coalition, opposed the Indo – US nuclear Treaty in Parliament and outside and even withdrew their support in 2008 when Prime Minister Manmohan Singh went ahead with it. Ironically it was a regional party headed by Mulayam Singh (Samajwadi Party), which came to the rescue of Dr Manmohan Singh in getting the measure passed in Parliament. In the early nineties some States like the Communist-ruled West Bengal opposed the World Trade Organisation (WTO) Treaty when they felt that it impinged on their right as they felt that it affected agriculture. In recent times some States like West Bengal and Tamil Nadu opposed the proposal for Foreign Direct Investment (FDI) in retail sector. In September 2011, at a bilateral summit meeting between the Prime Minister Dr Manmohan Singh and Bangladesh Prime Minister Sheikh Hasina a number of agreements were signed, but the Teesta River water- sharing accord was deferred due to West Bengal Chief Minister Mamata Banerjee backing out at the last minute. However, she came on board later and accompanied the present Prime Minister Narendra Modi when he visited Dhaka in June 2015 to sign the other important Land Boundary Agreement, which was finally endorsed by Indian Parliament after 41 years. These examples are suggestive of how federalism in India is gradually undergoing a change.

The Ascendency of Regionalism

The ascendancy of regionalism in recent years has come about in a natural way. Just as the social map of India is complex its political map is also changing with the growing regionalism. The traditional notion of foreign relations has also changed remarkably over the years. The nature of the diplomatic relations too has undergone changes, as they are no more limited to the earlier concept of national sovereignty, territorial integrity and nationality. Foreign policy included economic and cultural diplomacy apart from the normal diplomatic dialogue. It has now come to include security, social, environment, trade, investment another aspects. That is why the Indian government has started setting up separate wings in the embassies abroad to specifically deal with these issues. Although India is a diverse country with diverse culture many still debate whether it matters when it comes to foreign policy.

Economic Diplomacy

As the globalisation becomes the order of the day the economic diplomacy too has become a major part of India's foreign policy. Now broader issues of international affairs like the foreign trade, foreign aid, external investment, bilateral and multilateral economic negotiations, resolving trade disputes, and technological exchanges have become key ingredients of international economic affairs. Also unprecedented developments in trade and the industrial sector in recent decades have made involvement of the diplomats in the promotion of trade and business in the overseas market.

The economic cooperation in the region has become focused and growing, as most countries have realized the real importance of the economic clout. A shining example is how the United States and China are dealing with each other keeping aside their political and ideological differences. Interestingly, it is on the economic diplomacy that New Delhi has been able to achieve progress even with Pakistan and China.

Former Foreign Secretary Muchkund Dubey observes, "India's neighbours are its best and natural partners in economic cooperation. Geographical proximity, common languages, religion and consumption patterns and the inheritance of common institutional and physical infrastructures from its colonial past, confer on India, by way of reducing transaction costs, competitive advantages over countries outside the region, in trading and forging other links of economic cooperation with neighbouring countries.[3]"

Yet another factor was the overwhelming technological revolution, which has shrunk the world. Above all, the end of the Cold War, the collapse of the Soviet Union and the disenchantment with the ideological battles have also combined to give a higher profile to economic diplomacy. World over there is a new realisation that it is not power politics or war but the economic muscle and the economic ascendency, which yield results. China is a classic example of this awareness. From the nineties even India has acquired some economic muscle because of its attractive market and liberalisation. There is a growing realisation that war is becoming costly and avoidable.

During the Cold War days there were two blocks in the world, one led by the Soviet Union and the other by the United States. The non- alignment movement also saw some countries including India remaining neutral but this movement is no more relevant in a Uni -polar world as after the end of the Cold War in the nineties things had changed. Even countries like India are now leaning towards the United States of America.

South Asia had one of the highly regulated economies outside the Communist Bloc. Among the South Asian nations, Sri Lanka was the first country to liberalize its economy in 1977. Bangladesh followed in 1980, Pakistan in 1989, and India in 1991. Since then India has begun to use its economic card. New Delhi has been giving substantial amounts of money as aid and soft loans and entered in to trade pacts to serve dual purpose of market access as well as part of its security strategy with neighbouring countries. The Ministry of External Affairs too has realised the importance and allocates sizeable money for this purpose from its budget.

On August 3, 2014, Prime Minister Narendra Modi during his visit to Kathmandu announced $1 billion (Nepalese rupees 10,000

---

3   Muchkund Dubey, *'India's Foreign policy: coping with the changing world'*, Pearson, 2013, P. 11

crore) as concessional line of credit to Nepal.[4] News Portal "First Post" reported on June 7, 2015 Prime Minister Narendra Modi announced a credit line of 2 billion US dollars during his visit to Dhaka.[5]

New Delhi has also given aid and grants to other neighbours like Afghanistan, Nepal and Bhutan. New Delhi has spent a substantial amount of money on Bhutan to secure India's strategic interests. Diplomatic relations between India and Bhutan were established in 1968 with the appointment of a resident representative of India in Thimpu. India's Political Officer in Sikkim looked after the diplomatic relations earlier. The basic framework of India-Bhutan bilateral relations was the Treaty of Friendship and Cooperation signed in 1949 between the two countries. This was updated and signed during the visit to India of His Majesty Jigme Khesar Namgyel Wang chuck in February 2007. This special relationship has been sustained by the tradition of regular high level visits and extensive exchange of views at the highest levels between the two countries. In recent times, there had been some high level exchanges including that of His Majesty Jigme Khesar Namgyal Wang chuck, the King of Bhutan to India in 2013 as the Chief Guest to the 64th Republic Day celebrations. The young Bhutan King paid an official visit from January 6 to 10, 2014 at the invitation of President Pranab Mukherji. It has been the practice that India's External Affairs Ministers choose Bhutan for their first foreign visit.

The track record shows that most Indian Prime Ministers have left their imprint on India's foreign policy depending on their personality, their interest and their capacity to influence, manipulate and persuade the States. However, increasingly the Union Government has also seen that it has to take into account the special interests of the States. External Affairs Minister Sushma Swaraj points out "You have to take those concerns. When you say they are shaping it, it looks as if the States are hijacking the foreign policy of

---

4   News tracker, *'PM Narendra Modi announces $1 billion as concessional line of credit to Nepal,'* First Post, August 3, 2014

5   Rajeev Sharma, *'Will Narendra Modi's $2 billion loan to Bangladesh be a setback for China?'* First Post, June 7, 2015

India. That is not the case. The Centre will decide the policy but the concerns of the States expressed by the various Chief Ministers have to be addressed amicably. That is the thing.[6]"

Limitations of Regional Satraps

The Centre – State politics aside, there are limitations for the powerful regional satraps as carrying out an alternative foreign policy at their level is not possible without the Centre. The foreign countries also know their limitations. As former Bangladesh Prime Minister Khaleda Zia observes, "The principal focal points for bilateral relations between Bangladesh and India will have to be the capitals of the two countries. This is a universal principle. Foreign policy decisions are made in Dhaka and New Delhi and they are implemented accordingly. There is however nothing to prevent close cultural and social ties with the people of the Indian States that are in our immediate neighbourhood. A degree of engagement may also be cultivated with the governments of these federal units. The key contacts, however, will have to remain between the capitals of the two countries. At the same time it must be ensured that bilateral relations between Bangladesh and India transcend narrow regional interests and be seen in the larger bilateral context."[7]

The age-old practice of the Chief Ministers, Ministers and other trade and industry delegations taking clearance from the Centre to visit abroad still continues in India. Sometimes the Prime Minister includes some Chief Ministers in his delegation when he makes important visits abroad, which sends a healthy signal. For instance, Dr Manmohan Singh took Chief Ministers of North-eastern States during his visit to Bangladesh in 2011. Prime Minister Narendra Modi had also sent a good signal by including the opposition chief minister like Mamata Banerjee in his delegation to Bangladesh in June 2015,

Under the present system, the communication between the External Affairs Ministry and the States is on an ad hoc basis. Sometimes the Centre refuses permission, as it did in the case of

---

6   Author's interview with Sushma Swaraj, (March, 2015)

7   Author's interview with Khaleda Zia (6 March, 2014)

Narendra Modi when he was the Gujarat Chief Minister to visit Sri Lanka. Bihar Chief Minister Nitish Kumar was denied permission to visit Nepal to attend the post- death rites of former Nepal Prime Minister Girija Prasad Koirala in April 2010. India's then Railway Minister and former Chief Minister of flood-plagued Bihar State Lalu Prasad Yadav had to scrap his intention to visit Nepal after the External Affairs Ministry advised him against it. In 2015, Andhra Pradesh Chief Minister Nara Chandrababu Naidu was denied permission to participate in the funeral of the Singapore doyen Lee Kuan Yew as the Indian Prime Minister Narendra Modi was representing the country. When such a thing happens, the affected Chief Ministers try to make political capital out of it. On the contrary, the then Indian Prime Minister P.V. Narasimha Rao, when he launched economic reforms in the nineties encouraged them to seek foreign investment for their respective States. Even non-Congress Chief Ministers like Lalu Prasad Yadav, (Bihar) Chandrababu Naidu, (Andhra Pradesh) Jyoti Basu (West Bengal) and others utilized this opportunity to project their States abroad and attract the much-needed foreign investment. However one should not lose sight of the fact that the increasingly pro active role of the provincial chieftains in foreign policy is not always obstructionist.

Secondly quite often it is not only the opposition parties but also the allies in the coalition, who had become troublesome. The Dravida Munnetra Kazhagam, in the United Progressive Alliance and the Shiv Sena in the NDA are examples of this pattern. The DMK and the All India Dravida Munnetra Kazhagam and the Trinamool Congress are examples of a trend where the coalition constituents and States are bringing water and security issues to the bargaining table. The DMK had demanded that the UPA should pilot a resolution in the United Nations Human Rights Council demanding an international probe into the alleged war crimes in Sri Lanka. The other Dravidian parties joined the populist stand demanding a boycott of the Commonwealth Heads Of Governments Meeting in Sri Lanka, a ban on Sri Lankan cricket team in the Indian Premier League matches in Tamil Nadu, and also a resolution in the Tamil Nadu assembly asking the Centre to get the UN to create a separate Tamil Elam in Sri Lanka. Thirdly it is time that smaller

Border States like Nagaland and Manipur also have a say in India's neighbourhood policy than merely feel its impact

Evolution of India's Foreign Policy

To understand the growing influence of the regional satraps one had to understand India's foreign policy evolution in the last 70 years. Indian federal character has passed through evolutionary phases and it is still evolving. The first 17 years belonged to India's first Prime Minister Jawaharlal Nehru. He was a stalwart and a world-renowned leader who held the External Affairs portfolio with him until he died in May 1964.

The second was the post-Nehru phase, which was a transition from a single party rule to a system dominated by a few national parties. The past three or four decades have witnessed the decline of the national parties, emergence of the coalition politics and the ascendency of some 49 regional parties. Although the 2014 Lok Sabha elections have brought a single party rule, the regional players continue to dominate. This shows that the federal spirit has asserted itself. The question is whether it turns aggressive and confrontational, or constructive and cooperative. All these will depend on how the players at the Centre and the States handle it. There is no denying the fact that among such mixed determinants of foreign policy, the domestic factors are particularly important. Indeed, the domestic sources of foreign policy are so varied that the task of tracing the way in which they guide that policy would pose a challenge.

Nehru and India's Foreign Policy

During India's first Prime Minister Pandit Jawaharlal Nehru's regime, foreign policy was seen as an elitist exercise. Whatever Nehru decided was accepted as national consensus as no one contradicted him. **Nehru found a way of dealing with the Chief Ministers by befriending them with his frequent interactions and by corresponding with them and sharing his thoughts on various issues including foreign policy regularly. In his letters to the Chief Ministers, Nehru often took them into confidence on aspects of the foreign policy, but it was more to educate them and inform them rather than to consult or discuss with them. The Provincial leaders also responded to him**

with respect. Senior Congress Party leaders like Sardar Patel and Maulana Abul Kalam Azad were national leaders but even those who drew their power from their regional bases like Govind Ballabh Pant (Uttar Pradesh), Dr Bidan Chandra Roy (West Bengal), Morarji Desai (erstwhile Bombay presidency) or Chakravarti Rajagopalachari (Tamil Nadu) had a broad national outlook. In any case, as former Union Minister Saugata Roy (Trinamool Congress) observes that during Nehru's time all the States were ruled by the Congress and great stalwarts were State Chief Ministers. "Now stalwarts are not there either at the Centre or in the States. You can't impose from the Centre foreign policy directives any more.[8]"

In India the foreign policy has always been top down and not bottom up. Nehru generally ignored the foreign office because those who were influencing him were from outside the Ministry of External Affairs. Nehru set the benchmark and his word was final, as former Foreign Secretary Lalit Mansingh observes. He notes that diplomats were accustomed to not taking part in the evolution of the policy earlier assuming that those at the top would take decisions.

Indian polity has matured now and they don't need a Prime Minister to open their eyes, observes another former Foreign Secretary Kanwal Sibal. "Communications Revolution with the contacts we have with the rest of the world and economic integration has changed all this. Our free trade agreements and strategic partnerships and also have changed the world.[9]"

During the Cold War days there was a split in the Ministry of External Affairs between those who sought better relations with the West including senior bureaucrats Lakshmi Kant Jha and M.J. Desai and those who had links with Moscow belonging to the pro-Soviet group diplomats like K.P.S. Menon (Kumara Padmanabha Sivsankara Menon) and Triloki Nath Kaul even though India was pursuing non-alignment policy. For instance Kavalam Madhava Panikkar, popularly known as Sardar K.M. Panikkar and the then Defence Minister Krishna Menon mostly influenced India's China

---

8   Author's interview with Saugata Roy (17 July 2014)

9   Author's interview with Kanwal Sibal (13 July 2014)

policy. Nehru too had a positive view of China. Menon strongly argued in favour of India joining the Commonwealth. There were senior Foreign Service officers with South Asian Countries like Girija Shankar Vajpayee and Badruddin Tayyabji, who advised Nehru on having good relations with Southeast Asian countries?

Several factors were instrumental in shaping Nehru's foreign policy. He had a definite worldview and a vision for India. The period of initial fashioning and formulation of the Indian foreign policy ended with Nehru's death on May 27, 1964. "Since India's independence Nehru's foreign policy had moved from its idealistic and equitable rational place to more realistic moorings as he progressively adjusted the emerging realities of world politics. The adjustments made were a response to the pressures born out of these trends in India."[10]

As eminent political scientist Prof Sumit Ganguly of the Indiana University notes that in the initial stages Nehru's foreign policy could be defined fewer than three things. "First, India played a significant role in multilateral institutions and particularly in United Nations peacekeeping operations. Second, it also emerged as a critical proponent of the non-aligned movement. Third, as a leader of the non-aligned movement it also made a significant contribution toward the process of decolonization.[11]"

New Delhi took lead in the Non- Aligned Movement and participated in several multilateral fora including setting up of the United Nations and Asian Development Bank. As Sumit Ganguly points out, there was a change after the 1962 Chinese aggression, which shocked Nehru and India. Nehru was committed to a million- man army, a 45 squadron Air Force and a modern Navy. His Panchsheel (five principles) concept failed after the Chinese aggression. Even his Non -Aligned policy came under strain, as he had to request the U.S President John. F. Kennedy for military help

10 J.N. Dixit, 'Makers of India's Foreign policy,' HarperCollins, India, 2004, P 96

11 Sumit Ganguly, 'India's foreign policy, Retrospect and Prospect,' https://www.ufmg.br/cei/wp-content/.../indianforeignpolicy_ganguly.doc, 2010

to deal with the Chinese aggression. The United States of America promptly gave him help to meet the situation as the Americans were trying to contain communism.

Nehru Faces Pressure on Goa Liberation

Although Nehru was an undisputed tall leader he also faced some pressure from the States. These include the proposal concerning the ceding of a part of the Berubari Union No 12 to Pakistan in 1958, transfer of 900 sq. km of the Rann of Kutch to Pakistan in 1958, the Liberation of Goa (1961), and the status of Tamils in Sri Lanka.

Nehru faced pressure from Maharashtra and Goa for the Goa liberation. While the French transferred their settlements to Indian Union after India's independence in 1947, the Portuguese held on to their territorial possessions claiming them as part of Portugal and holding on to Goa for 14 years after India's independence. Nehru initially hesitated to use force to evict the Portuguese but ultimately abandoned his diplomatic efforts in favour of liberating Goa inviting international criticism.

'Operation Vijay' was the code name given to the military operation in December 1961 to liberate Goa. The armed action was a decisive victory for India, ending more than 450 years of Portuguese rule in India on 19th of December 1961. Thirty-four Indians and thirty-one Portuguese were killed in the conflict. The brief war drew a mixture of worldwide praise and condemnation. While India saw it as a liberation of historically Indian Territory, Portugal and North Atlantic Treaty Organization (NATO) countries viewed the war as an aggression against national soil. Maharashtra being a contiguous State hoped that Goa might become part of it when it was freed but the Goans wanted to remain a separate State.

Lal Bahadur Shastri's foreign policy

When Lal Bahadur Shastri succeeded Nehru in June 1964, some foreign powers including the United States of America were apprehensive of his role, as he had no experience in India's foreign policy. He was a contrast to Nehru with his low profile style of functioning. Shastri during his brief stint as Prime Minister faced two conflicts between April and October 1965 with Pakistan. One of his major foreign policy achievements was bringing an end to the 1965 Indo- Pak war and project India as a credible military power. While the Tashkent Agreement ended the conflict in 1966 it did not result in a long- term solution.

After Nehru's death Lal Bahadur Shastri felt that there should be improvement in the relations with the neighbours on the advice of Chandrasekhar Jha, a former foreign secretary. Shastri concluded an agreement with Sri Lanka amicably on the citizenship issue. The agreement with the Sri Lankan Prime Minister Sirimavo Bandaranaike was regarding the citizenship status of Indian Tamils in the island country. " The agreement on the question of citizenship for the persons of Indian origin signed with India in October 1964 (Sirimavo – Shastri Pact) with a provision for repatriation of 5,25,000 Plantation Tamils to India, though eased tension in India – Sri Lanka relations was as much a rude shock to the Plantation Tamils as to the ethnic Tamils. The Plantation Tamils were appalled that the Pact would render them refugees and force them to leave their homes and hearths to an uncertain future in India". [12]Under the terms of this agreement, 3,75,000 were to be granted Sri Lankan citizenship. This settlement was to be completed by 31 October 1981.

Shastri Ignores the voices of dissent from Tamil Nadu

Shastri ignored the voices of dissent from Tamil Nadu including those from his own party when he signed the Accord on 30 October 1964, a few months after he took over. Prof Suryanarayan points out "It was signed despite strong opposition from important political leaders like Kumarsamy Kamaraj Nadar, Vengalil Krishna Menon, Conjeevaram Natarajan Annadurai and comrade P. Ramamurthy. It was also a betrayal of Gandhi-Nehru legacy on Indians Overseas. Secondly, the conclusion of the India-Sri Lanka Maritime Boundary Agreements of 1974 and 1976, which ceded the island of Katchateevu to Sri Lanka and bartered away the traditional fishing rights enjoyed by the Indian fishermen, was preceded by strong Opposition from

12 Avtar Singh Bhasin, 'India and Sri Lanka: Between the Lion and the Tigers' Manas publications, 2004, P 40

various political parties in Tamil Nadu."[13] Dixit notes, "His (Shastri) tenure was too short, but all indications were that he would have oriented India's foreign policy towards political relations and towards a greater focus on the country's national interests."[14]

Indira Gandhi's powerful Prime Minister's Secretariat

Mrs Indira Gandhi, who succeeded Lal Bahadur Shastri in January 1966, continued the personalised style of her father Nehru in conducting her foreign policy. She was the first to setup a separate Prime Minister's Office, which became all powerful. That was still a very small office run by her Principal Secretary Parameshwar Narayan Haksar and it became a tradition that it was headed by a Foreign Service officer. He ran Mrs Gandhi's foreign policy from this office. She ruled from 1966 to 1977 in her first phase and from 1980 to 84 in her second stint. She had several experienced foreign ministers from Mahommedali Curim Chagla to Sardar Swaran Singh to Pamulaparti Venkata Narasimha Rao. But Mrs Gandhi maintained a dominant profile throughout and used to call the Foreign Secretaries directly. She carried on the foreign policy in her own way because of her powerful personality. Ambassador Lalit Mansingh notes, "This idea people have that the senior officers in the Ministry of External Affairs make the foreign policy and rubber stamped by the political leaders was not correct.[15]"

Annadurai's concern about Tamil labour from Myanmar

Yet another instance when the provincial aspirations came to light in the sixties was when the then Tamil Nadu Chief Minister C.N. Annadurai was "deeply concerned with the involuntary repatriation of Tamil labourers from Burma (Myanmar) consequent to the nationalisation of retail trade and the related issue of non-payment of compensation due to them. Annadurai wrote a letter to Prime

---

13 Prof. Suryanarayan, *'India and Southeast Asia, A personal narrative from Chennai,'* 'Institute of Peace and Conflict studies special report 139, March 2013

14 J.N. Dixit, *'Makers of India's foreign policy,'* Harper Collins, India, 2004, p 108

15 Author's interview with Lalit Mansingh (13, December, 2013)

Minister Indira Gandhi suggesting that India should enter into a long-term trade agreement with Burma for import of rice, and compensation due to Burmese repatriates could be adjusted in the proposed deal.[16] It may be recalled that in the mid-1960s, India was facing an acute shortage of food grains. There was no response from New Delhi on this concrete proposal.

Indira Gandhi's Foreign Policy

Although Mrs Indira Gandhi inherited the Nehruvian vision she did not share her father's idealistic view of Nation States. Also she came to power at the peak of the Cold War and Sino – Pakistani collaborations. J.N. Dixit notes, "She believed that India's foreign policy should be clearly and precisely related to the country's evolving political, economic and security interests at a given point of time. She also felt that safeguarding these interests primarily depended on India becoming self sufficient and strong."[17] That was why she went for the Green Revolution and White Revolution, which made India self-sufficient.

One of the major foreign policy initiatives of Indira Gandhi was the Liberation of Bangladesh in December 1971. With millions of refugees pouring in from East Pakistan to West Bengal and the Northeast, she had to address the problem in an aggressive manner. Bypassing the then External Affairs Minister, Gandhi's aide Durga Prasad Dhar supervised the Bangladesh operations and also the relationship with the USSR.

Gandhi's two-track policy on Bangladesh

Indira Gandhi adopted a two- track policy – one to help and train the Bangladeshi freedom fighters and the other to mobilise international opinion in favour of Bangladesh. While she succeeded in the former, she could not succeed much on the latter as the United States was backing Pakistan firmly and persuaded its allies to follow its thinking.

---

16 Author's interview with Prof. Suryanarayan (12, December 2014)

17 J.N. Dixit, *'Makers of India's foreign policy,'* Harper Collins, India, 2004, p 122

New Delhi signed a Friendship Treaty with the Union of Soviet Socialist Republics (USSR) much to the surprise of the United States. When Washington protested she told her Foreign Minister Sardar Swaran Singh to offer a similar Treaty to them making them speechless.

The refugee issue created political, economic, social and communal problems for West Bengal and the North- eastern States. **Mrs Gandhi shrewdly took these State governments on board. Almost all the political parties including the Communist Party of India (Marxists) had supported her move for the liberation of Bangladesh. That was one of the reasons for her success in the Bangladesh Liberation War.**

Interestingly, victory over Pakistan in 1971 also consolidated New Delhi's power in Kashmir. In 1975, Mrs Gandhi declared Jammu and Kashmir as a constituent unit of India. Realizing that she would make no major concession on Kashmir, the National Conference Chief Sheikh Abdullah had to recognize India's control over Kashmir. Abdullah agreed for a special autonomous status to Kashmir. The Kashmir conflict remained largely peaceful. She also decided to go for nuclear tests in Pokhran in 1974, which she attributed for peaceful purposes.

Tamil Nadu, Sri Lanka and Indira Gandhi

Tamil Nadu put pressure on the Union Government when Indira Gandhi signed a Treaty ceding Katchateevu, an uninhabited island administered by Sri Lanka to Colombo to help the Sri Lankan Prime Minister Sirimavo Bandaranaike by an agreement on 26 June 1974, and the maritime boundary between the two countries was re- drawn by another agreement on 23 March 1976. This provoked protests in Tamil Nadu with most political parties opposing the pact. The Katchateevu issue continues to be an irritant even today.

The All India Anna Dravida Munnetra Kazhagam (AIADMK) chief Jayalalithaa Jayaram and the Dravida Munnetra Kazhagam supremo Muthuvel Karunanidhi, who had been ruling Tamil Nadu alternately for the past twenty five years had challenged the ceding of Katchateevu in the Supreme Court arguing that it was done without following the Constitutional proviso and Indian Parliament's nod. The Union Government has filed an affidavit before the Madras High Court recently similar to the one it had filed in the Supreme Court earlier arguing that India had no sovereign rights over Katchateevu and that the maritime boundary was a settled issue. There is a running battle between Tamil Nadu and Sri Lanka on the question of fishing rights as fishermen from Tamil Nadu who are poaching on the Sri Lankan waters are often arrested by the Sri Lankan Navy.

Morarji Desai's Foreign Policy

When Morarji Desai became the Prime Minister in 1977 heading the Janata government, the neighbouring countries like Sri Lanka, Nepal and Bangladesh, which had some reservations about Indira Gandhi's neighbourhood policy, welcomed Desai hoping he might be friendly. As expected, Desai took a friendlier line on Sri Lanka, Nepal and Bangladesh. As Dixit observes the then Indian President Neelam Sanjiva Reddy and Desai's interaction with the Sri Lankan President Junius Richard Jayewardene constituted a persistent footnote to main trends in Indian foreign policy during that era. "The consequence was Reddy and Desai conveying all sorts assurances to Jayewardene about India's willingness to compromise on various pending issues with Sri Lanka. They also emphasised that Mrs Gandhi's intrusive interest in Sri Lanka, because of her friendship with Mrs Bandaranaike, would be removed under the Janata government.[18]"

Indira Gandhi's second stint

Indira Gandhi came back to power in 1980 as a mellowed person. It was then she began her covert designs to help the Sri Lankan Tamils who were being oppressed by the State. While she helped the Tamils by giving them support, she also continued the diplomatic dialogue with Jayewardene. Deposing before the Jain Commission, which went into the Rajiv Gandhi assassination, former Prime Minister Vishwanath Pratap Singh on November 5, 1995, officially confirmed that the first batch of training of the militants was given in 1983 by the Indira Gandhi government.

18 J.N. Dixit, *'Makers of India's Foreign policy,'* Harper Collins, 2004, p 137

Interestingly neither the Tamil Nadu Chief Minister Marudhur Gopalan Ramachandran nor Prime Minister Indira Gandhi supported the separate Eelam demand of the Tamil militants. This was for various reasons. The anti –Tamil July 1983 riots in Sri Lanka and the overwhelming support for their Tamil brethren from Tamil Nadu was the flash point. It was also in response to Jayewardene's encouragement to expanded military intelligence presence of the US, Israel and Pakistan in the island country. Dixit concludes that "the two foreign policy decisions she could be faulted are: her ambiguous response to the Russian intrusion into Afghanistan and her giving active support to Sri Lankan Tamil militants."[19]

Rajiv Gandhi and Sri Lankan issue

Her two Sikh bodyguards assassinated Indira Gandhi on October 30, 1984. Rajiv Gandhi, who succeeded her, followed the same imperious style of his mother. Guided by his handpicked aides, Rajiv Gandhi took bold and adventurous decisions on sensitive issues. He presided over a Prime Minister's Office, which became all powerful. His first major foreign policy initiative was to improve relations with Pakistan. The second was to break ice with China. His meeting with the Chinese revolutionary and Statesman Deng Xiaoping was a great hit, which opened up opportunities. The third was to mediate in the Sri Lankan Tamil issue. Rajiv Gandhi also made use of Chief Minister M.G Ramachandran in tackling the Liberation Tigers of Tamil Eelam. Dixit notes that, "He (Rajiv Gandhi) maintained continuity in Indian politics but with certain significant shifts in emphasis and nuances in its approach in order for the efforts to succeed."[20]

Jayewardene befriends Rajiv Gandhi

Rajiv Gandhi wanted to build his international image. In 1985, when the then Sri Lankan President Jayewardene met Rajiv Gandhi, it paved the way for cessation of hostilities between the Sri Lankan armed forces and the Tamil militants. Thimpu talks followed in which the militant groups also participated but it failed. Rajiv Gandhi

---

19 J.N. Dixit, 'Makers of India's Foreign Policy,' Harper Collins, 2004, P 147

20 J.N. Dixit, Editor J.N. Dixit, 'External Affairs, Cross-Border Relations,' Roli Books Pvt Ltd, p 62

began to mediate between the Sri Lankan government and the Tamil groups to bring about some solution. The Indo – Sri Lanka Accord is important in this regard. He made efforts to persuade the LTTE chief Velupillai Prabhakaran to lay down arms and opt for a political solution but could not succeed. Rajiv Gandhi also got embroiled in the Bofors gun deal scam and spent most of his time in defending himself and his family. It took almost three years of the Indian Peace Keeping Force operations to find that it could make no headway and ultimately when Ranasinghe Premadasa succeeded Jayewardene, the Indian Peace Keeping Force (IPKF) had to be pulled out at his request in 1990.

Minister of State for External Affairs Gen. V. K. Singh has said recently, "It was a policy failure that the Government of India and Sri Lanka had entered into an agreement, while the fight was between the Liberation Tigers of Tamil Eelam (LTTE) and the Sri Lankan Government. Neither there was control over the LTTE nor did they owe any responsibility." [21]Rajiv Gandhi paid for this mistake with his life as later the LTTE assassinated him on May 21, 1991 while he was on his campaign tour during the Lok Sabha elections in Tamil Nadu.

Echoing this, former External Affairs Minister Kunwar Natwar Singh, who was involved in the resolution of the Sri Lankan crisis, feels that "Rajiv Gandhi's visit to China was a great success but Rajiv Gandhi's Sri Lanka policy was a great disaster. He lost his life because too many people were advising him. He was changing his mind so often."[22]

V.P Singh's limited role

Viswanath Pratap Singh, who rebelled against Rajiv Gandhi, succeeded him in 1989 as Prime Minister supported by the right and left parties but did not have much time to focus on foreign policy, as he was bogged down with the domestic issues. His brief tenure was

---

21 Zee news, *Sending IPKF was a high level policy failure:* V.K. Singh, April 15, 2015 http://zeenews.india.com/news/india/sending-ipkf-to-sri-lanka- was-high-level-policy-failure-vk-singh_1578800.html

22 Author's interview with K. Natwar Singh (September 15, 2013)

turbulent with agitations and demonstrations. However, prodded by his Dravida Munnetra Kazhagam ally who was sympathetic to the Liberation Tigers of Tamil Eelam (LTTE), V.P. Singh completed the pull back of the Indian Peace Keeping Force from Sri Lanka in 1990. Rajiv Gandhi had already started the process acceding to the request of President Premadasa.

Coalition era begins

The 1989 Lok Sabha elections finally proved to be the turning point in the process of federalisation of the Indian political system, increase in assertion for autonomy of States and State units of national parties and the growing clout of the regional parties. Thus began the advent of the multi-party system with coalition governments, which allowed the regional parties to acquire a decisive balancing role in the Union government. The regional parties have not only influenced the States but also the national parties. They have made important inroads into the traditional support base of the Congress amongst Muslim, Dalits and Tribals.

P.V. Narasimha Rao and Foreign Policy

When P.V. Narasimha Rao took over heading a minority government at the Centre, his coalition partner and the All India Anna Dravida Munnetra Kazhagam chief Jayalalithaa came to power in Tamil Nadu in 1991. She was opposed to the LTTE. "She was very angry because they went to the DMK. She feared that the LTTE wanted to eliminate her as she was on their hit list. So she wanted to finish the LTTE.[23]" Jayalalithaa gave strict orders to her officials to eliminate the LTTE, which had assassinated Rajiv Gandhi. When Karunanidhi took over from Jayalalithaa in 1996, the LTTE got his support once again. His becoming the partner in the United Front Government enabled him to have influence on the Sri Lanka policy.

The increasing role of the States
Since the opening up of the Indian economy in 1991, States have consistently exercised their newfound economic policy latitude to craft their own strategies to woo foreign investors. On pure foreign policy matters, India's relations with its neighbours - whether it is

---

23 Author's interview with Prof Sahadevan. (28, August, 2013)

Pakistan to the West, Sri Lanka to the South, Nepal to the North or Bangladesh to the East--have for many years have been coloured by the respective positions of the ruling elites in the Border States of Punjab, Kashmir, Tamil Nadu, and West Bengal, North-eastern States, U.P and Bihar.

On the economic side, the decline in the role of the Union Government on account of privatisation and globalisation have bestowed new responsibilities on State governments like resource mobilisation, competitive bids for foreign direct investment. They began to court investment from the West and managed to get loans from the World Bank and other financial institutions for infrastructure and irrigation projects to develop their States. The liberalisation also enabled the economic interests overtaking all other interests in the States as people have begun to demand development and delivery of promises made by the political leaders. Secondly, the provincial level economic, administrative, and political reforms came to be focused more than ever before. The State chieftains began to indulge in competitive federalism. Chief Ministers like Chandrababu Naidu (Andhra Pradesh), later Nitish Kumar (Bihar) and Naveen Patnaik (Odissha) found that development was one way of getting votes. Prime Minister Narendra Modi, as Gujarat Chief Minister used the development mantra for his successive victory in the State as well as the 2014 Lok Sabha polls.

In the nineties, as mentioned above when politics changed from the single party domination to coalition politics, the States began to insist that the Centre must consult them and address their concerns on many issues including foreign policy. Despite heading a minority government, the Narasimha Rao regime took bold steps like recognising Israel and adopting a "Look East" policy for engagement with countries located in the Eastern side of India. Therefore countries like Singapore, Malaysia and Japan came in to focus. He took a conscious decision to deal with Myanmar's military junta to improve relations. As Bangladesh Prime Minister Khaleda Zia was hostile to India, he had to look for other avenues to secure the Northeast and turned to Myanmar and Bhutan. This was necessary in view of the security concerns in the Northeastern States and the militants were finding safe haven in Myanmar and Bangladesh.

Gradually most States are themselves getting affected by caste and identity politics, which is fracturing the polity. Barring some in the Hindi belt and Gujarat, every other major State is effectively run by a coalition, or was run till recently. **As equal players, the coalition partners began to assert themselves making the foreign policy formulation all the more complex. Participation of regional parties in the Union Government had also increased gradually since 1989.** The Grand Old Party of India – the Indian National Congress – lost its primacy though it remained the largest single party in the political system until recently. The BJP has overtaken it in 2015. But the BJP is not yet a pan- national party. The decline of the Congress dominance has resulted in its own failure to adapt to the growing democratisation and federalisation.

Rise of Regional Parties

There is a pattern in the rise of the regional parties. They tasted power after becoming stakeholders at the Centre in the National Front government led by V.P. Singh, as well as the two United Front governments led by Deve Gowda and later Inder Kumar Gujral. The emergence of coalition governments like the Janata Party, (1977- 80) the National Front (1989 to 91), the United Front, (1996 to 98) National Democratic Alliance (1998 -2004) United Progressive Alliance I and II, (2004 to 2014) and the NDA since 2014 gave the ruling coalition partners considerable leverage in the Union Government's policies. They were emboldened to pursue some foreign policy related activities without attracting censure from the Centre.

Regional chieftains try to influence Foreign Policy

"The share of votes won by regional parties cracked the 50 per cent mark for the first time in 1996. Then the engine sputtered somewhat. By 1999, vote share of regional parties had dipped to 48 per cent. By 2004, their vote share crept back up to 51 per cent, the same level it had been eight years earlier, before modestly rising again in the 2009 elections."[24] The same official statistics reveal that in 1989,

---

24 Milan Vaishnav, *'The complicated rise of India's regional parties,'* Carnage Endowment for international peace, carnegieendowment.org/.../

they won 27 seats in the Lok Sabha. In the 1999 elections, this figure rose to 158 and in the 2004 elections to 193. In 2009, with a total of 52.54% vote share, against 47.36% for the Congress and BJP clubbed together, regional parties attracted an absolute majority of voters. This speaks eloquently the case of the regional parties.

A good illustration of the electoral system is the collective strength of the regional parties in 2014. "**Despite the massive vote swings and seat variations of the Congress and the BJP, the representation of regional parties remains equal – at 212 seats – with the same vote share (46.6% against 46.7% in 2009).** Only five regional parties manage to get more then 3% of vote share and the gap between the largest regional party and the Congress is 15%. However, this apparent stability of the regional parties' score hides important variations among them. Put simply, the northern regional parties of the Hindi belt have been wiped out in the Lok Sabha polls, despite sometimes-good performances. The Samajwadi Party and Bahujan Samaj Party combined still represent 42% of vote share, the Janta Dal (United) and Rashtriya Janata Dal 38%."[25] Even parties, which suffered considerable loss of seats, such as the Samajwadi Party or the Dravida Munnetra Kazhagam – have maintained their vote share. The most striking result is the 2014nil score of the BSP, despite its 19% of vote share in Uttar Pradesh. However, this apparent stability of the regional parties hides important variations among them. "Put simply, the northern regional parties, particularly of the Hindi belt, have been wiped out in the Lok Sabha polls, despite good performances at times. The SP and BSP combined still represent 42% of vote share, the Janata Dal (United) and Rashtriya Janata Dal 38%. At the same time, regional parties contesting outside the Hindi belt, in States where the BJP was not a serious contender, have had their field day, thanks to the collapse of the Congress. The All India Anna Dravida Munnetra Kazhagam, the Biju Janata Dal, the

---

complicated-rise-of-India's-regional parties (accessed July 12, 2015)

25 Giles Verniers and the YIF electoral data unit, '*Everything you need to know about Lok Sabha verdict 2014 explained in 40 charts*', Scroll.in, June 6, 2014

Trinamool Congress, and three regional parties in Andhra Pradesh completely dominate their State."[26]

Since the decline of the Congress Party's nation-wide dominance in the late 1980s and the failure of any other national party's attempt to replace Congress by the mid-1990s India's polity has progressively splintered and regionalised. This has resulted in mushrooming of the regional parties and sub-regional parties and caste and religion -based parties in the past two decades. Only after the 2014, the BJP has overtaken the Congress and become the largest national party in the country.

The politics of the country has also changed due to the political assertion of suppressed masses as caste based parties like the Bahujan Samaj Party (BSP) and the Pattali Makkal Katchi (PMK), the Samajwadi Party, the Rashtriya Janata Dal and Janata Dal (U) began claiming their share in the political process demanding political power and also became part of ruling coalition in some States like Uttar Pradesh and Tamil Nadu. Riding on regional pride and regional development and supported by the new middle class, other parties like the Telugu Desam founded by N.T. Rama Rao in Andhra Pradesh also came to the forefront of politics in the eighties and nineties.

Former Union minister Yashwant Sinha observes that since then regional leaders had become more powerful. **This was because they had founded their own parties, as most of them were personality -oriented parties led by charismatic leaders with mass appeal.** Almost all parties except perhaps Shiv Sena, Aam Admi Party (AAP), National Conference and the Dravidian parties, the others are the offshoots of some national party mostly the Congress and the Janata Parivar. It is the emergence of these strong leaders in the States that changed the nature of politics. No doubt there were many stalwarts and Chief Ministers like Bidan Chandra Roy, (West Bengal) Sri Krishna Sinha, (Bihar) or Govind Ballab Pant (U.P), Biju Patnaik (Odisha) Chakravarty Rajagopalachari and Kumarasway Kamaraj

---

26 Giles Verniers and the YIF electoral data unit, *'Everything you need to know about Lok Sabha verdict 2014 explained in 40 charts,'* Scroll.in, June 6, 2014

(Tamil Nadu) but none of them was allowed to acquire the kind of stature Nehru had. The present day regional satraps have no high command as they believe in a kind of personality cult. Even the newly born Aam Admi Party (AAP), which has captured Delhi in 2015 Assembly polls, is a one-man show. "So the emergence of these strong State Chief Ministers and the weakening of the Centre is an important development in Indian politics, which the national parties are not able to contain or challenge. As a corollary, the pressure on the part of the national parties to join an alliance with the regional parties for the sake of power is also a new development. This is affecting the polity in various ways. It is affecting foreign policy, it is affecting economic policy, security policy it is affecting terrorism policy and it is now affecting the coalition governments.[27]"

The politics of regionalism has since matured to a large extent. Adam Roberts of the 'Economist' magazine points out how the regional parties fill the gap. "Usually built around a charismatic individual who becomes a State's Chief Minister, they wield near-presidential powers over a territory that often has a European country-sized population. These States control roughly half of all India's public spending. The most prosperous ones, which rely least on Delhi for discretionary funds, throw up the strongest leaders, who often influence what happens in Delhi too. The mightiest satraps pay the least attention to national parties.[28]"

No doubt the regional parties have been growing at the cost of the national parties and they will continue to grow. "Such is the emerging federal paradox in India: the States are losing financial autonomy to New Delhi but have growing political clout over the Union government. Powerful regional satraps are now in a position to leverage their political clout to demand funds from the Union Government."[29]

---

27 Author's interview with Yashwant Sinha (18 September, 2013)

28 Adam Roberts, 'Aim higher, Special report- India' The Economist, September 29, 2012, p 4

29 Niranjan Rajadhyaksha, 'The Indian federal paradox', Live Mint, 27 December 2015

The regional parties draw their strength on ethnic, linguistic, caste and sub-caste identities, which have gradually evolved and asserted over the years. Even though the BJP has come back with a majority in 2014, its influence continues to be only in pockets with the South and the East eluding to come under its fold so far. When the Modi wave swept India in 2014 there was a feeling that the days of regional parties were over. The subsequent Assembly polls in Maharashtra and Haryana showed that regional parties like the Shiv Sena, the Haryana Janhit Congress doing badly. But the Progressive Democratic Party in Jammu and Kashmir the Aam Admi Party in Delhi, and the Janata Dal (United) in Bihar have proved that regional parties are here to stay.

The splintered Janata Parivar has resulted in producing strong leaders of national repute with a significant identity, mass and caste appeal like Lalu Prasad Yadav, Nitish Kumar, Mulayam Singh Yadav, and Naveen Patnaik. There is also an interesting phenomenon of regional parties pitted against regional parties in some States- where the national parties have become irrelevant. A Mayawati versus Mulayam Singh, Jayalalithaa versus Karunanidhi, and Mufti Mohammed Sayeed versus Farooq Abdullah are examples of this trend. The centralized political model of the Congress has resulted in Sharad Pawar (Nationalist Congress Party), Mamata Banerjee, (Trinamool Congress), Jagan Reddy (YSR Congress) and G.K. Vasan (Tamizhaga Maanila Congress) leaving their parent party to float their own outfits with regional aspirations successfully. Later Sharad Pawar and Mamata Banerjee even had alliance with the Congress.

The current small and big regional players include the Samajwadi Party, the Rashtriya Lok Dal and the Bahujan Samaj Party in Uttar Pradesh, the Lok Janshakthi, the Janata Dal- (United) and the Rashtriya Janata Dal in Bihar, the Dravida Munnetra Kazhagam, the Anna Dravida Munnetra Kazhagam, the Pattali Makkal Katchi, and the Desiya Murpokku Dravida Kazhagam (DMDK) in Tamil Nadu, the Trinamool Congress in West Bengal, the Telugu Desam Party, the YSR Congress Party in Andhra Pradesh, and the Telangana Rashtra Samithi in Telangana, the Nationalist Congress Party (NCP), the Shiv Sena and the Maharashtra Navnirman Samithi in Maharashtra, the Janata Dal (secular) in Karnataka and the Biju Janata Dal in the

Eastern State of Odisha. There are many others like the Shiromani Akali Dal in Punjab, the National Conference (NC) and the People's Democratic Party (PDP) in Jammu & Kashmir, and the Asom Gana Parishad (AGP) in Assam. Apart from these the North-eastern States have a host of smaller regional parties like Sikkim Democratic Front. They invoke regional pride, regional identity, regional culture, history and language. Regional parties of the Northeast mostly combine identity issue with autonomy or Statehood demands.

Multiple stake- holders in Foreign Policy

No doubt, the emergence of multiple stakeholders has resulted in changes in foreign policy formulation. The earlier days of only the Ministry of External Affairs conducting foreign policy had stretched with other ministries like commerce and industry gradually becoming stake- holders after liberalisation. When the NDA government led by Vajpayee came to power in 1998 it further opened up more areas. With the opening of Defence sector, Defence ministry's inputs on the foreign policy were added. The armed forces began to think that security was their concern and demanded their say. When the National Security Council was set up in 1999 that too became a major stakeholder in the making of foreign policy as it became part of the Prime Minister's Office. Today it is accepted that there are multiple stake- holders in foreign policy formulation. But even now constitutionally under the allocation of cabinet posts, the ministry that speaks about foreign policy is the Ministry of External Affairs. .

Coalition Compulsions

The truth is that in a coalition era with a globally integrated Indian economy, managing a parliamentary coalition and also working with Chief Ministers from the opposition-ruled States is increasingly becoming difficult. This is a reality and a challenge to the Prime Ministers and the Ministry of External Affairs to conduct the foreign policy within these constraints. One cannot deny that in the present federal structure the limbs have become more important than the body. While the ideal situation would be strong States and a strong Centre but what is happening is that the States are becoming strong while the Centre is becoming weak. Former Union Minister Saugata Roy of the Trinamool Congress observes that it is important for the Prime Minister to have a good personal chemistry with the Chief Ministers. "Yes, it is important that Prime Ministers in the last few years have been concentrating on the high table in international conferences and have little time for other things or build relationship with the Chief Ministers.[30]"

Former Union Minister Natwar Singh notes that even during the Morarji Desai (1977-79) regime this kind of assertion of State chieftains did not happen. It was because the tradition was so strong and every one respected it. "Today Karunanidhi advocates a foreign policy in Tamil Nadu for Sri Lanka. So did M.G. Ramachandran and Jayalalithaa. Mamata Banerjee has her own foreign policy. This is a sign of weakness. This is because the regional parties have the power to make and unmake Central governments. With globalisation and economic reforms, ethnic, immigration and economic issues and even simple prejudices of regional leaders began to play a role in the making of foreign policy."[31]

Rao stresses on Economic Diplomacy

After the assassination of Rajiv Gandhi, Sri Lanka successfully portrayed itself as a co-victim of Tamil terrorism. During P.V. Narasimha Rao's regime, the Sri Lankan President Chandrika Kumaratunga visited India and the Indian government helped her to fight the Liberation Tigers of Tamil Eelam (LTTE), which was banned in India after the assassination of Rajiv Gandhi. On the one hand, Colombo argued it was helping India by fighting Tamil insurgents and on the other New Delhi tolerated Sri Lanka's defence transactions with China and Pakistan because there was realisation that armed Tamil insurgency was a threat to India's own maritime security. The Vajpayee government fully supported peace talks, which the Norwegians mediated between the LTTE and the Sri Lankan government in 2000. New Delhi stayed away from participating in it because LTTE was a banned organization. The Manmohan Singh government too helped Sri Lankan President Rajapakse in his efforts to finish the LTTE.

---

30 Author's interview with Saugata Roy (17, July 2014)

31 Author's interview with Natwar Singh (September15, 2013)

But after the end of the Eelam war 4 in 2009, the Rajapakse government stonewalled India's suggestions for political rehabilitation of the Tamil minorities. President Rajapakse failed to implement the 13th Amendment plus which he promised New Delhi. India's vote in favour of the United Nations Human Rights Commission (UNHRC) twice and its abstention in 2014 has called off this bluff. Sri Lanka was now free to further expand its ties with China and Pakistan and criticize India's human rights record in Jammu and Kashmir. However, the defeat of Rajapakse in the 2015 January presidential elections and the subsequent Parliament polls has opened up new opportunities for the Tamils. The new Srisena-Wickremesinghe government was willing to address their concerns as the entire Tamil population in the island nation supported them. The Parliamentary elections on August 17 gave a verdict in favour of Ranil Wickremesinghe of the UNP. The Srisena – Wickremesinghe combination have worked together since January 2015.

Is India's Foreign Policy going in the right direction?

This is to be viewed in the context of the growing assertion of the regional satraps. The growing number of regional parties as well as their increasing clout has resulted in the Centre waking up and listening to their voices already. The External Affairs Minister Sushma Swaraj is firm in her conviction that the Modi government's policy is going in the right direction. "We will be able to solve the problems in a very positive manner. So we are going in the right direction."[32]

Related to that is the question whether it is in the national interest to allow the regional chieftains to influence India's foreign policy. This cannot be answered now, as only time will tell. The States will have to understand the broader impact of foreign policy issues and the Centre the domestic side of the foreign policy. This can be done by taking the regional chieftains into confidence and also bringing them on board by persuasion. Modi has begun doing just that by talking about cooperative federalism and making them stakeholders.

---

32 Author's interview with Sushma Swaraj (March 2015)

Insurgency in the Northeast and Foreign Policy

There are two dimensions to dealing with the Northeast. One is domestic dimension and the other is the foreign policy angle. The North- eastern States have huge stakes on India's relations with Bangladesh, Bhutan, Nepal, China and Myanmar. For instance, take the case of Bhutan, which is located at the Eastern end of the Himalayas. Bhutan stands to be a triple buffer State between India and its crucial neighbours Nepal, Bangladesh, and China. Bhutan is important for India too, as it is close to the narrow "Chicken's Neck" corridor. Thus Bhutan happens to be a crucial link. It is clear that the foreign policy can only be built on domestic factors so that there could be a coherent external face. Then, of course, the implementation strategy of the Government of India is also important.

As former Foreign Secretary Kanwal Sibal points out Bhutan is very sensitive to what Assam does. Insurgency in the Northeast has been continuing for decades. Earlier it came only from Bangladesh but now it is extended to Bhutan and Myanmar. Infiltration was found even in the seventies but only from Chief Minister Hitendra Saikia's time insurgency started in Assam and it is still continuing although it is much less now. "There is need to look a little more deeply about Assam- Bhutan problems. The only entrance to Bhutan is through Assam. So this issue of the landlocked country becomes very important. What is the view of the Chief Minister of Assam to have an alternate route through Bangladesh to Chittagong to Bhutan? This needs to be taken into consideration. Then of course this larger question of the whole of North and the links with Myanmar and beyond that east.[33]" The field impact of Assam government's thinking on the United Liberation Front of Assam (ULFA) is very sensitive. New Delhi succeeded in getting the support of the King of Bhutan to throw out the insurgents. They were always worried that they might come back especially to Eastern Bhutan. So a lot depends on how serious the Assam government views all these. Assam chief Minister Tarun Gogoi argues that the States should have more say in India's foreign policy. "I feel States should be involved more and more. I went with Prime Minister Manmohan Singh to Bangladesh

---

33 Author's interview with Kanwal Sibal (13 July 2014)

in September 2011 and it sent a good signal. Supposing India wants to deal with Myanmar or even with South East Asia, we can play a vital role. My own idea is that in the foreign affairs the States have to play an important role. What is India? It is a federation of States"[34]

In recent times, Bhutan started drifting towards China and stepping up its contacts with Beijing, which has made New Delhi suspicious. Prime Minister Modi has tried to revive the defining spirit behind the Indo-Bhutanese friendship by making overtures even while stressing an equal relation. It was perhaps an attempt to win back Bhutan to balance the increasing Chinese influence in the Himalayan Kingdom and also to take into confidence a new democracy. He perhaps made the best blending of diplomacy and economy when he explained the idea of B2B (Bharat to Bhutan).

On the economic side, the two countries have had very good relations. India is not only Bhutan's main development partner but also its leading trade partner. A free trade regime exists between the two countries. Trade and Commerce Agreement between the two were first signed in 1972. This Agreement was renewed for a period of 10 years during 2006. It also provides for duty free transit of Bhutanese merchandise for trade with third countries. The entry/exit points for bilateral trade are given in the Trade Agreement.

India accounts for nearly 60 per cent of Bhutan's exports, and 75 per cent of its imports, as well as being a vital donor of economic aid to the country. Seeking to repair relations, India's Prime Minister Modi chose Bhutan for his first visit abroad, in 2014 and came bearing gifts in the form of a fifty per cent increase in aid and loans from the previous year. "The visit also raised the prospects of moving forward on Bhutan's 10,000 MW initiatives, in which the Indian government is to fund three hydroelectric projects that upon completion are expected to produce up to $1.7 billion worth of electricity."[35]

---

34 Author's interview with Tarun Gogoi (26, November 2013)

35 Brian Benedictus, *'Bhutan and the great power struggle',* The Diplomat , August 2,2014

Tarun Gogoi puts pressure on the Centre to contain the ULFA

Tarun Gogoi is one of those who had been putting pressure on the Centre to talk to Bangladesh, Bhutan and Myanmar to contain United Liberation Front of Assam (ULFA) and other insurgent groups who were operating in the Northeast. "The moment you go after them they sneak into the territory of the neighbouring countries, which are full of jungles. Bangladesh is a very porous border. Sometimes we ask for fencing although it is not always possible because of the hill area. We would like fencing not only in Assam but also in Bengal and other border areas. Now the Centre has done it. We are taking some measures but still there are some shelters here and there. Even in Bangladesh some insurgents are there. I don't say absolutely they are all removed. Myanmar government also is trying but they are still there in some areas where the government has no influence. Even the Military Junta rule could not do much. That area is very porous and adjacent to China also. Chinese arms are there. We can't say the Chinese government is encouraging but arms sales are there. They come through Myanmar and to the entire North.[36]"

Northeast and cooperation with Myanmar

Trans-border cooperation with Myanmar has to take place with the Border States of Mizoram, Manipur, Nagaland and Arunachal Pradesh. Myanmar, the only Southeast Asian country, which shares a 1,000-mile-long border with India, serves as its gateway to the other 10-member States of the Association of Southeast Asian Nations (ASEAN). Though the bilateral relations have been largely peaceful and mutually beneficial, recent border disputes in Manipur have caused concern among the local communities, as well as the State and Central government officials. The core concern is over the pending issue of alleged territorial encroachment.

India and Myanmar have traditional, cultural, historical, ethnic and religious ties, in addition to sharing a long land border and maritime boundary in the Bay of Bengal. India and Myanmar's relationship officially got underway after the Treaty of Friendship was signed in 1951. "The visit of the Prime Minister Rajiv Gandhi in

---

36 Author's interview with Tarun Gogoi (26 November 2013)

1987 laid the foundation for a stronger relationship between India and Myanmar. Since then, high level visits have been taking place on a regular basis between the two countries.[37"]

P.V. Narasimha Rao took it further by signing a trade agreement in 1994. He started building up relations with Myanmar and other Southeast Asian countries as part of his 'Look East' policy. India has set up a comprehensive security cooperation mechanism with Myanmar. In the past two decades, the drastic reduction in insurgency related violence in Manipur and Nagaland - States sharing borders with Myanmar - has allowed the two countries to seal the gains. These include India's generous supply of arms and equipment to Myanmar and setting up forums for the continuous exchange of ideas between the two countries.

From the security angle also Myanmar has become strategically important for India, as it is the only ASEAN country that shares a border with India. It is also the only country that can act as a link between India and Association of Southeast Asian Nations (ASEAN).

The Nationalist Socialist Council of Nagaland (NSCN) was formed in on 31 January 1980 by Isak Chishi Swu, Thuingaleng Muivah and S.S. Khaplang opposing the Shillong Accord, signed by the then Naga National Council (NNC) with the Government of India and established its headquarters in North-western Burma/ Sagaing region.[38]

Later, due to a disagreement within the outfit leaders over the issue of commencing dialogue with the Indian government, on 30 April 1988, the NSCN split into two factions; the NSCN-Khaplang led by Shangwang Shangyung Khaplang, and the NSCN- M (Isak Chishi Swu and Thuingaleng Muivah).[39] The split was accompanied by a spate of violence and clashes between the factions.

---

37 www.mea.gov.in/Portal/ForeignRelation/Myanmar_2015_07_20.pdf

38 https://en.wikipedia.org/wiki/National_Socialist_Council_of_ Nagaland

39 https://en.wikipedia.org/wiki/National_Socialist_Council_of_ Nagaland

Myanmar's Sagaing region became the base for these northeast insurgent groups. The Myanmar Military Junta had no control over this region. The NSCN got divided in 1988 but the NSCN (K) faction headed by S.S Khaplang, a Burmese Naga still remained in control of the region as the other faction NSCN (IM) shifted its headquarters to Dimapur after a ceasefire agreement signed in 1997 with the Government of India. In 2001 the NSCN (K) had also signed similar ceasefire agreement with New Delhi. In 2012 ULFA was split into ULFA- Independent (I) headed by Paresh Baruah with headquarters established in this region. The National Democratic Front of Bodoland (S) led by a non-Bodo I.K. Songbijit also shifted its headquarters to Myanmar. The People's Liberation Army (PLA), United National Liberation Front (UNLF), The People's Revolutionary Party of Kangleipak (PREPAK), Kanglei Yawol Kanna Lup (KYKL), and Kangleipak Communist Party (KCP) had also established their headquarters in this region. It is in India's interest to get integrated to the Southeast Asian economy.

Similarly, a peaceful Northeast has great potential to develop economically with its rich biodiversity, hydropower and precious mineral resources once it is integrated to the Southeast Asian economy. 'Look East' policy was meant for this economic integration with the countries in the East. India became the second largest importer of Myanmar's products and invested in the infrastructure development and energy sector keeping an eye on importing its gas and oil. New Delhi has also decided to upgrade the Kalewa-Yargyi road segment to highway standard, while Myanmar would develop the Yargyi-Monywa portion for better connectivity. This in turn would improve India's connectivity and relationship with both Myanmar and Thailand. Reforms presently underway in Myanmar have opened up enormous economic opportunities for several countries.

The then Prime Minister Manmohan Singh signed around a dozen MOUs, along with a line of credit for $500 million during his State visit in 2012. Prime Minister Narendra Modi used the ASEAN summit in Myanmar's capital Naypyidaw on November 17, 2014 to unveil India's new "Act East Policy," and convince his Southeast Asian counterparts that his government is serious about boosting ties with the region.

As Bibhu Prasad Routray, visiting fellow of the Institute of Peace and Conflict Studies (IPCS) notes that engagement with Myanmar had succeeded in partially countering the Chinese dominance in that country. "Perceptibly, New Delhi has followed a different approach to the Indo-Myanmar border. While fencing dominates its strategy along the Indo-Pak and Indo-Bangladesh borders, security along the Indo-Myanmar border is sought to be protected by establishing a cooperation mechanism between the border guarding forces.[40] "

Chief Ministers asserting on Foreign Policy

Foreign policy advocacy by certain States was not uncommon, For instance, the Indus Water Treaty could not have been concluded without a nod from Punjab. This only proves that any government, which wants to take sensitive foreign policy initiative, should be smart enough to take concerned States on board. Sri Lanka and Nepal policy of Government of India would be more successful if the Border States are taken into confidence.

In recent times leaders like West Bengal Chief Minister Mamata Banerjee, Bihar Chief Minister Nitish Kumar and Tamil Nadu Chief Minister Jayalalithaa, Odisha Chief Minister Naveen Patnaik -all have been assertive on issues concerning their respective States. Yashwant Sinha points out "In our case we had to keep the sensitivity of Chief Minister Jayalalithaa in mind on the Sri Lanka policy. The two years I was the External Affairs Minister, there was a proposal to start a passenger ferry from Tuticorin in Tamil Nadu to Colombo so that people can travel faster. It emerged from discussions that this kind of ferry service would make it easier. But we could not implement this because she said that the terrorists would come from that side."[41] Nitish Kumar wanted to project his State Bihar as a bridge between India and Nepal. Modi as Gujarat Chief Minister had demanded that the State chieftains should be involved in defining the country's climate change policy. Kerala legislature passed a resolution against the Indo-US nuclear deal during the Left Democratic Front (LDF)

---

40 Bibhu Prasad Routray, *'Myanmar and India's Northeast: Border cooperation, better connectivity and economic integration.'* India article 3788, Institute of Peace and Conflict studies, 10 January 2013

41 Author's interview with Yashwant Sinha. (18 September 2013)

regime. Kerala also has some genuine concerns about the Indian labour working in the Gulf countries and elsewhere. As Prof Raja Mohan points out, "Sikkim has long been an active champion of deeper economic cooperation with Tibet in China. But it is Delhi's security establishment that appears to be resisting the case for full-fledged trade across the Sikkim-Tibet border. The Northeastern States see connectivity with Southeast Asia as critical to their economic prosperity. While Delhi talks of the Northeast as the gateway to Asia, it has done precious little to improve transport infrastructure within the region over the decades."[42] Maharashtra and Tamil Nadu governments slowed down the Jaitapur and Koodankulam nuclear projects, Odisha forced a revision of a multi- billion dollar South Korean Posco project and recently the Congress led Kerala Ommen Chandy government took up the case of Italian marines, who had allegedly killed two fishermen off the Kerala coast. The list is long and growing.

Vajpayee extends a hand of friendship to Pakistan

When Vajpayee became the Prime Minister with 24 regional players as his coalition partners in 1998, he faced pressure form his numerous allies including those from Tamil Nadu. But Yashwant Sinha says, "I don't recall the regional chieftains creating problems like Mamata Banerjee is doing now. Bihar and UP were generally on board. Punjab had some interest in Pakistan policy but it was more due to sensitivity than anything else. On important issues we consulted the Chief Minister. Jammu and Kashmir is an important State but I don't think we consulted them on Pakistan policy. On the release of terrorists during the hijack drama, yes, Chief Minister Farooq Abdullah was consulted. He was opposed to their release. With regard to the formulation of Pakistan policy as such as for instance in 2004 Islamabad declaration it was not as if we consulted the State. It was not pronounced as in the case of Tamil Nadu or now in the case of West Bengal. Consultations mean new initiative to talk to them and take them on board. This was the way it worked.[43]"

---

42 C. Rajamohan, '*States and the SAARC*', Indian Express, November 29, 2014

43 Author's interview with Yashwant Sinha, (18,September 2013)

Pointing out that Jammu and Kashmir was a special case when it came to foreign policy, Yashwant Sinha notes that in the name of Pakistani sensitivities, the Jammu and Kashmir adopted positions, which the other States were not permitted to do. Moreover, Jammu and Kashmir has used the differences with Pakistan to push for its own autonomy in various ways. The role that the Hurriyat plays in relations with Pakistan is significant. These separatists meeting Pakistani leaders in India has almost become routine according to Yashwant Sinha.

Vajpayee took a bus ride to Lahore in 1999 to improve the Indo – Pak relations but within weeks Kargil War happened. This was one of the worst periods of tension between India and Pakistan when 100,000 soldiers were deployed on the border with eyeball -to -eyeball contact with the Pakistani soldiers on the other side. The situation eased only after the US President Bill Clinton stepped in to persuade Pakistan to fall in line. Vajpayee invited Pakistan president Gen. Parvez Musharraf for a summit in Agra in 2001 but that too failed. J.N. Dixit sums up, "The decisions taken between him (Vajpayee) and Gen. Musharraf about joint resisting of terrorism, and about recommencing official level talks on all items on Indo-Pak agenda as well as about continuing high level discussions are remarkable developments given the intense adversarial relations with characterised Indo-Pakistan interaction during the last four years.[44]"

Mufti Mohammad Sayeed was the Chief Minister of Jammu and Kashmir (2002 – 2005) when Vajpayee extended his hand of friendship to Pakistan and then the foreign ministry was asked to explore the areas New Delhi can cooperate with Pakistan. For example, Mufti pushed for the opening of the Srinagar-Muzzafarabad bus route, which received unflinching support from the Vajpayee government, even though the People's Democratic Party (PDP) was allied with the Opposition Congress Party. These good relations with the BJP came to his help in March 2015, when he formed the first ever PDP-BJP coalition government in Jammu and Kashmir embarking on a new experiment.

---

44 J.N. Dixit, *'Makers of India's Foreign policy,'* Harper Collins, 2004, P 269

Vajpayee's period saw a lull in the Indo- Sri Lanka relations because the Sri Lankan government and the militant groups were involved in peace talks, brokered by the Norwegians. New Delhi decided to keep out of the negotiations. Yashwant Sinha recalls, "That did not lead to a situation where India was isolated because the Sri Lankan government was briefing us fully every fortnight. They were briefing us on everything that was happening on peace talks." [45]On the Bangladesh side too, Begum Zia was the Prime Minister and there was not much movement on the bilateral relations but the Zia regime was not hostile. The Indo-Nepal relations saw high and low when the palace massacre took place in 2001 followed by the King Gyanendra's rule.

Manmohan Singh faces the ire of some regional chieftains

Prime Minister Manmohan Singh's rule saw more or less the continuation of Vajpayee's foreign policy. Whether it was India's nuclear strategy or the 'Look East 'policy, the engagement with great powers or an emphasis on the economic integration of the subcontinent, Singh's policy was not much different.

If anyone faced the brunt of the ire of the regional satraps it was Prime Minister Manmohan Singh who ruled from 2004 to 2014. The DMK became the UPA partner in 2004 and continued until 2013. The elimination of the LTTE by Sri Lankan President Rajapakse in 2009 at the end of the Eelam War 4 changed the political dynamics in Tamil Nadu once again. The line between sympathy for a humanitarian issue and support for acts of terror committed by the LTTE started blurring. This led to political posturing by different Dravidian parties for their electoral purposes. Fringe groups and the pro-LTTE voices like Vaiko (MDMK) and Nedumaran (President, Tamil National movement) have always enjoyed political space in Tamil Nadu. Even after the Rajiv Gandhi assassination, these groups remained active, though they were not allowed to dictate the mainstream political agenda. Interestingly, now the two frontline parties of the State, which do not see eye to eye on many things, have a similar stand as far as relations with Sri Lanka are concerned.

---

45 Author's interview with Yashwant Sinha, (18, September 2013)

The game changer of course was India's vote on March 21, 2012 at Geneva on the United Nations Human Rights Commission on the human rights situation in Sri Lanka. India voted with the USA, a departure from its stated policy of not voting for a country-specific condemnatory resolution. It was purely under pressure from the Tamil Nadu parties. Ultimately, the DMK left the UPA 11 protesting against the Centre's Sri Lankan policy on March 18, 2013. "The DMK chief said while the 'genocide' in Sri Lanka was a topic of discussion on the world stage, India's failure to understand the gravity of the situation and its indifference was anti-democratic. The Centre had let him down badly, he said, but rejected a suggestion that the general opinion was that the party should have quit in 2009 itself, terming it perverse." [46]

Prime Minister Manmohan Singh faced a problem because the Congress President Sonia Gandhi was the real power behind the throne and he had to go along in accordance with her wishes. This happened in Sharm-e-sheriff when he articulated his Pakistan policy. The Congress Party was up in arms against it and he had to face criticism. It happened in the case of Sri Lanka also when he was prevented from participating in the Commonwealth Heads meet in Colombo in 2013 despite the Ministry of External Affairs advising against skipping it. Even the decision on the vote against Sri Lanka was taken at the last minute. He faced the wrath of Jayalalithaa and Karunanidhi (Sri Lankan Tamil issue), the Left parties (Indo-US nuclear deal) and Mamata Banerjee (Teesta) at different times on different foreign policy issues. The Left Parties, which were supporting the UPA government pulled out on the issue of Indo-nuclear deal in 2008. In fact the Left had been at war with Prime Minister Manmohan Singh on various economic issues also. Although he stuck to the nuclear deal, he did not have the energy to defend his initiatives towards Pakistan and Bangladesh. No doubt he was operating under severe constraints, which few of his predecessors had ever faced.

---

46 B. Kolappan, *'DMK quits UPA ship but won't sink it'*, The Hindu, March 19, 2013

The UPA government took several initiatives but Sri Lanka became one of Manmohan Singh's main problems throughout. Tamil Nadu 's role in influencing the Sri Lanka policy was also significant, as the concept of Tamil nationalism became the primary aspect in influencing it. UPA's Tamil Nadu allies pulled him in different directions. To add to his woes, he did not have easy relations with the AIADMK chief Jayalalithaa. Also the Congress relations with the UPA ally DMK had become strained after the 2 G scam in which the DMK minister A. Raja and Karunanidhi's daughter Kanimozhi were alleged to have been involved. The DMK ultimately pulled out its support to the Manmohan Singh government in March 2013 on the Tamil Issue.

Sri Lanka policy hostage to Dravidian parties

Looking back, the Indian foreign policy agenda in Tamil Nadu became hostage to Tamil sub national interest and the regional Tamil politics tried to influence the Sri Lanka policy on a number of occasions. There is a long list including the issue of citizenship, ceding Katchateevu, India's support to LTTE, sending the Indian Peace Keeping Force (IPKF) to Sri Lanka, the official language legislation of 1956, the Republican Constitution of 1977 as all these discriminated against the Tamils of the island nation. As Jawaharlal Nehru University (JNU) Professor Sahadevan points out, "One thing in Tamil Nadu politics was the competitive rivalry among the political parties on the Sri Lankan issue."[47]

The expanding, aspirational and asserting role of the regional satraps is also on account of the economic liberalization launched in 1991. States are the key players in the implementation of the economic reforms. The main reason for India's attraction for foreign investors is its growing economic muscle, and the prospects for rapid growth as well as the growing middle class. This in turn, has given New Delhi a reason to look for improved relations with the West and elsewhere. Successive governments also took forward the 'Look East Policy' of Narasimha Rao to expand trade and commerce in the East. Prime Minister Modi now talks of 'Act East policy.'

---

47 Author's interview with Prof Sahadevan (28 August 2014)

Since the 1990s Indian States have been doggedly pursuing economic diplomacy with other countries. In recent years, States such as Andhra Pradesh, Maharashtra, Gujarat, Tamil Nadu and Bihar, West Bengal have been pro-active in their engagement with foreign governments. According to official statistics, from a $287 billion in 1991, Indian economy has now grown to become the ninth largest in the world. "Maharashtra contributes 14.10% of total India's Gross Domestic Product (GDP) with gross State domestic product around of 1,476,233 crore INR at current prices. India's most populated State Uttar Pradesh is at second position with a share of 8.24%. Tamil Nadu (7.93%) is at 3rd, India's most economically free State Gujarat (7.31) is at 4th and West Bengal (6.75%) is at 5th position in year 2013-14."[48]

Therefore the Chief Ministers have an effective say in economic diplomacy and rightly so. Some State governments such as Gujarat, Bihar, West Bengal and now Tamil Nadu have started global summits showcasing their States to attract potential investors from around the world.

When Bangladesh was born in 1971, West Bengal had higher stakes than other provinces when an overwhelming number of refugees landed up there. That was why the people of West Bengal had full sympathy for their Eastern counterparts and supported them in their liberation struggle in 1971. The various political parties in the State also sympathised with their cause. The Communist Party of India (Marxists) not only extended its full support but also called for a nationwide agitation. It also passed several resolutions in its party conclaves. The Jana Sangh, the earlier avatar of the BJP, the Praja Socialist Party and the Congress were also in favour of Bangladesh, which emerged as a separate entity on December 6, 1971. Throughout the 33 years of the Left rule in the State, the ruling party supported the refugees from Bangladesh and also helped them get ration cards and other necessary documents for their vote bank politics.

---

48 *Indian States by economic freedom,* Statistics Times.com, Statistics Times, 25 January, 2015

Should the Centre and States work together?

Gradually the strategic community and even those in government have begun to see the importance of these Border Provinces for economic and security reasons. This feeling has also increased because of comparisons with China. The Border States are not mere frontiers but they can act as bridges or gateways. It is the same connectivity problem in Arunachal Pradesh, Manipur and other border areas. Chief Ministers like Tarun Gogoi insist on border fencing for security reasons.

Positive and negative roles of Satraps in Foreign Policy

Ambassador T.P Srinivasan points out that there have been positive State interactions with neighbouring countries. "Pakistan announced its readiness to buy power from Gujarat, the Bihar Chief Minister has been hosting dinners for Nepal politicians and the Chief Minister of Punjab has received a gift of a buffalo from the Chief Minister of Pakistani Punjab."[49] West Bengal and Tripura have agreed to supply power to Bangladesh.

Even during the Janata Party regime there were signs of some positive movements from the regional leaders. "In April 1977, Defence Minister Jagjivan Ram visited Dhaka for finalising an interim accord for sharing of Farakka waters. Ram, who spoke fluent Bengali, stopped en route in Kolkata to consult the West Bengal Chief Minister Siddhartha Shankar Ray, before he inked the accord in Dhaka. The Union Cabinet, despite objections from Charan Singh, later approved this Accord."

Two decades later, the role of West Bengal government in India's pursuit of its foreign policy agenda became high profile when the Farakka Treaty was signed in December 1996 between India and Bangladesh. Prime Minister Inder Gujral held extensive discussions and even directly involved the West Bengal Chief Minister Jyoti Basu in finalising the Farakka Accord of 1996. It was during this time the regional players began to assume a bigger role in influencing foreign policy as part of the coalition stakeholders. It was the visit of Jyoti

---

49 T.P Srinivasan,'*How Modi will change India's foreign policy*' rediff.com. May 14, 2014

Basu from November 27 to December 2, 1996 to Dhaka, which ultimately clinched the Farakka issue. Gujral was also instrumental in reviving tariff and non-tariff barriers on Bangladesh's exports to India. Unfortunately, Gujral's tenure was too short to make more impact on India's foreign policy but his neighbourhood policy is still hailed as 'Gujral doctrine.'

Chief Ministers, particularly those from the Border States have played both positive and negative roles. An in-depth analysis of their role reveals that certain State governments like Punjab and Tripura have responded to New Delhi's overtures. Even Bihar chief minister Nitish Kumar has been making serious overtures towards Nepal. The State governments in the Northeast have been enthusiastically pushing for better relations with Bangladesh and Myanmar. Tripura Chief Minister Manik Sarkar had invited Bangladesh Prime Minister Sheikh Hasina to his State in January 2014. So enthusiastic was Sarkar for better relationship with Bangladesh that he even offered to mediate with Mamata Banerjee about Teesta River Treaty.

The Negative Role of some Regional Chieftains

The States have also become vocal in giving vent to their views, which affect their limited interests to protect their vote banks where foreign policy is concerned. These relate to areas of water sharing, land, security, agriculture, environment, and nuclear energy, social and cultural issues. It is because of this reason the regional parties like the Trinamool Congress, the Shiromani Akali Dal (SAD), the National Conference (NC), the Dravida Munnetra Kazhagam (DMK), the Pattali Makkal Katchi (PMK), the Marumalartchi Dravida Munnetra Kazhagam (MDMK,) the AIADMK, the Desiya Murpokku Dravida Kazhagam (DMDK), the People's democratic party (PDP) and others had asserted on foreign policy issues. There have been agitations about Koodankulam nuclear power plant, about the BT cotton, and land acquisition of the prestigious Korean financed Posco plant in Odisha.

With the change in the Writers building, in 2011 (where the government secretariat is located), Chief Minister Mamata Banerjee has her own way of dealing with the foreign policy issues pertaining to Bangladesh. Unlike her predecessors Jyoti Basu or Buddha Dev

Bhattacharya, Banerjee opposed the Teesta River water sharing agreement, on the ground that five districts of West Bengal would be deprived of water. She also opposed the exchange of the enclaves on both sides, which could mitigate the sufferings of the people living in these enclaves and give them identity. However, when the Modi government persuaded her providing a financial package, she agreed later.

Muchkund Dubey points out that "it would be difficult to imagine how to deal effectively with illegal immigration from Bangladesh without the cooperation of the governments of West Bengal, Assam, Tripura and Mizoram. Mamata Banerjee has become a little soft after her visit to Dhaka in February 2015 at the invitation of the Bangladesh Foreign Minister and has started talking of cooperation on issues like Land Boundary."[50]

Given the local politics of the Indian Border States often-electoral considerations factor into New Delhi's thinking. Recent examples include the UPA government's policies toward Bangladesh and Sri Lanka to accommodate the regional interests of chief ministers Mamata Banerjee and Jayalalithaa over water-sharing and fishing disputes, respectively.

First of all, as stake- holders, the regional parties held the balance in Parliament for more than two decades where the survival of the coalition governments depended upon their support. Be it the National Front, United Front or the National Democratic Alliance and a decade of United Progressive Alliance coalition governments, they had often forced the Centre to back down on a number of important legislations, policies and diplomatic positions. Some of the ruling coalition allies too had used this pressure tactics to get their way. The Centre then was forced to seek support from other regional parties.

The Manmohan Singh government often needed and took the support of both the Samajwadi Party and the Bahujan Samaj Party apart from the DMK to get some bills passed in the house. Despite the majority, the present the Modi government too has to depend

---

50 Author's interview with Muchkund Dubey, (10, July,2014)

on the support of the AIADMK, Biju Janata Dal (BJD) and other regional parties for getting the bills passed in Rajya Sabha where the NDA is in a minority.

The suggestion of the Assam Chief Minister Tarun Gogoi on setting up Brahmaputra River Valley Authority which should include China, Bangladesh and Bhutan is yet another example. On the eve of Chinese Premier Li Keqiang's visit to India in May 2013, Kiren Rijiju, presently a junior minister in the Modi government from Arunachal Pradesh but then a Member of Parliament maintained that by issuing stapled visas to Arunachal is instead of its earlier policy of denying them visas altogether, the Chinese government has softened its position and has virtually conceded that Arunachal Pradesh is a dispute.

The UPA Government's mistakes

The Manmohan Singh government in the past decade has mishandled some issues. The first was the fiasco over the Italian marines. "The Government was keen to give the benefit of doubt to the marines that they had shot dead two Kerala fishermen in the international waters off the Kerala coast, mistaking them to be sea pirates. However, once the Marxists in Kerala upped the ante and forced the State Congress Government to embrace the chauvinistic stand, a weak and wavering Centre felt obliged to toe the line."[51] The Centre was keen to give the benefit of doubt to the marines when they claimed that they shot two Kerala fishermen mistaking them for sea pirates. Prodded by the Marxists in Kerala the Congress ruled Ommen Chandy government embraced a chauvinistic stand with the result the Centre looked weak in the eyes of the people.

The second was the handling of the Sri Lankan Tamil issue. The way the Union Government first agreed to tone down the US sponsored resolution on Human rights issue in Sri Lanka and followed it by moving harsh amendments coming under pressure form the DMK and other Dravidian parties shows the weakness of the Centre. "While 13 countries, including Pakistan, voted against,

---

51 Virendra Kapoor, *'when foreign policy becomes foreign'*, Afternoon Despatch and Courier, April 01,2013

eight member-States abstained from voting on the contentious resolution that saw political tremors in India with the DMK pulling out of the UPA alliance and the government."[52] The United Nations Human Rights Commission fiasco has only helped to distance Sri Lanka further from India pushing it closer to China. However, this was rectified when the new Srisena – Wickremesinghe government took over in 2015.

The third was the Prime Minister's decision to skip the CHOGAM meeting in Colombo in November 2013. Had he taken the initiative to participate in the meeting and also travel to Jaffna to meet the newly elected chief minister of Northern Province Wigneswaran, it would have sent a very good signal to the Tamils. Instead, Singh decided to skip the meeting bowing to the pressure of the Tamil Nadu political parties.

The fourth was the Teesta River water sharing issue, which showed the failure of the Union Government to delink partisan domestic politics with that of the foreign policy. Manmohan Singh could have handled it with more finesse. On the other hand Prime Minister Narendra Modi utilized the services of his Foreign Minister Sushma Swaraj to get Mamata Banerjee on board on the Land Boundary Agreement resolution and also settling the enclave issue.

The Shiv Sena, a regional party from Maharashtra, had jumped into the foreign policy debate both with regard to New Delhi's Pakistan and Bangladesh policy. It indulged in vandalism during the cricket matches in Delhi and elsewhere when it was the NDA partner in the Vajpayee government. Even in October 2015, the Shiv Sena blocked the music concert of Pakistani singer Ghulam Ali in Mumbai and also a meeting of Board of Control for Cricket in India and with his Pakistani counterpart despite being a ruling coalition partner. In 1998 when the Maharashtra government attempted to deport some Bengalis to Bangladesh, West Bengal government protested against it. According to 'Frontline' magazine – The West Bengal government lodged a protest with the Centre and the Maharashtra Government on the issue of 'deporting infiltrators'. Describing the Shiv Sena-BJP

---

52 Press Trust of India, *'UNHRC adopts US sponsored resolution against Sri Lanka, India votes in favour.'* Economic Times, March 21, 2013.

government's action as uncivilized, Chief Minister Jyoti Basu asked: "Are they dealing with cattle?"[53]

At the time of the Indo- US nuclear deal, the Leftist government in Kerala campaigned strongly against it and also raised an alarm when a trade agreement between India and ASEAN came up. It argued that the loss of revenue to the State should be avoided even if there were benefits for the Centre. Kerala insisted that the bilateral relations between India and Italy should not be dragged into the legal case against the Italian marines even as the Manmohan Singh government felt that its jurisdiction was questioned by a State ruled by the Congress Party. Kerala held that a settlement could have been reached with the Italians with the help of the church, had the Centre not intervened.

As political analyst Mr Tridevesh Maini points out that the increasing role of States in foreign policy formulation raises some interesting points. **"First, State intervention in foreign policy is not always a bad thing; examples of Tripura, Bihar and Punjab clearly reiterate this point. Second, in the context of foreign policy issues, political parties that are not part of the central alliance, such as Bihar and Punjab, are usually more supportive of central government initiatives. Third, some leaders are very aggressive when it comes to engaging countries outside India's immediate neighbourhood, but fail to do so within it."[54]**

On the positive side, one would expect that States such as Punjab – which suffered a traumatic partition and wars with Pakistan – would be more jingoistic. On the contrary, Punjab is taking a lead role in acting as bridge in trade, commerce, sports and cultural areas with Pakistan. In fact, today if the two mainstream parties of Punjab, the Shiromani Akali Dal and the Congress are on the same page on any issue, it is for closer economic ties with Pakistan. The Punjab Chief Minister Prakash Singh Badal as well as his predecessor Captain Amarinder Singh had lobbied with New

---

53 Kalyan Chaudhary, '*Protest in West Bengal*' The Frontline, August 15 -28, 1998

54 Tridevesh Maini, '*India's foreign policy: the increasing role of regional satraps*', East Asia forum, October 25, 2012

Delhi for more trade promotion between the two countries through the two Punjabs. The Centre for Research in Rural and Industrial Development (CRRID) has been actively involved in promoting such connectivity at the people to people, serving different interest groups, such as media, agriculturalists and small and medium entrepreneurs. In the past three years three instances bear evidence to the closeness on both sides. One was the Atari function on 13th April 2012. It was the completion of the first Integrated Check Post (ICP) programme of the Home ministry and the border management. ICP combines both customs as well as immigration facilities at the check posts. The ICPs were proposed in two phases all along India's western border. Out of the 13 ICPs that was the first one, which was completed. The two Chief Ministers – Shehbaz Sharif from Pakistani Punjab and Prakash Singh Badal from the Indian side participated. The then Home Minister P. Chidambaram inaugurated it and the commerce ministers from both sides were also present. The two Chief Ministers made their speeches in Punjabi amidst great enthusiasm. At the inauguration, the Punjab Chief Minister Badal urged India's home minister to ease the visa regime for citizens of both countries in general and the two Punjabs in particular. He also spoke about the need for opening up more trade routes with Pakistan through his State. It brought home the point that both the Punjabs were very much interested in cooperation. The second was more recently, Badal's son and Deputy Chief Minister of the State, Sukhbir Singh Badal, urged the Centre to allow sale of surplus wheat produce to Pakistan during his visit to Pakistani Punjab in 2012 November as part of celebrating International Punjab day. Now there was a Kabbadi tournament in which both sides participated. The third was when Shehbaz Sharif visited Indian side Punjab on December 13, 2013. These were seen not merely trade but also people-to-people public relations. They also tried to increase cooperation in agriculture, animal husbandry, solar farms, biomass etc. in renewable non-traditional energy, which the Indian side of Punjab has done well. Shehbaz Sharif and the Badals as well as their predecessors had shown enthusiasm in developing these relations. There is a lot of potential in exporting energy to Pakistan and this could be exploited.

Bihar Chief Minister Nitish Kumar has been making serious overtures towards Nepal, as was evident from the Global Bihar summit in February 2012. He invited the Prime Minister of Nepal Dr Baburam Bhattarai to participate in the Bihar global summit on February 17, 2012. He had also extended his hand of friendship to other Nepal Prime Minister s including Prachanda and Sushil Koirala. While there can be no single explanation, it is perhaps a combination of various factors. The Himachal Pradesh government has been lobbying with the Centre for giving work permits to Chinese workers working in that State. State governments such as Gujarat, Bihar and Tamil Nadu have started global summits, which host potential investors from around the world. Modi, as the Chief Minister successfully attracted investment by holding" Vibrant Gujarat "showcasing Gujarat every year which is now continued by his successor Anandibhen Patel.

Secondly, the geographical proximity as well as ethnicity, religion and family ties makes these Border States get involved in shaping the foreign policy. India shares a border with Pakistan in Kashmir, Punjab, Rajasthan and Gujarat in the North and the West. Uttar Pradesh and Bihar have a border with Nepal. In the Eastern side, West Bengal and the North- eastern States share a border with Bangladesh while Tamil Nadu is much closer geographically to Sir Lanka. U.P, Bihar, West Bengal, Sikkim and Uttarakhand share the Nepal border.

Thirdly, with the emerging growth of aspirational voters who want development and governance, the Chief Ministers have to keep in mind how to deliver jobs and growth. They try to cultivate the ambassadors of various countries and try to market their States for investment. Telugu Desam chief Chandrababu Naidu who earned the name of "Flying Chief Minister" was enterprising in finding funds for the development of the united Andhra Pradesh when he was the Chief Minister earlier. Now that he has come back to power in 2014, Naidu has been visiting countries like Singapore to build his State's new capital at Amravati and also finding resources for the development of the bifurcated Andhra Pradesh. Because of these developments, the national parties also are forced to take a clear stand on foreign policy. Fourthly, several Indians from various States migrate to other countries for greener pastures. Slightest hardship for them becomes an electoral issue for the political parties. The head -gear controversy in France, ethnic Tamil issue in Sri Lanka and the racial attacks on Indian students in Australia are some other examples. Kerala has always taken up the cause of its workers who have gone to the Gulf countries for jobs who are estimated around three million. The Iraq crisis in 2014 brought tension in Punjab and Kerala when the workers from these States had to be evacuated.

Fifthly, States have become important in the context of neighbourhood policy through increased bilateralism. Two important policies of the Centre–The South Asian Association for Regional Cooperation and the 'Look East' policy have enabled the involvement of States in a big way.

Mr Bharat Bhushan, senior journalist and political analyst points out that the Tamil Nadu cabinet passed a resolution in 2012 against restarting work on the Koodankulam nuclear power plant - stalled by anti-nuclear protesters - knowing full well that it would impact on the Indo-Russian relations. "Later, Chief Minister Jayalalithaa was persuaded to change her stance. The price she is believed to have extracted was to get India to vote against Sri Lanka at the UN Human Rights Commission on the Tamil rights issue."[55]

Do States have a case for bigger role?

These go to prove that the involvement of States in foreign policy is not always a bad thing. Secondly, sometimes even some State governments, which are not part of the coalition, are supportive of the Centre. For instance, Chief Ministers like Narendra Modi when he was in Gujarat was keen to support trade with countries like China, Japan and Korea.

Nepal is another example where the Indian political parties take an active interest. The Indo-Nepal ties have seen the highs and lows over the years. The BJP looks to Nepal as the only Hindu Kingdom while the Left parties have friendship with their comrades. Chandrasekhar, D.P. Tripathi, Sitaram Yechury and CPI leader A.B.

---

55 Bharat Bhushan, '*Why is the US chasing India's regions*', BBC news, India, 8 May, 2012

Bardhan also have influenced the Indo – Nepal policy. The JD (U) has an interest in Nepal because of Bihar.

Jammu and Kashmir is yet another example of how the regional parties like the National Conference and the PDP, or separatist outfits like the Hurriyat had tried to influence in a limited manner India's Pakistan policy. Jammu and Kashmir still complains about the short shift it got in the matter of river waters when the Union government signed the Indus Waters Treaty with Pakistan. Chief Minister Mufti Mohammad Sayeed, a coalition partner with the BJP had been asking for more trade routes with Pakistan.

As for water sharing the Chief Ministers of Bihar and Assam too have important issues, which impinge on our relations with Nepal and China. As stakeholders, these States, which have special links with certain countries, either because of a common border or cultural and commercial affinities, expect to be consulted in framing policies towards those countries.

Foreign countries courting Regional Satraps

Increasingly, foreign governments have also realized the growing importance and assertion of the States. The foreign consulates have stepped up their activities in several States. Foreign governments have noticed the increasingly important roles the State governments play, and are beginning to actively engage with them. Requests for appointment of honorary consuls have multiplied. The States have begun to push for the internationalisation of education to gain benefits abroad. There is a growing appreciation on the one hand and concern on the other that regional satraps influence the foreign policy and its implementation, and thus there have been aggressive efforts to woo them.

A new development is that international diplomats are increasingly courting regional leaders. For instance in May, 2012, the then US Secretary of State Hillary Clinton directly held interactions with the West Bengal Chief Minister Mamata Banerjee and Tamil Nadu Chief Minister Jayalalithaa to probe the possibility of the US investments in their respective States. This was of course encouraged by the Union Governments to attract foreign investment. Mamata

Banerjee is opposed to the recent reform initiatives launched by the Modi government, especially easing up on Foreign Direct Investment and Land Acquisition Bill. Hillary Clinton also went to Chennai and discussed with Jayalalithaa about the Sri Lankan issue. Chinese President Xi Jingping breaking the tradition visited Ahmadabad first before starting his Delhi engagements in 2014. It has become a tradition for the visiting dignitaries from abroad to visit at least one or two States like Mumbai, Bangalore or Hyderabad while they are in India.

Nitish Kumar has received delegations from many countries, including those from the US, China and Pakistan. He even visited Pakistan in November 2012. Other Chief Ministers too have found diplomats knocking at their doors. It is, therefore, to be expected that trade delegations and diplomats will make aggressive efforts to court various players who can help improve trade relations.

Minister of State for External Affairs Gen. V.K. Singh agrees that domestic political compulsions should not make the foreign policy a hostage. "Irritants must be looked at and resolved. Good foreign policy implies that your neighbours live in peace with you. Domestic political compulsions will always create problems. It is for the Centre to ensure that they do not overshadow your foreign policy. I don't think the regional leaders are putting more pressure on the Centre and they are maintaining their stance. It is for the Centre to reach out and narrow down the differences and ensure that what the Centre wants gets done.[56]"

Why do Chief Ministers desire a greater role?

Meghalaya Chief Minister Mukul Sangma has proposed joint investment with his State given its rich deposits of granite and very high quality limestone. Sangma has invited Bangladesh for making joint investments in hydropower projects and the agro-forest sector in Meghalaya. Meghalaya has huge potential in hydro-electricity and Bangladesh could get electricity through investment.

Another North-eastern State, Tripura will be largely benefited from improved trade ties and connectivity with the neighbouring

---

56 Author's interview with Gen V.K. Singh (4, September 2014)

Bangladesh. This tiny State is surrounded by Bangladesh from three sides. The Manik Sarkar government, which enjoys a warm relationship with the Awami League regime in Bangladesh, has been seeking transit facilities through Bangladesh and access to Chittagong port. Indian government is providing financial assistance for the construction of a bridge on Feni River, building a 70-km road from Sabroom in South Tripura district to Chittagong port and laying railway tracks between Agartala and Akhaura (in Chittagong division).

"The Hasina government has already sought New Delhi's permission to open its Deputy High Commission in Guwahati and upgrade Agartala visa office to an Assistant High Commission to boost diplomatic and commercial presence in the Northeast."[57]

Former Prime Minister Manmohan Singh was aware of the growing influence of the regional satraps. A disappointed Singh while returning from Dhaka in 2011 September observed, "Provincial sentiments cannot be wished away in a multi regional set up. We are a country of great complexities and great diversity. There are different regions, they have different perspectives, and they have different problems. So we have to find pathways in which we can take along the regional parties, while trying to find out a coherence in our foreign policy relations with our neighbours and as well as with other countries. These problems are bound to arise for example when we go to negotiate on environment. Increasingly States are saying, 'Well, you are trying to barter away our interests. You must take us into confidence.' Although treaties are exclusively within the domain of the Centre but one has to take into account the political realities. So there I look ahead of us, and I think we must, open up more and more channels of communications with State governments and regional forces, to help build a coherent national perspective on these seemingly difficult issues."[58]

---

57 Rupak Bhattacharjee, *India Bangladesh business: Engagement of Northeast essential*, South Asia monitor. Updated September 17,2014

58 'Transcript of Manmohan Singh on board media interaction during return from Bangladesh, Pravasi Today,' NRI and PIO portal, September 7,2011

Modi Regime and Chief Ministers

Prime Minister Narendra Modi is busy building up his international image. The initial actions of his government seem to indicate that Modi wants a strong neighbourhood policy backed by economic and strategic diplomacy. Will he be able to have a free hand in the conduct of foreign policy or will he be constrained by the assertive role of the Chief Ministers? The Prime Minister is a great votary of federalism and often talks of working with the Chief Minister s as a team. He calls it as 'Team India.' Even as the Chief Minister of Gujarat he had demanded a bigger role for the States. As for legislative measures, there is no doubt that Prime Minister Modi needs the support of these regional satraps in Parliament as the BJP is in a minority in the Rajya Sabha. While the BJP-led National Democratic Alliance has 336 of the 543 seats in the Lok Sabha, they have just 57 seats in the Upper House. To play an effective role and obtain parliamentary approval on labour laws, Land Acquisition bill, Goods and Services Tax, regulatory clearances and creation of a pro-market environment, Modi needs the support of the States. Until 2019, the BJP will not be in a position to gain majority in the Upper House and therefore would need the backing of even hostile regional parties - such as the Samajwadi Party, the Bahujan Samaj Party and the Trinamool Congress. The DMK too won't dare cross swords with the BJP, given that the CBI sword is hanging over former minister A. Raja and Karunanidhi's daughter Kanimozhi's heads because of their alleged involvement in the 2 G scam. The SP and BSP share a love-hate relationship with the BJP but have also helped each other in the past. It will be of critical importance to Modi to keep them in good humour.

Prime Minister Modi had come up with the 'neighbourhood first' concept starting with his invitation to the SAARC Heads of State for his swearing in ceremony in May 2014. He obviously feels that the key to India's emergence as a regional and global power lies in New Delhi's ability in improving relations with its immediate neighbours. Modi articulated this view during his first foreign visit as Prime Minister to Bhutan in 2014. President Pranab Mukherji, outlining the Modi government's foreign policy in the first joint session of Parliament in 2014 said while the government was committed to work towards building a peaceful, stable and economically inter-linked neighbourhood, but clarified that they will not shy away from raising issues of concern to India at the bilateral level. This is where the Border States come in, as they certainly want to have a say in dealing with the neighbours and more connectivity and trade with them

External Affairs Minister Sushma Swaraj is quite candid when she admits that the Centre has to address the concerns of the States. "They are not asserting themselves. They express their concern about policies decided by the Centre. For example, the Land boundary Agreement between Bangladesh and India or when you talk of exchange of enclaves naturally you have to take the Chief Minister of West Bengal on board. For Teesta water issue you have to take the concerned Chief Minister on board. The earlier government also tried that and we are also trying to do that. We took Mamata Banerjee on board and she also expressed that she is ready for the enclaves' exchange as well as adverse possession. So there is no contradiction in the policy. She was only saying give me a financial package. That concern has to be addressed. For example she has not come on board on Teesta. Still we are positively discussing it. What she wants she has spoken to Prime Minister of Bangladesh during her recent visit to Dhaka but on Land Boundary Agreement she has come on board. Why, because the Centre has also said that we will give you financial package. So she has not stopped it. She has expressed her concerns and when the Centre is ready to address these concerns the policy is shaped. We cannot ignore the States especially when we talk of cooperative federalism. We have to address their concerns and take them on board."[59]

Ministry of External Affairs has a Division for States

It is heartening to note that the Modi government has taken a first step in improving relations with the States regarding foreign policy. The Ministry of External Affairs has setup a new division called States Division to interact with the Provincial governments. This division was setup in October 2014 headed by a senior level Indian Foreign Service (IFS) officer who reports directly to the Foreign Secretary.

59 Author's interview with Sushma Swaraj (March 2015)

Prime Minister Modi claims that he believes in 'cooperative federalism. "His observations during the 2014 campaign should be read with a foreign policy scene when the UPA government had already ceded the veto power to some States, particularly West Bengal and Tamil Nadu. Modi has now come up with a different idea and wants to make the Border States stake holders in deepening regional ties.

Sushma Swaraj points out: "Things have changed. That time it was unitary form of government. Now we are talking of cooperative federalism. Though Constitution provides for federal it was working like a unitary government. Since the coalition began things have changed. Manmohan Singh could not ignore Karunanidhi's views or Mamata Banerjee's views. As for us, we are always consulting. For example we talked to Mamata Banerjee when she went to Bangladesh recently to meet the Bangladesh Prime Minister Sheikh Hasina. My officers were there and the joint secretary in charge of Bangladesh accompanied her to Dhaka. So she was all the time on board. There was a meeting between Foreign Secretary, Home Secretary and Chief Secretary of West Bengal on the financial package. They sat and decided the fixed package and interim package. So political leadership is also talking and the executive are also talking.[60]"

In the coming months, Prime Minister Modi will face several contradictions as he tries to bring his foreign policy agenda. True federalism means voluntarily reducing the Centre's powers in several areas and handing them over to States to work as equal partners. Will he do this? The recent decision to accept the Finance Commission's recommendation to increase the share of the States is a welcome step in this direction. Setting up of the Niti Ayog in place of Planning Commission is yet another step. Modi's schemes will work only if the States agree to implement what the Centre has proposed.

In conclusion, **there is a case for institutionalising the process of consultation and involvement of States in foreign or security policy, trade and investment and people to people contact in the changing scenario where the regional satraps are demanding**

---

60 Authors interview with Sushma Swaraj (March 2015)

a greater role in foreign policy making because of the concerns pertaining to their states.

Former West Bengal Governor M.K. Narayanan observes, "The Centre should take the Border-States along with it and today there is no other choice. To what extent they should have a veto is a matter of opinion. When there is a question of land, water there is need for concurrence. There is also need for more consultations and interaction between the Centre and the States.[61]"

At the same time, the regional parties also should not use federalism for their anti-congress or anti – BJP sentiments. Several non-congress and non – BJP ruled States seem to be going this way with parties pursuing their own goals. While the Centre should not be patronising, the States too should not use emotiveness as an electoral tool.

Apart from this there is the problem of ethnicity. So in future India's foreign policy has to be calibrated keeping in mind the sensitivities of the people living in the Border- States. Saugata Roy asks, "Can we settle the Chinese border question bartering away Arunachal or the Kashmir question bartering away a part of Kashmir? As far as the States located in the Centre of India they have no problem. They have no border sharing and nothing affects them. For us this remains a serious problem.[62]"

A motley group of weak national parties and strong regional groupings had weakened governance and scuttle political consensus on policy reforms and foreign policy. **Federalism does not mean a weak Centre and combative States but there should be a strong Centre and strong States. A federation envisages decentralisation of power and not regionalisation of the nation. If the Union Government fails to address the concerns of the States, the regionalism will only grow further and the regional satraps will consider States as their personal or family fiefdom. Regional parties becoming powerful enough in their own States to win enough parliamentary seats have inadvertently strengthened Indian federalism. The numerical clout**

---

61 Author's interview with M.K.Narayanan (13, December 2014)

62 Author's interview with Saugata Roy.

of a regional party determines not only how many but also which particular ministries it can claim.

The big question is whether he can convince the Chief Ministers, particularly of the Border States to back his ambitious plans on his South Asia policy. Will what he calls 'cooperative federalism' really work at the ground level? It should if the Centre and the States understand their respective roles and address each other's concerns.

Chapter 2

India and Sri Lanka

Why does Tamil Nadu get disturbed if anything happens to their cousins in Sri Lanka across the Palk Straits? Is it because of the historical and cultural bond between the Sri Lankan Tamils and people of Tamil Nadu? Or is it the geopolitical location of the island country that compels not only Tamil Nadu but also New Delhi anxious over any destabilising development in Sri Lanka, which Marco Polo once described as the island paradise of the earth.

To understand the ethnic conflict in Sri Lanka, the rise of the LTTE and other militant groups, their armed struggle, Tamil separatism, India's role in the island nation and the part played by Tamil Nadu, one must trace the history and the context to tensions that began nearly eight or nine decades ago. What started as an agitation against the discrimination of Tamils by the Sinhalese in the forties and fifties had ended up as a demand for a separate Eelam in the seventies. The militant group, the Liberation Tigers of Tamil Eelam (LTTE) had fought four wars in the past four decades, which ended in 2009 with the killing of its leader Velupillai Prabhakaran. In the course of these conflicts, Tamil Nadu's regional chieftains became stakeholders because of their Tamil brethren.

Broadly, there are five landmarks in the ethnic conflict of Sri Lanka, which had repercussions in Tamil Nadu. The first was the 'Sinhala Only' Act of 1956, the second was the Republican Constitution, the third was the 1977 elections and the emergence of Junius Richard Jayewardene as President in 1978, the fourth was the 'Black July riots' in 1983 and the fifth the end of the Eeelam War 4 in 2009.

There were different phases in India's Sri Lankan policy. In the fifties, the Tamil question was not a big issue. The Tamil Nadu chieftains did not take much interest in the Sri Lankan affairs as the Congress was ruling in the State as well as at the Centre. In the sixties and seventies the Dravidian parties like the DMK and the AIADMK began to champion the Tamil cause. The local unit of the Congress also joined them. In the eighties, particularly after the 1983 Black July riots and Sri Lankan government's oppression of the Tamils, the interests of the Centre and the State began to converge. In the seventies and eighties, as author Aditi Mukherjee notes, **"What was sought and achieved with ease was the cooperation of the Tamil Nadu Government to the policies that were being formulated by the Central Government and assistance in their implementation. The State Government collaborated with such ventures keeping in mind the calculations of alliance politics."**[1]

Prime Minister Indira Gandhi began the double track policy of covert and overt designs to deal with the issue. In the mid eighties, her son Rajiv Gandhi started the mediatory policy between the Sri Lankan government and the Tamil militant groups and donned the role of an 'honest broker', but he failed. In the early nineties, there was a policy of non-intervention after the LTTE assassinated Rajiv Gandhi. This period also saw the growth of caste based and splinter groups of the Dravidian parties in Tamil Nadu.

In the late eighties and nineties there was a perceptible change in the Centre-State relations due to coalition politics and the growth of regional parties. **Moreover, the Dravida Munnetra Kazhagam (DMK) and the All India Dravida Munnetra Kazhagam (AIADMK) alternatively became part of collation governments which ruled the Country and they fell in line with the Centre's policy but the pitch of their support increased or decreased according to whether they were with the ruling coalition or in the opposition at the centre or the State.**

---

1   Aditi Mukherjee, ' *Tamil Nadu and the Sri Lankan conflict, evolving Centre – State understanding on the ethnic issue,* 'Mainstream weekly, 29 December, 2013

By this time, the Tamil issue became dominant in the Indo- Sri Lankan bilateral relations. In early 2000s, the Vajpayee government supported the peace initiatives brokered by Norway. The DMK was a partner in Vajpayee government. From 2004 onwards New Delhi adopted a pro – Sri Lankan government policy and supported the end of Eelam War 4. By this time the DMK became part of the ruling United Progressive Alliance. From then on the focus has been mainly on how to make Colombo implement the 13thamendment (giving, among other things, more regional autonomy to the Tamil majority areas) and find a political solution. The present Modi government too is continuing the same policy.

The interests of regional satraps in Tamil Nadu have often been in direct conflict with the larger interests of India's national foreign policy. As various interviewees point out later in this chapter, the regional concerns of Dravidian parties have focused on the protection of rights of their Tamil brethren in Sri Lanka rather than on the geo-political desire on the part of India to keep Sri Lanka out of China's sphere of influence and also its strategic interests. In short, they became complex problems involving two national governments and one state government.

As we shall see in this chapter, the Tamil Nadu regional players have five main concerns regarding India's Sri Lanka policy. They would like India to do the following:

(i) Restore the fundamental rights and liberties of Sri Lankan Tamils.

(ii) Retrieve Katchateevu, the territory ceded to Sri Lanka during the Indira Gandhi- Sirimavo period.

(iii) Protect the rights of the Tamil Nadu fishermen.

(iv) Persuade the Sri Lankan government to implement the 13th Amendment of the Sri Lankan Constitution as per the Indo Sri Lankan Accord.

(v) Return of the Tamil refugees presently living in Tamil Nadu refugee camps to the island.

The question posed in this chapter is under what conditions are these regional players able to influence or not influence the Central government's foreign policy? My hypotheses are:

1. **The regional players are more likely to carry weight when they are key partners of the Centre whether they are in a coalition or not.** This is true of the DMK and the AIADMK as they were able to influence the decisions pertaining to the Sri Lankan policy to some extent. While Chief Minister M.G. Ramachandran by and large went along with the Centre, two other Chief Ministers - Jayalalithaa Jayaram (AIADMK) and Muthuvel Karunanidhi (DMK) - at times took a hard line. For instance both opposed the Sri Lankan President Mahinda Rajapakse's war strategy during Eelam war 4, which they described as 'genocide' of the Tamils. Karunanidhi even pulled out of the UPA on the Lankan issue in March 2013 on the Sri Lankan Tamil issue. They were able to force Prime Minister Manmohan Singh to skip the Commonwealth Heads of Government Meeting (CHOGM) in Colombo in 2013 November.

2. **Regional players are less likely to be successful in influencing foreign policy when they are in the opposition.** During the initial phase (from independence to 1967), the strong position of the Congress Government at the Centre, its holding of power in Tamil Nadu, and the staunch opposition by the Dravidian parties foreclosed the possibility of cooperation. Initially when the Congress party ruled at the Centre and the State in the fifties and sixties, the Union Government took unilateral decisions in its Sri Lanka policy despite opposition from the Dravidian parties.

   As Prof V. Suryanarayan points out, "The first is the Sirimavo-Shastri Pact of 1964 and the subsequent Sirimavo-Indira Gandhi Pact of 1974, by which New Delhi agreed to confer Indian citizenship on thousands of people of Indian origin in the Island and decided to repatriate them to India as Indian citizens. The second illustration, where the Government of India was insensitive to the interests of the State of Tamil Nadu took place in 1974 and 1976, when the India-Sri Lanka maritime boundary agreements were concluded. They resulted in the ceding of the island of Katchateevu, which was a part of the Zamindari of the Raja of Ramnad, to Sri Lanka and also sacrificed the traditional fishing rights of the Indian fishermen in the Palk Bay region. But since fishermen are no respecters of maritime boundaries and move wherever there is fish, the Indian fishermen poach on the Sri Lankan waters and in that process get killed, injured, their boats get destroyed and the fish dumped into the sea. The rich fishing grounds on the Sri Lankan side of the Palk Bay have become a bone of contention among the fishermen of the two countries and the Sri Lankan Navy. " [2]

According to Suryanarayan, the Government of Tamil Nadu was completely kept out of the negotiations, on the delimitation of the maritime boundary. But before the agreement was finally signed, the then Foreign Secretary Kewal Singh, came to Madras, met Chief Minister Karunanidhi and a few of his colleagues. He explained the background to the signing of the Agreement. **This was the period when the Centre did not heed the dissident voices from Tamil Nadu even from Congress leaders like K. Kamaraj.**

3. **Regional players are more likely to be successful if their preferences match those of the Central governments.** For instance MGR was successful after the post 1983 July riots in persuading Indira Gandhi to take a hard line in dealing with the Sri Lankan government. Panruti Ramachandran, a trusted minister in the MGR cabinet who interpreted for him says Indira Gandhi and MGR were on the same page. Also both did not support the demand for a separate Eelam. Later, Karunanidhi as Chief Minister helped the then Prime Minister V.P. Singh in negotiating with the

---

2   V.Suryanarayan, 'India's Bilateral Agreements and Centre-State Relations – A Perspective from Tamil Nadu'. Published in South Asian Analysis Group on Monday, February 08, 2010. Paper no. 3655

Tamil militant groups as it coincided with his interests. Also in the seventies, the Tamil parties accepted the Central line for electoral purposes both in the State and at the Centre adopting a live and let live attitude towards the Centre.

In this chapter, I will test these hypotheses on the evolution of India's foreign policy towards Sri Lanka, and the changes in the policy.

Historic ties between India and Sri Lanka

The history of Sri Lankan Tamils and their relationship with India dates back to centuries. Before the arrival of Vijaya, the legendary prince from India with his 700 warriors who was the founder of the Sinhala race in the fifth century BC it was the home of the mythical Yakshas and Nagas. The first real occasion was when Elara, a prince form the Chola Kingdom in South India seized the Northern Sinhalese Kingdom, ruled it for 44 years and was ultimately dislodged by the Sinhalese warrior Duttagamani who brought the entire island under his sway. South Indian invasions reached their peak when the Cholas conquered most of the island in 1017 AD monopolizing trade to Malaysia and China. During the Chola occupation, the Buddhist and the Sinhalese suffered a great deal from neglect and oppression.

Buddhism came to Sri Lanka 2300 years ago and since then the island country remains steadfastly Buddhist. Sinhalese and Tamils had lived together and the Sinhalese accepted a Tamil as a King for the whole country much later. But that Tamil King was very benevolent to Buddhism. When the Portuguese landed in Ceylon, (Sri Lanka was known as Ceylon earlier) in the 16th Century they found two kingdoms – one ruled by the Tamil King in the Northeast and the other by the Sinhalese in the south. Then came the Dutch and the British. Soon Ceylon became a British colony. While the impact of the Portuguese and the Dutch was not that big, the British legacy in the island was quite evident. Though Tamils and the Sri Lankans have deep historical roots, the island became a multi- ethnic society. The Muslims whose origin is traced back to the 10th century arrived in Ceylon as traders from Arabia. They adopted Tamil as their mother tongue and settled down in Eastern and Northern districts.[3]

It was in 1815, with the conquest of the Kandyan Kingdom by the British, the history of the Tamil Plantation workers begins. "They setup coffee plantations and brought about a million cheap labourers from South India, particularly Tamil Nadu between 1840 and 1950 to work in the plantations."[4]

Given these historical antecedents, it is not surprising that when the Sri Lankan Tamils felt oppressed by the Sinhalese dominated government, they sought a separate Eelam. Anton Balasingham, the LTTE, ideologue, justifies the Tamil demand for a separate Eelam pointing out that " From 13th Century onwards, until the advent of the colonialism, Tamils lived as a stable national formation in their own Kingdom, ruled by their own Kings, within their own specified territory of traditional homelands embracing northern and eastern provinces".[5]

Former Sri Lankan Minister Udaya Prabhath Gammanpila notes that when the British came, the Sinhalese resisted them. The British had worked with the Tamils in South India and found them loyal and so they brought them to administer Sri Lanka. He points out that "The first layer was British; the second layer was the Tamils and the third layer the Sinhalese. Since the Tamils became the second layer of administration, they got good business opportunities, government supplies and soon became rich. Because they were affluent, they were able to afford education for their children in England. So the Tamils came to dominate and became the elite community of Sri Lanka. Naturally the Sinhalese resented this. This was the beginning of struggle."[6]

---

3   Prehistory The island of Sri Lanka... - We Accuse War ...https://www.
    facebook.com/eelamtamils/posts/38638042471

4   https://southasiarev.wordpress.com/2009/11/23/history-of-the-tamil-
    struggle-for-self-determination-in-sri-lanka/

5   Anton Balasingham, 'War and peace', Fairmax publishing Ltd, 2004, P 2

6   Author's interview with Udaya Prabhath Gammanpila (17-22 February,
    2014)

In contrast, the story of the tea estate Tamils known as Plantation Tamils was quite different. They were the migrant workers and became citizens much later. Most of them were from poor families from the Tamil Nadu districts of Tirunelveli, Madurai and Thanjavur. When the coffee plantation collapsed in the 1870s due to the spread of a leaf disease, the British shifted to the tea plantations. They built up the Tamil Plantation community within the heartland of Kandy and manipulated the Tamil – Sinhala differences to their policy of divide and rule. Social and economic factors during the early colonial period under the Portuguese and the Dutch contributed towards the freezing of ethnic boundaries. Thus came the consolidation of the Sinhala community in the Central and south western parts of the country and of the Tamils in the North and Northeast. The British colonisation of the island made it more complex.

Origin of Sri Lankan Tamil conflict

The trouble started soon after Sri Lanka's (technically Ceylon at that time) independence on 4 February 1948, with the restriction of citizenship rights to the Indian origin Tamils. "The major ethnic group, Sinhalese (70 per cent of the population in 1946), trace their ancestry to a group of North Indian 'Aryan' settlers believed to have arrived in the country around 500 BC. The second largest ethnic group, the Sri Lankan Tamils (11.0 per cent), claim to have lived in the country for at least two millennia. The Indian Tamils (11.7 per cent) are (mostly) descendants of migrant workers brought from South India by the British in the late 19th and early 20th centuries who came to work as indentured labourers on the tea and rubber plantations. The 'Muslims' (Moors) (6.4 per cent) trace their ancestry to the Arab traders involved in the millennia-old seaborne trade between the Middle East and South and Southeast Asia. A smaller group, the 'Ceylon Burghers', are descendants of various European settlers."[7] While the Sinhalese and Tamils are the two official languages, English continues to be the link language.

---

7   Thuppahi, *Victory in war and defeat in peace: Politics and economics of post conflict in Sri Lanka*. Thuppahi's blog, July 28,2015, https://thuppahi.wordpress.com/2015/07/28/victory-in-war-and-defeat-in-peace-politics-and-economics-of-post-conflict-sri-lanka/

Annamalai Varadaraja Perumal, former Chief Minister of the North-eastern Province of Sri Lanka, who has taken political asylum in India since the nineties, points out: "No Muslim had Sinhala as their mother tongue though over a period of time they speak Sinhala but traditionally they all were Tamils. Because of their interests, their economic issues were separate and they were from a different class also. The Sri Lankan origin Tamil group follow more Parliament -oriented politics. Among the Sinhalese, there were two kinds. One is the traditional Kingdom root Sinhalese. They are the higher-level Sinhalese. Then, the lower level Sinhalese live in the coastal areas. They indulged in fishing etc. The upcountry Sinhalese were more farming oriented while the coastal Sinhalese more industrial based."[8]

Demand for federalism in Sri Lanka

The demand for federalism came in the 1920s from the upcountry Sinhalese, who sought a Kandy- based province. But the Tamils did not support the demand because the Tamil elite and the local Sinhala elite were partners in power. But in 1931 things changed when universal franchise was introduced in Sri Lanka. It was the first country to get it not only in the region but also in comparison with many other countries in Europe. So naturally the majority Sinhalese became the majority in the State Councils. The Sinhala slogan, Sinhala unity, Sinhala pride, all these started emerging. As a counter to that in the 1940s Tamil leaders began demanding that the majority should not dominate the minorities. So they demanded fifty per cent for Sinhalese and the rest for others.

As Perumal points out "In Sri Lanka all the Hindus are Tamils. All the Muslims are Tamils. All the Buddhists are Sinhalese. But there are Christians among the Tamils and among the Sinhalese. So it was religion plus language. It was not that simple for the British as they felt 75 per cent were Sinhalese and they can't be given just 50 per cent."[9]

Tamils felt disgruntled and disadvantaged when the economic development took place mainly in the Central and Western parts

---

8 Author's interview with Varadaraja Perumal (14, September, 2013)

9 Author's interview with Varadaraja Perumal ((14, September, 2013)

of the island thereby creating an imbalance. "The ready availability of the English secondary schools benefitted the Sri Lankan Tamils especially the high caste Vellala community over the others with regard to higher education, colonial employment and other professions. This benefit was not available to all the groups in Jaffna but mostly to a group, which came to be known as 'First class Vellalas' in Sri Lanka".[10] The Sinhalese were not able to compete in exports trade with the British while the British bankers and the South Indian Chettiars controlled the finance.

Sri Lanka gets independence

One has to understand the background of the ethnic problem to understand its connection with Tamil Nadu's concern. In sharp contrast to India, Sri Lanka had little trouble in 'winning' its independence from Britain.

Ceylon Citizenship Act

The Tamils of Sri Lanka felt alienated when the Ceylon Citizenship Act of 1948, India and Pakistani Citizenship Act of 1949 and the Ceylon Parliamentary Amendment Act of 1950 were passed. The aim of these three legal measures was to disenfranchise the overwhelming number of Indian Tamils and to make it difficult for them to become citizens. In 1947 the Sri Lankan Parliament elected 7 Tamil members from the Plantation Tamil community. They were never able to elect any other member after that. Then in the first elections in 1948 not one Sinhalese member was elected from the Eastern Province. In 2015 there are as many as 16 members. That shows the demographic change. "The natural increase from 1947 to 1981 the Sinhala population was around 238 per cent, about two and a half times. In the Eastern Province, it was 888 per cent. These were the matters that caused concern for the Tamil people",[11] the Tamil National Alliance (TNA) leader Rajavarothayam Sampantham claims. It was the recognition that the Tamil speaking people had a genuine concern in the composition of the demography of the Tamil

---

10 . Author's interview with Varadarja Perumal, 14, September 2013)

11 Author's interview with Rajavarothayam Sampanthan (17-22, February, 2014)

speaking area in the Northern and Eastern Provinces. And here is where India and Tamil Nadu came in.

The Tamils thought that when the British left, they would hand over the country to them because they felt they were more mature and educated enough to rule. That was why they vehemently opposed introduction of universal franchise and had given evidence to the Donoughmore Commission against introduction of universal franchise. But the Commission rejected their suggestions.

Sinhala Official Languages Act alienates Tamils

"In 1956, eight years after Sri Lanka gained independence its Prime Minister Solomon Bandaranaike brought in the Official Language Act (No. 33), otherwise known as the 'Sinhala Only' Act."[12] He replaced English as the official language of Ceylon with Sinhala. He followed it by converting Ceylon into a Sinhala Buddhist nation. The new Act demanded proficiency in the Sinhala language in civil service while Tamil, spoken by about 29 per cent of the population, wasn't recognized. The Tamil civil servants were forced to learn the Sinhala language, deprived of increments and promotions and job opportunities for the Tamils.

Gammanpilla points out that in 1958 the Federal Party passed a resolution in its Trincomalee convention against what it called the Sri Lankan apartheid. It demanded two federal units one each for the Tamils and the Sinhalese and both as equal partners. The Sinhala community responded to this with anti Tamil riots.

This, and subsequent laws that discriminated against the Tamil population united the three groups, who came from different ethnic origin" the Jaffna Tamils, the Plantation Tamils, who had migrated from India to work on British plantations (and spoke a different dialect), and the Moors (Sri Lankan Muslims who spoke an Arabized form of Tamil). Calls for power-sharing and equal status soon became

---

12 Nandini Krishnan, *Prabhakaran's last throw*. Doug Saunders, March 30,2012, http://dougsaunders.tumblr.com/post/20165166365/prabha -karans-last-throw

demands for autonomy in certain areas, which eventually gave rise to a separatist movement."[13]

To understand the complexity of the Tamil problem one must understand the differences in their status. Mr Muthu Sivalingam, born to a plantation worker and leader of the Ceylon Worker's Congress (CWC) feels that when the plantation workers retired they had no place to go. They have no land holdings in Sri Lanka while the Sinhala and the Jaffna Tamils had their ancestral holdings. It was hard for them to find jobs as the plantations were shrinking. The younger generations of the Planters' families don't want to work in tea gardens. Muthu Sivalingam fears that in ten years time there would be nobody to work in the plantations. "There are 81 million people within the plantation and about 80 lakhs living outside the plantation. If there are 300 acres of plantation land about 30 or 40 acres of land is with us. We live there with our cattle shed and gardens. We have temples and we want the government to give us some land. This is our life in Sri Lanka."[14]

Plantation Tamils versus Jaffna Tamils

Former Sri Lankan President Chandrika Kumaratunga points out that there is a history for that. The Non- State Tamil people looked down upon the Plantation Tamils, as there was a class difference and caste also played a role. They were badly treated by the British and also by most Sri Lankan governments. There was another reason. The Plantation Tamils were uneducated and hapless. President Kumaratunga observes, "I created a new ministry for them. I called it the State Infrastructure and Development Ministry and gave it to them first to the grandfather Thondaman and after he died to his grandson but they did very little to uplift the plantation workers. Their leaders want to keep them like that and a few of them are now getting educated. Zero point zero zero zero one per cent has got good jobs "[15]

13 Nandini Krishnan, *Prabhakaran's last throw*. Doug Saunders, March 30, 2012, http://dougsaunders.tumblr.com/post/20165166365/prabha karans-last-throw

14 Author's interview with Muthu Sivalingam (17-22, February, 2014)

15 Author's interview with Chandrika Kumaratunga (3-7, March, 2014)

The Tamil Nationalist movement

There is a historical background for the Tamil Nationalist movement in Sri Lanka. In 1951 the Federal Party decided to have a country of its own. The DMK in India had the same dream of a separate Dravida Nadu. When the first Federal Commission was set up not only the Tamils but also the Southern Indian groups demanded for a separate federal setup called Dravidastan linking all the four Southern States but the British rejected it. The same request was made again in 1935 when the second Federal Commission was formulated. It was turned down again. Because of that the Tamils felt they had been side lined and rejected by the British. That was why they started the "Naam Thamizhar (we are Tamils)"movement after independence. It turned into a militant movement in India and Nehru crushed it.

According to the TNA leader Sampanthan "Tamils had a dream of having a country of their own. That was how the entire Tamil focus came to Sri Lanka. So the Tamil separatism was the creation of the British 'divide and rule' policy. But it has become the dream of the Tamils all over the world. There are a sizeable number of Tamil populations in a lot of countries of the world. Malaysia, Singapore, Fiji, Myanmar, Madagascar, South Africa. During the last 40 years European countries also began to receive lot of Tamils. There is a sizeable population in Germany, Canada and Norway. The biggest population is in Canada followed by the UK."[16]

In 1956, the Federal Party swept into power in several Tamil speaking areas and became the voice of the Tamil Nationalist Movement. It decided to intensify the movement to achieve its demands including that of a provincial autonomy. Bandaranaike, wanting to nip it in the bud agreed for several concessions for the Tamils and signed a pact with the Federal Party leader Samuel James Velupillai Chelvanayagam including assurances to stop the Sinhala colonization of the Tamil areas only to abrogate it soon on the pressure from his Sinhala colleagues.

The Kamaraj Congress leader Nedumaran, who had close association with the Sri Lankan Tamil Movement, points out that

---

16 Author's interview with Sampanthan (17-22, February, 2014)

Chelvanayagam resigned and started the Tamil National Alliance (TNA) and fought for the citizenship of the Plantation Tamils. "They won some seats and raised the Tamil issue in Parliament once again. The Sirimavo – Shastri pact agreed to send back some Tamils to India. The Jaffna Tamils stopped them and took them to Vanni and housed them there. Perumal was also from the Indian origin Tamil. They think that if they were educated they would not come for the plantation works."[17]

Civil disobedience movement

Sirimavo Bandaranaike who succeeded her husband after his tragic assassination tried to mollify the Tamils in 1958 by bringing in an Act to assure the reasonable use of Tamil in the Tamil speaking areas. But in 1961 she made the Sinhala as the official language throughout the country. Chelvanayagam started a civil disobedience movement but the government responded by imposing emergency in the North and the East.

Emergence of DMK in Tamil Nadu

Simultaneously, to understand the role of the Dravidian parties in the Sri Lankan ethnic conflict one has to go back to the forties. **The emergence of the DMK in Tamil Nadu coincided with emergence of the Tamil nationalism in Sri Lanka.** It was Periyar Ramaswami Naicker who founded the Dravida Kazhagam Party in 1944, which opposed the imposition of the Aryan Brahminical dominance, the imposition of Hindi and advocated a separate Dravidian country. In 1949 the Dravida Kazhagam split and the Dravida Munnetra Kazhagam was born under the leadership of Conjeevaram Natarajan Annadurai who in 1967 became the first DMK Chief Minister of Tamil Nadu.

This Tamil sentiment and affinity towards the Tamil cause on both sides of the Palk straits gave a momentum and the language was used as a tool to achieve their political goal. The DMK used this to attack the Centre and the Congress- ruled Madras State but did not succeed in the fifties and sixties.

---

17 Author's interview with Nedumaran (8,August 2014)

DMK gives up separate Tamil Nadu issue

When the language riots broke out in Sri Lanka in 1958, Tamil Nadu fully supported their Tamil brethren across the Palk straits. According to the DMK leader T.K.S. Elangovan "Homeland, the official magazine of the DMK carried full- length articles about the atrocities of the Sinhalese"[18]The DMK, which was in the opposition, criticized New Delhi and the Congress ruled State Government for not coming to the rescue of the Sri Lankan Tamils.

When the Federal Party leaders were arrested in 1961, the DMK made its protest once again and passed a resolution in a public meeting to support their Sri Lankan Tamil brethren. According to the DMK leader Elangovan the separatist movements like 'Naam Tamizhar' and the 'Greater Tamil Nadu' irritated Prime Minister Nehru. The State government fell in line with Nehru who was against internationalising the issue. "When India declared secessionist parties illegal in 1963, the DMK publicly gave up its demand for a separate Dravida Nadu."[19]The Constitution of India was also amended to make it mandatory to those who were running for public office to take oath within the framework of the Constitution

Rise of Tamil militancy in Sri Lanka

Though Bandaranaike brought Sinhalese as the official language in 1956 he was basically a federalist. "He made some sort of provision for the Tamils. But there were protests from the Buddhist Bikkus. Facing a crisis, he abrogated that pact. Similar thing happened in 1965 when Dissanaike came to power. So this created a suspicion in the minds of the Tamils. There were also anti- Tamil riots in 1956, 58, 61, 74, 77, 79 and 83. All these were responsible for the rise of Tamil militancy."[20]

---

18 Author's interview with Elangovan (25, March, 2014)

19 Vasanthi, 'From radicalism to accomodation' Hindustan Times, November 20,

20 Author's interview with Sampanthan, (17-22,February, 2014)

Sirimavo Bandaranaike and standardisation system

In 1970 when Sirimavo Bandaranaike came to power the Sinhala extremist movements came up with anti Tamil slogans. In India Indira Gandhi was getting stronger after the split in the Congress. She had good personal relations with Sirimavo. In Tamil Nadu the DMK leader M. Karunanidhi took over after the death of Annadurai in 1969. Karunanidhi was hostile to Indira Gandhi because of his local politics.

The first act of Sirimavo was to introduce a 'standardisation' system. It stipulated more marks for the Tamil students in the university admissions while Sinhalese with lower marks were admitted. This made the Tamil educated youth to agitate for their rights. "Their ideal was not Gandhi or his ahimsa movement. It was Bhagat Singh, Subash Chandra Bose, Lenin, and Fidel Castro and their chosen path of violence. So that made the youth movement to take to arms. When the movement picked up, the government used the army and the police to suppress them. When they used force against the youth the movement became more violent."[21]

In 1972, when Sirimavo brought in a new Constitution, Chelvanayagam and other Tamil Members of Parliament walked out while the Federal Party and the Tamil National Congress led by Thondaman joined hands to form Tamil United Liberation Front (TULF). The DMK government in Tamil Nadu supported the Tamils against Bandaranaike.

The Sri Lankan Tamils move from autonomy to separatism

While the DMK gave up its secessionist tendencies, the Tamils of Sri Lanka moved their demand from autonomy to separatism in the seventies. Even as the Sri Lankan Tamil political parties such as the Tamil United Liberation Front (TULF) put their faith in talks, other groups saw armed resistance as the only solution. In 1972, 18-year-old Velupillai Prabhakaran founded the Tamil New Tigers (TNT), which later became the militant Liberation Tigers of Tamil Eelam (LTTE) in 1976. This militant outfit waged guerrilla war, gaining control of vast territory in the North and the East of the island,

---

21   Author's interview with Varadaraja Perumal, (14 September 2013)

where it established a quasi-government. It raised its own army with sophisticated weapons, and a suicide squad called Black Tigers, which carried out political assassinations.

The Plantation Tamils did not join in their struggle or in their training and their armed battles. Muthu Sivalingam points out that "We did not want to fight for Eelam and we did not want to involve in any struggles for them. Our identity is separate and we live in the midst of the Sinhala people."[22] They also did not support the Vattukottai resolution, which demanded a separate Tamil State. They chose another path and fought for their voting rights, citizenship rights and achieved them without a war. When Thondaman entered the Parliament for a second time in 1965 he was able to talk to the government and get the full citizenship.

In the 1950s and 1960s, relations with Sri Lanka did not become a matter of concern in Tamil Nadu because none of it touched the people directly. The support was merely rhetorical. **But later when the problems like the repatriation of the Indian Tamils and the settlement of maritime boundaries emerged; Tamil Nadu posed strong resistance to the Union Government policies. During the Congress rule in the sixties and seventies the Centre had often ignored the sentiments of Tamil Nadu.**

Two bilateral agreements between Sri Lanka and India caused tension in Tamil Nadu. According to the 1964 Sirimao- Shastri pact "India agreed to confer citizenship on 5.25 lakh persons, with their natural increase, over a period of fifteen years. The agreement was followed by another in 1974, as a result of which India was to receive another 75,000 persons of Indian origin, within a period of two years, after those under the first agreement had been repatriated. The entire process was expected to be completed by October 1981. Sri Lanka agreed, in turn, to absorb 3, 00, 000 persons and their natural increase under the first agreement and another 75,000 persons under the second as its nationals, at the ratio of four Sri Lankan nationals for every seven repatriated to India. These two agreements sealed the

---

22 Author's interview with Muthu Sivalingam (17-22, February2014)

fate of the overwhelming majority of the people of Indian origin in Sri Lanka."[23]

In 1974 the DMK opposed the maritime boundary agreement surrendering Katchateevu between Indira Gandhi and Sirimavo Bandaranaike as they argued that besides the territory, the agreement took away the traditional fishing rights of the Indian fishermen. This fishermen issue is still not resolved.

According to Prof Suryanarayan "M. Karunanidhi, the then Chief Minister of Tamil Nadu, has maintained that the Government of India did not have the courtesy to discuss the provisions of the agreement with the Government of Tamil Nadu, though it adversely affected the interests of the State. Even then he called on the Prime Minister and senior officials of the Ministry of External Affairs. He reiterated that the island belonged to India and should not be ceded to Sri Lanka. An all- party meeting was convened on 20 June 1974 to express the anguish and indignation of the people of Tamil Nadu. The matter was debated in the Tamil Nadu Legislative Assembly on 21, August 1974. The Chief Minister requested the Central Government to reconsider the provisions of the Agreement."[24]

The opposition from the regional leaders was mainly because it affected the State. Former Governor General and Tamil Nadu Chief Minister C. Rajagopalachari, the leaders of the Communist Party of India, and the Dravida Munnetra Kazhagam expressed their strong resentment. C. Rajagopalachari echoed the feelings of the vast majority of the Tamils in India when he stated, "Why should nearly a million children and grand children born in Ceylon to parents who toiled and sweated for Ceylon and who had gone there from South India and settled down in the plantations be disentitled to be citizens of Ceylon? Why should a single child born in Ceylon and desiring

---

23 V. Suryanarayan, India's Bilateral Agreements and Centre-State Relations – A Perspective from Tamil Nadu, Published in South Asian Analysis Group on Monday, February 08, 2010. Paper no. 3655

24 Prof Suryanarayan, 'One up-manship in Tamil Nadu Assembly on Katchativu.'. 24/6/2016, Spith Asia Analysis Group., paper no 6138,www.southasiaanalysis.org/node/2017

to be in Ceylon, and be a working citizen thereof, be turned out to wander as homeless refugees in India?" [25]

Prof Suryanarayan's analysis too buttresses my first hypothesis. "1) In the name of good neighbourly relations, the Government of India has sacrificed the interests and views of the federal units. 2) India has not yet evolved a mechanism by which the federal units could make benign inputs into the making of India's neighbourhood policy. In the negotiations which took place preceding the Sirimavo-Shastri Pact, a member of the Tamil Nadu cabinet was included in the Indian team, but he did not carry out his responsibilities as the representative of his government or of the political party of which he was a member. In the case of the maritime boundary agreements, the Chief Minister of the State was formally informed about the provisions, after an informal agreement was reached with Colombo; but the views of the State were not sought on the subject nor was any representative of the State included in the Indian team. 3) The political exigencies of the time and the desire to seek the Congress Party's support in order to remain in power made Chief Minister Karunanidhi not to resort to legal remedies to protect the interests of the State."[26]

DMK leader T.K.S. Elangovan points out that the leaders of the LTTE shared a rapport with leaders of the Dravida movement in Tamil Nadu right from the beginning. Most Tamil Nadu leaders including Kalaignar Karunanidhi visited Sri Lanka in the early fifties and sixties. At that time the question of a separate Eelam did not arise. It was all about giving rights to the people of Tamil origin.

The DMK became moderate in its views about the Sri Lankan Tamils after it came to power but strongly criticized the Congress-ruled Centre for not supporting the Tamil cause. The DMK's support

25 V. Suryanarayan, 'A Tamil Nadu Perspective On India's Bilateral Agreements, Center-State Relations', February 8,2010, Eurasia Review, http://www.eurasiareview.com/

26 V. Suryanarayan, 'A Tamil Nadu Perspective On India's Bilateral Agreements, Center-State Relations', February 8, 2010, Eurasia Review, http://www.eurasiareview.com/

for their Tamil brethren was also part of its anti-Congress agenda. Karunanidhi could not influence its policy.

Karunanidhi succeeds Annadurai

The next phase started in the 1970s by which time the Dravidian parties had become strongly rooted in the Tamil Nadu politics and the Congress, which had lost its hold in Tamil Nadu in 1967, started to ride piggyback either on the DMK or the AIADMK since then for its electoral politics. New Delhi continued its Sri Lanka policy more or less in the same vein till the 1980s. The Centre however, perceived the DMK activities as prejudicial to the Constitution and dismissed the Karunanidhi government in 1976.

MG Ramachaandran launches AIADMK

This also coincided with the rule of the matinee idol turned politician M.G. Ramachandran, who broke away from the DMK in 1972. He floated the All India Anna Dravida Munnetra Kazhagam and came to power in 1977. The LTTE also emerged as a powerful militant group by this time. In 1979 MGR broke his political ties with Indira Gandhi. She wanted to contest a bye- election in the South in 1978. MGR, who was supporting her, changed his mind. So she went to Karnataka and contested from Chikmaglore and won. When Indira Gandhi came back to power in 1980, prompted by her ally the DMK, she dismissed the MGR government in the same year but MGR came back to power in 1981 and also later joined hands with the Congress after the virtual break up of ties between the DMK and the Congress. **MGR's relationship with Indira Gandhi and later her son Rajiv Gandhi remained cordial and they were on the same page on the Sri Lankan issue. MGR could persuade Gandhi to take on Sri Lankan government after the Black July carnage and when Indira Gandhi wanted his support in covertly supporting the Tamil militants by giving them arms, he agreed. He remained as Chief Minister till he died in December 1987.**

Jayewardene and rise of Tamil tigers

When J.R. Jayewardene came to power Morarji Desai succeeded Indira Gandhi in Delhi almost at the same time. The two developed good relations, as Morarji Desai wanted to have good relations with the neighbours.

Jayewardene introduced a new Constitution in 1978, giving primacy to the Sinhala language and the Buddhist religion relegating the Tamils to a secondary role. Upset by all these, the Tamils did not participate in the promulgation of the new Constitution.

Prof Ralph Buultjens of the New York University, a close confidant of Indira Gandhi notes that personalities were one of the key reasons for deterioration of Indo- Sri Lanka relations after 1977. Indira Gandhi's warnings to a certain extent prevented President Jayewardene from imposing further restrictions on Sirimao Bandaranaike in the 1980-84 periods. "Jayewardene also believed that the short confinement of his son Ravi was responsible for his ill health thereafter."[27] Jayewardene's speech at the banquet on October 27, during his visit to New Delhi referred to this. "I will not go into recent history but there are many parallels that can be drawn between the events that took place in your country during the last two years and events that took place in our country during the same period. You may not know but my one and only son was put into jail and up to this date he has not been charged for any offence. I was put in jail because our position was too powerful to put the Leader of the Opposition into jails as they did in the case of Morarji Desai."[28]

State repression of the Tamils in Sri Lanka

On 20 July 1979, the Jayewardene government repealed the Proscriptions of Liberation Tigers law and replaced it with the Prevention of Terrorism Act, a Draconian law. Emergency was declared in the Jaffna area and there was State repression of the Tamils. Soon after, the LTTE suspended all hostile activities against the State concentrating on the expansion of the organization. By early eighties, millions of Tamils fled to Tamil Nadu to escape the harsh treatment meted out by the Jayewardene government. The citizenship issue of these Sri Lankan Tamils also became a sore point.

---

27 Author's interview with Prof Ralph Buultjens, (September 5, 2014)

28 Avtar Singh Bhasin, 'India in Sri Lanka between Lions and Tigers', Manas Publications, 2004, P 67

The Tamil Diaspora also expanded in many countries like U.K, USA. Canada and Germany and started sending money for the LTTE.

A Sri Lankan source claims that Prabhakaran had faith in three things. The first was history. The Island of Sri Lanka had never been united. Only after the British came in 1915 it was united. That unity continued after independence. Traditionally there was Tamil unity in the North and the South. Prabhakaran thought this was coming to an end and he would therefore engineer the northern breakaway. He had a second belief that the Tamils were going to break away from the Indian Union. So he visualized that there could be a greater Tamil Nadu including Sri Lanka. The third belief was that he was a man of destiny and he would be leader of that group. He wanted a better deal for the depressed sections of theirs Lankan Tamil community.

Indira Gandhi helps the militant groups

President Jayewardene's action of suppressing the Tamils resulted in a steady influx of Sri Lankan refugees from the Jaffna and North -Eastern provinces to Tamil Nadu after a huge crackdown on the Tamils by the Sri Lankan government in the early eighties. This was the beginning of the third phase when New Delhi decided to intervene with the pressure from Tamil Nadu increasing. When the Tamil Nadu leaders like Nedumaran were helping the militant outfits finding a base in the state, it was then the July 1983 riots took place. **Chief Minister M.G. Ramachandran as well as the Leader of Opposition M. Karunanidhi and the other Dravidian leaders gave full support to the Sri Lankan Tamil cause and Tamil Nadu liberally helped the militant groups.**

There are enough interviews, books and articles to show that the Indira Gandhi government gave support to the fleeing Tamil refugees from Sri Lanka from 1980 onwards. As Varadaraja Perumal, former Chief Minister of the North-eastern Province points out, "It was the RAW (Research and Analysis Wing) the India's external intelligence agency, which helped various Tamil militant groups, which had taken shelter in Chennai and other parts of Tamil Nadu. They were given arms for what is described for self- protection. They were trained in Dehradun and other places."[29]

---

29 Author's interview with Varadaraja Perumal, (14,September 2013)

Perumal explains that by and large five groups had come up. The Eelam People's Revolutionary Liberation Front (EPRLF) and the Eelam Revolutionary Organisation of Students (EROS) were from one group. Within the Tamil Nationalist Movement they were left oriented. The LTTE got divided and became three groups. Umamaheswaran, Prabhakaran and Sabarathnam headed these three groups. The EPRLF was more organized at the rural level. The LTTE was engaged in violence while the EROS was subtler. The Umamaheswaran group took a left oriented line but it was more like the LTTE. The Parliament leaders of the TULF also did not attempt for any coordination and always kept aloof. "But Jayewardene's anti -Tamil activities made the groups fight more vigorously. These groups were functioning more and more independently and there came a time when they turned against the TULF. Now the TULF came to a situation when it could not play its game. They were not for the Tamil Eelam but for some compromise like a council and autonomous region. The brutal suppression of the Jaffna Tamils under the emergency and the destruction of the Jaffna library in 1981 rendered the moderate TULF style of politics untenable giving place to militancy. So that created a problem and then came the 1983 riots."[30]

The Black July riots and Indian intervention

The situation became uncontrollable when the Sri Lankan government used force to suppress the Tamil movement. The Black July communal clashes on July 23, 1983 provided that space, the right conditions and the need for the Indian intervention in Sri Lanka. This ended only in 1990 with the withdrawal of Indian Peace Keeping Force (IPKF) from Sri Lanka brining to an end to a critical period in the Indo- Sri Lanka relations. **This engagement assumed different forms at different stages gradually evolving into an extremely complex engagement as well as political, military and strategic ramifications.**

At the political level the process began as an urgent humanitarian intervention to prevent the genocide unleashed against the Tamils. This politico-diplomatic effort soon changed into a mediatory effort

30 Author's interview with Perumal

in Rajiv Gandhi's time, which ended up in the bilateral Indo – Sri Lanka Accord in 1987. On the geo- strategic level, the Indian intervention sought to remove the external forces and this strategic objective was achieved with certain binding classes in the accord.

Indira Gandhi intervenes in the Tamil cause

There were a number of reasons as to why Indira Gandhi decided to intervene. As Varadaraja Perumal notes President Jayewardene was not ready to hold elections and extended the life of the Sri Lankan Parliament by a referendum for another six years. "So in 1983 the State aided riots started taking place against the Colombo traders and shops of the Tamils were burnt. The competition between the Muslims and the Tamils and the Tamils and the Sinhalese was there."[31]

Secondly the sentiments whipped up by the alleged genocide of the Tamils in Sri Lanka generated apprehensions in Delhi about the possible revival of secessionist tendencies in Tamil Nadu. The people of Tamil Nadu were agitated. **The AIADMK led by Chief Minister MGR, an ally of the Congress and the other Dravidian parties competed with each other in staging protests and demonstrations against the Sri Lankan government building pressure on the Centre.**

Thirdly, as Prof Ralph Buultjens notes that Mrs Indira Gandhi was worried about the Southern States where elections were due. "She told me, 'we will clean it all up after the elections.' She was very much against the terrorists but did not want to do anything drastic before the elections."[32]

MGR and Indira Gandhi on the same page

Fourthly, **Panruti Ramachandran, a minister in the MGR cabinet who also acted as his interpreter confirms that the Centre and the Tamil Nadu government worked in tandem.** "At that time this question of separate Eelam did not arise. The Government of India and the Tamil Nadu government were not interested in promoting that idea. The aim was to defend the civilian population. That was

---

31 Author's interview with Varadaraja Perumal (14,September 2013)

32 Author's interview with Prof Ralph Buultjens, (5,September 2014)

all. Whatever Government of India did, they took us into confidence. And whatever we wanted them to do we prevailed upon them. We were with the Government of India policy just to arm the Tamil civilians and protect them and that was all.[33]"

Fifthly, not only the Tamil Nadu Assembly but also the Indian Parliament faced noisy scenes on the Tamil massacre with the result the Indira Gandhi government was compelled to take note of the plight of lakhs of refugees pouring into Tamil Nadu. Colombo proscribed the TULF and they began operating from Chennai.

Sixthly, as Anton Balasingham claims "Of the half a million people uprooted by the racial cataclysm, two hundred thousand sought asylum in India and the rest fled to the Western Europe, Canada, and Australia as political refugees. Hence the ramifications of the July riots precipitated critical conditions in Tamil Nadu compelling the Government of India to take action."[34]

Seventhly, D.R. Kartikeyan, former Central Bureau of Investigation (CBI) Director points out, "Prabhakaran was at some point talking about larger home for Tamils including Tamil Nadu. So the Indian government wanted this to be confined to Sri Lanka insisting that Tamils should be given equal rights. At that point of time they thought that it was the right policy for India to support them – overtly and also covertly.[35]"

Eighthly, one has to see the international and regional background in this regard. It was the last phase of the Cold War. While India aligned with the Soviet Union, the United States entered into a strategic relationship with Pakistan in the early eighties. "Israel began to build up the Sri Lankan naval capacity and brought in intelligence agents from the Internal Service Security to train the Sri Lankan armed forces, especially the special task force in counter insurgency

33 Author's interview with Panruti Ramachandran (13 December, 2014)

34 Anton Balasingham, 'War and Peace', Fairmax Publishing Ltd, 2004, P 51

35 Author's interview with Kartikeyan (11, September 2014)

warfare."[36] It was at this point of time that Sri Lanka opened up its doors to the United States and other Western Countries. "In the meantime the US expanded the 'Voice of America', relay station with electronic intelligence facilities in Chilaw, north of the capital Colombo. Furthermore, the Americans also attempted to gain contract for the Trincomalee oil contract for the tank through overseas American firm. The visits of General Vernon Waltairs, a senior figure in the US defence and intelligence establishment to Colombo in October 1983, followed by Casper Weinberger, US Defence Secretary further heightened Indian apprehensions concerning greater American involvements in Sri Lanka."[37] Balasingham notes further, "Additionally China was supplying a substantial amount of military equipment to Sri Lanka. At this juncture Delhi conceived this steady build up of external forces inimical to Indian interests as a serious threat to her security and geo strategic environment."[38]

Former Foreign Secretary J.N. Dixit, observes that the "1983 riots gave Indira Gandhi not only a handle but also the justification to caution President Jayewardene about his non- responsive attitude regarding Tamil aspirations." [39]Delhi had a strong feeling that Jayewardene would not take the Tamils seriously unless they posed a threat to him and to the unity of Sri Lanka. Indira Gandhi was advised to provide some training to the militant groups to defend themselves. But neither the Tamil Nadu government nor the Centre was in favour of breaking up of the island nation. All that they aspired for was the autonomy short of independence, Dixit claims.

Tamil Nadu hosts Sri Lankan Tamil refugees

The 1983 July riots naturally resulted in sympathy from the people of Tamil Nadu, which put pressure on Delhi to come to their rescue. Tamil Nadu showed its anger by demanding that Indira Gandhi should take

36 Anton Balasingham, '*War and Peace*', Fairmax Publishing Ltd, 2004, P 49-50

37 Ibid P 49-50

38 Ibid P 50

39 J.N. Dixit, '*Assignment Colombo*' Konarak Publishers Pvt. Ltd, 1998, P 15

action to put an end to the genocide. Massive demonstrations were held in front of the Sri Lankan High Commission. "Chief Minister M. G. Ramachandran and the Opposition Leader M. Karunanidhi issued statements condemning the Colombo government for the atrocities. Ramachandran's statement said fifty million Tamil hearts in Tamil Nadu bled in sympathy with the Sri Lankan Tamils. He pledged assistance to the sufferers. Karunanithi's statement urged Prime Minister Indira Gandhi to act quickly to safeguard the Sri Lankan Tamils."[40]This convergence of the interests of the State leaders and the Centre had resulted in a united action.

Indira Gandhi intervenes

Soon after the Black July riots, Indira Gandhi dispatched her Foreign Minister P.V. Narasimha Rao to Colombo to initiate mediatory process choosing a political option than a military option. In his meeting with Rao, Jayewardene gave the background of the riots and blamed the TULF, the LTTE and the Tamils. P.V. Narasimsha Rao conveyed Indira Gandhi's message that India was willing to mediate for a negotiated settlement and Jayewardene agreed. Thomas Abraham points out that on the one hand she did what any country might be expected to do by troubles in a neighbouring country. She offered her good offices to the Sri Lankan government to mediate between it and the Tamil political party TULF. "But more controversially she also took the first step towards involving India deeply into the Sri Lanka conflict by arming and training the fledgling Tamil militant groups."[41]

G. Parthasarathy deputed as mediator

Indira Gandhi chose G. Parthasarathy, a Tamil Brahmin who was chief of the Policy Planning cell in the Ministry of External Affairs, as the mediator. His brief was to bring round the Jayewardene government to meet the legitimate aspirations of the Tamil groups. He came up with a set of proposals called "Annexure C" after consulting both

---

40 T. Sampantham, from Volumne 2, http://www.sangam.org/articles/view2/422.html

41 Thomas Abraham, *Negotiating peace in Sri Lanka,* Edited by Kumar Raisinghe, Volume 1, Second edition, P

sides. This proposed regional administrative structures devolving power to the provinces. Parthasarathy also met Karunanidhi on his way back from Colombo and briefed him about the sensitive situation.

Mrs Gandhi's covert operations

Knowing that President Jayewardene was not fully supportive of the Parthasarathy proposals as the President favoured military option to deal with the increasing militancy, Indira Gandhi began covert operations by giving training to the militant groups.

In the author's perception and also from information gathered from several sources, while Gandhi played up the overt attempts, the covert projects were kept as a secret. Balasingham notes that Indira Gandhi chose a three -men team for this purpose. The main strategist was Rameshwar Nath Kao, her National Security Adviser, the man who executed it was Girish Chandra Saxena, Chief of Raw and the third was Sankaran Nair, Director in Gandhi's PMO. The plan was to secretly fund, train and arm the militant groups.

Mrs Gandhi arms the militants, keeps MGR informed

It was Jayewardene and Indira Gandhi who did not see eye to eye, which resulted in Gandhi giving some small arms to militant groups thinking that the militants would go back and fight the army or destroy some police stations so that it would make Jayewardene to re -think. "That might be her assessment but President Jayewardene had his own plans. He got the help of the South Africans, which was under the white rule. The Mossad, the MI 5 of Britain, the CIA and Pakistan's ISI were also roped in. China was not pro- Jayewardene and he was also not pro- China but he was of course pro- Japan. But Japan did not involve in any military activities. So these were the five countries that helped him but Mossad was the main. South Africa also was supplying some vehicles.[42]"

Indira Gandhi telephoned to M.G. Ramachandran about her double track policy. **While MGR hesitated at first, he fell in line with her proposal and directed his trusted minister Panruti**

---

42 Author's interview with Varadaraja Perumal, (14,September 2013)

Ramachandran to work on this line. According to the latter, "the strategy pursued by Mrs Gandhi was to help the 'boys' in the Tamil areas to protect the lives of the Tamil people locally from the onslaught of the Sri Lankan army. To that extent the training was given and also some arms and it worked well. However, the State government was not involved in the training of the militants.[43]" Perumal's assessment was that Gandhi did not give any importance to the militant groups as they were only to be used as tools to give some pressure to Jayewardene.

The fact that MGR helped the LTTE has been confirmed by many sources. Deposing before the Jain Commission which went into the Rajiv Gandhi assassination, former Prime Minister V.P Singh on November 5,1996, officially confirmed it. He said, ".... the first batch of training of the militants was done in 1983 under the Congress Government. I will not disclose the place where this training was held. It was done in Chakarata. Then in 1984, weapons were given to all the militant groups. The camps were set up in Tamil Nadu. Monetary help was given. MGR in his statement in the Assembly of Tamil Nadu said that he has given Rs4 crores aid to Tamil Militant Groups. The other information I will not give to the Commission, which I believe is sensitive."[44]

Karuna, a onetime close aide of Prabhakaran and a minister in the Rajapakse government admits that he had met MGR many times along with the LTTE chief. "When we went there he would ask Prabhakaran whether he needed anything and whatever Prabhakaran asked, he gave them. He gave them money, weapons and every other help. He gave the LTTE base for training in Salem Mavattam (district) and other places. Tamil people also appreciated him.[45]"

Panruti Ramachandran also confirms that whenever Prabhakaran needed money MGR funded him without hesitation.

---

43 Author's interview with Panruti Ramachandran (13, December, 2014)

44 Tamil Nation. Org, *'Growth of Sri Lankan Tamil Militancy in Tamil Nadu',* Jain Commission interim report, Chapter I - Phase I (1981-1986), section 3, Para 15, 7-9

45 Author's interview with Karuna (17- 22, February, 2014)

"I myself have seen MGR giving money. Once MGR gave it officially from Fort St George. I was with MGR in all his political activities – political and administrative matters whichever department I was holding. I was the person authorized to do these and it was I who handed over the Rs four crore cheque to the LTTE from Fort. St. George."[46]

Tamil Nadu gets flooded with the Sri Lankan Tamil refugees

The 'Black July' riots became a watershed because the Federal Party became the Tamil United Liberation Front (TULF). Its leader Amrithalingam was very much influenced by the Dravidian parties in Tamil Nadu and adopted the same symbol also. The TULF wanted the LTTE to put pressure on Jayewardene but Amrithalingam underestimated Prabhakaran and did not calculate that it would get out of hand.

By the time the 1983 July riots broke out these Tamil militant groups had already had their presence in Tamil Nadu. Varadaraja Perumal recalls that the LTTE was close to Nedumaran but it did not have any office in Chennai. Prabhakaran was operating from Jaffna. The Tamil Eelam Liberation Organisation (TELO) was close to Karunanidhi and the TELO leaders including Sabaratnam met him regularly. The People's Liberation Organisation of Tamil Eelam (PLOTE) was in touch with M.G. Ramachandran through his trusted minister S.D. Somasundaram. The PLOTE leader Umamaheswaran was given some facilities like accommodation in the MLA hostel and land for training Centre etc. The Eelam People's Revolutionary Liberation Front (EPRLF) was close to naxalite groups and its leader Pathmanabha was operating from Jaffna. Perumal notes, "All five groups were given training. Shankar led the Eros and Prabhakaran was the LTTE chief."[47]

LTTE seeks the help of RAW

It is interesting to see how the LTTE found its feet in Tamil Nadu. The author gathers from sources that it was in the early eighties that

---

46 Author's interview with Panruti Ramachandran, (13,December 2014)

47 Author's interview with Varadaraja Perumal, (14,September 2013)

Prabhakaran asked his alter ego Balasingham and his wife Adele to shift to Chennai from London. Balasingham came to know about the secret training operations through an acquaintance Prof Rajendran of the Singapore University. Dr Rajendran informed Balasingham that the three Tamil militant organizations - the TELO, the EPRLF and the EROS had already been accepted by the Government of India for the project and were in the process of sending their cadre to the military training camp, somewhere in north India. By September 1983, Chennai was full of Sri Lankan Tamil boys.

The Research and Analysis Wing (RAW) was responsible for the programme and Samuel Chelvanayagam Chandrahasan, son of the late S.J.V Chelvanayagam, and the leader of the Federal Party was coordinating the whole clandestine affair from the Tamil side. Balasingham claims, "We made a conscious, calculated choice to participate because we had no alternative other than to swim with the currents of inexorable historical process."[48] Delhi agreed to train 200 LTTE cadres, beginning from November and like Perumal, the LTTE leaders too could grasp the motive behind the Indian action and understood that in this grand clandestine scheme, the Tamil militant movement had been allocated a specific, limited role. "The ultimate objective was to militarily compel Jayewardene to seek a regional political Settlement with the Tamils.[49]"

Karunanidhi and his lieutenant Anbazhagan resigned their Assembly seats protesting against the plight of the Sri Lankan Tamils soon after the Black July riots. Not to be outdone, MGR announced that the AIADMK would not contest the bye-elections to Anna Nagar and Purasawalkam constituencies arising out of the resignation of the two DMK leaders.

---

48 Anton Balasingham,' War and peace', Fairmax Publishing Ltd, 2004, p 59

49 Anton Balasimgham, 'War and Peace', Fairmax Publishing Ltd, 2004,P 59

"He also directed his party men to wear black shirts for a month from 16th August to express their solidarity with the Sri Lankan Tamils."[50]

An ailing MGR wins Tamil Nadu again

Soon MGR fell ill and went to New York for treatment. His number two in the cabinet Nedunchezhian ran the government in his absence. Indira Gandhi's assassination on October 30, 1984 by her security guards brought some uncertainty in India's Sri Lanka policy. Indira's son Rajiv Gandhi, who succeeded her went for elections in December – January 1985 to establish his legitimacy and came back with a thumping majority. The Congress and the AIADMK fought the elections together in Tamil Nadu. MGR appealed from his hospital bed in New York through a video message and the Congress - AIADMK combination swept the polls. It was during this time that Jayalalithaa; MGR's protégé campaigned for the party and made her mark. The AIADMK got 133 seats while the Congress won 62 and the DMK got just 20 seats. In the Lok Sabha also the combine got a majority of seats.

MGR returned from the US and was sworn in as Chief Minister again on February 10, 1985. The Sri Lankan problem was one of the top priorities of the new government. As Mohan das, MGR's Intelligence Bureau chief describes that apart from the refugee inflow the militant groups also tried to annihilate each other. "Meanwhile the opposition of Tamil Nadu people towards the abuse of their hospitality extended to the militants was growing."[51]

Jayewardene befriends Rajiv Gandhi

After Indira Gandhi's assassination the relationship between Delhi and Colombo began to change. When he came to attend the funeral of Indira Gandhi in 1984, "Rajiv Gandhi had indicated to Jayewardene that he was willing to make a fresh start in India's

---

50 K. Mohan das, '*MGR: the Man and the Myth*' Panther Publishers, 1992, P 79.

51 K, Mohan das, '*MGR: The man and the Myth*'. Panthers publishers, 1992,P 136

mediation efforts. He also told Jayewardene that India would move away from the partisan role it was playing in dealing with the Sri Lankan situation. He however emphasized that a solution would only be possible if the legitimate aspirations of Tamils were met by the Sri Lankan Government."[52]

Those who participated in the evolution of Rajiv Gandhi's Sri Lanka policy included his Foreign Secretary Romesh Bhandari, joint secretary in the Prime Minister's Office Ronen Sen, RAW chief Gary Saxena, Intelligence Bureau chief M.K. Narayanan, the then Indian High Commissioner to Sri Lanka J. N. Dixit, Rajiv Gandhi's ministers P. Chidambaram and K. Natwar Singh. By and large it was through them that Rajiv Gandhi operated his new Sri Lanka policy. **In any case he found MGR supporting his policies. After Rajiv Gandhi decided to modify his Sri Lanka policy, he telephoned to MGR and sought his cooperation, which he got fully.** It was then the Foreign Secretary Romesh Bhandari entered the picture. "Before I took over, the problem was that the negotiations were conducted by G. Parthasarathy. I am not questioning his competence. But he was perceived in Sri Lanka as a Tamil. They felt that the foreign policy of India was being formulated in Chennai. Jayewardene was not accepting it. When Rajiv Gandhi took over and when we were on a flight to Moscow he discussed the issue with me and said he wanted to have a new look at the Sri Lanka policy. That was when I came in."[53]

Romesh Bhandari mediates

Jayewardene heaved a sigh of relief after Rajiv Gandhi decided that India would be committed to the unity, sovereignty and territorial integrity of Sri Lanka. Soon Indira Gandhi's covert operations were stopped and a ceasefire was announced for negotiations. In his first visit to Colombo Bhandari conveyed the concerns of Gandhi to Jayewardene. When they started the dialogue, the major issue was that Jaffna and Northeast Tamils had to have a proper deal. Then

---

52 J.N. Dixit, *'Assignment Colombo,'* Konarak Publishers Pvt. Ltd, 1998, P 24

53 Author's interview with Romesh Bhandari (6April, 2013)

there was the whole question of political solution as Rajiv Gandhi was not keen on disturbing the unity of Sri Lanka.

Bhandari impressed upon the Sri Lankan president that conditions must be created for the refugees to go back to Sri Lanka. By this time the number of refugees stood at 90,000, which was causing concern. On April 25, 1985, Prime Minister Rajiv Gandhi told the Lok Sabha that Chief Minister M.G. Ramachandran had personally expressed concern at the growing number of refugees. He repeated this in the Rajya Sabha on May 3 saying, "Our concern is for the Tamils in Sri Lanka. The concern is not only of people in the South but also it is of everyone in India. We have to see that the refugees go back, go back in honour, go back in safety, and go back with the security of expecting and getting full freedom to express themselves, to work, to live with the integrity of Sri Lanka.[54]" **This was another instance when the Centre understood the concerns of the State chieftain and acted on them.**

Karunanidhi demands military action

After 1985 August 2 bomb blast near the Madras airport, things became worse. Karunanidhi kept up the agitation demanding that India should invade Sri Lanka. He also wanted India to snap all diplomatic ties with the island nation and urged New Delhi to support a separate Elam. He courted arrest along with 8000 followers. Nedumaran and Dravida Kazhagm leader Veeramani formed an organisation called the Tamil Eeelam Supporter's Organisation (TESO) on 24, April 1985.

LTTE becomes dominant group

Meanwhile the LTTE gained strength with the support of MGR and became the dominant group but the distance between New Delhi and these groups widened. The LTTE began to finish the other groups, as New Delhi was not willing to talk to the LTTE alone. Bhandari recalls, "It first destroyed the TELO, and by the end of 1986 it could order the EPRLF and the PLOTE to disband. By 1987, it declared that it was going to take over the administration

---

54 A.S. Bhasin, 'India in Sri Lanka, Between the Lion and the Tigers', Manas Publications, 2004 P 107

of Jaffna. Prabhakaran told me that he would not stop until they achieved the Eelam. I tried to convince him in every way I possibly could and I took him to Arun Nehru and Rajiv Gandhi. I was unable to do anything.[55]"

SAARC Conference and Rajiv Gandhi's diplomatic misadventure

The next important development in the mediatory effort was the South Asian Association for Regional Cooperation (SAARC) summit held in Bangalore in 1986 on November 16 and 17, which further exposed the growing distance between the LTTE and New Delhi. Although disheartened, Rajiv Gandhi had not given up his efforts to find a solution to the Tamil problem. By this time Bhandari had retired. Jayewardene came up with a proposal for the trifurcation of the Eastern Province. "Under this project the boundaries of Trincomalee, Batticaloa and Amparai districts would be redrawn to carve out three regions for the three communities – the Tamils, the Muslims and the Sinhalese – living in the Eastern Province."[56] New Delhi wanted to bring Prabhakaran and Jayewardene to come to some understanding. Rajiv Gandhi requested MGR to fly down to Bangalore and persuade the LTTE chief. Prabhakaran and Balasingham were also brought from Chennai to Bangalore for what was described as the 'proximity talks' on November 17 but the meeting ended as a complete disaster.

Rajiv Gandhi uses MGR as mediator with LTTE

Panruti Ramachandran, who accompanied MGR to Bangalore, recalls that the Chief Minister played the role of the messenger conveying what Rajiv Gandhi said to Prabhakaran and the latter's response to Rajiv Gandhi. "But ultimately the Sri Lankan government did not agree as particularly the merger of the Northern and the Eastern provinces became a bone of contention. Tamils demanded that at least their homeland should be defined. Jayewardene was not for the merger at all."[57] The LTTE leaders rejected Jayewardene's proposals.

---

55 Author's interview with Romesh Bhandari (6, April 2013)

56 Anton Balasingham, *'War and Peace,'* Fairmax Publishing Ltd, 2004, P 87.

57 Author's interview with Panruti Ramachandran, (13,December 2014)

Rajiv Gandhi turns peacemaker

However New Delhi took it as a snub, as it turned out to be another diplomatic misadventure. Dixit advised Rajiv Gandhi for change of tactics realizing that India's purely mediatory efforts were not likely to succeed. So New Delhi shifted its role from that of a mediator to a peacemaker and the guarantor of such peace if the crisis in Sri Lanka was to be resolved. Getting the message from New Delhi, Prabhakaran soon saw that he could not depend on the Indian support and quietly left for Jaffna in early January 1987.

Collapse of the Thimpu talk

By June 1, 1985, Rajiv Gandhi was able to persuade Jayewardene to announce a four-phase framework for a ceasefire. Bhandari was one of the main players. "For India, Thimpu marked for the first time the two track of Indian policy- diplomacy and the militants, engaged in the open together."[58] Tamil groups representing all shades of opinion participated in the talks. The LTTE was a reluctant partner. They did not send their top leaders but as a united front of Tamil organizations the Eelam National Liberation Front (ENLF) played a crucial role. The Sri Lankan government came up with a set of proposals. In response to this the Tamil groups put forward four cardinal principles. According to Perumal, who was a participant they spelt out these principles. They are –

"1. Recognition of the Tamil groups of Sri Lanka as a distinct nationality.

2. Recognition of an identified Tamil Homeland and guarantee of its territorial integrity.

3. Right of self determination of the Tamil nation and

4. Recognition of the right to full citizenship and other fundamental democratic rights of all Tamils, who look upon the island as their country. "[59]

---

58 Thomas Abraham, *'Negotiating peace in Sri Lanka: efforts, failures and lessons learnt',* Volume 1, second edition, P no 17

59 Author's interview with Varadaraja Perumal (14,September 2013)

In the first round of Thimpu talks in July 1985, the Tamil groups rejected the Sri Lankan proposals. In August when the talks resumed, the Sri Lankan delegation rejected the Tamil proposals, as it was not prepared to accept Tamils as a distinct nationality. Neither Romesh Bhandari could succeed in his efforts nor the Sri Lankan delegation could match the clever tactics of the Tamil groups. With both sides taking a hard line, the first round of talks conducted from July 8 to July 13, 1985 failed. Rajiv Gandhi was disappointed that his mediatory efforts could not succeed. The second round began on August 12. H.D. Jayewardene, who was leading the Sri Lankan delegation, denounced all but one of the four demands. With both sides taking an uncompromising position there was an impasse.

The collapse of Thimpu talks was a severe blow to India's mediatory diplomacy and a lesson that militants were not as pliable as New Delhi expected. Secondly Tamil groups resented the role of the Indian intelligence agencies and their attitude that they could be manipulated. "On the one hand all the militant groups were to a lesser or greater extent dependent on India. Without a secure hinterland in Tamil Nadu to which they could retreat, train and acquire arms Tamil militancy would not have emerged as a dominant force it has now become. But there were also limits as to how much India can influence the militants."[60]

Sri Lanka hardens stand

Soon the Sri Lankan government began to believe that India had lost its influence over the Tamil groups and hardened its stand. From the beginning of 1987, the Sri Lankan government launched an offensive on the LTTE and the Tigers hit back with equal force. **Coming under the pressure of the Dravidian parties and unable to forsake the Tamil groups, New Delhi put Colombo on notice on February 9, 1987 warning that if the offensives were not stopped negotiations would not be resumed.** By May the situation worsened and Rajiv Gandhi came under constant domestic pressure. Tamil Nadu was seething with anger.

---

60 Thomas Abraham, *'Negotiating peace in Sri Lanka: efforts, failures and lessons'* Volume 1, second edition, P 18

Natwar Singh notes that Rajiv Gandhi felt that the grip of Jayewardene was tightening on the Tamils and he decided to send humanitarian aid on June 5, 1987, which was called "Operation Poomalai". Meanwhile, pushed to the wall, a frustrated and cornered Prabhakaran was planning to leave Colombo in May 1987. Perumal claims that "If New Delhi had not resorted to sending the food supplies, Prabhakaran would have fled to Chennai".[61] India's aggressive gesture in violating Sri Lanka's air space and the LTTE's counter attack on the military headquarters made President Jayewardene turn to New Delhi for mediatory efforts. Thus came hectic activities in Colombo and New Delhi to prepare a bilateral agreement incorporating a package of devolution of powers to the Tamils to resolve the ethnic conflict.

Indo – Sri Lankan Accord

Rajiv Gandhi came up with the Indo-Sri Lankan Accord as a solution to the Tamil problem. Ronen Sen, who was fully involved in the exercise, says it was difficult to say when exactly it all began as the reality was completely different. In Sri Lanka, a lot of people contributed to the process and it evolved over a period of time. Then there was also the force of circumstances, which brought it. "Of course there were certain steps New Delhi had taken which precipitated the issue like the rapid military movement towards Jaffna and the violation of State sovereignty by supplies, airdropping food deliberately. It was an open deliberate violation of sovereignty just to show it was food today and it could be something else tomorrow. They got the message and it was a message to others also.[62]"

With the help of the then Hindu Editor N. Ram both the countries began to look at a fresh set of proposals to resolve the issue. Dixit and Sri Lankan minister Gamini Dissanaike prepared the draft, which culminated into the Indo – Sri Lanka Accord of July 29, 1987. Jayewardene's priorities were that the militant groups including the LTTE would participate in the elections under the accord. Secondly the militants would not use the Indian Territory once the Accord

---

61 Author's interview with Varadaraja Perumal, (14,September 2013)

62 Author's interview with Ronen Sen (27 November 2014)

was signed. Thirdly, he had no option but to deal with India within the accord.

India tries to persuade Prabhakaran to accept the Accord

According to Hardeep Puri, then First Secretary in the Indian High Commission in Colombo, the contact with the LTTE leaders began when he went to Jaffna in 1987 in connection with some work. It was then he had come into contact with the LTTE leaders who later took him to meet Prabhakaran in the jungle.

When Hardeep Puri met the LTTE leader he had discussed the draft of the Accord, which he had taken with him. He told Prabhakaran that the draft was prepared on the lines of the demands of various Tamil groups including the LTTE. Prabhakaran listened to it carefully and finally said he was agreeable to the solution. Puri came back to Colombo after his discussions on July 19 and 20. "The LTTE chief had only two pre-conditions: (a) the Sri Lankan forces should close down all the military camps set up in the Vadamarachi region after May 25, 1987 and withdraw to the barracks; and (b) he should be taken to Madras and Delhi in an Indian Air Force plane and dropped back safely." [63] Hardeep Puri conveyed the categorical assurances from New Delhi about Prabhakaran's safe passage.

Subsequently, on July 23, 1987, two Air Force helicopters airlifted the LTTE leaders Prabhakaran, Yogarathnam Yogi and Dileepan to Delhi accompanied by Hardeep Puri while Balasingham joined them in Chennai. Black cat commandos guarded the entire top floor of the five- star hotel Ashok in the capital. For the next four days, some intelligence officials, Dixit and other officials visited them but Prabhakaran was not convinced. "Prabhakaran told Balasingham" Bala Anna, I am trapped again."[64]Dixit firmly told them "whether you accept or not, the agreement will be signed. This is a bilateral agreement between two countries you will face far reaching consequences if you oppose."[65]

---

63 Author's interview with Hardeep Puri (21, October, 2014)

64 Anton Balasingham, 'War and Peace ', Fairmax Publishing Ltd, 20014, P 100

65 Anton Balasingham, 'War and peace', Fairmax Publishing Ltd, 20014,

Rajiv Gandhi uses MGR for negotiations with the LTTE

On July 26, 1987 MGR arrived in Delhi at the request of the Prime Minister Rajiv Gandhi to persuade the Tamil Tigers. As a reporter for the United News of India, the author had covered their meetings. MGR met them in the Tamil Nadu Bhavan and Dixit was also present at this meeting. Prabhakaran explained his apprehensions to MGR who understood their concerns. MGR got frustrated when his persuasive powers did not work. Later at the at Ashok hotel when he returned the LTTE chief told the author "We had been fighting the Sri Lankan government so far. Bur from now on we have to fight the Indian Government also."[66] A disappointed MGR boarded the plane and went back to Chennai leaving behind Panruti Ramachandran in Delhi to deal with the defiant Tigers.

Panruti Ramachandran claims that he explained to the LTTE leaders that there were three things to their advantage. One was that for the first time Sri Lanka had allowed another country to enter into a pact to solve the problems of Tamils. The Sri Lankan government agreed to enter into an agreement with the Sri Lankan Tamils. This was the first time India had taken the responsibility to see to it that even if the Sri Lankan government tried to wriggle out, it could not go back. The second advantage was that for the first time Sri Lankan government had agreed to merge the Northern and the Eastern provinces but after two years. The third was that whatever might have been the claims of these different groups there was no legitimacy. So by forming an interim council they would get the legitimacy. 'I made them agree on these three arguments,"[67] claims Panruti Ramachandran.

Rajiv Gandhi meets LTTE leaders at midnight

Panruti recalls that he took the LTTE leaders to meet the Prime Minister that night and Prabhakran told Rajiv Gandhi 'Sir we used to get money from the Tamil population. After the Accord we will not be able to raise the funds.' The Prime Minister asked how much money was required. Prabhakaran said they would need fifty lakhs

---

66 Author's meeting with Prabhakaran at Hotel Ashok (26, July 1987)

67 Author's interview with Panruti Ramachandran, (13, December 2014)

of rupees every month. "When we came out, Rajiv Gandhi gave Prabhakaran fifty lakhs of rupees. After that first instalment no more money was given. He handed over his own bullet- proof jacket as a protection to Prabhakaran as a gesture. What happened later was a mystery to me. When he went back perhaps his cadres did not agree."[68] India also gave the necessary assurances of the LTTE's future security and participation in Sri Lankan politics he claims.

Rajiv Gandhi also made several other assurances including an LTTE controlled interim administrative authority. Gandhi further assured them "Please don't worry. I'll definitely fulfil my pledges. Let us take this as a gentleman's agreement, as minister (Panruti Ramachandran) correctly characterized." [69]

Balasingham confirms that in that midnight meeting Rajiv Gandhi heard them patiently. He even jotted down some points and explained, "We have to proceed stage by stage. It is very difficult to get everything at once. With great effort, we have secured regional autonomy for the Tamils in the United Province. This represents a major advance."[70]

On July 29,1987, when Prime Minister Rajiv Gandhi visited Colombo, "India and Sri Lanka came to an understanding that the Sri Lankan government would devolve powers on the Indian model to a new merged Northern and Eastern Province, to be called the Northeast Province, where Tamils were concentrated and grant official status to the Tamil language (through the 13th Amendment to the Sri Lankan Constitution) India and Sri Lanka signed an agreement that made it possible for India to dispatch an Indian Peace Keeping Force (IPKF) to accept surrender of arms by Tamil militants as part of a general ceasefire. All groups, including Prabhakaran personally agreed to this. But these arrangements soon broke down." [71]

---

68 Author's interview with Panruti Ramachandran, (13,December 2014)

69 Anton Balasingham, 'War and Peace,' Fairmax Publishing Ltd, 2004, P 109

70 Anton Balasingham. 'War and Peace', Fairmax Publishing Ltd, 2004, P 1

71 Shiv Shankar Menon, 'Choices: Inside the making of India's foreign policy' Published in Allan Lane by Penguin random House, India, 2016

Rajiv Gandhi took care to take Karunanidhi on board. He consulted him though his nephew Murasoli Maran, (D.M.K M.P) and Karunanidhi wanted a peaceful settlement and did not oppose it as long as all groups agreed to the Accord. So when the Indian Peace Keeping Force (IPKF) went to Jaffna the DMK did not oppose that. "But after that when we heard reports that Tamil women were raped by the IPKF men and the Tamil groups complained to our leader that the IPKF was intimidating the Tamil groups then Karunanidhi did not go to receive them when the IPKF came back. By that time he had become the Chief Minister, he wanted the IPKF to come back because of the atrocities committed by the IPKF.[72]"

Rajiv Gandhi considered the Accord as his personal achievement. Many of his advisers thought that it had many plus points. India wanted peace in Sri Lanka as Tamil Nadu was flooded with the Tamil refugees. Secondly, politically it was a good strategy to throw the ball back at Jayewardene's court. Thirdly and more importantly, MGR was ill and Rajiv Gandhi was keen to utilize MGR's services to influence the LTTE. Also he knew that any Accord was possible only when Jayewardene was in power, as his Prime Minister Premadasa was known for his anti – India feelings. The Accord was not only for settling the Tamil issue but also to address New Delhi's security concerns, "like the use of Trincomalee port, future of the Voice of America broadcasting station, presence of foreign military advisers in Sri Lanka etc. These were the one sided obligations thrust upon Sri Lanka."[73]

Rajiv Gandhi signs Indo Sri Lankan accord

While Rajiv Gandhi flew into Colombo the next morning to sign the Accord, the LTTE delegation left for Jaffna. The moment he went back Prabhakaran declared that he would not give up arms when he addressed a large public meeting on August 4 on the grounds of the Sudumalai temple. The tone and tenor of the speech was totally contrary to the commitments he had given to Rajiv Gandhi in Delhi.

---

72 Author's interview with Elangovan, (25,March 2014)

73 Avtar Singh Bhasin, ' *India in Sri Lanka; Between Lion and the Tigers,*' Manas Publications, 2004, P 154

By October 1987, things had changed. The LTTE leaders Pulendran and Kumarappa, who were being transported to Colombo for interrogation swallowed cyanide capsules in a mass suicide attempt. The repercussions were felt in Colombo as well as in Tamil Nadu. On October 7 Indian Defence minister K.C. Pant and army chief K. Sunderji flew into Colombo and informed Jayewardene of India's decision to disarm LTTE by military force. 'Operation Pawan'- a major offensive against the LTTE was launched on October 10. Romesh Bhandari was not in favour of the IPKF going there and he came up with a three-point formula. "There were three possible scenarios. One was commonwealth and the second was England. The third was sending our forces. I put the third option never to be exercised. They chose the last one.[74]"

IPKF in Sri Lanka

This IPKF war with the LTTE continued for two years and seven months, the longest war that India ever fought. Perhaps in a tactical way, on October 12, Prabhakaran wrote to Rajiv Gandhi appealing for peace. "I humbly appeal to you in the name of peace and goodwill and on the basis of our relations with the people of India, to instruct the IPKF to cease military offensive operations."[75] Two days later he wrote a more detailed letter to Rajiv Gandhi in which he said "I humbly request you to initiate a process of negotiations with our liberation organisation to affect a ceasefire of hostilities and to restore peace, normalcy and ethnic harmony."[76] In his third and final letter to Gandhi on January 13, 1988, Prabhakaran pledged to lay down all weapons when the Interim administration was formed in accordance with the secret agreement with Gandhi. But there was no response from Gandhi, as the Indian government took it as the LTTE's weakness.

---

74 Author's interviewwith Romesh Bhandari (April 6, 2013).

75 Anton Balasingham, 'War and Peace,' Fairmax Publishing Ltd, 2004, P 124.

76 Anton Balasingham,'War and Peace ', Fairmax Publishing Ltd, 2004, P 127

Failure to disarm the LTTE was a big failure of the Accord and an embarrassment to the Indian government. The unfortunate thing was that had Rajiv Gandhi taken note of Prabhakaran's softening, history would have been different. However, by this time he also got submerged in the Bofors gun deal scandal facing a belligerent opposition. He got busy with the domestic problems.

Karuna, a minister in the Rajapakse government and a one time close aide of Prabhakaran who had fallen out admits that Prabhakaran had committed many mistakes. The first was that he did not accept the Accord. The second was his decision to attack the IPKF. "We advised him against it but Prabhakaran would not listen. We fought against the Indian army and even after that there was a chance. Though we fought against the IPKF, Tamil Nadu leaders supported us. I mean moral support. They told the Centre not to kill Tamils etc. Then soon after that Prabhakaran killed Rajiv Gandhi."[77]

After MGR passed away on 24, December 1987 the AIADMK faced a split with MGR's wife Janaki claiming the leadership of the party and Jayalalithaa staking political legacy of MGR. Janaki became the first woman Chief Minister of Tamil Nadu in January 1988 but her government collapsed in 24 days. The President's rule was imposed then.

Perumal becomes North-eastern Province chief minister

Meanwhile changes were happening in Sri Lanka. Jayewardene retired and Premadasa assumed the presidency of Sri Lanka on January 2, 1989. The Janata Vimukhti Perumana (JVP) and Sirimavo were openly against the accord. In November 1988, the North-eastern Provincial Council elections were held and the EPRLF leader Varadaraja Perumal became the Chief Minister.

Perumal had been lobbying for the elections even though the other parties including the LTTE were not enthusiastic. The LTTE decided to boycott it. The exclusion of Sinhala mainstream politics also put a question mark on the legitimacy of the elections. Therefore the council, which should have been a representative character of Northeast, failed to present itself as a bridge. Perumal found it difficult

---

77 Author's interview with Karuna (17-22, February, 1984)

to sustain, as the elections were held without devolving powers and both Premadasa and the LTTE resented his presence. Perumal was neither a Jaffna Tamil nor from the East. He was an Indian origin Tamil settled in Jaffna. Ironically while President Premadasa was making efforts to throw out the IPKF, Perumal was walking on the support of India and the IPKF. The LTTE offered to fall in line with the Sri Lankan government if the IPKF were withdrawn. This suited Premadasa.

D.R. Kartikeyan, who was then posted as Inspector General of Police of the Border Security Force (BSF) was sent to Sri Lanka to make an on -the - spot assessment of the situation in June 1989. After spending a fortnight and meeting many people, he came up with a report in favour of talking to the LTTE and withdrawal of the IPKF. He felt that though Varadaraja Perumal was loyal to India he lacked the strength and popularity and the morale of the IPKF was very low. "If you see my report, on my way to Sri Lanka our soldiers were asking why are we here? If there is a war between the Sinhalese of Sri Lanka and Tamils of Sri Lanka why should we suffer? If it is Kashmir or Punjab it is for our land. Their morale was low and I came back and reported here also."[78]

Rajiv Gandhi's Sri Lanka policy came under fire in Parliament and outside as also in Tamil Nadu as it was seen as a misadventure. On June 1, 1989, the new President Premadasa called upon India to withdraw the IPKF by July 1989 giving an ultimatum to Rajiv Gandhi. On July 28, 1989, the two countries formally announced the withdrawal of the IPKF with immediate effect. **It was not a big secret that neither Rajiv Gandhi, nor the Tamil leaders in Tamil Nadu had any great love for Premadasa, who they believed was not a friend of India.**

Rajiv Gandhi defeated; V.P. Singh takes over

By December 1989, there was a regime change in New Delhi. Rajiv Gandhi was defeated in the elections. V.P. Singh, a former minister in the Gandhi cabinet who was crusading against corruption took over the reins supported by a strange combination of the right

78 Author's interview with Kartikeyan, (11,September, 2013)

wing BJP and the Left parties. The formation of the National Front government, with Gujral as its External Affairs Minister couldn't have come at a better time for President Premadasa. Had the Congress regained power, he would have had to face a hostile Indian government. Against the backdrop of Premadasa's hostility towards India and the Gandhis, this would have placed Sri Lanka in an extremely difficult position.

V.P. Singh was keen to have good neighbourly relations. I.K. Gujral too wanted to adopt a 'neighbours first' policy. Not only V.P Singh but also the National Front chairman N.T. Rama Rao was spearheading the withdrawal of IPKF. **So there was a common cause among V.P. Singh, Gujral, Karunanidhi, Namdamuri Taraka Rama Rao and also the LTTE. Premadasa responded warmly when Singh ordered final pull out of the IPKF by 31 March 1990.**

Karunanidhi uses his good offices as mediator with Tamil groups

In January 1989, Karunanidhi once again took over as chief minister following his party's decisive victory over the split AIADMK. The DMK also became a partner in the National Front government led by V. P. Singh at the Centre. This was the time Karunanidhi openly became a mediator between the LTTE and the Indian government. The LTTE sent personal emissaries to Karunanidhi seeking his support in their battle against the IPKF. It was at this point of time that V.P. Singh assigned him the task of opening the dialogue with the LTTE, as Premadasa also wanted it. Karunanidhi had the advantage as he had good relations with most of the Tamil groups. So as soon as V.P. Singh asked him to play the role of a mediator, he called the LTTE leaders including Balasingham and Yogi. "He revelled in the publicity it brought him, he did everything concerning the issue transparently and in the eye of publicity.[79]" Karunanidhi undertook a very delicate and difficult responsibility of balancing the various Tamil groups and bringing them together. He more or less donned the role of MGR in his mediatory efforts. The LTTE wanted supremacy and had already finished the other groups. Perumal had dug his heels in the North-eastern Province. There was

---

79 Lakhan Mehrotra, *'My days in Sri Lanka,'* Har Anand Publications, 2011, P 188

fighting between the LTTE and the Civil Voluntary Force known as the Tamil National Army, raised with the help of the IPKF in the North-eastern province for protection of the civilians.

Perusal announces Eelam, seeks asylum in India.

Meanwhile Perumal drifted apart from Premadasa. The reason was simple, as they were working on parallel lines. When New Delhi agreed to withdraw the IPKF at the instance of Premadasa, Perumal was perturbed. Dismayed, he air- dashed to Delhi in January1990 pleading for continuation of the IPKF. When V.P. Singh rejected his request, Perumal rushed to Chennai and met Karunanidhi to persuade him to use his influence with Singh. The DMK chief asked Perumal to enter into an agreement with the LTTE and hand over the provincial administration but Perumal refused. Ambassador Lakhan Mehrotra who was then the Indian High Commissioner in Sri Lanka notes, "Karunanidhi said he was prepared to receive all his (Perumal's) men in Tamil Nadu and help them settle down. Perumal, on the other hand considered the proposal preposterous, treated it as 'LTTE's booby trap' to destroy rival Tamil groups and responded with the "Declaration of the State of Eelam."[80] However neither the LTTE nor the Sri Lankan government accepted this.

Perumal thought that if they had to go down fighting why not become a hero and declared Eelam on March 1. His unilateral Declaration of Independence by introducing a resolution in the Council to establish a sovereign democratic republic of Eelam took Colombo unawares. Obviously it was meant to outdo Prabhakaran who was still trying to establish his dream Eelam. Perumal was facing pressure from New Delhi till the last minute. "On the day before my resolution a senior Indian official came to request me to agree to the dissolution of the council. This request came directly from Prime Minister V.P. Singh who was under pressure from Karunanidhi but I refused."[81] It was his parting shot to both the LTTE and the

---

80 Lakhan Mehrotra, *'My days in Sri Lanka,'* Har Anand Publications, 2011, P 222

81 Author's interview with Varadaraja Perumal, (14,September 2013)

Sri Lankan government. President Premadasa was outraged at this declaration of independence.

India agreed to take genuine refugees on humanitarian ground but made it clear they would not be allowed to indulge in any other activities. Cornered from all sides, on March 24, a week earlier than the schedule, when the last of the IPKF batch left the island Perumal and other EPRLF leaders also fled and Perumal sought political asylum in India. Preceding the escape of Perumal from Sri Lanka, Mehrotra went to Delhi and discussed the political future of Perumal with V.P. Singh in the light of the Sri Lankan President's request to India to take Perumal away. Seeing the changed atmosphere Perumal himself sought political asylum in India. "He then requested me and the External Affairs Minister that he and his family be flown in the first instance to Mauritius where he wanted to spend some time after their traumatic years in Sri Lanka. What followed was a rescue operation on 10th March 1990 with the Sri Lankan government's knowledge and permission to fly Perumal and his family out of stronghold of Trincomalee in a special IAF aircraft to Mauritius. The operation was made public after Perumal's entry into India later."[82] The Sri Lankan government too did not wish to create a diplomatic crisis. The next day, a cargo aircraft, which landed in the China Bay had picked up about 250 of Perumal's supporters and flown them to Odisha. Perumal was taken to Mauritius and later on to Lakshadweep. Then he was moved to Madhya Pradesh and ultimately he is now living in Delhi and has become an Indian citizen. Thus ended Perumal's role in Sri Lanka. **The Perumal episode and the exit of the IPKF also show that when V.P. Singh and Karunanidhi were on the same page, there was full cooperation.**

The IPKF misadventure

The IPKF operations in Sri Lanka turned out to be a misadventure. "The IPKF came out of Sri Lanka after paying a heavy price. Its task remained unfulfilled. Its reputation was sullied and battered. In human terms the price was quite high. Total number of all ranks killed was 1155 of which the officers were 55, an indication of the

---

82 Lakhan Mehrotra, '*My days in Sri Lanka*', Har Anand Publications, 2011, P223-224

leadership qualities of the Indian army provides. The number of disabled was 36. The number of wounded was 2854. The IPKF killed 2592 Tamil guerrillas. Wounded 1199 and captured 1185."[83]

LTTE having a free run in Sri Lanka

The exit of the IPKF and Perumal left the field free for the LTTE. Soon it took control of almost all the districts of the Northeast. But the confrontation continued as Premadasa was seeking a solution within the unitary State while the LTTE was looking for a separate Eelam. When the Tamil Tigers refused to lay down arms, which was Premadasa's condition for holding fresh elections, the frustrated President chose the military option. By the end of May 1990, fresh contingents of the Sri Lankan military moved into the Eastern Provinces. The truce between the LTTE and the Sri Lankan government collapsed resulting in large-scale violence.

Chandrashekhar takes over as Prime Minister

Meanwhile by early November 1990, the V.P. Singh government was voted out and Rajiv Gandhi was virtually back in power, as his Congress Party supported the successor Chandrashekhar government from outside. Tamil Nadu was under President's Rule and there was chaos in the AIADMK. Meanwhile the people of Tamil Nadu were getting wary of the activities of the LTTE in Chennai and other places creating lawlessness.

Significantly, Rajiv Gandhi, while speaking on the no confidence motion against V.P. Singh on November 7 had referred to the fact that the LTTE was having the run of the place in Tamil Nadu. Confirming this, the then President of India R. Venkataraman has pointed out in his autobiography 'My Presidential Years ' that the IB (Intelligence Bureau) has briefed him from time to time on Kashmir, the North-eastern States and Tamil Nadu. "In one of its briefing it told me that the LTTE was infiltrating into Tamil Nadu and creating a law and order situation. It was reported that the LTTE had made Tamil Nadu the base of its operations and was actively indulging in smuggling petroleum products and food articles and also in sale of

---

83 Avtar Singh Bhasin, 'India in Sri Lanka: Between Lion and the Tigers,' Manas publications, 2004,P 246

arms to other anti social elements. In particular a mention was made of the supply of AK 47 rifles to naxalites in Andhra Pradesh and to the ULFA of Assam. Though I had passed on the information to both Prime Minister V.P. Singh and Home Minister Mufti Mohammed Sayeed they did not respond, presumably because the DMK was a constituent of National Front."[84] President Venkataraman goes on to say that he also got information from Thanjavur and other areas about extortion by the LTTE and the indifference of the local police when complaints were made.

Chandrasekhar gets Karunanidhi government dismissed

During the second week of January 1991, the pressure on Chandrashekhar for removal of the Karunanidhi ministry increased from the local Congress unit. When the President visited Tamil Nadu, he told Karunanidhi that he should not only take action against the LTTE, but also that action should be demonstrable. Karunanidhi responded by saying that he was doing his best to contain the LTTE. "This was, however, at variance", says Venkataraman, "with the refusal to receive the IPKF personnel on their return from Sri Lanka on the plea that the IPKF had killed Tamils in Jaffna and therefore did not deserve a reception."[85]

On January 30, 1991, the Prime Minister called on the President and informed his government's decision to get rid of the DMK government. He also told the President that since the Tamil Nadu Governor Surjeet Singh Barnala, a friend of Karunanidhi, had declined to dismiss the government he was proceeding under the provisions of the Constitution which enabled the Central Government to act either on the advice of the Governor or 'otherwise.' Bhishma Narain Singh, a senior Congress leader replaced Governor Barnala. Karunanidhi lost his government once again but this time because of his sympathy for the LTTE. **This was one instance when the regional chieftain did not toe the line of the centre and he got dismissed.**

---

84 R. Venkataraman, 'My Presidential years,' Harper Collins, 1995,P

85 A. Balu, '*The Sri Lanka imbroglio, desperate situations, desperate measures,*' The Tribune, June 4,2000

The Chandrashekhar government also fell in March 1991 after the Congress withdrew its outside support on a flimsy excuse. Fresh elections were ordered but the LTTE suicide squad assassinated Rajiv Gandhi on May 21, 1991 during the midst of poll campaign at Sri Perumbudur near Chennai.

Kartikeyan, who headed the special investigation team that probed the Rajiv Gandhi assassination case, notes that even afterwards the LTTE chief sent an emissary to Rajiv Gandhi. They met him two months before the elections in February 1991. "He sent Tiruchelvam, a chartered accountant to Rajiv Gandhi but there was no record of their meeting. Even Vincent George (Gandhi's private secretary) did not know. We produced former Foreign Secretary Romesh Bhandari (who fixed up the meeting) in the court also. They said 'mistakes were committed but let us forget.' But they wanted a separate Eelam. Rajiv said no and the Congress was the only party, which said no division of the country. Prabhakaran also knew after Rajiv Gandhi the leadership would be weak.[86]"

Imposition of the President's rule in Tamil Nadu was a major setback for the LTTE. The DMK government was obviously in the dark regarding the LTTE plan to liquidate Rajiv Gandhi. The Research and Analysis Wing (RAW), was equally clueless about the existence of the plot or else the assassination could have been prevented. A highly placed official familiar with the Sri Lankan affairs confirmed to this author that they had no information about the assassination plan, which was plotted in a highly secretive way. After the IPKF de- induction in March 1990, India washed its hands off Sri Lanka. Few in India supported deployment of the Indian troops in the island even if Colombo were to ask for it. The sympathy for the Tamil militants had evaporated even in the Indian Parliament.

Narasimha Rao government bans the LTTE

One important factor at the government level since the 1990s was the change of governments in both the countries. As power moved from the UNP to the Sri Lanka Freedom Party in Sri Lanka, the Congress Party came back to power led by P. V. Narasimha Rao in

---

86 Author's interview with Kartikeyan, (11, September, 2013)

1991. Added to that was the change of government in Tamil Nadu. In the 1991 elections, the AIADMK, which was the Congress partner, came to power in Tamil Nadu led by Jayalalithaa. So there was cohesion about the Sri Lanka policy and LTTE.

India keeps aloof, switches to economic diplomacy

Rao, who had dealt with Sri Lanka as External Affairs Minister of both Indira Gandhi and Rajiv Gandhi, declared that India would not desire to take any active part in resolving the problems of Sri Lanka. New Delhi showed more interest in developing the framework for a working relationship with Sri Lanka, rather than identifying itself with the Tamil cause. Rao decided that the only way to salvage ties with Colombo was to create a stake for the Sri Lankans through economic ties. Since India had launched liberalization measures, he oversaw the biggest expansion in bilateral economic engagement between Colombo and New Delhi. He spotted opportunities in the island's growth rate of about six per cent year after year despite the ethnic clashes.

Narasimha Rao banned the LTTE in May 1992, a measure that found all round support while the DMK, which was defeated in the elections, remained silent. At the same time, assuming office as Tamil Nadu Chief Minister Jayalalithaa ordered crackdown on the LTTE, which for long had operated openly in the State. "A bureaucrat, who held a key security portfolio at the time, told post (embassy officials) that Jayalalithaa ordered him to do 'whatever it takes to finish off the LTTE' in Tamil Nadu, even if it required extra-judicial killings of LTTE associates in the State," said a dispatch sent by the then US Consul General in Chennai, Andrew T Simkin. The cable further added that she is an "iron lady" and "even her fiercest critics acknowledge that Jayalalithaa's aggressive approach went a long way towards pushing the LTTE out of Tamil Nadu".[87] **This was a case when the interests of the Centre and the State coincided.**

While some in Sri Lanka also favoured the banning of the LTTE, the Sri Lankan government wanted to keep the Tigers engaged.

---

87 Times News Service, *'US cable credits Jaya with flushing out Tamil Tigers',*
April 10, 2013

In January 1993 Premadasa made a stop over in Delhi during his pilgrimage but things did not improve as the mistrust continued. On May 1, 1993, the LTTE assassinated President Premadasa after which the UNP was defeated.

Chandrika comes to power in Sri Lanka

Correspondingly, Chandrika Kumaratunga, daughter of the Bandaranaikes' came to power seeking a mandate on peace initiatives with the LTTE, leading a coalition of parties called People's Alliance on 19 August 1994. Facing a crisis economically, politically and militarily her only option was to go for peace and a negotiated settlement. "I talked of peace because I like peace. And also because my knowledge of world affairs (gained from being the daughter of two Prime Ministers) and history and world affairs made me no war could ever be completely settled with war. Finally whatever you do is through a negotiated settlement. That is why I was always for negotiated settlement and also because of the terrible devastation that war and violence can wreck a country."[88]

LTTE invited for talks

Within ten days after she took over Chandrika invited the LTTE for talks and Prabhakaran was quite responsive. He offered to release some policemen and soldiers kept under his custody as a goodwill gesture. The riot- ravaged Tamils also welcomed it as an opportunity to finally resolve the ethnic conflict. There were four rounds of direct talks between the LTTE and the Chandrika government each lasting two or three days and the rest were held through lengthy correspondence. The two sides agreed on many things.

"Then the LTTE asked for fishing rights, which was also agreed to. Our commanders were quite against it and advised 'don't give this Madam; they will start the war again.' But I said 'let us give it' because the civilian rights also were affected. Then they came and blasted one by one using the facilities we gave and then the war began. So I made a public statement that 'if it is peace it is peace and if it war it is war. 'Then the State had to wage war. Right through

88 Author's interview with Chandrika Kumaratunga (17-22, February 2014)

that period I kept sending messages to Prabhakaran to lay down their arms temporarily and come for talks again. There was no response,"[89] Chandrika recalls. Obviously Prabhakaran was sceptical about the peace talks and by 1995 Chandrika's strategy collapsed.

Recalling the reasons for the failure of talks Kumaratunga claims that it was because Prabhakaran wanted a separate State and she was agreeable to anything but a separate State. Very extensive devolution of powers like what is in India was offered to them. He was not satisfied but more than that he was obsessed with Eelam. "No doubt he was an extremely talented leader and a god -like figure for the Tamils. But he was so obsessed with war and not willing to give that up. If he had agreed then he would have become the Chief Minister of a Province and lived democratically. We had told some Indian diplomats that he was worried about peace and what his people will do to him. He was a tyrant to his people also. So he did not want peace altogether.[90]"On June 3, India put forward the request for Prabhakaran's extradition after the talks had collapsed. The period after 1995 saw unprecedented escalation of war resulting in a humanitarian crisis in the Northern provinces.

Karuna observes that killing of Rajiv Gandhi was the biggest mistake Prabhakaran had committed and because of that India banned the LTTE. Following that decision more than 26 countries banned the LTTE as a terrorist organisation. "I told Prabhakaran before I broke away from the LTTE that a separate country will never happen because India totally opposed it. Without India's consent those days we could not do anything. The last chance was a very good chance facilitated by the Scandinavian countries. That also he did not accept. He bought more weapons and he did not accept.[91]"

The Congress party was defeated in the 1996 elections and for the next two years United Front leaders Deve Gowda succeeded

---

89 Author's interview with Chandrika Kumaratunga (17-22, February 2914)

90 Author's interview with Chandirka Kumaratunga (17-22, February 2014)

91 Author's interview with Karuna (17-22, February 2014)

by his foreign minister I.K. Gujral ruled India. Meanwhile the Jain Commission, which was set up to go into the Rajiv Gandhi assassination came out with its interim report. Based on the deposition of what it called key and credible witnesses, the report singled out the DMK for its severest indictment.

The Commission came down heavily on Karunanidhi for abetting the LTTE prime suspects in the case. It also blamed Prime Ministers V.P. Singh and Chandrashekhar for their laxity in assessing the threat perception to Rajiv Gandhi. "While conceding that both the Congress government at the Centre and M.G. Ramachandran's AIADMK government in the State were responsible for the initial impetus to Tamil militancy, Jain holds the DMK guilty of encouraging and assisting the LTTE even after the Indo-Sri Lankan accord of 1987 pitted the Indian Army against the Tigers."[92]

The Congress saw an opportunity in the aftermath of the report. The then Congress President Sitaram Kesri insisted on Prime Minister Gujral dropping the DMK ministers from his cabinet. He drove to Rashtrapathi Bhavan (presidential palace) on November 29, 1997 and withdrew the Congress support plunging the United Front into a crisis as Gujral refused to drop the DMK ministers. The Gujral government collapsed and fresh elections were ordered in 1998.

Sonia Gandhi leads the Congress party

This was the time when Sonia Gandhi, widow of Rajiv Gandhi, decided to come out and lead the party after seven years of mourning. She campaigned heavily for the party but the Congress had to sit in Opposition after the 1998 elections winning only 141 seats.

Jayalalithaa pulls down Vajpayee government

While it is true that India took a detached view of the ethnic conflict in the aftermath of Gandhi's killing, things changed shortly after the BJP led National Democratic Alliance took office in 1998. There was a tilt in the balance of power in Tamil Nadu also as

92 Prabhu Chawla, '*Damning the DMK, Rajiv Gandhi killing: Jain commission indicts DMK for colluding with LTTE,*' India Today, November 17,1997.

the AIADMK became a partner in the Vajpayee led a 24-partner coalition government. Jayalaliathaa continued to oppose the LTTE.

As in the past the Sri Lankans were the first to land in Delhi to get reassurance of support from Vajpayee towards the ethnic issue. The new government did not mind giving that assurance. In return, Sri Lanka kept mum when Vajpayee went for the Pokhran nuclear blasts in May 1998, which shocked the entire West resulting in sanctions against India.

The DMK was languishing after the rout in the 1998 elections for some time. Karunanidhi was biding time, as the DMK was not in power either at the Centre or in the State. Within 13 months the National Democratic Alliance partner Jayalalithaa pulled down the Vajpayee government in collusion with the Congress party. Vajpayee lost by one vote but he came back with an impressive majority in 1999 and formed the government. By this time the DMK had become the NDA partner replacing the AIADMK. Vajpayee took the view that it was time for a major peace push in Sri Lanka and got into the act of ushering in peace in Sri Lanka, quietly. Almost all the Tamil Nadu parties went along with this stand.

LTTE attacks military forces

Correspondingly, there was a regime change in Sri Lanka also as Chandrika Kumaratunga became the president in 1999. When she took over, the LTTE operations were at its peak. The Tamil Tigers had launched "Operation unceasing waves" in November 1999. Within a month they had captured the North-eastern coastal belt Vettikerni. Five years after the Sri Lankan troops triumphantly drove out the Tamil Tigers from the Northern Jaffna peninsula; it was the turn of the battle- weary troops to beat a hasty retreat. This was in the face of the biggest offensive launched by the LTTE for a separate Eelam. Its push towards Jaffna and its savage attacks on the military installations forced President Kumaratunga to virtually declare a State of emergency.

Karunanidhi's tight rope walking in Tamil Nadu

By the late nineties, the power of the Dravidian parties began to increase in the national coalition politics. Karunanidhi was facing problems in dealing with the strident fringe groups in Tamil Nadu who had taken up the cause of the LTTE. He was anxious to ensure that they did not try to whip up public sympathy and turn the Sri Lankan situation into a poll issue in the State Assembly elections due after a year. The NDA government was under pressure from its Tamil Nadu allies including the DMK, the PMK and the MDMK not to help the Sri Lankan government. His alliance partner, S. Ramdoss of the PMK, had taken the stand of open support to the LTTE, urging immediate recognition of Tamil Eelam. Ramdoss had even gone to the extent of appealing to the United Nations to intervene and help create an independent Tamil State in the island nation. The MDMK leader, Vaiko, who has been an ardent champion of the LTTE and Tamil Eelam, was against extending even "non-military logistics" to Sri Lanka. The AIADMK leader, Jayalalithaa, favoured a political solution and India offering its good offices to Sri Lanka in bringing about an end to the conflict. The Tamil Manila Congress (TMC) leader, G.K. Moopanar, wondered whether the Centre would permit its constituents like the PMK and the MDMK to support terrorism and militancy, both inside and outside the country. Before the eruption of the crisis in Sri Lanka, the DMK government had drawn flak from the opposition for recommending clemency for Nalini, one of the four accused sentenced to death in the Rajiv Gandhi assassination case.

Elephant Pass falls

The Sri Lankan situation turned worse with the LTTE attacking the Sri Lankan military forces. By December 1999 they captured the North- eastern coastal belt Vettikerni. The most drastic shift in the military balance came after the fall of the Elephant Pass on April 22, 2000. Located at the neck of the peninsula, Elephant Pass, the gateway to Jaffna was vital for its defence. The Tigers with their meticulous planning and strategy, succeeded in inflicting the most humiliating defeat on the Sri Lankan troops.

When the Sri Lankan government, facing a military crisis sought India's help in April 2000, Prime Minister Vajpayee's response was muted due to the pressure from his Tamil Nadu allies. The Dravidian parties including the DMK, PMK and MDMK opposed this. President Chandrika Kumaratunga was in need of urgent outside help. She sought India's help to evacuate the Sri Lankan troops from Jaffna if necessary. New Delhi's initial assessment was that the fall of Jaffna was imminent and the Sri Lankan army was on the retreat. The government, which stuck to its policy of non-interference, was also clear that there could be no solution outside the framework of Sri Lankan Constitution. The Cabinet Committee on Security (CCS) considered the options and decided that New Delhi would send humanitarian supplies. The Dravaidian parties opposed this tooth and nail.

Karunanidhi talks of separate Eelam

On June 3, 2000, Karunanidhi dropped a bombshell at a public meeting on his 77th birthday, that the creation of a separate Tamil State in the Northern and the Eastern provinces of Sri Lanka would be the most feasible solution to the island's ethnic conflict; this was clearly contrary to the declared position of the NDA government. This created shock waves in New Delhi forcing Vajpayee to launch an urgent damage control exercise. "Karunanidhi had strenuously lobbied with the other constituents of the ruling alliance and successfully stymied government's initial efforts. In a bid to reassure his allies Vajpayee was forced to reiterate that the government had 'ruled out the sending or selling of arms 'to Sri Lanka."[93]**This period showed that the Tamil Nadu parties opposed the Centre giving any help to the Sri Lankan government. Soon New Delhi began to adopt a gradual low profile shift towards Sri Lanka from an earlier stance of neutrality from 2000. The Dravidian parties began to balance their interest at the Centre and the State. The escalation of the civil war between the Sri Lankan government and the Tigers and growing refugee inflow from across the Palk straits created a**

---

93 John Cheiran, *India's policy dilemma,* Front Line, Volume 17, 10 May, 13 -26, 2000

situation in Tamil Nadu when the issue once again started having resonance in its public life.

New Delhi for peace talks with LTTE

In the 2001 Assembly polls, there was a regime change in Tamil Nadu. Karunanidhi lost power and the AIADMK chief Jayalalithaa took over. But within months she had to resign after the court disqualified her and she put her puppet Chief Minister O. Pannerselvam till she was cleared. During his short stint Pannerselvam opposed the suggestion that the peace talks should be held in Chennai and the LTTE leaders should be allowed to remain in Chennai. **Responding to his letter, the Centre took a decision that it would not permit such a thing. "On January 10, Union Minister of State for home I. D. Swamy talking to reporters at Kanyakumari said that with the Karnataka government too joining Tamil Nadu in opposing the LTTE's plea, there was no scope to examine the demand as the outfit had been banned."**[94]

Yashwant Sinha recalls that Karunanidhi and Jayalalithaa had to show politically that they were more concerned about the attacks on the Tamils. Vaiko, Veeramani and Nedumaran were fully on the side of the LTTE. Yashwant Sinha notes, "It was more often the Tamil parties came to us and represented their case. We did not face the problems the congress led government faced. The Centre's policy was reconciliation and peace talks. Then came the ceasefire of 2002.[95]"

Ranil becomes Prime Minister

Meanwhile, in Sri Lanka, Ranil Wickremesinghe, the Opposition Leader, became Prime Minister in December 2001. Unfortunately Wickremesinghe and President Kumaratunga, instead of complimenting each other, functioned as rivals.

Wickremesinghe announced talks when he came in. Diaspora was sending money and arms from different sources. Ranil got the

---

94 Special correspondent, '*T.N. CM cautions Vajpayee against providing base to LTTE*,' The Hindu, January 11, 2002

95 Author's interview with Yashwant Sinha, (18, September 2013)

blessings of New Delhi when he visited the Indian capital soon after he took over in December 2001. "I also asked Norway to keep India in the picture on the negotiations with LTTE."[96]

While backing the negotiation process Kumaratunga had been critical of the negotiating strategy of her Prime Minister. However, Wickremesinghe points out that in 2000 Norwegians were working with Kumaratunga. They did not make much progress. "Then in 2001 April – May after the army attack failed the LTTE retaliated on the Bandaranaike airport and there was another round of peace talk and secret talks. Tiruchelvam used to meet the Norwegians. But the army patrol that penetrated the area ambushed the vehicle. Tiruchelvam escaped and said he couldn't deal with it."[97]

A truce document was drafted. Yashwant Sinha observes that India could not join the peace talks openly because the LTTE was participating. Prabhakaran was a proclaimed offender and the main accused in the Rajiv Gandhi murder case. The LTTE was a banned outfit in India. Without undoing these India could not join the negotiations. "That did not lead to a situation where India was isolated because the Sri Lankan government was briefing us fully every fortnight. They were briefing us on everything that was happening on the peace talks."[98]

Eventually, on 21 February 2002, the LTTE Chief Prabhakaran signed the ceasefire agreement and Wickremesinghe put his signature a day later without consulting the President who was the executive head of the government. He was alleged to have kept back information from the President on the agreement. Chandrika naturally was upset. But Wickremesinghe claims that he had held no secret talks. "There were one or two persons who conveyed messages. Then I kept the facilitators informed. President Chandrika knew some of it but not all. They knew that I was keeping the facilitators informed. There were no secret deals. If I had a secret deal with Prabhakaran he would have been the winner. The LTTE would have been defeated at that

---

96 Author's interview with Wickremesinghe (17-22. February 2014)

97 Author's interview with Wickremesinghe,(17-22, February, 2014)

98 .Author's interview with Yashwant Sinha, (18, September, 2013)

time if India did not do the food drop and saved them. The main issue was linkage of North and the East. It cost so many problems with the Sinhalese. Prabhakaran attacked the IPKF thinking we were all bogged down here.[99] "

Kumaratunga points out that she offered much more in a devolved federal State. The LTTE completely rejected it. Then she made efforts to separate the Tamil Tigers from Tamil civilians. The talks went on for eight months and finally the LTTE turned it down. Chandrika encountered a problem, as she did not have the required two-thirds majority to change the Constitution. Although her party won 82 per cent of the votes their seats were less with only one member more than the opposition. This was the electoral system her predecessor had changed. "Then at the end finally little by little the opposition MPs started crossing over to us. At one point I needed only seven more votes. Now I feel I could have done it if I had been less democratic. I already had a simple majority and I would have become dictator for only one month and go back then this country would have been a better place.[100]

Tamil Nadu seeks extradition of Prabhakaran

While the peace talks were in progress, on April 16, 2002, the Tamil Nadu Assembly passed a government - sponsored resolution urging that Prabhakaran should be extradited to India to stand trial on the Rajiv Gandhi assassination case. "In a strongly-worded reference, the motion urged the Centre to dispatch the Indian Army to capture Prabhakaran and bring him to Tamil Nadu to face trial in the Rajiv Gandhi assassination case, if the Sri Lankan government could not extradite him."[101] **Tamil Nadu political parties including the DMK did not want India to take kindly to the LTTE suggestion that New Delhi should mediate. But this was one thing that the Centre was not willing to consider.** Pointing out the difficulties

---

99 Author's interview with Ranil Wickremesinghe, (17-22, February, 2014)

100 Author's interview with Chandrika Kumaratunga (17-22, February 2014)

101 N.Sathiya Moorthy, ' *TN Assembly urges Centre to seek Prabhakaran's extradition,* ' rediff.com April 16, 2002.

in the extradition of Prabhakaran former External Affairs Minister Yashwant Sinha notes, "There were two issues. While the official Indian position was the continued demand for his extradition, India also blessed the Norwegian mediation. Secondly on October 2, 2002, a Colombo court had handed down a 200-year sentence to Prabhakaran in the 1996 Central Bank bombing case. This shut the possibility of extradition."[102] He observes that the Tamil issue could not be resolved because the LTTE wanted much more. They wanted almost an independent army, independent navy and that was something like dividing Sri Lanka. But India was firm in the territorial integrity and unity of Sri Lanka. The RAW tried its best to convince the LTTE but failed.

Why did the Norwegian initiative fail?

The Norwegian efforts did not result in resumption of peace talks or lead to a formal ceasefire. The Norwegians had best intentions but could not succeed. "The failure of the Norwegian initiative in Sri Lanka in 2000- 2001 was primarily due to the absence in Sri Lanka's policy of conditions conducive for political engagement with the LTTE."[103] Secondly a reformist regime backed by reformist forces would have had a better chance of advancing a peace project in Sri Lanka. Thirdly the transformation of a peace initiative to a peace process was a difficult journey. Domestic conditions were crucial to make the external inputs yield results.

Interestingly the Plantation Tamils kept away from all these. The Ceylon Workers Congress (CWC) delegation led by Thondaman met Prabhakran in Killinochi twice during the ceasefire time. Saravana Muthu who was part of the delegation recalls, that Prabhakaran recognized their problem when they urged him not to recruit boys from their side. "He understood our position but unfortunately Tamil Nadu politicians don't understand us. They use us for their domestic politics."[104]

---

102 Author's interview with Yashwant Sinha, (18 September 2013)

103 Kumar Rupesinghe, '*Negotiating peace in Sri Lanka*', Research & Documentation Centre, Foundation for Co-Existence, 2006, P 265

104 Author's interview with Saravana Muthu (17-22, February, 2014)

Setback to Prabhakaran

Prabhakaran also suffered setbacks. The first was the defection of one of his top commanders Karuna to the Sri Lankan army in 2004. Prabhakaran was not one to tolerate disobedience and often got the rebels killed. Karuna, who was getting enough signals that Prabhakaran, was getting suspicious of him managed to escape along with 2000 of his supporters. This was the first split of the LTTE and Karuna had given valuable information about Prabhakaran's tactics and other secrets to the Sri Lankan government and its military to help them in their efforts to nab Prabhakaran. The second was a natural calamity when Tsunami struck the Sri Lankan shores, particularly the areas dominated by the LTTE.

Rajapakse wipes out the LTTE

In the November 2005 presidential elections Mahinda Rajapakse won with a slim majority defeating his opponent Wickremesinghe. With his rural background, Rajapakse soon established himself appointing people of his confidence and members of his family to top posts in the government. Rajapakse was a determined man and decided to wipe out the LTTE. Ironically, this was the time when Prabhakaran decided he was strong enough to break the ceasefire agreement with the Sri Lankan government. So in 2006 the final Eelam War kicked off.

Wickremesinghe points out that "Rajapakse had only to take the LTTE out of Vanni. Neither Chandrika nor I could have done it because the army was weak then. After taking over, Rajapakse built up the army and purchased arms. Chandrika's mistake was that she overstretched herself."[105] However, Kumaratunga observes, "I took an army that was defeated. I don't think Rajapakse would have won in 2005 or 2006. He did it in 2009. He took on a weakened Prabhakaran with a strong army. We had different strategies."[106]

---

105 Author's interview with Ranil Wickremenghe, (17-22, February, 2014)

106 Author's interview with Chandra Kumaratunga, (17-22, February, 2014)

Rajapakse adopted mainly the military strategy and his political strategy was keeping his Sinhala voters in one block.

President Rajapakse decided to go for war when the LTTE blocked the Mavilla anicut. The Eelam War IV began with the Sri Lankan Air Force launching an offensive on 26th July 2006. Rajapakse, who openly opposed the peace process, planned for a big offensive against the LTTE. Learning lessons from the earlier defeats he concentrated on mustering necessary support- economic, military and political- from other countries particularly India and China when he prepared for a final assault. He also unleashed a diplomatic offensive against the LTTE, particularly in the Western countries, where the LTTE had strong support in the Tamil Diaspora.

Tamil Nadu puts pressure on Manmohan Singh

One year before Rajapakse became the president, the Congress Party came to power in India leading the United Progressive Alliance defeating the BJP- led NDA in 2004. The DMK had quit the NDA and had become a partner in the UPA by this time. The basic policy was clear. The thrust at the level of the National Security Adviser M.K. Narayanan was to see whether India could make Rajapakse implement the 13th Amendment. But New Delhi found that it could not push him beyond a point because of political constraints.

There was an anti - LTTE sentiment in Tamil Nadu as the AIADMK was opposed to it after the assassination of Rajiv Gandhi. This was a domestic constituency, which New Delhi could not ignore. Moreover, the DMK was the UPA alliance partner. Shiv Shankar Menon, who was one of the policy makers at that time as the then Foreign Secretary, observes, "For Indian policy makers, the priority was clear to ensure that the least harm possible fell on the civilian population trapped in a military war, whatever their ethnicity- Tamil, Sinhala or Muslim. This was a moral as well as a political imperative, with Indian general elections coming in May 2009 and Tamil Nadu the state that swung the balance in 2004 elections in favour of the ruling UPA. After all for every Tamil in Sri Lanka, there were about 27 Tamils in India who were emotionally affected by and invested in what happens to Tamil in Sri Lanka[107]." All these perhaps made New Delhi assist Rajapakse to help annihilate the LTTE.

At this point, the international interest in Sri Lanka and the LTTE had declined. A top Intelligence official admits that the LTTE never realised that it was becoming weaker and the Sri Lankan government was becoming stronger. By this time Prabhakaran had reached a stage when he felt everybody was his enemy. If there was a dialogue with Prabhakaran face to face, New Delhi could have conveyed this information. Shiv Shankar Menon confirms that "By 2009, there was no one left in the LTTE leadership to tell him the truth in the last months of his life. They had either fallen by the wayside, like Anton Balasingham or had been eliminated by Prabhakaran himself."[108] In any case Rajapakse was determined to finish the LTTE and went about in a systematic manner. It was a combination of things that worked for the success. There were lots of sacrifices but ultimately the war ended.

Rajapakse plans final assault on the LTTE

Gotabhaya Rajapakse, brother of Mahinda Rajapakse and the former Defence Secretary of Sri Lanka asserts that firstly they were able to finish the LTTE because of the political will. Militarily, the leadership realized that a large expansion was needed within a very short period. In short the troops had to occupy the liberated land so that the LTTE or the terrorists can't come back. The troops had to perform the operations continuously and take on the LTTE from different fronts. The troops strongly occupied the South so that the LTTE did not come back and it was the same thing in the North so that LTTE could not attack from behind. The Tigers were not allowed to cut down the military lines of communications. Gotabhaya recalls, "We assessed this and briefed the President that we needed to expand a lot

107 Shiv Shankar menonr, 'Choices : Inside the making of India's Foreign policy', P 139, Published in the Allen Lane by the Penguin Random House, India , 2016.

108 Shiv Shankar menonr, 'Choices : Inside the making of India's Foreign policy', P 143, Published in the Allen Lane by the Penguin Random House, India , 2016.

within a short period. This was not an easy thing. You need to recruit people, train people fast and also equip them."[109]

Gotabaya Rajapakse notes that the President knew that the normal system of working through the foreign ministry was not enough to deal with the LTTE. So he created this troika with India. "From our side Basil Rajapakse, Veeratunga who was President's Secretary and myself and from the Indian side their National Security Adviser M. K. Narayanan, Foreign Secretary Shankar Menon and V.J. Singh who was the Defence Secretary were involved. We coordinated everything. We went to India and they came to Sri Lanka and we discussed everything even the operational plans and intelligence inputs. The Tamil Nadu Chief Minister Karunanidhi knew everything."[110] The two sides managed to settle many sensitive issues. Even when Karunanidhi went on hunger strike the Indian side went to Rajapakse and sorted out things and Karunanidhi ended his breakfast to lunch fast. This shows that Sri Lanka kept India informed throughout about the war.

Shiv Shankar Menon also confirms about the troika and that New Delhi was in "intense and constant" touch with Colombo. The Prime Minister and the then External Affairs Minister Pranab Mukherji took personal interest and was actively involved throughout according to him. "I vividly remember the atmosphere of the crisis that built up during that period and the repeated visits from and to Colombo in the first five months of 2009. Particularly memorable were the midnight visits to Colombo with Pranab Mukherji when we flew into Colombo at 8 PM, went straight to the presidential palace for a military briefing by Fonseka and a political one by President Rajapakse and had long conversation exploring options until we left the palace after midnight to fly home on the Indian Air force Emperor jet. By mid January 2009, the SLA (Sri Lankan Army) and leadership were convinced that they had the measure of the LTTE and that victory would be theirs." [111]

---

109 Author's interview with Gotabhaya Rajapakse (17-22, February, 2014)

110 Author's interview with Gotabhyaa Rajapakse, (17-22, February, 2014)

111 Shiv Shankr Menon, *"Choices, Inside the making of India's Foreign policy"*, *P139-140*. Allan Lane, by Penguin Random House, India, 2016

Explaining why they did not stop the war despite international pressure Gotabaya notes that if they had done so at any time they would have gone back to square one. Prabhakaran would have been doing the same thing over and over again. "This was the only opportunity we had and we used it. Whatever anybody says we wanted to end that."[112] **It should be noted that Tamil Nadu put tremendous pressure on Manmohan Singh government to stop the war while DMK adopted a strategy of running with the hare and hunting with the hounds. He covertly supported New Delhi while openly opposed Rajapalkse's strategy of war.**

Army Chief Sarath Fonseka's strategy to finish LTTE

The President had the confidence in his brother and also the army chief Gen. Sarath Fonseka who had been dealing with the LTTE for about 30 years. Fonseka knew its strengths and weaknesses as an army insider. He decided to take on the LTTE in the jungle and not in the conventional way the army dealt with it so far. As to how they trapped the LTTE, Gen. Fonseka recalls that they decided to enter the jungle in areas where the Tigers were strong but the army weakened them slowly. The LTTE fought till the last day. They started in the East. Gen. Fonseka kept them tied down in the North and also in the East. By 17th May 2009, the troops cornered the LTTE by 400 /400 meters area. On 17th night they tried to escape. There were three defence points the LTTE tried to break but they were prevented. The final fighting developed and continued from 17 to 19. Prabhakaran had jumped into the lagoon with his 100 men cadre. "I was confident. I said I would finish the LTTE in three years. I did it in 2 years and nine months. Prabhakaran was not weak. He had equipped himself with artillery and aircrafts. He had even tanks. I formed small, highly mobile, independent and lethal commando teams, who often infiltrated behind the enemy lines to isolate and then demolish LTTE defences,[113]" declares the victorious General.

Gen. Fonseka recalls that Prabhakaran's body remained there. On 18th (May) night, the topmost LTTE leadership divided itself

---

112 Author's interview with Gotabaya Rajapakse, (17-22, February 2014)
113 Author's interview with Gen. Sarath Forseka, (17-22, February2014)

into three different groups. They attacked the army's forward defence line along the Nandikkadal lagoon and did manage to break through. But they had reckoned without the army's second and third tier defences. Jeyam, Pottu Amman and Soosai led these three groups. Prabhakaran and his closest bodyguards thought they would manage to escape, but in reality all these LTTE fighters, around 250 of them, had got trapped between the army's first and the second defence lines. "After fierce fighting that night, almost all the top LTTE leadership got killed in the area. We discovered Prabhakaran's body on the 19th morning. I got the news of Prabhakaran's death around 11 pm on May 19. I got a phone call from the commander who gave me the information."[114] Gen. Fonseka also confirms that the **"Tamil Nadu government knew that LTTE was going to be finished. Karunanidhi knew about the annihilation. The Indian High Commissioner was monitoring the war."[115]"**

Tamil Nadu leaders like Nedumaran allege that India helped the Sri Lankan government in ending the war. New Delhi gave all the intelligence inputs. The Indian government had used its navy to surround the place and shot them. "Did not Rajapakse say after the war that they were fighting India's war? Did the Indian government deny this? They had used the weapons and radars given by India in the war. India did not deny all these," claims Nedumaran. A top official in India who dealt with the problem admits that everybody knew the big picture. After the end of the Eelam War, there was a change and a tendency to help the Tamils in Jaffna because of their sufferings in the war.

Confirming this, Shiv Shankar Menon points out that during their conversations with Sri Lankan leadership "one thing they would not agree to, however, was any understanding on keeping the LTTE leaders alive and taking them prisoners for the purpose of putting them on trial. Nor were they willing to see any form of international moderation or a ceasefire that would enable the top LTTE leadership to survive to fight another day. There were also obvious limits to what India could press for in terms of treatment of the convicted

114 Author's interview with Gen. Sarath Fonseka (17-22, February, 2014)

115 Author's interview with Gen. Sarath Fonseka, (17-22, February 2014)

killers of Prime Minister Rajiv Gandhi, who are still wanted by the law in India." [116]

Where did Prabhakaran go wrong?

What went wrong in Prabhakran's calculations? The TNA leader Sampanthan does not think that Prabhakaran had the political acumen to convert his military strength into political strength. "He was a failure in that respect and eventually destruction was due to the fact that he never respected human rights or democracy and he became too authoritarian. Many opportunities that came for a settlement were missed. [117]" In his opinion, the Indo- Sri Lanka Agreement fundamentally recognized various features that had hitherto been not recognized. The Tamils, Muslims and the Sinhalese had a right to preserve their identity and live with equal rights. The Northern and the Eastern Provinces were areas of historical importance for the Tamils. The 13[th]amendment of the Constitution that came out through the negotiations was a good beginning. Then Kumaratunga came out with a proposal in 1995. Those were opportunities that were available for the Tamil people but LTTE was the main negotiator on the other side. To bring them on board was difficult. The Sri Lankan government also was somewhat short sighted. It hoped to succeed militarily. Secondly, the war had gone on too long with almost two generations missing out the normal life. They became weary of war and were yearning for peace. Thirdly, Rajapakse was determined to finish the LTTE with the support of India and he did it.

Could India have stopped the genocide?

Former Foreign Secretary Shiv Shankar Menon explains "to my mind, it was the conjunction of factors, not just the conduct of war and the use of force that brought about the defeat of the LTTE. The international community's disenchantment with the LTTE after 2005, and India's response after the LTTE assassinated former Prime Minister Rajiv Gandhi held the ring enabling the political

116 Shiv Shankr Menon, "*Choices: Indise the making of India's Foreign policy,*" P 140 -141, Published in the Allan Lane, By Penguin Random House, India, 2016.

117 Author's interview with Sampandhan, (17-22, February 2014)

military and social isolation of the LTTE and Prabhakaran. Finally, Prabhakran and the LTTE's inability to innovate or change in response to the new SLA tactics and the shifting environment after 2005 brought about their end in Sri Lanka." [118]

There are many who blame India and Tamil Nadu Chief Minister Karunanidhi for not doing enough to stop the genocide. Western countries did little to curb the flow of funds to the LTTE from the Diaspora. But they have censured the Sri Lankan government at the U.N. Human Rights Council (UNHRC) every year since 2011, when a resolution was introduced by the United States, for the violations of human rights in the final days of the war.

Shiv Shankar Menon notes that India's policy options in that situation were limited. " If India had stood aside or asked him (President Rajapakse) to desist, in effect, defending the killers of an Indian Prime Minister, we would have effectively written ourselves out of Sri Lanka for the next decade or more, sacrificing our maritime and other interests in Sri Lanka and adhering a geopolitically strategic neighbour to other powers. More than 90 per cent of our foreign trade and most of our energy supplies came along the sea-lanes that Sri Lanka sits astride and we could hardly abandon Sri Lanka to potentially hostile influences. In effect, Sri Lanka is an aircraft centre parked fourteen miles off the Indian coast. This is the perpetual dilemma of India's Sri Lanka policy: We must engage in order to defend our interest in keeping Sri Lanka free of antagonistic outside influences while also trying to prevent the growth of extremism and separatism that could affect Tamil Nadu."[119]

Yashwant Sinha notes that by now India had become weak and did not have the same clout which Rajiv Gandhi had to deal with Sri Lanka. It might not have been possible for the Government of

---

118 Shiv Shankar menon, 'Choices" The inside the making of India's Foreign policy', P 151-152, Published by Allan Lane by Penguin Random House, India, 2016.

119 Shicv Shankar menon, 'Choices: Inside the making of India's Foreign policy'. P 146. Published in Allan Lane by Penguin Random House India,. 2016

India to stop the brutal wiping out of the LTTE. The Rajiv Gandhi-Jayewardene Accord came along with the 13ᵗʰ Amendment. That was the clout India had at one point of time. Rajapakse has made sure that he took the fullest advantage of New Delhi's weakness and he did not go beyond a point. "India could not do much and just watched the killing of the LTTE men. The tragedy is that sequel to that the Government of India had not been able to persuade Rajapakse to engage in purposeful discussions. He was doing nothing."[120]

Who killed Prabhakaran's son?

When the War ended in 2009, slowly the details of genocide and the alleged killing of Prabhakaran's teenage boy Balachandran emerged. The outrage in Tamil Nadu was enormous with the Tamil youth in the State coming out on the streets to protest against it. There was public anger. The Dravidian parties too took up this issue in a competitive spirit and put pressure on the Centre to take up the war crimes with the Rajapakse government.

Gotabhaya points out that there was heavy fighting. The boy died with his father. Even at the last minute Prabhakaran broke from the line and went to the island in this small place with his bodyguards and when people were looking for the bodies they thought that he was burnt in a vehicle. But still they were searching because he was the most important character even after the war ended for their leaders. They confronted the troops. "Do you think Prabhkaran will just give in? K. Pathmanabha, (KP) the LTTE financier spoke to Prabhakaran in January 2009 over the phone. We intercepted that conversation. KP said 'I would create an opportunity and take you out. I will find a safe place and then you can reorganize,' he suggested but Prabhakaran refused. He said 'No, no. I am going to fight. I am going to change the situation.' Then two weeks before the war ended KP spoke to him again and asked him to escape. He said no. 'I can fight, I can break and I will restart this.' This was his mentality. Do you think that such a person will come out holding his hands up and surrender? The other son died in a different place where he was fighting."[121].

Why Tamil issue becomes an election plank in Tamil Nadu?

Interestingly, nobody seems to have consulted the Sri Lankan Tamils or taken note of their views. Do they want Tamil Eelam? Are they enthused about the support from Tamil Nadu? They have got some Tamil MPs in Parliament. Some of them are ministers. Has anyone discussed with them? The view from across the Palk Strait is contrary to the position taken by the Tamil Nadu political parties.

Apparently, Tamil Nadu politicians exploited the Sri Lankan issue – either to stay in power or to capture power. There are some Sri Lankan Tamils like Sampanthan who feel that even if it did not get them votes it did not weaken their vote bank. This is because there is a strong underlying sentiment in Tamil Nadu about their brothers in Sri Lanka. **For New Delhi and Tamil Nadu it is a balance of what one needs to do and what one can do.**

The AIADMK, which had taken a non-reactive approach to the Sri Lankan Tamil problem from 1991 when Jayalalithaa came to power, started voicing its concern from 2001. Karunanidhi did not lag behind in his competitive politics. In successive general elections, the Tamil issue figured in campaigns with the DMK and the AIADMK trying to outperform each other in their support for the cause and so did the other Dravidian parties. **From 1999 to 2004 Karunanidhi, who was part of the NDA also had to keep in mind his alliance politics and therefore co-operated with Delhi's Sri Lanka policy by turning a blind eye to the brutal methods employed by the Sri Lankan army against the Tamils. Naturally the AIADMK and other Tamil Nadu parties criticized Karunanidhi for this doublespeak.** The next ten years from 2004 to 2013, the DMK was a UPA partner.

---

121 Author's interview with Gotabhaya Rajapakse, (17-22, February, 2014)

Karunanidhi puts pressure on Manmohan Singh

Karunanidhi played his politics well. In 2008, he had taken the resignations of all the DMK MPs to demand New Delhi's intervention to stop the war in Sri Lank despite being kept informed by the Centre on the Centre's stand on the War. After a few diplomatic exercises by the then External Affairs Minister Pranab Mukherji, Karunanidhi withdrew the threat. He needed a few political gimmicks to prove his sincerity in saving Lankan Tamils. On April 29, 2009, the Chief Minister surprised everyone by reaching the Anna Samadhi on the Marina beach in Chennai around 6 AM, on a Monday morning, sat in his motorised wheelchair near the memorial. As the crowds swelled, Karunanidhi declared he was prepared to sacrifice his life to protect the Tamils in Sri Lanka. "As it happened, Colombo announced cessation of hostilities later in the morning and the DMK patriarch called off his protest before lunch, not having missed a meal but having made an electoral point." [122] With the Eelam issue picking up in the run-up to the elections in Tamil Nadu, Prime Minister Manmohan Singh - on the insistence of his key ally, Karunanidhi - hurriedly deputed his National Security Advisor M. K. Narayanan and Foreign Secretary Shiv Shankar Menon to Colombo to urge Rajapakse to halt killings. At stake were the 39 seats in Tamil Nadu for coming back to power. Karunanidhi termed his fast as a success while the AIADMK and his other detractors ridiculed it calling it a tokenism. **The AIADMK chief Jayalalithaa too hardened her stand on the ethnic crisis, insisting that a separate Eelam was the only lasting solution. In fact almost all the Dravidian parties as well as the Congress believed that ignoring the Tamil issue might cost them their votes. But the Centre did not heed their demand because it was committed to the unity of Sri Lanka.**

---

122 M. Gyanasekharan, *'Karuna goes on sudden fast, ends it even faster.'* Times of India. April 28,2009

Jayalalaithaa's stand on LTTE

Jayalalithaa continued to support the anti-Tamil racialist war in Sri Lanka after President Mahinda Rajapakse resumed it in 2006. Even during the final phase of war, she cynically justified Tamil civilian casualties, claiming that civilian deaths are "inevitable in a war." **Jayalalithaa as well as other Dravidian parties were totally opposed to Rajapakse.**

A few weeks before the military defeat of the LTTE in May 2009, Jayalalithaa changed her tune and became a "defender" of Sri Lankan Tamils. Changing her stand, she delcared at an election rally, "We will fight to attain that independent, separate Eelam. Till today, I have never said that a separate Eelam is the only solution. I have spoken about a political solution, this and that. But, now I emphatically say a separate Eelam is the only permanent solution to the Sri Lankan conflict."[123]

Jayalalithaa focused on her demands for a political solution, a referendum for creation of a separate Eelam, supporting the international action against the Sri Lankan army for its alleged war crimes and imposition of economic sanction until Colombo agreed to a solution. The other parties had no other option than to go along and even demand more. Jayalalithaa's proposal to send a fact-finding mission comprising of Tamil Nadu M.Ps to Sri Lanka, her strong opposition to the training of the Sri Lankan military personnel in India were all part of a competitive Dravidian politics.

The 2009 Lok Sabha polls were important because the Eelam War had ended just then. Fortunately for Karunanidhi, despite all these problems the Congress- DMK alliance performed well in the 2009 Lok Sabha elections while the Manmohan Singh government came back to power for a second consecutive term at the Centre." The immediate reaction in Tamil Nadu, which was voting in the Indian general elections at the same time in April –May 2009, seemed to bear this assessment out. The war in Sri Lanka and the government of India's response did not prevent the DMK from

---

123 **Athiyan Silva**, 'India: Tamil Nadu chief minister tries to exploit issue of Sri Lankan Tamils', World socialist website, wsws.org

taking an overwhelming majority of Lok Sabha seats in Tamil Nadu despite the disadvantages of the incumbency and its membership of the ruling coalition in Delhi."

Soon after the war the DMK started demanding de-militarisation, democratisation and development in Tamil areas, which Rajapakse promised after the end of war but Karunanidhi's detractors questioned why did he not stop the genocide when he could have done so and exposed his double speak. Karunanidhi's proposal for giving citizenship to the thousands of refugees who had fled from Jaffna during the war had been nipped in the bud as it could have adverse impact on other refugee groups in India. Meanwhile the DMK chief was trying to find his lost space by reviving the TESO. Along with the Viduthalai Chiruthaikal Katchi and the Pattali Makkal Katchi, the DMK leader wanted to keep up pressure.

The Dravidian parties on the same page on Tamil issue

The AIADMK came to power with a massive majority in the 2011 Assembly elections. Jayalalithaa became the Chief Minister once again and the tug of war between the two main parties began but both took a similar stand regarding their Sri Lankan Tamil brethren. Immediately after she took over, playing the Sri Lankan card, Jayalalithaa demanded that economic sanctions should be imposed on Sri Lanka if it did not cooperate for an international tribunal to try President Rajapakse for alleged war crimes. **The Centre did not oblige her because the South Block did not see it feasible.**

The DMK got involved in the 2 G scam (Telecom scam) with DMK minister A. Raja and Karunanidhi's daughter Kanimozhi jailed on corruption charges. The echo of that was the DMK was wiped out in the 2014 Lok Sabha elections. It got zero seats plunging the party into a depression. Now that the DMK is not in power either in the State or at the Centre and the wily DMK chief is biding his time and also keeping the Tamil issue alive on issues like Katchateevu and fishermen.

Sri Lankan Tamil leaders criticize Tamil Nadu parties

The Tamil groups see through their political game. Sri Lankan leader Saravanamuthu explains that it was because, "it galvanizes people behind an emotive issue. It is politically organized. I think in the last Assembly elections I was told that lots of young people came out to vote and the Sri Lankan factor was there.[124] "He believes that the Tamil Nadu parties had not understood the basic thing. It was an ethnic issue with regard to the Tamils in the Northern and Eastern parts of the island. For Northern Province Chief Minister Wigneswaran and the Tamil National Alliance (TNA) their priority has always been a political settlement. "This has got to be understood and the emotive concern of those people in Chennai or the diaspora. I don't think that the people in Tamil Nadu or the Diaspora fully understand and are acquainted with dynamics of the politics here.[125]"

Muhammad Hizbullah, Rajapakse's Minister for Economic Development claims that neither Karunanidhi nor Jayalalithaa were keen to get the issue resolved. But politically they had to raise it because of their vote bank politics. Jayalalithaa's move to release Rajiv Gandhi killers in February 2014 showed that she wanted to capture the Tamil votes in the State. "We are also politicians and we know. Because of their actions our relationship is affected some times." [126]

There are several Sri Lankan leaders who are critical of the Tamil Nadu politicians for not doing enough to stop the Eelam War in 2009 when the Sri Lankan military finished the LTTE in a brutal manner. Muthu Sivalingam notes that "At that time the Tamil Nadu and India should have come forward and stopped those horrible killings. They had all opportunities. Only when the elections come they start talking about Tamil issue.[127]"

Echoing similar feelings the TNA leader Sampanthan points out that Tamil Nadu never took a united stand with regard to the

---

124 Author's interview with Saravanamuthu, (17-22, February, 2014)

125 Author's interview with Saravanamuthu, (17-22, February, 2014)

126 Author's interview with Hizbullah (17-22, February 2014)

127 Author's interview with Muthu Sivalingam (17-22, February 2014)

Tamil question. This affected their efficacy. But the notion persists that they were using the Tamil issue for their own political ends which was unfortunate. "The failure to evolve a common policy which was reasonable, rationale and acceptable to international community and which the Sri Lankan government could not have denied – if they had done that it would have been much more effective.[128]"

Northern Province Chief Minister Wigneswaran points out that when politicians in Tamil Nadu say separation was the only solution, the Sinhalese feel very apprehensive. What was being said in Chennai affected the Jaffna Tamils. The Tamil Nadu political parties were using their own narrative. The situation on the ground was different. "We are in a different type of world than the Tamil Nadu politicians are living. One has to be very careful in what you say. It makes the Sinhalese more apprehensive of what would happen. The Tamil Nadu politicians do not realise this and because of this we are having more problem, as the Sri Lankan President is not able to give us any more powers. They are unable to see that they are not helping us and on the contrary make it more difficult. They do not know what is their role in our political settlement. We need their moral support and nothing more."[129]

Gotabaya Rajapakse argues that for whatever reason they indulged in it, it did not help the Tamils in Sri Lanka in any way. They encouraged the LTTE and Prabhakran; they gave safe houses and training camps in Tamil Nadu. What did ultimately happen, he questions. "The Tamils were very peaceful people 30 years back and they were very well integrated in Sri Lanka with the other communities. But all this was destroyed because of terrorism. They have not helped their cause in any way.[130] "

Post Eeelam war Tamil Nadu turns against Sri Lankan government

At no point of time had the pro-Tamil Eelam activism in Tamil Nadu been so politically charged as in the years following the Tamil

---

128 Author's interview with Sampanthan (17-22, February, 2014)

129 Author's interview with Chief Minister Wigneswaran (17-22, February, 2014)

130 Author's interview with Gotabhaya Rajapakse, (17-22, February, 2014)

genocide in May 2009. After the end of Eelam War 4, Tamil Nadu leaders stepped up their agitation for the Tamil cause. The AIADMK chief Jayalalithaa has taken up the Tamil cause and provides staunch support besides raising other contentious issues like the fishermen poaching, Katchateevu and demand for trying Rajapakse for the genocide in the United Nation Human Rights Council. She also demanded action against President Mahinda Rajapakse for his ruthless human rights violations against the Tamils. **Interestingly, after the end of the war, the DMK and the AIADMK had taken a common stand supporting New Delhi's view that a political solution and devolution of power was required to mitigate the Tamils in Sri Lanka. This was what the Centre and the State want. The interests of the Tamil Nadu ruling party, its opposition parties, and the Centre converged.**

The end of the Eelam War 4

The Dravidian parties protested against the visit of President Rajapakse to India in September 2013 when he was on a private visit to Bodh Gaya. They did the same when he participated in Modi's swearing in ceremony in 2014 May. When Rajapakse was on another private visit to Tirupathi in Andhra Pradesh to pay obeisance to Lord Venkateswara just before the Sri Lankan presidential election in December 2014 they protested again. They even organized protest demonstrations when the Hindi film star Salman Khan went to Colombo to campaign for Rajapakse.

Ultimately when the 2014 elections came the Congress fought alone without any allies and drew a blank. The DMK too lost the elections and for the first time it won no seats in Lok Sabha since 1952 while its rival the AIADMK swept the polls getting 37 of the 39 seats. Since the Modi government took over in 2014, Jayalalithaa has been pressing for the resolution of the fishermen issue and Katchateevu.

Competing with each other, they began their vocal protests about human rights violation in the Jaffna area and war crimes in the final phase of the war. The new generation activists had created tremors in the State in their protests against the US resolution in 2013. The heat generated by the Tamil Nadu youth, besides the Diaspora also compelled the Tamil Nadu government to pass resolutions "urging the Centre to stop calling Sri Lanka a 'friendly nation,' and the Assembly demanded that an independent international inquiry be conducted into 'genocide' and 'war crimes' committed in the final phase of the Eelam War in 2009; those found guilty be produced before an international court and given appropriate punishment; and till the Sri Lankan government stopped repression of Tamils, an economic embargo be imposed on the island nation. **But the Centre was lukewarm to these demands because New Delhi did not want to antagonize Colombo.**

Can LTTE regroup?

There are mixed reactions to this question. Tamil Nadu parties allege that New Delhi's reticence even to discuss these issues in public domain had added to the suspicion that its acts of omission are partly to blame for the plight of Tamils. There is no doubt that the Sri Lankan Tamil Nationalist movement produced a whole lot of new generation leaders like Prabhakaran, Pathmanabha and Sabaratnam who believed in militancy and armed struggle. After the 9/11-terror attack on the twin towers in New York by the Al Qaeda in 2001, the situation has changed. There is a Western coalition of war against terror. The Tamil community in the island became weary of war after losing two generations of their kith and kin. In spite of all the support from the Diaspora, the LTTE may not revive. Above all there is no leader of the stature of Prabhakaran or even his second rung leaders to keep the Organisation alive. But with the exit of Prabhakaran, the violence part had ended in the island. Gen. Fonseka admits that it can regroup if there was an international support.

Karuna, a onetime close aide of Prabhakaran, agrees that it would not be possible because the organisation depended on one leader Prabhakaran. He never built up second rung leaders. "After I had left he was the only leader. People are fed up and now they can't go the people for regrouping.[131] "

Sampanthan does not rule out the possibility but with a rider that it depends on how the Sri Lankan government treats the

---

131 Author's interview with Karuna, (17-22, February, 2014)

Tamils. That is going to be the key issue. "If the government takes time to address the Tamil problem it may give rise to another such movement," he predicts. [132]

Nedumaran, a staunch supporter of the LTTE, believes that Prabhakaran is still alive. "Where is the death certificate?" he asks. "Sri Lanka claims Prabhakran is dead but why have they not produced his death certificate? Till today it has not been given to India. I believe that Prabhakaran is still alive and is in hiding." [133]According to him in the last Assembly elections the DMK lost because of their betrayal of the Tamils. The AIADMK chief Jayalalithaa realized the importance of this. "She was against the LTTE earlier and she got me and Vaiko arrested and put us in jail under the draconian law- the Prevention of Terrorism Act, 2002 (POTA) for months. After the elections she realized that this was the major emotive issue and got hold of it to beat the DMK and the Centre. She did not say much before the elections but after the elections she saw what impact it had in Tamil Nadu." [134]

However, the Commander of the Sri Lankan army in the Jaffna peninsula, Major Gen. Mahinda Hathurusinghe, told an Indian correspondent that with the Tamil National Alliance (TNA) glorifying the slain Tamil Tiger leader Prabhakaran in its campaign for the Northern Provincial Council (NPC) elections, there was a possibility of reactivating former Tiger combatants. "There are about 4,000 former cadres of the LTTE who have not undergone rehabilitation. These could be mustered by the TNA leadership." [135]

The authorities fear that the Tamil Diaspora, mostly in Canada, Australia and UK, has been donating millions of dollars for the LTTE cause. Chief Minister Wigneswaran believes that the story of the LTTE re-emerging was being floated in order to justify the heavy military presence in the north.

---

132 Author's interview with Sampanthan, (17-22, February, 2014)

133 Author's interview with Nedumaran, (8 August 2014)

134 Author's interview with Nedumaran, (8,August 2014)

135 P. K. Balachandran, 'Sri Lanka fears regrouping of 4 K LTTE cadres,' The New Indian Express, 16 September 2013

Northern Provincial Council elections

Coming under pressure from India and the Western countries Rajapakse eventually ordered elections to the Northern Provincial Council in September 2013. Also, Colombo was to play host to a meeting of the leaders of Commonwealth countries in November 2013. Just before that Rajapakse was compelled to allow a tour of the Northern Sri Lanka by the United Nations' High Commissioner for Human Rights, Navi Pillay. Internationally the elections were considered as free and fair.

The TNA that contested the election was composed of five parties: the EPRLF, the Peoples' Liberation Organisation of Tamil Eelam (PLOTE), TELO, the Tamil United Liberation Front (TULF), and the Ilangai Tamil Aras Katchi (ITAK). The TNA won 30 seats in the 38-member council, while the ruling United Peoples Freedom Alliance (UPFA) secured only 7 seats and the Sri Lanka Muslim Congress (SLMC) one seat. The TNA secured a record 78.5 per cent of the votes polled. The people of the Northern Province sent a message that they expected the TNA to keep Tamil nationalism alive despite the failure of Tamil insurgency. The Global Tamil Forum in the hands of the moderates worked to help TNA's pursuit of the Tamil cause within united Sri Lanka. Many believed that the end of the war and elimination of the LTTE would open space for greater political debate and moderation among Tamils, but this has not happened.

Manmohan Singh skips Commonwealth Heads meeting

For months before the crucial Commonwealth Heads of Government Meeting (CHOGM) hosted by Sri Lanka in November 2013,it was seen as a problematic event - as the Tamil Nadu leaders including the local Congress unit put pressure on New Delhi to send a stern message to Sri Lanka over its treatment of Tamils. Added to that was the pressure from the Tamil Diaspora in USA, U.K., Canada and Australia who demanded that their governments should boycott the event. Manmohan Singh's cabinet was divided. In an unusual manner four ministers – P. Chidambaram, G.K.Vasan, Jayanthi Natarajan and V. Narayanaswamy impressed upon the Prime Minister that he should not attend the meeting. Backing them was the Defence Minister A.K. Antony. Opposition came from the External Affairs Minister Salman Khursheed and Minister of State for Commerce E.M. Sudarsana Natchiappan and the Tamil Nadu Congress Committee president B.S. Gnanadesikan. Political calculations obviously weighed with Chidambaram and others who impressed upon Prime Minister Manmohan Singh that it would not be easy for the Congress to perform electorally as it had no allies to face the 2014 elections. The DMK revived the Tamil Eelam Supporters' Organisation (TESO), with Karunanidhi as its chairman and criticized the Centre for even sending External Affairs Minister Salman Khursheed to Colombo to attend the CHOGM meeting. The ruling AIADMK also did not lag behind in putting the UPA government on the mat.

Ironically, the Northern Province Chief Minister Wigneswaran made it clear that he did not share the objections of the Tamil Nadu leaders. In fact he was hoping to have consultations with Prime Minister Manmohan Singh if he had attended the meeting. It was a mistake on the part of Manmohan Singh to skip the event as his visit to Jaffna, symbolising India's commitment to their welfare, would have given a great boost to the morale of the people of the Northern Province. What helped the Jaffna Tamils was the British Prime Minister David Cameron's visit during the CHOGM and his commiserating with the suffering Tamils there. **Overall, Dr Singh's absence at the CHOGM signified a symbolic victory for Tamil Nadu and loss to New Delhi's diplomatic efforts as well as the influence of the regional satraps on the Centre. New Delhi had wanted to avoid a situation to prevent Tamil Nadu from turning volatile. When the regional satraps are strong, the Centre falls in line. Secondly it was also because the Sri Lankan policy could not be blind to the power bloc of Tamil Nadine Delhi could not ignore the pressure from Tamil Nadu where the popular sentiment was against the Sri Lankan genocide.**

UNHRC resolutions

India's stand on the United States sponsored resolution in the United Nations Human Rights Council (UNHRC) against Sri Lanka after the Eelam War 4 needs a special mention here. Sri Lanka had come under increased international pressure to probe allegations of excessive civilian deaths during the final battle between the Army and the LTTE that ended in May 2009. Colombo had earlier rejected a call by the UN for an independent international probe into allegations of war crimes and slammed it as "unwarranted interference."

Initially New Delhi could not take a pro-Sri Lanka stance due to two major reasons. First, the US was keen on getting the support of India for the resolution as the US and its allies did not want it to be termed as a pro- Western project against Sri Lanka. India's support would give the resolution a regional concern. Second, the Tamil Nadu pressure could not be ignored. India had voted in favour of the 2009 UN resolution bowing to the pressure from the Tamil Nadu. It did the same in 2012 and 2013 and this pushed Colombo away from New Delhi and closer to Beijing. **The resolutions passed in the UNHRC had its echo in Tamil Nadu, which wanted action against President Rajapakse and others who were involved in the war for what it called the genocide. Once again, fearing a backlash in the State India voted in favour of the resolution in 2012.**

But by 2013, when the U.K's Channel 4 television came out with the killing of Prabhakaran's young son Balachandran by the Sri Lankan army, the public outrage in Tamil Nadu and elsewhere was huge. Likening the killing of Balachandran with the killing of Jews in Nazi Germany, Tamil Nadu Chief Minister Jayalalithaa demanded that New Delhi should hold discussions with the US and like-minded countries and should pass a resolution imposing economic sanctions against Sri Lanka. For her part, she called off the 20th Asian Athletics Championships scheduled to be held in Chennai in July 2013, saying that the Sri Lankan players had no place in the State. M. Karunanidhi was one with her on this question: Support for this stand came from other unlikely quarters as well: The Communist Party of India leader D. Raja and former Chief Justice of Delhi High Court and noted defender of human rights, Rajinder Sachar, demanded that India vote against Sri Lanka at the UNHRC session. The Tamil Nadu unit of CPI (M) too, demanded that India support the US-sponsored resolution. **The issue was serious enough for the DMK, to walk out of the UPA on March 19, 2013 when it could not succeed in influencing the Sri Lanka policy on the ground** that India had incorporated none of the amendments sought by the DMK in the resolution. Karunanidhi announced his party's pull out from the UPA and the resignation of DMK ministers from the Singh cabinet. On March 21, India voted for "a watered down" U.S.-sponsored resolution which merely wanted Colombo to conduct an independent and credible investigation into allegations of violations of international human rights law and international humanitarian law, as applicable. If New Delhi's earlier position was about pandering to the Congress allies in Chennai, its U-turn came in 2014. **With apparently little to gain from further appeasement of the Dravidian parties, the UPA government abstained in the UNHRC voting hoping to better its relations with Colombo, which had been strained for some time. And in the process gained some geo-political mileage with Sri Lanka in 2014. The centre ignored the Dravidian parties when it was not in its interests.**

Before the 2014 elections, Jayalalithaa took a position to propose a resolution by India in UNHRC to punish those guilty of genocide and war crimes in Sri Lanka if an AIADMK inclusive government were elected at the Centre. However, that did not happen even though the AIADMK got 37 seats in the Lok Sabha polls while the BJP emerged as the single largest party and formed the government. When Prime Minister Modi took charge in May 2014, within a month Jayalalithaa visited New Delhi and called on Modi. She once again urged the Prime Minister to get India sponsor a resolution in the UN against genocide Sri Lanka.

India plays a role in rehabilitation of Tamils

Although the Government of India had vacillated in voting at the UNHRC over the Western-sponsored censure of the Sri Lankan government, it had prioritised the rehabilitation of the infrastructure of the Northern Province. "India is engaged in projects worth over $1 billion in the North and the East. This includes a $270 million commitment to build 50,000 housing units across affected areas, the rehabilitation of Kankesanthurai Harbour, Palaly Airport and Duriappah Stadium in Jaffna, and building a 500-megawatt coal power plant at Sampur in the Eastern Province." [136]When Prime Minister Modi visited Sri Lanka in 2015 March about 27000 houses had been handed over.

Katchateevu and Fishermen poaching from both sides

Tamil ethnic conflict is not the only irritant between India and Sri Lanka. There are others, which arise from time to time. Katchateevu is yet another issue for Tamil Nadu. Originally the Raja of Ramnad, a Tamil Nadu Zamindar had leased it to Ceylon. In 1974 India ceded to Colombo's claim on the island. Tamil Nadu leaders and the Tamil Nadu fishermen, who traditionally fished around the island, opposed this as it affected their livelihood. The agreements signed with Sri Lanka on June 28, 1974, March 23, 1976, July 31, 1976 and November 22, 1976 not only fixed the maritime boundary between India and Sri Lanka but also fixed all other related matters like fishing and exploitation of marine resources. As senior journalist Sam Rajappa notes, after the signing of the 1976 agreement, there was an exchange of letters between Kewal Singh, India's Foreign Secretary, and W.T Jayasinghe, Sri Lanka's Defence and Foreign Secretary. The letter says: "The fishing vessels and fishermen of India shall not engage in fishing in the historic waters, the territorial sea and the exclusive economic zone of Sri Lanka nor shall the fishing vessels and fishermen of Sri Lanka engage in fishing in the historic waters, the territorial sea and the exclusive economic zone of India, without the express permission of Sri Lanka or India, as the case may be."[137]

Unfortunately on the issue of fishermen poaching on the Sri Lankan Waters confusion still prevails. Although it had been settled four decades ago by the Sirimavo- Indira pact, the two major political parties – DMK and the AIADMK – as also the other Dravidian parties speak for the Indian fishermen. Colombo strictly enforces its authority over the island by arresting the Tamil Nadu fishermen who poach on their waters. **Jayalalithaa, Karunanidhi, as well as leaders**

136 Neelam Deo and Karan Pradhan, '*India's imperatives in Sri Lanka,*' *Gateway House, Indian council on global relations,*'17 October 2014

137 Sam Rajappa,'*Why no Modification on Kachchativu*', The weekend Leader, Vole 6 Issue 27, July 3 - 9, 2015

of other Dravidian parties use this to whip up emotions in their competitive politics. The Centre has informed the Supreme Court that it was a settled issue and there was no question of reopening it. The Centre has no intention of playing along with the State.

Meanwhile despite New Delhi advising Tamil Nadu to stay away from poaching, the State government is not interested or unable to restrain the fishermen. There are also allegations that some Tamil Nadu politicians own the trawlers used for poaching. The stance taken by Sri Lankan government and the Tamil Nadu government, is deeply affecting the fishermen on both sides. The election manifesto issued by Jayalalithaa's ruling AIADMK called for appropriate action against those responsible for the genocide of Sri Lankan Tamils and further actions including Sri Lankan Tamils to live with full freedom and dignity. **She also called for action to achieve a separate Tamil state in Sri Lanka and for India to grant dual citizenship right for Sri Lankan Tamils who have been living inside and outside of refugee camps for many years in Tamil Nadu. But Centre certainly does not believe in dividing Sri Lanka.**

When the Sri Lankan President Rajapakse came to New Delhi to participate in Prime Minister Narendra Modi's swearing -in ceremony in May 2014, he ordered a few Tamil Nadu fishermen to be released as a goodwill gesture even as Tamil Nadu protested against his participation in the function. A few months later, bowing to the pressure from Tamil Nadu to free five Indian fishermen sentenced to death by the Sri Lankan court Prime Minister Modi used the diplomatic channel to resolve the issue temporarily. However, this frequent arrest and release of fishermen from both sides will not be the solution. A joint working group was formed in 2004 involving officials from both sides. But it has met only four times so far.

External Affairs Minister Sushma Swaraj admits that there is no fish on the Indian side and naturally the Tamil Nadu fishermen went to the Sri Lankan side. But that is not one-way traffic as their fishermen also cross the line. "That is why when I spoke to Prime Minister Ranil Wickremesinghe, I told him that not only the Indian fishermen but also the Sri Lankan fishermen were coming this side. So they are arrested on both sides. There was a day when there were zero arrests. We have plans; the plan is to take them to deep-sea fishing. If they do that we will have so much fish on outside they don't have to go there. They go there for their bread and butter. We are already in the process of making that effort."[138]

According to the minister, they are working out the financial package first and then the training so that they can earn ten times more. The government is hopeful as Jayalalithaa is on board, all the fishermen associations are on board and they have also given their package. Meetings are taking place even at the minister level and joint meeting with the Sri Lankan fishermen Associations. Apart from this, there could also be joint development of coastal areas. There is some working relationship between Sri Lankan navy and Indian navy and Sri Lankan Coast Guard and Indian Coast Guard. The military relationships are good and Lanka is very much dependent on India. But Tamil Nadu's cooperation is also necessary. Both sides should avoid shooting incidents due to what they describe as mistaken identity. Tamil Nadu could be developing fishing farms extensively in the Indian waters and leasing fishing blocks from Sri Lanka, imposing strict restrictions and complete ban on mechanised trawlers and proper fisheries resource management.

Udaya Gammanpilla, the Sri Lankan leader argues that by poaching on the Sri Lankan waters, the Indian fishermen snatch away the opportunities available to the Sri Lankan fishermen whom they claim as their brothers. He complains that, "Chief Minister Jayalalithaa does not take any action to prevent the Tamil fishermen crossing over to Sri Lankan territory. It could easily be done, as it is a matter of coast guards and navy taking a patrolling boat along the maritime border. So this clearly shows that the DMK competes with the AIADMK shouting the very same slogan with a louder voice.[139]"

When Prime Minister Ranil Wickremesinghe visited New Delhi in September 2015 Prime Minister Modi said in a joint press conference "I am confident that with the wisdom and will of the leadership in Sri Lanka and the support of the people, Sri Lanka

---

138 Author's interview with Sushma Swaraj (March2015)
139 Author's interview with Gammanpilla (17-22, February, 2014)

will achieve genuine reconciliation and development, so that all Sri Lankans, including the Sri Lankan Tamil community, can live a life of equality, justice, peace and dignity in a united Sri Lanka." [140]

Politicians in Tamil Nadu know that the issue cannot be solved in a hurry given the fact that coastal fishermen are a huge and organized community, a vote bank eyed by every political party in the South Indian State. **So the regional satraps have not been able to make much headway because of the complexity of the issues unable to force the issue.**

Return of the Refugees

The Tamil refugees who have slipped into Tami Nadu is yet another issue of concern. The successive sympathetic governments in the State accepted them due to humanitarian and political considerations, though India has not signed the UN convention or protocol on refugees to guarantee refugee rights. **Though the two major political parties, the DMK and the AIADMK, have demanded Indian citizenship for the refugees many of whom are residents of India since 1983, nothing concrete has happened, as the Centre has to consider the problem, which might arise from refugees from other countries.**

Many refugees living in India prefer to return, as it might give them a chance to go back to normal life. After the Maithripala Srisena government took over in January 2015 the new President has sent positive signals that he might give a better chance for the peace process. New Delhi is now mulling with the idea of sending back over a lakh of refugees in view of the changed circumstances. The subject came up when Srisena's new Foreign Minister Mangala Samaraweera visited New Delhi and discussed this problem with his Indian counterpart Sushma Swaraj in January 2015. But this could succeed only if Colombo creates the proper environment like improving the conditions of the Tamils in Jaffna. This was not the first time this idea had come up for discussion, as even in 1987 it

---

140 Press Trust of India, *'India, Sri Lanka talk on Tamil community, fishermen issue;* PMs resolve to intensify cooperation,' First Post, India, September 15,2015

was debated. Now that the war is over and there is little chance of an armed conflict in the island nation. Wigneswaran has also welcomed the return of the refugees. "He said that over 1.2 lakh Tamil refugees from Sri Lanka were living in India, and their presence back home was necessary to ensure Tamil representation in parliament."[141]

"There are five categories of refugees in the State. The first is those who live in government camps, second category (about 30,000) is those who do not live in the camps but have the status of refugee, the third is the Sri Lankan nationals with valid documents but stayed after their visa expired, fourth is the former militants sheltering in the camps, and the fifth is those who have recently arrived with the help of Sri Lankan armed forces for jobs. The refugee influx started from the days of the July 1983 riots. The Tamil Nadu government gives Rs 1000 to every head of the family, Rs. 750 to each adult and Rs.400 to every child. Each refugee family gets 20 kgs of rice every month and ration cards are provided to them. Refugee children are allowed to study up to class 12 free. The Tamil Nadu political parties also give support to the refugees. Both the DMK and the AIADMK governments had demanded citizenship facilities or permanent resident status."[142]

Wigneswaran demands that India should make efforts to send back the more than one lakh refugees who are now staying in refugee camps in Tamil Nadu. It would increase the Tamil electorate in the island and counter the Sri Lankan government's efforts to make the Tamils become further minority there; he told reporters when he was on a visit to Chennai in November. "India should push for a change in the Lankan Constitution, which would protect the interests of Tamils living in the united Sri Lanka but not in a unitary framework."[143]

---

141 Special correspondent, '*Wigneswaran wants Tamil refugees sent back*', The Hindu, November 11,2014

142 Arun Janardhanan,'*explained: The Sri Lankan refugee question.*' The Indian Express, January 31,2015

143 Press trust of India, '*Send back Tamil refugees to SL: Wigneswaran.*' Daily mirror, 10 November, 2014

The refugee issue needs to be settled soon and this requires the support of the Government of Tamil Nadu, Government of India and the government of Sri Lanka.

The Indo Sri Lanka economic relations

The trade and economic relations between India and Sri Lanka go back a long way. In the pre-colonial days there were strong economic relations between the two countries but they got diluted during the colonial rule. Soon after independence in both countries economic relations strengthened, but not significantly. This was due to the inward-looking economic policies dominating in both economies until about the mid-1980s. The economic links began to pick up in the 1990s during the Narasimha Rao regime with a liberal economic outlook in both the countries. It received a further boost in 1998 when the two countries signed a bilateral India–Sri Lanka Free Trade Agreement (ISLFTA), which came into operation in March 2000. This pioneering attempt in trade liberalisation in the region involved the liberalization of trade in goods. Sri Lanka began economic liberalisation, after the UNP's defeat of the left-leaning SLFP government in 1977 Sri Lanka adopted export-oriented policies, which was a shift from a reliance on agricultural exports to an increasing emphasis on the services and manufacturing sectors

Today, India and Sri Lanka enjoy a robust trade and investment relationship. Last decade had seen rapid growth of bilateral trade, which has reached nearly US$ 5 billion. "Sri Lanka is India's major trading partner in South As bilateral trade in 2013-14 was $5.2 billion with Indian exports amounting to nearly $4 billion and Sri Lankan exports to $678 million."[144]

For Sri Lanka, India has emerged as the number one source country as far as Foreign Direct Investment and tourist arrivals are concerned. Nearly 40 per cent of all trade with Sri Lanka takes place through Tamil Nadu, involving thousands of people in the State. The informal trade through the State is estimated to be nearly double the formal one. "Apart from Indian-origin Tamils — about 40,000 in

---

144 Nayanima Basu, '*India pushes for comprehensive economic partnership with Sri Lanka,*' Business Standard, March 14.20

number, people of Indian Origin in Sri Lanka also include Sindhis, Borahs, Gujratis, Parsis engaged in various business ventures. They number about 10,000 mostly from the economically prosperous lot. Also, India is a major contributor to Sri Lanka's tourism industry. Tourism forms an important link between India and Sri Lanka with every fifth tourist comes from India. Therefore, there is much scope between the two countries to increase the volume of trade and commerce in the coming years. Indian tourists – 1,76,340 in number – made up nearly 18% of the total tourists visiting the island nation in 2010. Sri Lankans also visit India in large numbers, for pilgrimages to Bodh Gaya, Tirupati, Sai Baba's Ashram at Puttaparti, Velankani Church and temples in Tamil Nadu." [145]

Big Indian companies like the Indian Oil Corporation, Tatas, Bharti Airtel, and Taj Hotels have invested in Sri Lanka. Sri Lanka also has invested in India, which has grown in the last few years. These include Ceylon Biscuits (Munchee brand) and Carsons Cumberbatch (Carlsberg) apart from other investments in the freight servicing and logistics sector. India's major exports to Sri Lanka include automobiles, mineral fuel, pharmaceuticals and iron and steel, while imports include natural rubber, poultry feed, copper and paper and paper production.

Despite the FTA being in force for 17 years, the trade balance continues to remain in favour of India. As a result, Sri Lanka had been reluctant on signing the Comprehensive Economic Partnership Agreement (CEPA) although it was negotiated after 13 rounds of talks and concluded in 2008. The CEPA which begun initially in 2003, is yet to be implemented by Sri Lanka and India. The majority of the Sri Lankan business community and professional bodies were not convinced about the benefits from CEPA.

With the change of government in Sri Lanka in 2015 there are expectations that the bilateral ties may see more focus on its Economy. Indian investments in Sri Lanka have grown. Sri Lanka is also dependent on India for much of its fuel. The Indo-Lanka bilateral economic relations will have a significant impact on Sri

---

145 Hari Narayan, '*Engaging Sri Lanka is the best way forward,*' The Hindu, March 22, 2013

Lanka's ability to realize the full potential of the current favourable set of circumstances.

Modi's visit to Colombo in 2015, which took place after 27 years was important in many ways. The trip has marked the beginning of a new leaf in India-Sri Lanka ties, signalling a renewed interest of the Modi government to set things back on track. "In a bid to counter China's offers of substantial investments, Modi promised a further $US 318 million for railway infrastructure. India has already been involved in rebuilding Sri Lanka's northern railway line."[146] Modi opened the last leg of the Indian-built northern rail line to Talaimannar. "He also announced a $1.5 billion currency swap agreement between India's Reserve Bank and Sri Lanka's Central Bank. Sri Lanka's biggest natural harbour, at Trincomalee, was another focus of Modi's attention."[147]

The changing scenario and the future

The Indo-Sri Lanka relations are undergoing a change since 1990. With India emerging not only a regional power but also aspiring to become a global power they are affected by the regional power dynamics. For instance, India is the most important foreign supporter of Sri Lanka. Beijing is trying to expand its influence. China is currently one of Sri Lanka's major military suppliers, but also has a potential for economic investments and infrastructure projects. President Rajapakse was trying to exploit the geo-political struggle between China and India for dominance in the region to his advantage, while the United States had its own agenda for retaining its influence.

In the post-LTTE era after the end of Eelam War 4 Sri Lanka had come much closer to China, Pakistan and Israel because of their political and military support to Colombo during the war. China has partly filled the vacuum created by India's reluctance to openly participate in the Sri Lanka's war effort. **While the Indian government declined to provide military equipment, citing**

---

146 Wasantha Rupasinghe, '*Modi visits Sri Lanka to push for closer ties against China*', world socialist website, wsws.org, March 18,2015

147 Wasantha Rupasinghe – ibid

political compulsions and concern over the use of force against the LTTE, China filled in the gap with liberal supply of a wide variety of armaments. This has enabled China to gain more strategic space in Sri Lanka. The Chinese are constructing a commercial port in Hambantota in the south. This is certainly a great concern for New Delhi.

Relevance of Indo- Sri Lanka accord

The implementation of the 13ths Amendment flows from the Indo Sri Lanka accord. The end of Eelam War 4 has not resolved the Tamil problem. The LTTE is no more, Prabhakaran is dead and the civilians are reconciled to live a life of peace and progress. But reconciliation and rehabilitation is not easy. The Sri Lankan government has to come to grips about how to deal with the dominant and minority communities. One question arises whether the Indo- Sri Lankan Accord holds good today as some like Prasad Kariawasam thinks that "The Accord is important but it is not sacrosanct because a lot of provisions are irrelevant. 13[th]Amendment is a product of the Accord. The primary requirement is to make Tamils feel secure. What should we do? The Sri Lankan economy 70 per cent is in the hands of Tamils already. So what is left is very little.[148]"

But there is all-round consensus that a political solution should be found to resolve the ethnic problem- from the Sri Lankan side, from the Indian side and also from the affected Tamil community. An inclusive approach will start with the full implementation of the 13th Amendment and proceed with the stalled political discussions. For this there should be political will, commitment and sincerity of purpose on both sides.

For one thing, the Northern Province is still under the military despite a popularly elected government. Chief Minister Wigneswaran has been demanding more powers including land and police powers while President Rajapakse was not willing to give those. The TNA supported the Srisena - Wickremesinghe government on their electoral promise. Wigneswaran finds no elbow space with regard to relief and rehabilitation work. The Provincial Governor found it

---

148 Author's interview with Kariawasam (14, May, 2013)

difficult to share power with him. Wigneswaran argues, "We have a right to govern under the 13th Amendment and we are entitled to all those powers. I wanted to change the chief secretary who is close to the President Rajapakse as well as the Governor. I am not able to get a person of my choice to run the administration. She goes to the Governor and gets my orders countermanded. We have shortage of nurses. During the earlier time they had been brought from the south. We wanted them to remain for some more time. There is a death of nurses.[149]"

Srisena government and Tamils

When Srisena replaced Rajapakse, there were cheers not only in New Delhi but also in Chennai. **Tamil Nadu welcomed Srisena election. Across the political spectrum politicians such as the DMK chief Karunanidhi, the MDMK General Secretary Vaiko, the Bharatiya Janata Party Tamil Nadu president Dr Tamilisai Soundararajan and the BJP Global Convener Vijay Jolly in their press Statements welcomed the new leadership and showed a sense of overriding jubilation**

For the first time since Sri Lanka became independent in 1948, an incumbent President Rajapakse was voted out of office. In 2014 November when he announced the presidential snap polls two years ahead of schedule, neither his defeat nor his conceding it seemed likely as he was confident of winning a third seven year term. The move was to renew his mandate before a worsening economy began. The joint opposition candidate and his former colleague Srisena won because he offered the prospect of return of the rule-of-law including the abolition of the executive presidency. For the opposition simply getting rid of Rajapakse was a sweet revenge. Even the largest Tamil party in Sri Lanka, the Tamil National Alliance openly supported Srisena as also Muslims though he comes from the same Sinhalese Buddhist nationalist background as the Rajapakse. Moreover, the UN Human Rights Council (UNHRC) voting is an example of how Rajapakse has lost the international confidence. The CHOGM meet further demonstrated it.

---

149 Author's interview with Wigneswaran (17-22,February, 2014)

Sri Lanka has voted for change not once but twice in 2015, first in the Presidential elections in January and Parliament elections in August. The most difficult challenge for the new government will be reconciliation with the Tamils and the Muslims. Ranil Wickremesinghe, known to be pro - India, pro-business and pro-West, believes in far more conciliatory policies towards minorities. Prime Minister Wickremesinghe is also familiar with the Tamil problem, as he had dealt with it earlier. Since the new government has taken over, the international community has shown signs of friendly relationship with the Srisena administration. This is indicated by the visits of high level visits from the US and the UK.

Srisena has sent a positive signal and chose India as his first port of call, when he took over. Of all the agreements signed the one on cooperation in the peaceful uses of nuclear energy was the most significant, as it underscores a strategic bilateral shift, in that both Beijing and Islamabad have till now been overlooked for the purpose. The accord will facilitate the use of nuclear energy in industrial applications, as well as in fields such as medicine and agriculture. Exchange of knowledge and expertise, sharing of resources and capacity building and training of personnel will be an enriching experience for the neighbours. Two years ago, Sri Lanka expressed safety concerns arising from the geographical proximity of the Koodankulam nuclear reactors. The two sides have also agreed to enhance their defence and security cooperation in the existing trilateral format with the Maldives.

The Western countries as well as British Prime Minister David Cameron had been putting pressure on Sri Lanka for facilitating an UN investigation on human rights violation by the Sri Lankan army on the LTTE and its sympathisers. It is perhaps in acknowledgement of this that Prime Minister Modi visited Jaffna in March 2015. It provided new impetus for reconciliation by winning the confidence of Tamils and stressed that Colombo has no reservations about India's show of support for Sri Lankan Tamils in their own territory. The UNHRC report released in September 2015 had called for a special international court to prosecute Sri Lankan war crimes and has identified patterns of grave violations in the island country between 2002 and 2011. While the UNHRC report found fault both with the authorities and the Liberation Tigers of Tamil Eelam (LTTE) in respect of "unlawful killing", it pulled up the former on several counts, including "sexual and gender-based violence", "enforced disappearances", and "torture and other forms of cruel, inhuman or degrading treatment". As regards the detention of internally displaced people, the report said: "Almost 300,000 IDPs were deprived of their liberty in camps for periods far beyond what is permissible under international law." The report was critical of the LTTE in respect of "recruitment of children and their use in hostilities".[150] In all these Rajapakse has to face the music, as there are no LTTE leaders left to take the blame. Rajapakse knew what was coming and that was why he was desperate to become the President in 2015 January and at least Prime Minister in August polls but the country rejected him both times. However, despite all these he has some solid supporters and he continues to be a powerful force in Parliament unless his supporters defect.

As expected, the day the report was released, the Tamil Nadu Assembly passed a unanimous resolution urging the Union government to move a strong resolution in the UNHRC for an international investigation. **Chief Minister Jayalalithaa said in the Assembly: "in case the US takes a pro – Sri Lanka stand, India should make diplomatic efforts to change that."[151] Although the Sri Lankan government has promised due attention to the report it is to be seen how it handles the issue. However top officials who had dealt with the Sri Lanka problem from the Indian side feel that a permanent solution would be giving them the kind of autonomy that exists in Indian States. Without this there cannot be permanent peace. This should be the Indian objective to see to what extent Sri Lankan could be persuaded. The underlying need for the implementation is still there because the Sri Lankan government will find it difficult to resolve the issue without some degree of support from New Delhi.**

150 T. Ramakrishnan, *Sri Lankan war crimes horrific: UN report*, The Hindu, September 17,2015

151 B Arvind Kumar, *'Press for international probe, TN Assembly urges Centre.'* The Hindu. September 17, 2015

As Yashwant Sinha observes New Delhi's options are limited. It cannot ignore the importance of the growing Chinese influence in the neighbourhood including in Sri Lanka. China has funded larger projects across Sri Lanka. **More importantly, most Dravidian parties including the DMK have weakened and also electorally not doing well while the AIADMK continues to be on the top. When there are no coalition compulsions and Modi has emerged as a strong Prime Minister, it is difficult to predict the role of Tamil Nadu in shaping the Sri Lankan policy.**

Sushma Swaraj is optimistic when she says, "As for our concerns regarding Tamils we are pressing for it. Because the new government has been mandated to do that. President Srisena had got the Tamil votes as well as the Sinhalese votes and the TNA supported him publicly. They have also done some things. For example there was a demand to remove the governor and a civilian governor should be appointed and they have done that. They wanted another chief secretary and they have done that. President has appointed a task force for release of detunes. Former President Chandrika is heading that task force. PM Modi has spoken to President Srisena. He also talked about devolution of powers and the 13th amendment and so the mechanism is there and they are working on that[152]"

Srisena has pledged to free hundreds of minority Tamil detainees and return much of the Tamil land in the north and the east that the military seized. The other issues like military withdrawal transfer of land and police powers to the Provincial administration have not yet been addressed. The new Sri Lankan government has promised to reconsider the multi-billion dollar Chinese-funded Colombo Port City project. The Srisena – Wickremesinghe duo wants a more balanced with greater sensitivity to India's concerns about Chinese influence in the India ocean region

The Future of Indo–Sri Lankan ties

The Sri Lankan government has to actually move beyond the war – and this will happen if they demilitarise the North-east, restore full civil liberties in those areas, engage in a meaningful dialogue

---

152 Author's interview with Sushma Swaraj, (March 2015)

to address the ethnic conflict, ensure accountability for abuses, and effect reconciliation. There are at least four main challenges for the new government: the first is continuing the agenda of the internal governance, the second is the implementation of the economic reforms, the third is to deal with the minority issues including power sharing with the Tamils and the fourth is improving international relations, particularly with India, China, US and the Europe

The next transformative phase in the Indo-Sri Lankan relations has just begun with Prime Minister Modi's significant visit to Colombo in March 2015. Ranil Wickremesinghe's visit to New Delhi in mid September 2015 after his election as Prime Minister was equally important. India is recalibrating its Sri Lanka strategy with the Modi government making all the right noises and moving forward in many contentious issues like fishermen and ethnic Tamil issues.

The Indo-Sri Lankan ties are at a very delicate and crucial stage and the future is just unfolding with an unpredictable but promising scenario. One thing is certain. A strong, stable and above all a peaceful Sri Lanka in the neighbourhood is an imperative for India for various including security concerns. This is because if the island country is disturbed its echoes can be heard in Tamil Nadu. The stability will come to Sri Lanka only if the Tamil ethnic issue is settled. India should do all it can to achieve that.

Chapter 3

India and Bangladesh

Bangladesh is the newest State in the Indian subcontinent, which was born on December 16, 1971 after 13 days of fierce war with Pakistan. The Pakistan Army commander Gen. Niazi surrendered to the successful joint command of the Indian army and the Mukhti Bahini, the liberation force of Bangladesh, which was known as East Pakistan. The Liberation was the result of a long political evolution since India and Pakistan were partitioned. However, despite India's role in the liberation struggle the relationship between India and Bangladesh does not remain as strong as it should have been. While there was a brief honeymoon period soon after the liberation from 1971 to 73, things began to sour afterwards. Instead of being friends, Bangladesh looks at India with suspicion and resents New Delhi's 'big brother' attitude towards its smaller neighbour. Prime Minister Narendra Modi is trying to change this situation. The recent positive changes in the bilateral relations have led to considerable movement on almost all issues of contention.

Dhaka's perception of India, and its approach towards its Western neighbour, has remained varied under different governments. The three Awami League governments (1971-75, 1996-2001, 2009-present) found some ideological similarity with the Congress Party and had more positive ties with India whereas the more nationalist governments and military regimes did not have good relations with New Delhi while balancing against their larger neighbour China.

The five and a half decade old ties with Bangladesh have seen ups and downs over the years. Contentious issues between the two countries covered various areas from diplomatic, economic, trade, border security, boundary lines, sharing of common and trans-boundary waters, communication and transit, to regional and national security. In all these the Border States on the Indian side has concerns.

As veteran diplomat Deb Mukharji, who was Indian High Commissioner to Bangladesh earlier, points out that the relationship between India and Bangladesh can be divided in to five phases. "The first was from 1971 to 75 when each side basked in the glory of having defeated the enemy. Indian troops left Bangladesh within a remarkably short space of time. A 25 year Treaty of Friendship, Cooperation and Peace were signed, as also the Indira- Mujib Agreement on the land boundary."[1] Bangabandhu Mujibur Rahman was grateful for India's help and New Delhi supported the new- born Bangladesh with generous economic aid as well as its planning.

The second phase was between Mujib's assassination in 1975 and Prime Minister Morarji Desai's assumption of office in 1977. This period saw a mutual mistrust and suspicion.

The third phase was between 1977 and 1979, which saw the Morarji Desai regime until the return of Indira Gandhi as Prime Minister in 1980. Desai was friendlier with President Gen. Muhammad Zia Ur Rahman and tried to convince him of New Delhi's intention of non-interference in the Bangladesh affairs. The result was the interim Farakka Accord, which ensured a five- year water sharing formula between the two countries.

The fourth phase from 1980 to 1995 was one of non -engagement with no progress in any area. During this period Gen. Zia Ur Rahman was assassinated, Gen. Hussain Muhammad Ershad ruled for eight years and Begum Khaleda Zia, wife of Gen. Zia for another five years. In India it coincided with the Indira

---

1   Deb Mukharji, *Editor J.N. Dixit. 'External affairs: Cross border relations, Bangladesh chapter,'* Bangladesh chapter, Roli Books, 2003, P 196

Gandhi's regime followed by Rajiv Gandhi, Viswanath Pratap Singh, Chandrashekhar and P.V. Narasimha Rao.

The last phase began with Deve Gowda in 1996, as Prime Minister followed by Inder Gujral, then Atal Behari Vajpayee in 1998, Dr Manmohan Singh in 2004 -2014 and from 2014 Narendra Modi. In Bangladesh there was the rule of Sheikh Hasina, daughter of Mujib, followed by Khaleda Zia, wife of Gen. Zia and a second and third term of Begum Hasina. This period was one of high and low depending on who was at the helm of affairs in both countries. This was true at the State level also that for most of this period Jyoti Basu ruled West Bengal, followed by his comrade Buddhadev Bhattacharya and now the Trinamool Congress chief Mamata Banerjee.

The role of Indian States bordering on Bangladesh has become quite important over the years in the Indo -Bangladesh ties in view of the growing number of strong regional leaders ruling the Indian States and also asserting their rights. West Bengal and the Northeast have four important concerns pertaining to the Bangladesh policy of the Government of India. It is about the land, water, connectivity and security on the border.

My Hypothesis

1. **The regional players are likely to be successful in influencing the national foreign policy if their preferences match those of the Central government or if the Centre is able to take them on board. When the interests of the regional satraps and the national foreign policy objectives align, then it creates a synergy between the Centre and the State.** For example the then Foreign Minister I.K.Gujral utilized the services of the then West Bengal chief minister Jyoti Basu to clinch the Farakka treaty in 1996. Basu used his personal equations with the then Bangladesh Prime Minister Sheikh Hasina in clinching the issue. States like Tripura and Meghalaya also played a positive role. Mamata Banerjee played a positive role later during the present NDA government by accompanying Prime Minister Modi during his visit to Bangladesh in 2015 to sign the Land Boundary agreement. **Mamata had agreed after the Centre**

promised funds for rehabilitation of the people returning to Bengal from the enclaves, where stateless people from both sides were living for decades.

2. **The regional satraps are not likely to be successful when their local interests are opposed to the Centre's broader view of foreign policy.** Mamata Banerjee is a classic example in this regard. She had opposed the Teesta Treaty in 2011 citing that it would affect farmers in five districts of West Bengal. Assam is yet another example where the State opposes illegal immigration.

Indo - Bangladesh Historical ties

To understand the role of the regional chieftains from the Northeast and West Bengal in the conduct of India's foreign policy one has to understand the historical ties between the two countries. History shows that Bangladesh was under the Turkish, Afghan or the Mughal rule until the British entered the scene. Dr Deb Mukharji points out that there was an uninterrupted rule by the Sultan and the rulers of the Islamic faith for over 500 years before that. The Portuguese traders and the missionaries were the first Europeans to reach Bengal in the latter part of the 15th Century. The Dutch and the British East India companies followed them. Historical records show that the Mughal Subadhar of Bengal Kasim Khan Mashadi completely destroyed the Portuguese forces in the Battle of Hooghly in 1632. The decline of the Mughal Empire followed the rise of independent Nawabs of Bengal.

During the reign of Aurangzeb, the local Nawab sold three villages, including Calcutta to the British. While Calcutta remained the first focal point of the British economic activity, they gradually extended their commercial contacts and administrative control to the rest of Bengal. The defeat of the Mughals and the consolidation of the subcontinent under the British East India Company followed soon. After the battle of Plassey in June 1757, the British emerged stronger over the other European competitors like the Dutch and the Portuguese. After the Sepoy Mutiny, the power was transferred to the British crown.

Bengal prospered under the British, and Calcutta became an important Centre for commerce, education and culture in the subcontinent. They also encouraged the Zamindari system. While the Hindus welcomed the British presence and cooperated with them the Muslims resented the British. They resorted to riots whenever crops failed. "This was the clear policy of the British to reward the Hindus who helped them and to punish the Muslims who not only disobeyed them but also continued to be defiant.[2]"

Then came the Permanent Settlement Act of 1793. As Mahfuz Anam, the well known editor of Bangladesh newspaper 'Daily Star' points out that the Permanent Settlement redistributed the land on a permanent basis to a new set of gentry. Because of that arrangement the Muslims got totally wiped out. The Hindu Zamindars replaced the Muslim Zamindars. This broke the back of the Muslim gentry. There emerged a new class of Hindu traders but the Muslims never traded. So the Permanent Settlement became a very strong instrument of the economic disempowerment of the Muslims. This resulted in the Muslims leading most of the anti- British movements.

The economic division, with its class character, also became identified with a religious divide. The Hindus were seen as the oppressors and the Muslims the oppressed. Bengal was divided into West and East Bengal in 1905 under Viceroy Lord Curzon. The Dacca University was established and a High Court was setup in Dacca. A new presidency was formed to make East Bengal, a Muslim majority province. While the Muslims welcomed these developments the Hindus saw them as an attempt to divide them and opposed it. The Bengali Muslims looked at it as an economic benefit and administrative authority for them but the Hindus called it the Bengali nationalism. When it was annulled in 1911 the Muslims saw it as a defeat. This was the time they decided that they had to launch a political struggle. There was a whole bunch of political players who understood the issues both in Delhi and Dhaka.

---

2   Author's interview with Mahfuz Anam (3-7 March, 2014)

The Lahore resolution and demand for single nation

The 1940 Lahore Resolution did ask for a separate 'autonomous and sovereign' State but ultimately it became a demand for a single nation, with religion as the common base. As late as April, 1946, " the Muslim League convention held in New Delhi where the newly elected Muslim League legislators gathered, Muslim League legislator Abul Hasham, a member of Bengal provincial Muslim League delegation strongly opposed the draft resolution, which called for an independent and sovereign State of Pakistan comprised of Eastern and North Western zones on the ground that it was contrary to the letter and spirit of 1940 Lahore resolution."[3] He called for a separate State in the East. On April 9, 1946, finally and unanimously they passed a resolution for a single State- Pakistan that later became the basis for Mountbatten Plan of June 2, 1947. Abul Hasham once again opposed it but he was overruled. Thus the genesis for Bangladesh began as early as 1946. It was a question mark whether the Indian National Congress would have accepted the trifurcation.

Then came the Partition of India and Pakistan in 1947. East Pakistan was formed in 1947 and in 1948 Jinnah gave that famous speech that Urdu will be the official language. The moral of the story was that it was the Bengali Muslim who tilted the balance in the formation of Pakistan. Historically, events proved that it was the Muslims in the East who brought the birth of Pakistan not the Muslims of Punjab or of the Sind or Baluchistan. Without their support Pakistan would have remained a dream. It was the great Calcutta killing in 1946, which made Pakistan inevitable. It was when the Muslim League became the majority party in the 1946 elections that basically sealed the fate. The Cabinet Mission Plan was the last attempt to keep India united. Ironically the Congress Party opposed this plan and both Jawaharlal Nehru and Mohammed Ali Jinnah scuttled it. So when Pakistan was formed the Muslims of Bengal saw it as their victory. But the euphemism did not last long as within 18 months the Bengali Muslims began to oppose Pakistan. East Pakistan soon became the scene of recurring communal violence

---

3   Avtar Singh Bhasin *'India Bangladesh relations –Volume* 1, Documents 1971 to 2002.' Geetika Publishers, 2003, P x111

forcing the Hindus to flee to the neighbouring States in India. First it was the language issue, then economic independence and then came the demand for a separate country. Paradoxically, it was the Bengali Muslims again that broke Pakistan.

Mahfuz Anam explains that there was a strong Muslim attachment and a strong Bengali attachment. "So the Bengali attachment brings the Bangladeshis close to West Bengal and the Muslim attachment distances them from Bengal. This is the paradox."[4] It was this sentiment that provided the sustenance for the BNP (Bangladesh Nationalist party), which exploited the Islamic attachment while the Bangabandhu Mujibur Rahman's Awami League was intellectually and culturally committed to secularism. There should have been a convergence between the two philosophical heritages and it should have blended into one heritage. But history and politics made the two fighting with each other rather than unite. This controversy has been artificially exploited by the politicians, as there was no intellectual leadership to blend these unscrupulous political forces, which divided and exploited the people. It was basically this, which has brought differences between India and Bangladesh, Mahfuz Anam explains.

The Economic divide

If the Partition was painful for Punjab, which was divided into Eastern and Western Punjab, the situation was more complicated in Bengal, which also was divided into East and West Bengal where the major cash crop jute was produced in the Muslim-dominated East, but processed and shipped from the Hindu-dominated city of Calcutta in the West.

West Bengal's stake in Bangladesh

What happened in East Bengal always had its echo in West Bengal. If religion was the common bond between the East and West Bengal, soon the inequalities between the two regions stirred up the Bengali nationalism. The Bengali Muslims not only realized but also resented that they had become second- class citizens in Pakistan while West Pakistan dominated over the East. People in East Pakistan feared that

---

4   Author's interview with Mahfuz Anam (3-7 March 2014)

certain provisions of the Constituent Assembly were obstructive to their development. When Pakistan declared Urdu as the national language, the Bengali pride provoked the East to assert, which was followed by the language movement in February 21, 1952. This was triggered by the shocking way the police shot students of the Dacca University agitating for a rightful place for Bengali. It took the shape of demand for self- rule manifested by the huge win for the Awami League led by Mujibur Rahman in 1970 elections. Neither President Agha Muhammad Yahya Khan nor the Pakistan People's Party (PPP) chief Zulfikar Ali Bhutto expected it.

The origin of demand for a separate country in East Pakistan

The seeds for the birth of Bangladesh were sown much earlier before the general elections to both Pakistan in 1970 and India in 1971. As noted historian Robert Dallek points out "there were two major concerns of the Bengali population residing in Pakistan. One was about the Bengali language and the second was their representation in the legislature. The language issue led to more animosity between the two sides"[5].

Pakistan military ruler Yahya Khan was unprepared for the 1970 election results. He was expecting a fractured mandate, which would make him the arbiter but Yahya was in for a shock. While the Awami League led by Mujibur Rahman swept the polls in East Bengal, the Pakistan People's Party (PPP) of Zulfikar Ali Bhutto won a handsome victory in West Pakistan. The demand for a full autonomy became stronger after the Awami League's landslide victory. "While Yahya was struggling to deal with the situation, it became worse when his government was unable to deal with the devastating cyclone, which killed 20,000 people in East Pakistan and left thousands homeless." [6]When things went out of hand Yahya, who went to Dacca for talks, left in the middle and returned to Islamabad on 25, March 1971 as the talks broke down when the three leaders could not find a solution. Before returning, on 24 March, Yahya Khan met the army

5   Kalyani Shankar, *'Nixon, Indira and India'*, Macmillan Publishers India Ltd, 2010, P 213

6   ibid P 213-214

officers in Dacca and gave a go ahead and the next day at 11.30 AM, 'Operation Searchlight' began. He banned the Awami League, sent the army to quell the riots, arrested Mujib and put him in jail, which aggravated the situation further.

The US watching the subcontinent

There is an American angle in the birth of Bangladesh as the Nixon administration was closely watching the unfurling of events in the subcontinent. President Nixon succeeded Lyndon Johnson in 1968 and also inherited the Vietnam War. Both Nixon and his National Security Adviser Henry Kissinger found a friend in Yahya Khan. Nixon remembered how Pakistan received him with honour when he was out of office while India cold- shouldered him. President Nixon was involved in a major secret diplomatic exercise and wanted to normalize the relationship with China. Yahya Khan obliged them when he agreed to be a go- between.

The ferocity of the 'Operation Searchlight' stunned the East Pakistanis. The Pakistani army led by Gen. Tikka Khan was well prepared for the brutal operation while the poor innocent people in East Pakistan were not. But the refugee situation became alarming and what started off as a trickle to India soon became floods by mid April 1971. The Indian States of West Bengal, Tripura, Assam, Meghalaya, Bihar and Madhya Pradesh bore the brunt of the refugees. "By the end of May, for instance, 900,000 refugees had swept into the small State of Tripura, which had a population of only of 1.5 million. In West Bengal, the 3,00,000 refugees who arrived in just two months inundated places such as Bongaigaon, whose population was only 5000. Parts of Assam too faced similar situation". [7]

Nixon had his own interests to guard

Gen. Yahya Khan arranged for Kissinger to visit Beijing to hold secret talks with the Chinese leaders in July 1971 paving the way for Nixon's visit later. The whole operation was secretly planned and executed. Kissinger points out their dilemma in his memoirs: "There was no doubt about the strong arm measures of Pakistan military.

---

7   Srinath Raghavan, '*1971, A global history of the Creation of Bangladesh*,' Permanent Black, 2013, P 76

But Pakistan was our sole channel to China; once it was closed off, it would take months to make alternative arrangements."[8] This explains the reason for Nixon's aversion to the birth of Bangladesh. Yahya Khan was in touch with President Nixon throughout the Indo -Pak war period. "There was 'no option but to take that decision,' Yahya Khan explained to the President. Elaborating his reasons for sending the troops to crush the East Pakistanis, Yahya referred to the concentration of Indian troops on the borders as an additional reason. He urged Nixon to intervene and impress upon the Indian leaders the need for refraining from any action that might aggravate the situation." [9]

New Delhi helps the rebels in East Pakistan

Meanwhile the Awami League established contact with the Indian government. Mujibur Rahman had been seeking support from India since March 1971. He had deputed his General Secretary Tajuddin Ahmad to seek the Indian government's help to provide them political asylum in case Pakistan attacked East Pakistan. Mujib's request reached Indira Gandhi's office on March 19, 1971. The Deputy High Commissioner K.C. Sengupta gave a vague assurance on behalf of India to Mujib.

Hossain Toufique Imam, Political Adviser to the Bangladesh Prime Minister Sheikh Hasina, who was an important player during the Liberation War, recalls that initially in 1971 the 'Government of Bangladesh in exile' was located in India. By the time it was liberated they had their own governmental apparatus. The government was sworn in at Meherpur in Bangladesh and the place was named Mujibnagar. It was symbolic and the government of the People's Republic of Bangladesh came in to existence formally much later. Informally it was 25th night of March when the Bangabandhu declared independence through wireless and sent it throughout the country. Later on Zia Ur Rahman picked up the message and made

8   *Nixon presidential materials staff, NSC files, Indo-Pak war, Pakistan chronology,* Kissinger to India chronology, Dr Kissinger, Pak chronology Dr Kissinger, 1971 of 3 box no 578

9   Kalyani Shankar, *'Nixon, Indira and India,'* Macmillan India Pvt. Ltd, 2010, P 215

a declaration on behalf of the Bangabandhu on 27ᵗʰMarch. That was informal. "Only the Peoples' Representatives - who were members of the National Assembly and members of the Provincial Assembly, could make the formal declaration. They gathered at Siliguri and elected Prof Yusuf Ali and he read out the proclamation on behalf of the Constituent Assembly. That created the State of Bangladesh. On the very same day he was made the president in absentia. Nuzrul Islam became the acting president and vice president. Date is again April 10, 1971. These dates are confused even in Bangladesh."[10]

Indira Gandhi's strategy to liberate Bangladesh

The first major international crisis after Indira Gandhi took over in January 1966 was perhaps the Bangladesh War in 1971. India as well as Nehru's humiliation during the Chinese aggression in 1962 was still fresh in her memory. New Delhi felt that in view of the popularity of the Awami League things might work out in Bangladesh. But when the refugee flow began to continue New Delhi had to change its mind. The whole country felt the pain of the refugees fleeing from East Pakistan. Several political parties organized protests in front of the Pakistan High commission. There were protests in other States also. **This was a case when these Border States including West Bengal and Tripura were on the same page. Gandhi had the total support from the political parties and people in these States.**

Indira Gandhi decided that she had to move fast and also with tact. Initially New Delhi was willing to give general political support to the cause of the Bangladeshis and there was no intention to intervene militarily. In fact some of Mrs Gandhi's senior colleagues, like Sardar Swaran Singh who initially opposed any intervention in Pakistani affairs, were of the opinion that India should mobilise international support for the return of the refugees to East Pakistan. They also wanted to make the Pakistan government respect the results of the general elections and allow Mujibur Rahman to develop a new constitutional process, which would meet the aspirations of the people of East Pakistan. The Pakistani leadership however did not help matters. "The Yahya regime as well as Bhutto compounded their lack of judgment in dealing with their internal crisis by immediately

---

10 Author's interview with H.T. Imam (3-7 March, 2014)

launching a massive diplomatic and propaganda campaign against India."[11] Kissinger and Nixon gave their sympathetic ears and heard Yahya's side of the story with all attention. However, events moved too fast. News reached Delhi that Tajuddin Ahmed had crossed the border in the early hours of March 30. Indira herself moved in Indian parliament on March 31, 1971 to adopt a resolution in support of Bangladesh's liberation that said, "This House records its profound conviction that the historic upsurge of the 75 million people of East Bengal [Bangladesh] will triumph. The House wishes to assure them that their struggle and sacrifices will receive the wholehearted sympathy and support of the people of India."[12]

The distinguished Bangladeshi diplomat Rehman Sobhan, who became the Bangladesh High Commissioner to India later, was one of the first to visit Delhi and brief Indira Gandhi's close adviser P.N. Haksar in March 1971. On April 1, the Awami League leaders were flown to Delhi and had long discussions with Mrs Indira Gandhi and other leaders. She decided in May that they would have to find a final solution. "But when we went to Delhi they were not sure that people in Bangladesh were completely committed to independence. We had to persuade them. Haksar in particular was very crucial in persuading Mrs Gandhi.[13]"

Then Indira Gandhi suggested that the liberation leaders should first setup a government in exile so that New Delhi could deal with the liberation struggle properly. "Secondly since we had decided to declare independence we have to have a State. There must be a government and other things required for the Statehood like judiciary, armed forces and bureaucracy. The executive was most important during the war. So the Bangladesh government organized itself. I was one of the few who joined, as I was a civil servant of Pakistan earlier,"[14] recalls Imam. He was Deputy Commissioner of

---

11 J.N. Dixit, 'Makers of India's Foreign policy,' Harper Collins, India, 2004, P 130

12 Julfikar Ali Manik and Hasan Jahid Tusher, ' one person made a big difference', Daily Star, July 26, 2011

13 Author's interview with Rehman Sobhan (3-7 March, 2014)

14 Author's interview with H.T. Imam, (3-7, March, 2014)

Hill Tracks. He gathered the border police, armed forces and others and setup their own headquarters. The first thing they did was to establish contact across the border with the Tripura authorities. The Tripura government was quite supportive just as the West Bengal government and the other Border States were. On the Western side others were also contacted. "The top leaders came back from Delhi when the Assembly was in session in Siliguri and then the proclamation of independence was made on April 10, 1971. While the Pakistani army went on rampage before the war, Mujib himself was taken to West Pakistan where he underwent a trial at the end of which he was found guilty of trying to break up Pakistan and was awarded death sentence. The next day Tajuddin Ahmed made an address to the nation and this government formally took office at Mujib Nagar on April 16. But the government was formed earlier and that was the government, which continued throughout the war of liberation," [15]Imam recalls.

Research and Analysis Wing (RAW), India's external intelligence agency continued its presence in Bangladesh even after the latter's independence by training Chakma tribes and Shanti Bahini to carry out subversive activities in Bangladesh. Prime Minister Indira Gandhi wanted to undertake military intervention in April 1971 concerned by the events in the neighbourhood but she was dissuaded by the then army chief Sam Manekshaw who was later conferred the Field Marshall, India's highest military honour. "After outlining his reasons for avoiding a war, Manekshaw was claimed to have said at a cabinet meeting 'if you still want me to go ahead, Prime Minister, I guarantee you 100 per cent defeat. Now give me your orders.' Manekshaw added that he even offered to resign if the Prime Minister did not agree with his judgment. 'So there is a very thin line' reminisced Manekshaw, 'between becoming a Field Marshal and being dismissed!' Not to be left behind, Lt. Gen. J.F.R. Jacob, chief of staff of the Eastern Army Command, claims that Manekshaw was wobbling under political pressure and that he had stiffened his chief's spine."[16]

---

15 Author's interview with H.T. Imam (3-7,March 2014)

16 Srinath Raghavan, '1971, *A global history of Creation of Bangladesh*', Permanent Black, 2013, P 67

Mrs Gandhi, calculating other concerns finally decided against India's military intervention after the April 25 cabinet meeting. But the General knew what was expected of him and began preparations for the war even as India deferred any plan it had to invade Pakistan. New Delhi decided to sit through the monsoon season and continued to support the Mukhti Bahini.

Indira Gandhi's two- track policy

The Indian military forces performed brilliantly not only because of their preparedness but also because of the superb diplomatic moves made by Indira Gandhi. On the one hand India sought to put pressure on Pakistan to accept the electoral verdict of December 1970 in Bangladesh and on the other hand tried to mobilize support from the international community including the United Nations and also through bilateral contacts for Mujibur and his supporters. While Mrs Gandhi could manage to achieve the first she was not so successful in her second track.

Armed with the full support from the domestic side, Indira Gandhi launched a diplomatic offensive by deputing credible and senior political leaders like K.C. Pant and Sardar Swaran Singh to various countries. She herself visited many important countries including the USSR, Germany and the USA just before she finalised her war strategy. While there was sympathy for East Pakistan, the Western powers were unable to comprehend the real situation on the ground.

President Nixon blindly supported Pakistan by ignoring the reports from the US Consul General in Dhaka Archer Blood projecting the ground realities and the atrocities. The famous 'Blood Telegram' sent by the US Consul General on April 6, 1971 said "Our government has failed to denounce the suppression of democracy. Our government has failed to denounce atrocities. Our government has failed to take forceful measures to protect its citizens while at the same time bending over backwards to placate the West Pakistan dominated government and to lessen any deservedly negative international public relations impact against them. Our government has evidenced what many will consider moral bankruptcy, (...) but we have chosen not to intervene, even morally, on the grounds that the Awami conflict, in which unfortunately the overworked term genocide is applicable, is purely an internal matter of a sovereign State. Private Americans have expressed disgust. We, as professional civil servants, express our dissent with current policy and fervently hope that our true and lasting interests here can be defined and our policies redirected." [17]This bold and blunt telegram from a diplomat should have been an eye opener to Nixon but the U.S. President chose to ignore it because as mentioned earlier, he wanted to go ahead with his proposed China trip.

The Mukti Bahini formed in Bangladesh

Meanwhile the Mukti Bahini, a volunteer force comprising of motivated rebel Bangladeshis was formed. This suited Indira Gandhi, as she wanted to send a message to the world that it was the people of East Bengal who had taken up the arms against the West Pakistan. "By September 1971, though, Indian training operations had expanded dramatically in scale, processing a staggering 20,000 guerrillas each month, eight Indian soldiers were committed to every 100 trainees at 10 camps. On the eve of the war, at the end of November 1971, over 83,000 Bahini fighters had been trained, 51,000 of who were operating in East Pakistan- a guerrilla operation perhaps unrivalled in scale until that time. In the Chittagong Hill Tracts, Brigadier Uban sent in Indian soldiers or, to be more exact, CIA-trained, Indian-funded Tibetans using hastily-imported Bulgarian assault rifles and U.S. manufactured carbines to obscure their links to India. Fighting under the direct command of RAW's legendary spymaster Rameshwar Kao, Brig. Uban's forces engaged in a series of low-grade border skirmishes." [18]

The formation and training of the Mukti Bahini by the Indian army was a conscious strategy. Recalling his training days during the liberation struggle, Mr Assaduzaman Noor, a minister in the present Sheikh Hasina government describes how he and other enthusiastic youngsters got sucked into the Liberation War. The Indian army

17 Wikipedia, https://en.wikipedia.org/wiki/Archer_Blood

18 Praveen Swamy, *India's secret war in Bangladesh* The Hindu, December 26,2011

trained Noor and other youngsters in the jungle somewhere near Siliguri. "I entered the Bangladesh territory on Dec 14, 1971. We occupied my place because that was very close to Indian border, perhaps 30 or 40 kilometres. We did not know that they were going to surrender but we knew we were marching forward and we were on the point of conquering the enemy.[19]"

Kissinger meets Indira Gandhi before his secret visit to China

Before going on his secret mission to China on behalf of President Nixon, Kissinger met Indira Gandhi in New Delhi on July 8, 1971. She obviously had no knowledge about his proposed visit to Beijing. In that meeting she explained frankly and brutally the seriousness of the problem and told Kissinger that the settlement should be between the East and West Pakistan while he conveyed the basic message from Nixon that India should not support the liberation struggle. Kissinger saw two problems after the meeting. "The first was how to settle the refugee problem and the second was how to put the US- India relations on a stable basis over long years."[20] He even warned Yahya Khan about any misadventure when he stopped over in Islamabad.

Kissinger returned to Washington after his South Asia trip with the premonition fearing a 'disaster.' He suspected that India would launch an offensive against Pakistan after the monsoon. "In the first half of November the US received reports that some Indian officials were talking of a possibility of a war by the end of the month,"[21] Kissinger noted in his memoirs adding that they proved to be off the mark only by a week.

Gradually sympathy towards the Bangladesh refugees began to swell in the United States and elsewhere. "The famous band Beatles, Indian Sitar Maestro Ravi Shankar and American singer Bob Dylan performed to a packed house in New York for two days to

---

19 Author's interview with Noor (3-7 March, 2014)

20 Kalyani Shankar, *'Nixon, India and India'* Macmillan India, 2010, P 218

21 ibid, P 224

collect money for the cause, which raised millions of dollars for the refugees."[22]

Indira Gandhi visits Washington.

With Nixon adopting a tilt towards Pakistan, Gandhi's two-day State visit to Washington on November 4 and 5, 1971 was a 'disaster.' There was cold vibe between the two leaders, as Nixon hated Indira Gandhi's guts. In his private conversations with Kissinger and other officials Nixon used abusive language against Mrs Gandhi as the declassified records now reveal. As diplomat and author Dennis Kux points out "sceptical about the prospects, not trusting Nixon's bona fides, and having by then decided to use force to solve the problem, Mrs Gandhi remained silent. The Nixon – Gandhi talks were the dialogue of the deaf."[23]

New Delhi supports Bangladesh government in exile

Meanwhile New Delhi was preparing the ground for the liberation on the border. March 25, 1971 was the crackdown by the Pakistanis and the same day Bangladesh government was formed in exile. West Bengal and the other North-eastern States played a crucial role in helping the rebels. Mrs Gandhi swiftly opened an office in Calcutta of the Ministry of External Affairs. Arundhati Ghosh, a young Foreign Service officer was sent to Calcutta by the beginning of May to coordinate with the 'Bangladesh government in exile.' Their major preoccupation at that time was getting recognition from India. She was also helping the Bangladeshi diplomats who were defecting from the Pakistani mission. "I would pass on whatever messages Delhi sent to them and coordinate with the military and intelligence people. During the crisis everybody worked together for those nine or ten months."[24]

22 Kalyani Shankar, 'Nixon, Indira and India', Macmillan Publishers India Ltd, 2010, P 220

23 Kalyani Shankar, 'Nixon, Indira and India,' Macmillan India, Ltd, 2010, P 222

24 Author's interview with Arundhati Ghosh (28 April, 2013)

Yahya Khan declares war

Even as Gandhi was preparing for a war on the East, Yahya chose to launch the attack on December 3, 1971 on India's Western border making it easy for Indira Gandhi to be on the defensive. New Delhi would have launched the offensive on December 4, had not Yahya forestalled it. Kissinger says "On December 3, he (Yahya Khan) launched his army into an attack in the West that he must have known was suicidal. In simple minded soldierly fashion, he decided as I told Nixon, that if Pakistan would be destroyed or dismembered it should go down fighting."[25]The Indian army's brilliant strategy gave a big morale boost and restored the national pride to the armed forces which were humiliated by the 1962 Chinese aggression trauma.

India recognizes Bangladesh

On December 6, 1971, Indira Gandhi informed the Lok Sabha, "I am glad to inform the House that in view of the existing situation and response to the repeated requests of the Government of Bangladesh, the Government of India have after the most careful consideration decided to grant recognition to the Gana Prajatantri Bangladesh."[26] She was confident of the victory because the people of the Border States in the region were fully with her. West Bengal was under President's Rule then but almost all the political parties including the opposition CPI-M were fully supporting her moves. Tripura, Meghalaya and other states in the northeast were also fully on board. **This was how the Centre and the State continued to be on the same page because of convergence of local and national interests.**

On December 16, Mrs Gandhi triumphantly declared in Indian Parliament that Dacca was now the capital of a free country. She said, "The West Pakistan forces have unconditionally surrendered in Bangladesh. Lt. Gen. A.K. Niazi signed the instrument of surrender in Dacca at 16.31 hours I.S.T today on behalf of Pakistan Eastern Command. Lt. Gen. Jagjit Singh Aurora, GOC-in-C of the Indian

---

25 Kalyani Shankar, '*Nixon Indira and India,*' Macmillan India Ltd, 2010, P 226.

26 Avtar Singh Bhasin, '*India Bangladesh relation: Documents 1971-2002,*' Geetika Publishers, 2003, P

and Bangladesh forces in the Eastern Theatre accepted the surrender. Dacca is now the capital of a free country." [27]The same night she also announced a ceasefire in the west.

Kissinger notes that Indira Gandhi agreed for a ceasefire bowing to the pressure from the Soviets. " I have no doubt in my mind that it was a reluctant decision resulting form Soviet pressure, which in turn grew out of American insistence, including the fleet movement and the willingness to risk the summit."[28] Confirming this former Foreign Secretary J.N. Dixit observes, "the Soviets had indicated to India that they would not be able to resist the UN --sponsored compromise if the war was prolonged without any decisive results."[29]

After the war, India's first priority was to clean up the mess, redefine its relations with Pakistan and also cement its ties with Bangladesh. While Indira Gandhi consciously and wisely decided to lower India's profile, she had no intention of disengaging. The Yahya military regime fell in December and Zulfikar Ali Bhutto took over as Chief Martial Law Administrator and President of Pakistan.

Mujibur Rahman takes over Bangladesh

On the other side of West Bengal, Mujibur Rahman was released on 7th January 1972 and he travelled via Turkey and London passing through New Delhi on January 9, reaching Dacca on the same afternoon. H.T. Imam recalls that after he came back Mujib was sworn in as president. Preferring a parliamentary form of government he decided that there would be elections. Accordingly there was a new Provincial Constitution, which came into effect on December 1972 based on the four pillars of nationalism, socialism, democracy and secularism. The Mujibur government continued until the end of 1972 when the Constitution was approved by the Constituent Assembly. When elections took place in March 1973, the Awami

---

27 Avtar Singh Bhasin, 'India Bangladesh relations: Documents 1971-2002', Geetika Publishers, 2003, P 11

28 Henry Kissinger, 'The White House Years,' Cannada, Little Brown and company, 1979, P 913

29 J.N. Dixit, 'Makers of India's Foreign policy,' Harper Collins, India, 2004, P 135

League won a massive majority bagging 291 of the 300 seats. Mujib became the first Prime Minister of Bangladesh, Imam recalls.

Anti- India feelings emerge in Bangladesh

If New Delhi expected lasting friendship, loyalty and gratitude from Dacca it did not happen due to various factors. Although India helped the creation of Bangladesh, first by accepting the millions of refugees and then helping militarily in its liberation, Bangladesh felt no particular reason to be grateful to the 'big brother' India whom they saw as a 'big bully'. On the contrary there was resentment and mistrust. "The pronouncement of the Indian leaders of the early years which frequently recalled Indian contribution to Bangladesh liberation struggle were not only not appreciated by the intelligentsia but also were seen as giving offense to Bangladesh nationalism and sensitivities and undermining the struggle and sacrifices of the people of Bangladesh for their own liberation."[30]

Secondly, some Mukti Bahini elements, which occupied important positions in the new government, resented the Indian army cornering the glory ignoring their role in the liberation struggle. Most East Pakistan bureaucrats who were in Bangladesh after the liberation had continued their antagonistic and aggressive position against India.

Noor points out that even from 1947 till 1972 anti -India feelings had always been there. When the Indian army was in Bangladesh, a small section (mostly left -oriented and pro- China) started this propaganda. They started a subtle campaign that the Indian army had looted and taken away all the machineries after the Liberation War. People slowly started believing that India was planning to occupy Bangladesh. "That is why the Bangabandhu requested Indira Gandhi to call back the Indian army. Gandhi also understood the situation and took a very bold and strong step and withdrew the army within three months."[31]

---

30 Avtar Singh Bhasin, *'India Bangladesh Relations: Documents 1971-2002,'* Geetika Publishers, 2003, p xvi

31 Author's interview with Noor (3-7 March 2014)

Thus emerged a climate of distrust, suspicion, and misconception that prevailed at various levels of administration and mostly believed by the people in the post liberation Bangladesh. It did not show immediately because of the euphoria of liberation and Mujibur Rahman was personally grateful to India. Therefore soon after the War of Liberation, New Delhi and Dacca developed a close relationship, with Mujibur pursuing a "clear pro-India policy" between 1971-1975.

Indira Gandhi visits Dacca

Indira Gandhi visited Bangladesh- her only visit to the country in March 1972, four months after the liberation. The highlight of the visit was that she signed the Treaty of Friendship, Cooperation and Peace with Dacca on March 19, 1972. The two countries also established a Joint River Commission to coordinate water sharing interests and resources in the fields of flood control, river basin development, and the promotion of hydroelectric power and irrigation. While the Joint River Commission was entrusted with studying flood control and irrigation projects to ensure water resources were utilized on an equitable basis, it had little power to challenge unilateral actions.

Mujib becomes unpopular in Bangladesh

Mujibur Rahman was feeling quite uncomfortable about the international environment. Many countries had not yet recognized the new State. The Islamic countries, siding with Pakistan, would have nothing to do with Bangladesh even as Pakistan was trying to do everything against the international recognition of Bangladesh. The US was withholding recognition. China was far from friendly as Beijing and Islamabad had close connections and worked in tandem. In such a scenario, Mujib naturally wanted India to safeguard their territorial integrity. While the Bangabandhu wanted to continue his close ties with India, his critics viewed it as a kind of slavery to India. The resentment continued with the result this Treaty was not renewed in 1997 when it expired.

The next few years after the liberation were a bumpy period in the history of Bangladesh. There were several reasons for this.

There was a terrible famine in 1974, global oil prices were rising, lawlessness was growing, Mujibur's party men and relatives were clamouring for benefits, the underground movements were gathering momentum and all these showed that Mujib was not able to cope with the responsibility of steering a nation from political independence to peace and stability. He wanted East Pakistan to remain an independent entity with a Muslim identity. "He was also not involved in building democratic institutions of governance and interpreted democracy as a mass movement and finally he remained apprehensive of Indian domination in Bangladeshi politics.[32]

So it was only natural that differences cropped up from 1973 onwards. New Delhi's failure to perceive the undercurrents of discontent and distrust proved fatal to the development of a friendlier relationship. Even as mistrust against India grew in Bangladesh " India felt that since she had helped in the liberation of the country with blood and sweat and eliminated the hostile Pakistani factor, the ground was ripe for resolving the problems left over from the Pakistani days whether relating to borders, water or otherwise."[33]

Mujibur Rahman assassinated.

On August 15, 1975, the Bangabandhu was assassinated in the early hours of the morning when a group of Bangladesh army personnel went to his house and shot dead almost his entire family and also shot him in his chest near the stairs. His daughters Sheikh Hasina and her sister were the only family members who escaped because they were abroad. The assassination shocked the entire world.

Mujib's exit from the scene resulted in a fundamental shift in Bangladesh foreign policy. After his assassination, the Awami League became an orphan. Bangladesh began a short-lived experiment with democracy in 1979, when led by the popular President Zia, who established good relationships with the West, China and the oil-rich Islamic countries took over. Gen. Zia was a military man. Zia and

---

32 J.N. Dixit, '*Makers of India's foreign policy*', Harper Collins India, 2004 P 113

33 Avtar Singh Bhasin, '*India Bangladesh Relations: Documents 1971-2002*,' Geetika Publishers, 2003, P xviii

his supporters started their anti - Mujib campaign in the next few years. He felt that he must go beyond his military strategies and create his own popular base.

Bangladesh slowly gave up its secular character after Zia took over, as he wanted to reduce the emphasis on secularism and socialism. Socialism was replaced with a commitment to economic and social justice. He began to build his country's nationalist identity around a mix of distinctly Bengali traditions, with a moderate Islamic flavour. While those emphasizing the values of the freedom struggle against the Pakistan army focused more on their Bengali identity those opposing it were keen on fomenting anti-Indian sentiments. There was no surprise that the political party he founded was named the Bangladesh Nationalist Party (BNP). The BNP projected itself as the right of Centre party to differentiate itself from the Awami League, which was perceived as left of the Centre party.

Gen. Zia made some bold changes in the Constitution in 1977. He removed the word 'secularism' and re-designated the citizen from a 'Bengali' to 'Bangladeshi'. As Deb Mukharji points out this nationalism was based on the identity of Muslim Bengal and, in effect went back to the Lahore Resolution of March 1940, calling for the creation of one or more Muslim majority States. "Born in cantonment, the Bangladesh Nationalist Party became the torch bearer of the ideology of the Muslim League."[34]

New Delhi's ruling Congress party had more warmth for Sheikh Hasina.

She and her sister escaped death because they were in Germany when the Bangabandhu was assassinated. She came to India, lived in New Delhi in the early eighties and the present President Pranab Mukherji was put in charge of looking after her. She lived in a small apartment in Pandara Road until she went back and plunged into politics and became the leader of the Awami League.

Begum Sheikh Hasina came back to Dacca from New Delhi. In any case by this time the Awami League had become weak and

---

34 Deb Mukharji, *Editor J.N. Dixit, 'External Affairs, cross- border relations, Bangladesh chapter'* Roli Books, 2003,P194

rudderless. Hasina had declared no political ambition but the fact that she was Mujib's daughter was enough to attract the Bangabandhu's supporters. Gen. Zia too did not survive for long. On 30[th]May 1981 in the early hours of the morning he was attacked in the circuit house in Chittagong, and assassinated. The BBC reported, "President Zia is believed to have died at 04.30 local time when rebels stormed a government guest house. He is reported to have been killed by sub-machine-gun bullets when he opened the door of his room to see what was happening outside." [35]This tragedy ultimately returned the country to a military government that periodically assured that elections would be held soon.

Morarji and Farakka interim agreement

Meanwhile Indira Gandhi declared emergency in 1975. She was defeated in the 1977 elections and Morarji Desai came to power heading the Janata government comprising of several anti- Congress parties. Dacca saw an opportunity to mend fences with New Delhi and Desai too reciprocated but the Janata government lasted just for two and a half years. During this brief period he struck some friendship with Zia. Morarji Desai was keen to project an image of non-interference in the Bangladeshi affairs and also believed in good neighbourly relations. One of the major achievements was signing a five –year interim agreement on sharing of Ganga water at Farakka with Zia on 5 November 1977. West Bengal had huge stakes on this treaty.

Muchkund Dubey, who was then the Indian High Commissioner in Dacca, prepared the draft agreement in consultation with Jagjivan Ram, who was the concerned minister. "The agreement expired in 1982. It was renewed year after year until the new agreement was signed."[36]

After the two sides signed the Farakka Agreement Bangladesh was convinced that it was Mrs Gandhi who was the villain. The Congress Party, which was then the main Opposition party in the

35 BBC on this day, *'1981, Bangladesh President assassinated,'* BBC news Mat 30, 1981

36 Author's interview with Muchkund Dubey (10, July 2014)

Lok Sabha, was critical of the Accord. Morarji Desai also assured that Indian soil would not be used for anti – Bangladesh activities. But all this bonhomie was short- lived as Indira Gandhi came back to power in 1980 after which the old animosities resurfaced between the leaders of the two countries.

Gen Ershad and Delhi

Vice President Abdus Sattar took over after Gen. Zia's assassination and was elected in a popular vote in 1981. Sattar tried to reassert the civilian authority but Gen. Ershad had his eyes on the presidency. In March 1982, he removed Sattar and took over the reins under the martial law. Refuting the allegation that he had usurped power, Gen. Ershad claims that there was some division in his cabinet and the whole country was waiting for a change. "Ultimately they forced me to take over and I was hesitant to do so. I talked to my Generals. Ultimately pressure was so high from the bureaucrats and others that we took over. It was easy and it was peaceful. Everybody was mentally prepared for this. There was no bloodshed. We went to the TV and made a Statement. So that is how I came to politics. I never thought I would rule the country and I wanted to retire as I had reached the highest position in the army and was chief of staff for eight years, "Gen. Ersahd recalls.[37] He suspended the Constitution and political parties and in 1983 became the President.

Gen. Ershad had no power base of his own and therefore felt insecure. One of the things he did was to re establish his credentials as a Bengali and changed the name of Dacca into Dhaka in 1983. After usurping power, he dissolved the Parliament but co-opted many of the same elite who had helped the Zia rule. He more or less followed the same path adopted by Gen. Zia but moved much faster in the Islamization of Bangladesh. Like Zia, he also donned the mufti and created his own political party and called it the Jatiya Party in 1986 for consolidating power. He declared Islam as the State religion. To establish his credentials Gen. Ershad went on Haj and invoked Allah in his speeches. A consummate political manipulator, he established a kind of pluralistic image. He tactically allowed Awami League to come back, which could act as a check on the BNP.

37 Author's interview with Gen. Ershad (3-7 March 2014)

President Ershad undertook visits to India three times. When the General visited New Delhi in October 1982, he warned that the relationship would be strained if India went ahead with the proposed wire- fencing to stop infiltrators questioning the very need for such a measure when there was zero influx while West Bengal, Assam and other Border States were flooded with illegal immigrants from Bangladesh. At the time of the Sri Lankan July 1983 riots against the Tamils and the 1984 Sikh riots in India Bangladesh blamed New Delhi on both counts.

Assam Accord and apprehensions in Bangladesh

When Rajiv Gandhi succeeded Indira Gandhi after her assassination in 1984, he brought back the border-fencing proposal, which created further apprehensions in Dhaka. Then came the Assam agitation. Illegal immigration from Bangladesh into Assam has been a major political, economic, social and security issue for Assamese society, so much so that it evoked the highly visible Assam agitation (1979-1985) spearheaded by the All Assam Students Union (AASU). Assam shares a highly porous 262- kilometre border with Bangladesh with portions of it left completely unchecked due to the difficult nature of the terrain. The vigorous anti-foreigners movement in Assam led by Prafulla Kumar Mohanta of the All Assam Student's Union (AASU) continued from 1979 to 1985. When it ended with the signing of the Assam Accord, Mohanta became the country's youngest Chief Minister at the age of 33 and headed the State's first government run by a regional party, the Asom Gana Parishad (AGP). The Assam Accord stipulated that anybody settled in Assam from Bangladesh after March 25, 1971 is not a citizen but an illegal immigrant. However, this provision of the Accord has not been implemented by the Centre and the State faithfully and has therefore failed to change the nature of Bangladeshi immigration into Assam. **This was the time when the State could put pressure on the Centre and got what it wanted. The Centre had to bow down to the youth power because it had complete public support.**

Ershad wants good relations with New Delhi

Meanwhile Gen. Ershad felt that he should keep good relations with New Delhi. When the South Asian Association for Regional

Cooperation (SAARC) was formed it was Gen. Ershad, who hosted the event in Dhaka on 8th December 1985. In a conciliatory tone he claims, "We have a big neighbour surrounded by small countries. That is very much the reality. We can't ignore India. So whatever we do we have to keep good relationship with India? That is the primary thing. I did try to keep good relationship with India."[38]

Gen Ershad loses elections

Soon people got disenchanted with Gen. Ershad and there was unity between the two women leaders of Awami League and BNP -Sheikh Hasina and Khaleda Zia, who came together for their political survival. Gen. Ershad called for presidential elections to legitimize his rule in 1986. He was elected to a five- year term and lifted marital law after reinstating the Constitution. The next year, emergency was declared after Opposition demonstrations and strikes. In 1987 both parties decided to boycott the polls but suddenly Hasina changed her mind and chose to participate. Others saw this as a betrayal and some sort of hand shaking with Gen. Ershad. "Sheikh Hasina had always been ambivalent and did not know whom she hated more – Gen. Ershad or Begum Khaleda. Hasina's friends claim that she could not really look Khaleda in the face and not remember that she was the wife of the alleged killer of her father. So there was always this ambivalence. That one decision suddenly brought Khaleda to power as a steadfast uncompromising leader."[39]

Gen. Ershad held another election in 1988 that the two Begums boycotted. Ershad stepped down following mass protests in 1990. On 4[th]December 1990, two months after the Opposition began a new campaign to obtain "truly" free elections and forced President Ershad to resign, the latter was compelled to give up power. On 3[rd,] December, Gen. Ershad stated that he was ready to make concessions. However, the Opposition rejected his "peace plan". Mahfuz Anam notes that, "On 4[th]December, 100,000 people marched in the streets of Dhaka demanding the President's immediate resignation. Shortly after his resignation, he was arrested, convicted and jailed

---

38 Author's interview with Gen. Ershad, (3-7, March, 2014)

39 Author's interview with Mahfuz Anam (3-7 March 2014)

for corruption and illegal possession of weapons. He was released in 1997 from prison."[40]

Begum Khaleda becomes President

Hasina lost the 1992 elections contrary to expectations. Mahfuz Anam recalls, "Low and behold surprising everybody the BNP won. This was really a puzzle and a wake up call to all of us who were freedom fighters and secularists. We felt if there were free and fair elections, the Awami League would come back. Begum Khaleda was Zia's widow who did not know much politics. I remember sitting in the central election board in the Election Commission office. As the results started coming the BNP leaders' eyes started widening and they were totally surprised. They were hoping for a good show and good place in Parliament but not to form the government."[41] Khaleda Zia became the first woman Prime Minister of Bangladesh.

Bangladesh unsympathetic to India's concerns

Over the years Bangladesh remained unsympathetic to many issues pertaining to India. Begum Zia continued her husband's policy of an anti- India stand. The anti- India politics was also anti- Delhi. She was critical of the Indian role in Sri Lankan affairs and viewed it as an undesirable interference in the internal affairs of Sri Lanka. Bangladesh's stand on Kashmir was also equally unsympathetic. Mujibur was not called upon to take sides as Shimla Agreement had put the controversial issue on the back burner but later Bangladesh took a stand that it should be resolved between the two countries. However, when the Kashmir problem worsened Gen. Ershad expressed concern about their Muslim brethren and demanded immediate stoppage of their oppression. Begum Zia continued this ambivalent policy. When the damage to the Charare Sharif in Kashmir in 1995 happened, the initial reaction of Bangladesh was one of "deep concern." Bangladesh government's attitude at the time of Babri Masjid demolition and the subsequent riots also lacked understanding. The atmosphere became so vitiated that the 1993 SAARC summit had to be postponed. Political parties of Bangladesh

---

40 Author's interview with MahfuzAnam, (3-7, March 2014)

41 Author's interview with MahfuzAnam (3-7, March 2014)

also considered the insurgents in the India's Northeast as freedom fighters, who found safe haven in Bangladesh. Throughout her second term from 2001 -2006, New Delhi alleged that Bangladesh gave shelter to the terrorists who were active in India's North-eastern States.

Why the anti-India sentiments?

It was indeed a tragedy that Bangladesh - a country which was born with India's help should put India on the dock suspecting New Delhi's action as those of threatening her security and sovereignty. To the dismay of India, Dhaka slowly began to move towards China, a country that was opposed to the birth of Bangladesh and even withheld diplomatic recognition for some time. China even vetoed the admission of Bangladesh in the United Nations.

New Delhi perceived that there was a strong anti-India rhetoric and blamed Dhaka for collusion with Pakistan's Inter services intelligence (ISI) to destabilise India's North-eastern States. Over the years, this perception that India was a dominant power had become more of a popular sentiment. But neither country addressed this issue seriously or tried to correct the misperception. Internal political dynamics also played a role when Khaleda, came to power. Both Dhaka and New Delhi made blunders with the result the relationship went on a wrong track and the bilateral ties became part of a domestic political process in Dhaka.

The beginning of the strain between the two countries started even during Mujib's rule with small irritants. The public perception changed when anti- India elements spread rumours that some rogue elements of the Indian army took away valuable items from different military establishments. H.T. Imam notes that soon after the liberation these sentiments spread because there were hoards of businessmen who had come to Bangladesh to sell clothes and other things. They deliberately made profit as they did in India. Imam recalls "We worked it out with the Indian authorities, with Eastern Command and also with the Centre. We planned where to receive the refugees, their requirements like sugar salt etc., shelter and even bullocks had been worked out. We had a planning cell and a planning commission in Kolkata under the government. I was the common factor because I was the Cabinet Secretary. So I used to maintain relations with D.P. Dhar's office.[42]"

Strangely, these anti- India sentiments continue to this day. Begum Khaleda Zia observes that there is a general perception, and arguably so, that a prevailing sense of trust- deficit impede the development of the relations into one of strong bonding. "I think it is important to objectively analyse what has brought this about. I feel the inability to find mutually acceptable solutions to our critical bilateral issues, especially the sharing of the waters of our common rivers, the killing of Bangladeshis along the borders by the Indian BSF personnel, the unresolved Land Boundary issue and the huge trade imbalance are the principal causes for this."[43]

Begum Khaleda Zia cites several reasons for the distrust. She observes that it was important to objectively analyse what had brought this about. "I feel the inability to find mutually acceptable solutions to our critical bilateral issues, especially the sharing of the waters of our common rivers, the killing of Bangladeshis along the borders by Indian Border Security Force personnel, the unresolved Land Boundary issue and the huge trade imbalance are the principal causes for this."[44]

Moreover, some believe that after Mujib was assassinated, President Zia Ur Rahman who succeeded him had to prove that everything Mujib did was not correct and particularly the Farakka Treaty was not in the interests of Bangladesh. So he tried to internationalize the issue by taking it to the United Nations. He also suggested that to depict their toughness against India they should demand other things. So the dynamics became such that cooperation was not what made one popular. Confrontation got one votes though there was not that many free and fair elections. So anti -Indian sentiments became part of Bangladesh internal domestic politics. The BNP inherited that legacy. They started talking about Bangladeshi nationalism as against Bengali nationalism. As Mahfuz

---

42 Author's interview with H.T.Imam, (3-7, March, 2014)

43 Author's interview with Khaleda Zia (3-7, March 2014)

44 Author's interview with Khaleda Zia, (3-7, March 2014)

Anam asks what makes it separate? "It is the religion. If you talk about one culture, one language, and one legacy then where is the difference? So the difference is religion. So they brought in that and Gen. Zia made it into part of domestic political issue."[45]

Another military ruler Gen. Ershad advocates several reasons for these anti- India feelings among the Bangladesh public. He points out that there was the whole Pakistani propaganda since 1947 that India was their enemy. During the Bangladesh liberation period it changed a bit. Many people started understanding that India had liberated Bangladesh. At that time India was very popular. But soon after that came the Ganges water Treaty and it became a sore issue, as the anti India elements believed it was a 'sell out' to India. There was a psychological feeling that India might dominate Bangladesh. "We felt that we were not getting our due share of water during the dry season. There came a feeling that India was neglecting us. Our economy is mostly agricultural based. The propaganda was that India was trying to kill us."[46]

When the military rulers came to power, they revived the religious parties and all the anti India elements, which were basically collaborators of Pakistan. If Gen. Zia was the beginning of the revival of anti India forces, Gen. Ershad was clever and he blatantly nurtured Islamic forces. He was less openly confrontational with New Delhi. But he also played his political games. He chose other sources to create his political base. These other elements were Islamic forces or Muslim League type of people

These leaders admit that water sharing was one of the most sensitive issues that create tension in both the countries. Bangladeshis think they had not been given their due share of water. They also believe that their markets were being exploited. It may not be real but it was the perception that influences the people of Bangladesh. **This was one area the regional satraps like Jyoti Basu and Mamata Banerjee played a role, sometimes supporting the Centre (Jyoti**

---

45 Author's interview with Mahfouz Anam, (3-7 March 2014

46 Author's interview with Gen. Ershad, (3-7 March 2014).

Basu) and at other times (Mamata Banerjee on Teesta) differing with the Centre's views.

Khaleda and P.V. Narasimha Rao

Meanwhile P.V. Narasimha Rao became the Prime Minister in 1991 after Rajiv Gandhi was assassinated in the midst of the poll campaign. Relations with New Delhi during Begum Khaleda Zia's regime became strained and several issues like illegal immigration, insurgency in Northeastern States of India with the help of Bangladesh, water sharing, maritime boundary and Chakma refugees became irritants.

During his entire five-year term Rao (1991-96) did not visit Dhaka except attending the SAARC meeting in 1994. Instead, the Rao government obtained the cooperation of Myanmar by opening up a channel with the military Junta rulers in dealing with the Khaleda government's alleged involvement with armed insurgents in Northeastern States like Manipur, Assam and Nagaland. **The Satraps in these Northeaster states had expressed concern about the insurgency and were fighting it. The Centre too agreed with their arguments and went ahead in tackling the insurgency.**

Allegations were that the ISI/Bangladesh combine had helped these insurgents clandestinely from Thailand and transported them to Bangladesh. Begum Khaleda Zia herself acknowledged the existence of this problem when she visited India in 1992. The meeting between Rao and Khaleda did not remove the mistrust on both sides. The Bangladesh rulers also had their line to the West Bengal leaders. Former Bangladesh Foreign Secretary Farooq Sobhan, who accompanied Begum Zia, recalls that during her visit she wanted to meet the West Bengal Chief Minister Jyoti Basu and the latter had promised to give a red carpet reception if she stopped over in Calcutta. However, Delhi did not like the idea and ultimately a via media was found that she should make a brief stopover in Calcutta's Dum Dum airport on her way back from New Delhi. Jyoti Basu came to the airport and the two had a private meeting at the VIP lounge. But Margarat Alva, who was the minister- in-waiting, insisted that she too would be present at the meeting. "She could not understand a word of what was talked about as the two leaders conversed in Bengali. Begum Zia was keen to touch upon the

Farakka issue."[47] Rao could have utilised Jyoti Basu on the Farakka issue, as Hasina was keen to discuss it.

Paying glorious tributes to the Communist leader, Begum Khaleda says, "As a politician, and indeed as a statesman, Jyoti Basu enjoyed great respect among the people of Bangladesh. He was also highly regarded. I do recall my meeting with him, however brief. I did raise the Farakka issue with him. But as I said earlier, the resolution of this was not in his hands, the decision had to come from New Delhi.[48] "

Sheikh Hasina comes to power

Only when Sheikh Hasina took over in 1996, things began to look bright for the Indo – Bangladesh relations when she attempted some damage control exercise. The three secular Awami League governments (1971-75, 1996-2001, 2009-present) historically have held an ideological similarity to the Congress Party and, have usually proposed a more positive policy regarding India. The BNP governments and military regimes have believed in putting a distance between Dhaka and New Delhi.

Begum Hasina firmly believed that all the important and contentious issues could be sorted out through dialogue. In her first term, two of them – Farakka and Chakmas – were resolved to the satisfaction of both countries as well as the affected parties. Meanwhile there was change of government in India too. The Narasimha Rao government lost the elections in 1996 and the United Front government led by Deve Gowda took over, supported by the Congress from outside.

Farakka Treaty signed

The first thing that happened within months of Hasina taking over was the landmark 30-year agreement of Farakka Treaty on December 12, 1996, which sent positive signals. This was soon followed by the Chakma peace agreement. Chakmas occupy the Chittagong Hill Tracts (CHT), which lies on the border of Myanmar and India.

---

47 Author's interview with Farooq Sobhan (3-7 March, 2014)

48 Author's interview with Khaleda Zia, (3-7 March 2014)

The British annexed the CHT in 1860 and restricted the migration of outsiders in 1900. The 1935 Government of India Act declared the area as "excluded area". At the time of Partition, it had 97 per cent non –Muslims mainly tribal and Buddhist and expected to be included in West Bengal. Despite this, the inclusion of the area to East Pakistan under the Radcliff award came as a rude shock.

Lord Mountbatten shrewdly did not announce the demarcation until he presided over the partition with the result no one knew that ultimately it would go to East Pakistan on an economic ground, as it was the source of hydropower for the East Pakistan. As expected, a large number of Bengalis in the region began to make it a demographic problem for the Chakmas who fled across the border to India. The construction of Hydro- electric dam in CHT also caused havoc for the Tribals. After the liberation of Bangladesh Dhaka showed a deaf ear to deal with their problem. The Mujib government, branding them as secessionists, rejected their demand for autonomy, restoration of special status abolished in 1964 and a ban on Bengalee settlement. "On the contrary, the Tribals were advised to merge their identity with the Bengalee mainstream. Zia Ur Rahamn and Ershad administrations too failed to show them any accommodation. Instead, thousands of Bengalee Muslims from the plains were brought to the CHT for settlement at the cost of the tribals."[49]Facing the challenge to their very existence the Chakmas took to arms and organized a voluntary force called Shanti Bahini. Dhaka accused Delhi of helping the Chakmas and used the Bangladesh army to repress the rebels. During this period there was the influx of Chakma refugees, who found safe haven for those indulging in insurgency in India's northeast. "Almost 60,000 Chakmas found refuge in camps in Tripura in the post Bangladesh period."[50]

So when Hasina came to power, she wanted to tackle this problem with the help of the Indian government. In December 1997 her government signed a bold agreement with the Chakmas

---

49 Avtar Singh Bhasin, '*India – Bangladesh Relations; Documents 1971 to 2001'*, *Geetika Publications, 2003. P ciii*

50 Avtar Singh Bhasin, '*India –Bangladesh Relations; Documents 1971 to 2001'*, Geetika Publications, 2003. P civ

bringing peace after 20 years of conflict. Shanti Bahini stopped their insurgency after that. This facilitated the dispossessed Chittagong Hill Tribes return to Bangladesh. The Chakma Accord was another peaceful resolution of a tricky problem.

Essentially the Awami League government during 1996 to 2001 changed the rules of the game at the political level but it could not change the mind-set of the bureaucracy, which continued to nurse anti -India feelings. The BNP successfully propagated that Hasina had signed the Farakka Treaty by conceding a larger share of water to India and Bangladesh was cheated of its rightful share and also managed to paralyze the Hasina regime.

Therefore despite good intentions, Hasina could not deliver the sale of gas, the transit and shipment facilities sought by New Delhi, which naturally got frustrated that whether it was Begum Hasina or Begum Zia nothing much changed in Dhaka. Hasina was handicapped in her first term because she had a precarious majority in Parliament. Awami League had won 146 of the 300 seats and relied on other parties to run the government. But in 2009, when she came with a strong majority she had more manoeuvrability and could deliver what New Delhi wanted.

The insurgents, though keeping a low profile continued to be active in India's northeast. Hasina also maintained the same stand as Khaleda that there were no insurgents in Bangladesh in her first term. But New Delhi understood her helplessness and did not make much of the issue.

Khaleda Zia and Vajpayee

Prime Minister Vajpayee dealt with both Begum Hasina and Begum Khaleda during his six-year rule from 1998 to 2004. When he took over in March 1998, he inherited a by and large tension- free Indo – Bangladesh relations. While Hasina welcomed the new government Vajpayee responded warmly by promising that he would make all efforts to maintain friendly ties with the neighbour. Hasina's bilateral visit in 1998, the first by a foreign Head of State after the Pokhran nuclear explosion, went off well with promises of good neighbourly relations. After the May 11 blasts in the Pokharan desert, Nepal and

Bangladesh issued routine Statements of dismay, while Sri Lanka took 48 long hours to phrase its reaction.

The Bangladesh-India bilateral relationship froze once again when the BNP returned to power in 2001. During her second term, there was a shift in Khaleda's foreign policy. She was moving closer to China and signed a military cooperation agreement with Beijing in 2001. She tried to counter-balance the Bangladesh relations with China while continuing her anti – India stand. The Jamaat's coalition with the BNP provided it the required muscle and some of its members became cabinet ministers in Khaleda government attaining political power. Gradually the differences in security perceptions between the two countries resulted in a hardening of their policies towards one another.

Khaleda's second term was turbulent as she faced a stiff Opposition from the Awami League. Hasina took to the streets and there was civil unrest and violence. The Jamaat was flexing its muscles as a coalition partner in the Khaleda government. From 2006 to 2008, the Bangladesh military resumed its rule of the country through a caretaker government. Slight progress was made when both countries agreed to cooperate on counter-terrorism in 2007. During the first term of Manmohan Singh from 2004 -2009 there was political instability in Bangladesh.

Hasina and Manmohan Singh

Eventually, when general elections were held on December 29, 2008, the 14-party coalition led by the Awami League won by a significant majority and formed the government in January 2009 led by Begum Hasina once again. The political alignment in Dhaka was complemented in New Delhi, with the Congress led UPA winning for a second time with more number of seats ensuring stability and continuity in 2009. While making a deal with Bangladesh was important for Prime Minister Manmohan Singh, Hasina decided to redefine the relationship with New Delhi after her massive mandate. Since 2009, the Sheikh Hasina government has been building a stronger bilateral architecture with India in almost all sectors. Her government moved quickly to address Delhi's concerns on cross-border terrorism and promised connectivity to the Northeast. Moreover, while forming her government, Hasina included the

Harvard-returned academic Gowher Rizvi as her adviser and the highly regarded Tariq A. Karim as the High Commissioner to India, who was given Minister of State rank to emphasize the importance she gave to New Delhi. There was warmth once again between the two governments.

Begum Hasina has largely delivered on India's security concerns by cracking down on terrorism directed against India from Bangladesh soil. One of them was handing over to India the United Liberation Front of Assam (ULFA) terrorists who had taken shelter in Bangladesh. This positive step on the security front continued when Dhaka took action against other insurgent groups, including handing over two members of Lashkir eTaiba who had been operating from Bangladesh. Appreciating this gesture New Delhi also reciprocated a number of positive gestures. Additionally, her government was trying to keep in check Islamic fundamentalism in Bangladesh, represented by outfits like Harkat-al-Jihad-al-Islamic (HUJI), the recently banned political outfit Jamaat-e-Islamic, others like Hefajat-e-Islam, Jagrata Muslim Janata, and HUJI-B whose links to Al Qaeda are well known, at some cost to the Awami League rank and file.

Hasina visits New Delhi

Exactly one year after assuming office, Prime Minister Hasina travelled to New Delhi for a high profile State visit in 2010. At this summit, both sides agreed to build an irreversible cooperative relationship between the two neighbours. "The two governments looked to formalize security cooperation and agreed on three points, including Mutual Legal Assistance on Criminal Matters, the Transfer of Sentenced Persons, and provisions Combating International Terrorism, Organized Crime, and Illicit Drug Trafficking. India has recently adopted a policy of restraint at the border and ordered the Border Security Force to avoid firing and to instead detain illegal migrants until they can be given to local police. The Indian BSF and the Border Guards of Bangladesh have even begun a series of coordinated patrols." [51]

---

51 Cody M Poplin, *'India Bangladesh relations: Review of bilateral Opportunities,'* Indian Development corporation research, February, 20, 2013

In turn, Dhaka agreed to provide transit facilities through Bangladesh to India in January 2010, and to allow the use of the Mongla and Chittagong ports for the movement of goods to and from India. **This has been the demand from the chieftains of Northeastern region.** New Delhi welcomed the offer announcing increased assistance for the upgrade and expansion of the Bangladeshi transit system. However, the agreement has not been implemented because Singh could not sign the Teesta River water sharing agreement.

During Hasina's visit, she expressed her strong desire to see the border issue resolved. The Government of India too agreed. After year- long negotiations, land surveys and joint visits to disputed areas by officials finally a protocol was announced when Dr Manmohan Singh visited Dhaka. The Foreign ministers of India and Bangladesh S.M. Krishna and Dipu Moni signed the protocol on 7, March 2011. There was full -scale cooperation between the two sides to implement many projects especially under the supplier's credit of $ 1billion loan, the biggest ever credit to Bangladesh by India (out of which $200 million was later converted into grant).

Mamata Banerjee opposes the Teesta Treaty

This was followed by exchange of high level visits from both sides. The return visit of Mamohan Singh in September 2011 to Dhaka was equally responsive. There was high expectation that Singh's visit would remove most of the apprehensions accumulated in the past and launch relations on a more pragmatic and practical level. What would have been a watershed visit did not meet the expectations because he could not sign the Teesta Treaty. The Teesta water sharing, which was touted as a biggest deliverable, could not be delivered because Mamata Banerjee donned the role of a spoiler backing out at the last minute embarrassing both sides who walked the extra mile to find solutions for many issues. It was seen as a historic opportunity to open the doors and reach out to each other.

Mamata claimed that the Union Government had not consulted her even as West Bengal was the most affected when it came to border and water issues between the two neighbours. Banerjee was riding high after her landslide victory in the 2011 Assembly elections, which saw her overthrowing the 33 year- old Left Front rule in the State. As the UPA alliance partner she was expected to cooperate with New Delhi on the Teesta Treaty. **Sheikh Hasina also had good personal relations with Mamata and did not expect her to put a spoke on the Teesta treaty. To Singh, who did not expect this from an alliance partner, Mamata played the spoiler on an important foreign policy initiative because it did not suit her local interests.**

Despite all this, the visit did not go in vain as both sides felt the need to address the other pending issues quickly, taking forward things achieved during 2010 Hasina visit to Delhi. The main concession India wanted was the overland access through Bangladesh to India's seven land-locked North-eastern States. This would help open up the region to mineral exploration, including oil, gas and coal and be an important step toward realizing New Delhi's ambition of using the region as a gateway to Southeast Asia and 'Look East' Policy. But Bangladesh put off overland access when India could not sign the Teesta Treaty.

However, the presence of the chief ministers – Tarun Gogoi of Assam, Manik Sarkar of Tripura, Mukul Sangma of Meghalaya, Lalthanhawla of Mizoram gave the visit a new dimension. "During their interactions with the government, business and the civil society leaders, the chief ministers sought increased trade, investment, and connectivity. They offered joint venture industrial projects and promotion of tourism. The failure to sign a "letter of exchange"- the transit deal – did frustrate them but they were in unison pursuing their common goal- connectivity." [52]**This is an example of how the regional satraps win over the Centre when they have similar interests on Delhi's Bangladesh policy. All these regional chieftains had been pressing for closer connectivity and more trade with Bangladesh so that both countries can benefit. The five crore people of the Northeastern States needed this for improvement of their economy. Moreover, they had been insisting on access to Bangladesh's Chittagong port, just 75 km from Tripura.**

---

52 Haroon Habib, *'Northeast gatway to Bangladesh ties'*, The Hindu, September 24,2011

President Pranab Mukhejri visits Dhaka

When Pranab Mukherji became the president in 2012 July, his first foreign visit was to Bangladesh. It had considerable symbolic weight, raising hopes on both sides. Apart from the fact that his wife Suvra hailed from Nariel and he is a Bengali himself, the President's visit from March 3 to 5, in 2013 despite the unstable political situation in Dhaka proved Delhi's commitment towards Bangladesh. According to the then Minister of State Adhir Ranjan Choudhary who accompanied the President, the government took a calculated risk by sending Mukherji to Dhaka at a troubled time because the gesture could give confidence to the international investment community over the Hasina government's grip on the situation. The presence of Mukul Roy, a Trinamool Congress MP from West Bengal, was significant because local resistance among the people of West Bengal has been one of the main sticking points that has thwarted a deal.

Water disputes and Farakka Accord

One contentious issue, which is of concern to West Bengal and the Northeast region, is the sharing of water between the two countries. This includes the Farakka treaty and now the Teesta Treaty. The origin of the water disputes can be traced back to the 1972 Treaty of Friendship, Cooperation and Peace. It is not surprising considering the two countries share 54 trans-boundary rivers big and small! As per the Peace Treaty, the two established a Joint River Commission to work on the common interests and sharing of water resources, irrigation, floods and cyclone control.

The Farakka Barrage was built in 1974, about 10 kilometres from the border of Bangladesh, controlling the flow of the Ganges, diverting some water into a feeder canal linking the Hooghly River, keeping it silt free. With increasing demands for water in Kolkata for industrial and domestic use, and for irrigational purposes in other parts of West Bengal, dispute over the sharing of water remains a problem.

Muchkund Dubey points out that "We built the Farakka Barrage despite Pakistani opposition. We did not divert it because we wanted to do it under the law. When Mujib came to power we made him sign the agreement but it was temporary. India may draw water of 40,000 cusecs until a final agreement was reached. The 1975 agreement with Mujib was the basis for drawing water from Farakka. We were Treaty bound but they started complaining that you are drawing away all water."[53]

As Gen. Ershad notes this water dispute has been going on since Gen. Zia's time. Bangladesh was supposed to get 40,000 cusecs of water. It came down to 35,000 and Zia tried to reach some agreement but failed. Farakka was in focus even during Ershad's time also as efforts were made to reach an agreement. Gen Ershad notes, "Our demand was 40,000 cusecs. But India was not willing to give it. At that time, sharing was difficult because India needed some more water. The problem was during the dry season only. And then there was a link canal between the Ganges and the Brahmaputra. That worried Dhaka a lot. There was some misunderstanding during Rajiv Gandhi regime. Jyoti Basu was not involved at that time. Actually we had no direct communication with West Bengal."[54]

Agreement on Farakka water sharing

However, the basic issue remained unaddressed, leading to its lapse in 1982. Ultimately, it was resolved in 1996 mainly due to the pro-active role of Deve Gowda's Foreign Minister I.K. Gujral. **It was in a way a combined effort of the Centre and State coming together on a vital issue.**

Former Bangladesh High Commissioner to India Rehman Sobhan claims that Gujral first flagged the issue with him when Sobhan visited India to participate in the Indo-Bangladesh dialogue on water. He conveyed this to his brother Farooq Sobhan who was the Foreign Secretary and the move was taken forward.

Jyoti Basu plays a positive role

Gujral used his biggest trump card by seeking the help of the then West Bengal Chief Minister Jyoti Basu to resolve the Farakka issue. **It was a classic example of how a regional leader could play a positive role in diplomacy when their interests converged.** He was

---

53 Author's interview with Muchkund Dubey, (3-7 March 2014

54 Author's interview with Gen. Ershad, (3-7 March 2014)

a card- carrying member of the CPI-M who studied law in London where he was involved in anti imperialist struggle. The people of Bangladesh had a soft corner for Jyoti Basu because he hailed from a Bangladesh village. He had a good relationship with Gujral. Being a statesman, Basu went to Dhaka on a private visit and clinched the deal with Begum Hasina. "Prime Minister Hasina could capitalise on this aspect. She had decided that if we have to have settlement on these two issues - Farakka and Chittagong Hill Tract -we have to do it in this short window. She also had the political sense to assess the State of Indian politics that the Deve Gowda government was not going to last.[55]"

Farakka Treaty signed

Basu assigned the job to his Finance Minister Asim Das Gupta who worked out the draft with the experts and finally Deve Gowda and Hasina signed it on December 12, 1996. Ultimately Basu succeeded in finding a short and medium term solution to the Farakka issue. **As Deb Mukharji points out the agreement came because each, while protecting their own interests, was assured of the bona fide of the other and also trusted each other. Bangladesh was assured of a reasonable deal without unduly straining Indian interests.** "Besides the sharing of water of an agreed basis, the 30-year span of the duration of the agreement made it virtually permanent, ensuring that Bangladesh would never again have to face the uncertainty of a no Treaty regime and could embark upon its own development programmes with a degree of certitude.[56]"

The brief from Hasina to the Bangladesh Foreign Secretary Farooq Sobhan who negotiated the Treaty was that they should try and get something better than the 1977 agreement. Hasina who envisaged initially a much more ambitious target agreed to scale down her demand and dropped down their minimum guaranteed flow throughout and accepted this alternate ten- day formula. Her view was that she personally and the Awami League as a party had

55 Author's interview with Rehman Sobhan (3-7, March, 2014)

56 Deb Mukharji, *Editor J. N. Dixit, External Affairs, Cross Border Relations, Bangladesh chapter*, Roli books, 2003, P202

much closer ties with India and wanted to match and improve the minimum guaranteed flow that had been provided for in the 1977 agreement. The two sides were looking at this almost 20 years after and they had to accept that the flow in the river had declined. By 1996 the water was being utilized more for irrigation purposes rather than for the de- siltation purposes. The big difference was that in 1977 there was a guaranteed flow. In the 1996 agreement there was no guarantee clause or an arbitration clause. If the agreement ran into any difficulty it was for both sides to sit down and sort out. There was no third party involvement. Two other key elements in the agreement were the understanding that Bangladesh would use this agreement, to build a barrage on its side and that would then provide sufficient water for the dry season for irrigation purposes. India agreed to help raise the funds for construction of the barrage with an estimated cost somewhere between 8 to 10 billion US dollars. There was also an understanding that India would speak to Bhutan on behalf of Bangladesh to see if some water from Bhutan could be diverted to augment the Ganges. These were the two approaches that were recommended. "It was not by any means a perfect Treaty. If we compare it with some of the earlier agreements it had no arbitration clause and no guarantee clause. We said in principle we will share water. The fact that water is a State subject makes it a very complicated issue. West Bengal was right to a certain extent in thinking 'why should we be punished and why should we share the little water that we have with Bangladesh.' According to international law as the lower riparian State Bangladesh have rights. So this is a matter that needs better leadership and some better water management.[57]"

Farooq Sobhan observes that the most important aspect of the Farakka Agreement was the clear signal from New Delhi that they would accept whatever West Bengal was willing to accept. Basu was not only able to persuade the Bangladesh government but also the people of West Bengal because of his stature and Statesmanship. "Basu had a carte blanche to clinch the deal. This was a marked change from what was New Delhi's policy in the past,

---

57 Author's interview with Farooq Sobhan (3-7 March, 2014)

which was that Delhi would decide what was best for India and the States had to accept it."[58]

While the sharing of the Ganga waters was successfully agreed upon, the major area of dispute remains on India's construction and operation of the Farakka Barrage to increase water supply to the River Hooghly. "The main provisions of the Farakka Treaty were that India would ensure release of maximum water to meet the needs of Bangladesh for thirty years subject to the availability of water flow in the Ganges above and below the Farakka Barrage. Bangladesh would get between a minimum of 35,000 cusecs and maximum of 70,000 cusecs depending on the water available in the upper trenches."[59]

Hasina faced a virulent propaganda from her opponents led by Begum Khaleda Zia who even today believes that the 30 year- old Ganges Water Treaty constituted a setback for Bangladesh for several reasons. "First it saw a further drastic reduction of water available to Bangladesh during the dry seasons as compared to the Farakka Agreement of 1977. I would like to emphasise here that the Farakka Barrage is located only eleven miles from the Bangladesh border. This means that India was in a position to unilaterally withdraw waters from the upstream, which covers 90% of the total length of the Ganges River. Second, the Ganges Treaty does not have a guarantee clause ensuring a minimum flow of water for Bangladesh during the dry seasons. Third, one has also questioned the absence of transparency leading up to the signing of such a crucially important bilateral Treaty that has long-term implications for us as a lower riparian country. Since the Treaty provides for periodic reviews, these matters must be rectified as a top priority.[60]"

Begum Hasina's critics led by Begum Khaleda Zia complained that Bangladesh did not get a fair share of water in the dry season and some areas got flooded when India released excess waters during the monsoons. The pro-Pakistani elements in the country were not pleased by the manner in which she had firmly dealt with cadres

---

58 Author's interview with Farooq Sobhan, (3-7 March 2014)

59 Author's interview with Farooq Sobhan, (3-7 March 2014)

60 Author's interview with Khaleida Zia, (17-22 February 2014)

of separatist Indian insurgent groups such as ULFA and taken on Islamist terror outfits such as the Harkat- ul- Jihad-al-Islami (HuJI).

Jyoti Basu appreciated for his positive role

Interestingly both the countries appreciated the role played by Jyoti Basu. Soon after the Farakka Accord was signed, Gujral praised Jyoti Basu in a suo- motto statement in the Rajya Sabha on December 12, 1996, on signing of the Farakka Treaty. **Gujral had placed on record the Union Government's appreciation and the "very constructive role played by the Chief Minister of West Bengal and his Cabinet colleagues in bringing about an improved atmosphere in which the Treaty between India and Bangladesh has become possible."[61]** Prime Minister Deve Gowda also praised Basu for his role in clinching the accord.

However, the Trinamool Congress leader Saugata Roy argues that in the end the Treaty went against the interests of Bengal. "Jyoti Basu wanted to play the statesman. He had a lot of hold on his own party, which was very strong in the State at that time. He rode rough shod."[62] The CPI-M leader Mohd Salim disagrees with any comparison of Jyoti Basu with Mamata Banerjee with the kind of personality Basu had, his political acumen and his statesmanship. He was never in Parliament but he had a national stature. "But Mamata was in Parliament and a Central minister but she never developed a national outlook. She only tried to create a constituency at the regional level although she was groomed in a national party like Congress.[63]"

Despite all these criticisms many believe that the Treaty has worked well by and large. Bangladesh now has enough water during the monsoon season and too little water during the dry season. But there is need to revisit this question of augmentation. The lesson learnt from the Farakka Treaty is how to use water and how to conserve water but water management should be the priority to both

---

61 Statement in Rajya Sabha by Gujral on December 12, 1996

62 Author's interview with Saugta Roy (17 July, 2014)

63 Author's interview with Mohd. Salim (16 September 2014)

the countries, which would help both in judicious use of the water resources.

Khaleda takes over again

Begum Khaleda Zia took over from Sheikh Hasina in 2001. Khaleda's government adopted an unusual toughness against India. Before the election the BNP even threatened that it would either re- negotiate the Treaty or rescind it altogether but after coming to power it was caught in a dilemma. New Delhi's sharp warning that in any revision of the Treaty there was no guarantee that already allocated water would remain sacrosanct made the Khaleda government think twice.

During the three successive democratic regimes, three significant developments had taken place. The first was the handing over of the Teen bigha corridor in perpetuity by India in the early nineties. Second was the repatriation of Chakma refugees. Third was in 1999 Kolkata - Dhaka bus service inaugurated.

When the Vajpayee government took over in 1998, it inherited a number of problematic issues between India and Bangladesh including illegal migration. The BJP has always made a distinction between the Hindus and the Muslims emigrating from Bangladesh considering the former as refugees and terming the later as illegal immigrants. However, when it was in power the reaction remained muted to the post-election violence in Bangladesh in 2001, which led to the large scale displacement of the Hindus in Bangladesh. Rather, the Vajpayee government took a pragmatic view.

The human rights issue regarding the Hindus in Bangladesh has always been a sore point. During Khaleda's second term, many Hindu refugees fled to West Bengal. The Vajpayee government was so concerned that he deputed his National Security Adviser Brajesh Mishra to Dhaka as Prime Minister's special envoy to establish contact with the Khaleda government that assumed power on October 28, 2001. Bangladesh allayed India's fears and guarded the Hindu temples in the wake of Godhara riots in 2002.

For instance, "In 2003 a crisis erupted when 213 nomadic people especially the snake charmers from Bangladesh were stranded in no-man's land and Dhaka refused to take them back. This led to border tension and a bilateral political crisis as both India and Bangladesh refused to own these people creating a humanitarian crisis. Finally these people were mysteriously made to vanish from the no-man's land as a face saving measure. To deal with the issue in 2003 the BJP government introduced an Amendment to the Citizenship Act which for the first time defined 'illegal migrants' by inserting clause b to section 2 of Citizenship Act 1956." [64]

Hasina's second term

Begum Hasina wanted to resolve the Teesta water dispute when she came to power for the second time. Recalling the course of events the then Bangladesh Foreign Minister Dipu Moni says that during Prime Minister Sheikh Hasina's visit in January 2010 they expected something concrete might emerge, perhaps signing an interim Treaty but it did not come. "I think we talked about our intention to do something. The discussions and negotiations went fairly well."[65]

During her three-day visit to India Prime Minister Sheikh Hasina exchanged draft agreements with India, as it would provide key support to agricultural production in the northwest region of Bangladesh, which accounts for 14% of the total cropped area. Around 63% of the total cropped area in the region is irrigated with Teesta water.

After a two day ministerial level meeting of the Joint River Commission, Dhaka favoured a draft interim agreement while New Delhi came up with a draft of a Statement of Principles on the sharing of river water during the dry season. It was also felt that a decision should be taken within a year.

Mamata Banerjee plays spoiler on water and land issues

But the problem arose from the West Bengal side. As Mamata had good relations with Hasina and also with Bangladesh, no one expected any problem from her side on the Indo – Bangladesh

---

64 Smuriti S.Pattanaik, '*Politics of illegal immigration and India Bangladesh relations,*' Institute of Defence Studies, May 16, 2014

65 Author's interview with Dipu Moni (3-7 March 2014)

relations. But to their horror, Mamata Banerjee held that West Bengal would not like to trade away their water.

Singh includes Northeastern Chief Ministers in his delegation

Recognising the political sensitivity of the issues Manmohan Singh included Chief Ministers of Assam, Tripura, Meghalaya, Mizoram and West Bengal, in his delegation when he visited Bangladesh, which paid off. Mamata Banerjee was considered absolutely essential in forging any agreement on the sharing of Teesta water. She took away the sheen from the Prime Minister's historic Dhaka visit in 2011. Referring to this, her predecessor Buddha Dev Bhattacharya asked, "Was it really necessary to create an impasse on water sharing and the enclaves? The matter could have been solved rationally" adding "Comrade Jyoti Basu took it on himself to pilot the Farakka Treaty. He acted responsibly. But now look at what Mamata Banerjee is doing! She is opposing all the legitimate moves taken by India to meet the aspirations of Bangladesh. She is proving to be the stumbling block, Bhattacharjee said.[66]" Obviously, the Centre had discussed with him about the LBA before Mamata dethroned him.

Dr Singh terming it as "a special moment," said that the inclusion of the Chief Ministers – Tarun Gogoi of Assam, Manik Sarkar of Tripura, Mukul Sangma of Meghalaya and Lal Thanhawla of Mizoram -- indeed gave the visit a new dimension, as it had direct ramifications for trade and connectivity through Bangladesh. **This has been the demand of the Northeastern chief ministers, which the Centre has accepted.**

During their interactions with the government, business and the civil society leaders, these regional chieftains emphasized increased trade, investment and connectivity and offered joint venture industrial projects and promotion of tourism. They laid stress on improving Bangladesh's relations with the "Seven Sisters" in all sectors and proposed an increase of land ports. They also wanted cooperation in health, education and environment.

---

66 Kolkata correspondent, *'Buddha attacks Mamata on Teesta,'* BD news 24.com, 29 January, 2014

Dhaka saw the failure to sign the Teesta Agreement as a setback to Hasina with the BNP swinging into action to attack her. Importantly, the water issue also has a bearing in the Bangladesh domestic politics because of its primary agrarian economy. Moreover, the BNP, whenever in power had taken a rigid stand on the issue. But it should not be overlooked that local politicians in North Bengal, cutting across party lines, have diligently opposed the Teesta deal because five districts, namely Darjeeling, Jalpaiguri, Cooch Behar, North and South Dinajpur, claiming that it would adversely affect the people in North Bengal. Mamata or even her predecessors had to keep this domestic politics in mind. Manmohan Singh also "announced 24- hour access to Bangladesh nationals through the Teen Bigha corridor besides duty free access to 46 textile items with immediate effect."[67]

Why did Mamata play a negative role on Teesta?

Why did Mamata go back on the Teesta Treaty? According to Muchkund Dubey the agreement was almost finalised before Manmohan Singh's September 2011 visit. It was broadly agreed that 50 per cent would be the total flow when the river enters into the plains. Between the entry and where the barrage is where the sharing will take place and 50 per cent will be given from there. The assumption was that during this period there will be regeneration and therefore what will be shared would be much less than 50 per cent. The two governments had agreed to this formula. The Government of India's brief was that they would not give 50 per cent. The Bangladesh brief was that they would not take less than 50 per cent. "So the solution was that 'we will give you 50 per cent of the total flow when the river enters into the plane. You will be able to draw it only when the river water is let from the barrage. Between the place when the river enters and reaches the barrage, there is an accretion because of rainfall.' Therefore the 50 per cent of the total flow at the barrage would be much more than when the river enters the plains. In the text they had not mentioned the percentage when it reached

---

Bangladesh. This is the basis on which the National security Adviser Shankar Menon must have explained to Mamata.[68]"

Hasina's Adviser Gowher Rizvi, who was involved in the negotiations was disappointed that the Treaty was not signed after all the hard work put in from both sides. Dhaka found it difficult to understand why Mamata did not agree. "What we understand is that her objection was more due to domestic reasons than anything in Bangladesh.[69]" He confirms that the draft Treaty was definitely shown to Mamata Banerjee but she never once raised any objections with Rizvi who met her a few days before Singh's visit or any other Bangladeshi officials who called on her. Rizvi claims that there has never been any suggestion that the formula be changed. Also both sides had initialled the formula. It was wholly based on what was available at the barrage point and it was an agreement that would benefit both countries. "We are not privy to what happened in between our visit and Manmohan Singh's visit. And nor have we been ever told. And that is why we are not raising this issue with Mamata Banerjee because it is a dispute between Delhi and Kolkata and not between Dhaka and Kolkata.[70]"

Trinamool Congress leader Saugata Roy defends Mamata asserting that she took a stand in the interests of the State because she had to ensure that the Teesta water sharing should benefit West Bengal. Justifying Mamata's ego problem, he observes that in his opinion "the Foreign Minister or Prime Minister should have called her and not a 'retired diplomat who was on an extended tenure.[71]"

Others think that it was her way of putting pressure on the Centre to get a special financial package she was demanding for Bengal. Secondly Mamata Banerjee was also upset that Prime Minister Singh decided to take the other four Chief Ministers of the Northeastern States in his delegation while Mamata expected that she alone would accompany Manmohan Singh and get a pride of place. The objections to equal sharing are because in lean season

68 Author's interview with Muchkund Dubey, (10Ju;y, 2014)

69 Author's interview with Gowher Rizvi (3-7 March, 2014)

70 Author's interview with Gowher Rizvi, (3-7, March2014)

71 Author's interview with Saugata Roy(17 July 2014)

West Bengal is reportedly left with insufficient water flow to meet its own irrigation needs. The West Bengal State Irrigation Minister Rajib Banerjee claimed in 2013, "at least five districts in the State depend on the Teesta for irrigation. Of these five districts, Cooch Behar, Jalpaiguri, South and North Dinajpur have a considerable percentage of minorities. While North Dinajpur has 47% minority population, the other districts have about 30%. We need to irrigate around 1.20 lakh hectares during the lean period, between October and May. The Chief Minister wants to protect the interest of the farmers in the area." [72]

Who is to be blamed for the Teesta fiasco?

Ultimately, questions arise whether it was a case of lack of communication between the federal and the State government, or a case of personality and ego clash? Was it a clash of domestic politics vis-à-vis foreign policy issues? Prime Minister Manmohan Singh was explicit when he claimed that he had done all he could to take Mamata on board. During an on -board media interaction on September 11, 2011 Singh explained "I was in touch with Mamataji for quite some time, and in fact I sent Shankar Menon, who is my National Security Adviser to meet Mamataji, to seek guidance from her, more than a month ago. And I was told that all technical details were sorted out. And subsequently for the first time in the Political Affairs Committee Meeting of the Cabinet, Dinesh Trivedi (Trinamool Congress minister) raised some objections and that time I again sent Shankar Menon to visit Kolkata. He had a meeting. What the Chief Minister said and what Shankar Menon understood, he undertook to get it done. He visited Dhaka and arrangements were made. But in the meanwhile obviously some other factors must have intervened and therefore Mamata Banerjee said she would not accompany me. It is only subsequently I learnt that the reason was disagreement with what was being attempted with regard to Teesta. So I think we are all in politics, senior advisors when they are sent they have a political mission, but one learns from ones mistake.[73]"

---

72 Madhuparna das, *'West Bengal CM Mamata Banerjee may be eyeing bigger compensation,'* Economic Times, 13 June 2015

73 'Transcript of Manmohan Singh's on board media interaction during return from Dhaka,' Pravasi Today. Com, news portal, September 7,

Should Foreign Policy play a second fiddle to domestic compulsions?

Mamata Banerjee's opposition to Teesta has brought to focus whether foreign policy should become the hostage of domestic politics pushing the national interests to the background. At the same time, West Bengal's concerns cannot be undermined either. **The point is that the view from Delhi is different from the view from Kolkata and North Bengal. This is because of the travesty of democracy. This is where the question comes about how New Delhi can manage these contradictions.**

The then West Bengal Governor M.K. Narayanan says he has seen how strongly North Bengal felt about Teesta waters. Any democratic political party could not afford to ignore that and that was exactly the compelling reason for Mamata Banerjee to take the line she takes. Narayanan notes, "Teesta is a problem, which is not just how many TMCs of waters are going to Bangladesh. How do you meet the concerns of political leaders of both sides? Both West Bengal and Bangladesh want a Treaty that will protect them in the future. Everything we are doing on the Tessta issue now is concerning the present. It is also difficult to foresee what would be the picture 20 years hence. The resolution requires the Prime ministers of both the countries, Chief Minister of West Bengal and political parties of both sides. Jyoti Basu did not agree; Buddha Dev did not agree, Mamata did not agree and there is no formula right now on the table, which will satisfy all parties. There has to be a give and take. It is really how you work the whole thing out involving the leaders, political parties, the intellectual and others."[74]

Should foreign governments talk to Indian provincial chieftains?

Begum Khaleda Zia is very clear that Dhaka must deal only with the Federal government. The role of regional leaders had no bearing for Bangladesh, she claims. She was categorical that the onus of negotiating and signing an agreement on the Teesta or any other common river vests exclusively on the Government of India. Taking

(2011)

74 Author's interview with M.K. Narayanan (12 December 2014)

cognizance of their opinion on this would give an added outreach to the Central government to alter any commitment it has undertaken. The way to resolve the issue was for the Indian government to abide by its decision with Bangladesh. The critical factor was reaching agreement on the basis of equity, i.e. a fair and reasonable share of a recognized scarce commodity. "The situation prevailing now at the Teesta area has become alarming. The plight of those whose life and livelihood depends on the waters of the Teesta are beyond description. A fair, just and a long-term arrangement must be reached without any further delay through an open and transparent process."[75]Begum Rowshan Ershad, wife of Gen. Ershad and Leader of Opposition in the Bangladesh Parliament echoes similar sentiments claiming, "Everything depends on how you talk and how you develop the relationship between the two countries. I think gradually and definitely we will win over.[76]"

Dhaka disappointed on not singing Teesta agreement

Bangladesh was disappointed with the turn of events. Bangladesh leaders confide their dismay in private about this setback. But none of them, either from the Bangladesh government or from the opposition, were willing to openly criticize Mamata. Two things dominated the Bangladesh restraint. One was that the Hasina government's overwhelming desire to have good relationship with India. The second was that they should say nothing, which could further aggravate the issue. This policy paid because Mamata made a successful visit in February 2015 to Dhaka at the invitation of the Bangladesh Foreign minister with full blessings from New Delhi. Hasina gave her a red carpet welcome.

Rehman Sobhan points out that in a way it has affected Hasina's political stakes because much was made about the Teesta Agreement. The Opposition parties have been putting her on the defensive as they did earlier when the Farakka Accord was singed. "She was willing to make concessions for India and took major steps on the security issue. She took a big risk while activating the whole

---

75 Author's interview with Khaleda Zia, (3-7, March 2014)

76 Author's interview with Begum Rowshan Ershad (3-7 March, 2014)

process. Very serious elements form the Northeast were involved. Domestically it was also a factor. Hasina was a secularist but none of these were adequately reciprocated by India." [77]

Lessons for the Centre

The first lesson for Dr Manmohan Singh on his Bangladesh policy was that he should have taken Mamata Banerjee on board. He also should have seen that he could not ignore the claims of a strong State chieftain. Secondly, as Deb Mukharji points out both India and Bangladesh constructing barrages on miles within each other where the water is not adequate even for one structure has to be addressed. What are lacking from both sides are efforts for water management. Bangladesh, quite understandably from its perspective, wants assurances that traditional flow will not drastically diminish and is not willing to talk of management. It is impossible for India to give such an assurance over a long period because of the needs of nearly 300 million people who inhabit the Ganga - Brahmaputra basin. "The answer has to lie in management, augmentation and not in the least in cooperation and understanding of the genuine needs and concerns of all parties involved.[78]"

Modi government and the Indo- Bangladesh relations

Teesta continues to be a sensitive issue even after the Modi government has taken over in May 2014. Added to that is the differences between Mamata and Modi on policy issues and ideological issues. Mamata is worried about the growing influence of the BJP in her backyard, as she had to protect her turf.

The visit of the new Foreign Minister Sushma Swaraj to Dhaka soon after the Modi government took over was a good beginning. This first stand-alone bilateral visit in June 2014 reiterated unequivocally New Delhi's willingness to further enhance the Bangladesh-India relations. The visit also raised the level of confidence and comfort between the two governments.

---

77 Author's interview with Redman Sobhan, (3-7, March, 2014)

78 Deb Mukharji, *Edited by J.N. Dixit, 'External affairs: Cross Border Relations.' Bangladesh Chapter*, Roli books, 2003, P 211

Land corridor problem

The land corridor through Bangladesh to connect the Northeastern States of India was yet another irritant. Right now, the only land connection between these two parts is the 20 to 25 km wide area known as India's Chicken Neck. This transit was used till the 1965 Indo – Pak war. Immediately after the Liberation War, the new government allowed transit in air and sea routes to India while the transit through road remained unaddressed. **New Delhi has been urging the reopening of the Northeastern routes through Bangladesh to its West, and with Myanmar and Southeast Asia to the East bowing to the demand of the Border States.**

The opening of the road route would help both the countries in many ways. While there would be huge direct economic gain from transit fees to Dhaka the mutual transit facilities will give Bangladesh a much shorter route to China and an initiative to link the Chinese province of Yunan with the Seven Sisters of India, Myanmar, Thailand and Bangladesh. The region is also rich in energy resources like natural gas and hydro-electricity.

Connectivity with Northeast

Manik Sarkar, Chief Minister of Tripura, the State which shares a 856km long border with Bangladesh, has been stressing the need for transit and trans-shipment facilities including road, rail and waterways connectivity through Bangladesh. He has been demanding India's intervention in persuading Dhaka to allow multi-modal transportation of goods through Bangladesh with Ashuganj as the port of call, including a related infrastructure boost. Tripura's desire to have the waterways access through Bangladesh is a demand voiced by the entire Northeastern region. In return, Bangladesh will gain access to the rest of India. There is the Bangladesh, China, India and Myanmar Economic Corridor (BCIM); there is the Asian highway and Asian railway. But both sides need to develop infrastructure and a regulatory framework through which there can be free movement.

As H. T. Imam points out "We are not connecting with India alone. Through India we are connecting with Nepal, Bhutan and other countries. Northeastern States are entirely dependent upon the Kolkata port. It is horrendously expensive for them. Through Chittagong it is much cheaper. There are goods now produced in Bangladesh like pharmaceuticals, garments and leather goods. Bangladesh has setup companies in Tripura. We entered into a trade pact and for the first time we created border huts. This is possible because of the regional leaders. We have good relations with Meghalaya, Tripura and Assam.[79]"

Dhaka's issues with Northeast

The Siliguri corridor, a narrow stretch between the North-Western head of Rajsahi Division and Jhapa district of South-eastern Nepal, is the only access for Indian transmission lines, road and rail. Transport through Bangladesh is vital for India on several planes: for the mainland to reach the Northeast in a straight line, for the landlocked Northeast to get to the sea, and to access Southeast Asia through the Bangladesh rather than the roundabout North-eastern hills. Over the decades Dhaka has filibustered on the transit matter, in the hope of extracting huge concessions.

Bangladesh has three important issues with the Northeast. One was mistrust because of the perception that Bangladesh was providing base for ULFA and other the threat from the insurgency groups. Dhaka had similar complaints that New Delhi was supporting the Shanti Bahini, the Chakmas and the Indian intelligence agencies were playing the destabilizing games. Secondly there is the issue of illegal immigration, which Dhaka feels is not properly understood in the region while it has become a political problem in India. Thirdly there are some apprehensions about how much freedom of action the Northeast region really has with Delhi to move forward in relations with Bangladesh to utilize the enormous economic opportunities. Successive Prime Ministers have been promoting an economic union with Bangladesh.

The Chief Ministers of the North-eastern States including Assam and Tripura have been putting pressure on New Delhi to improve connectivity with the neighbouring countries like Bangladesh and Myanmar. **Had the Northeastern States more clout in New Delhi,**

---

79 Author's interview with H.T. Imam, (3-7,March, 2014)

South Block would have concentrated to sort out the transit matter much earlier. This proves the hypothesis that if the regional satraps are weak they do not get what they want.

Former Prime Minister Dr Manmohan Singh acknowledging the importance of the 'Seven Sisters' says, "We have to create a climate conducive to investments and what we have done today, we have tried to create an environment that would strengthen the cause of peace and friendship in the North-eastern region of India and Bangladesh. The very fact that I took four Chief Ministers of the North- eastern States having borders with Bangladesh is a visible proof that winds of change are blowing in this region. I am confident that if border incidents become a thing of the past, if we develop border infrastructure, modernise it, if we deal with the problems arising out of connectivity issues, I think we will all benefit from the economic potential of both Bangladesh and the North-eastern States of India."[80] Singh should know the problems of the Northeast because he had been representing Assam in the Rajya Sabha for the past two and a half decades

Assam Chief Minister Tarun Gogoi is of the view that India's 'Look East Policy' might benefit the region. Assam is the gateway to Myanmar. "India is planning road routes, water route and even had a car rally recently, which began in Assam and ended in Indonesia. The route needs to be developed further. Earlier also there was a road during British time called Steel well road. It started from Assam and ended in China. Our part is yet to be made all right but Myanmar has just started. Assam is pressing for opening the route."[81]

Tripura's positive role in Bangladesh relations

The Border States should learn a lesson or two from Tripura. It has shown the way to leverage the national foreign policy thrust to improve the relations with Bangladesh and other neighbours. Agartala figures in the narrative of the Bangladesh liberation struggle as no

---

80 'Transcript of Manmohan Singh's on board media interaction during return from Dhaka,' Pravasi Today. Com, news portal, September 7, 2011

81 Author's interview with Taren Gogoi (26, November, 2013)

other Indian State. "It is the Agartala conspiracy case that propelled Mujibur Rahman to the cult figure status of the Bangabandhu after the Pakistani military regime accused him of sedition and said he had travelled to Agartala to ask for Indian help to secede. Tripura sheltered 17-18 lakh refugees in 1971 when her own population was merely 15.56 lakhs -- and it did so without a hiccup. The leading figures of the Liberation War, including Zia Ur Rahman first regrouped on Tripura's soil after his group of Bengali soldiers, tired and battered, were received at Sabroom by BSF office P K Ghosh (F company, 92 battalion) and my late father-in-law Nirmal Majumder (then in charge of Sabroom PS). From Sachin Singh to Nripen Chakrabarty to Manik Sarkar, all Tripura Chief Ministers have been unusually friendly to Bangladesh, except when its military and quasi-military regimes sponsored insurgents attacking targets in Tripura." [82]It not only has excellent relations with Bangladesh but also been able to implement its ambitious 726MW gas-fired Palatana power project after Bangladesh allowed transhipment of its heavy equipment through Chittagong port and Asuganj land port.

Modi moves closer to Dhaka

External Affairs Minister Sushma Swaraj points out,"You see the demonstration of our relations. We talked to the Bangladesh Prime Minister Sheikh Hasina that we want to take our Public Distribution System (PDS) goods through transit of Bangladesh to Tripura. It is just 40 kms to Tripura via Dhaka. She allowed us. She also offered that if you upgrade this road heavy vehicles like bigger truck could go. We are in the process of doing that. So our relations with Bangladesh today are at our best."[83]

It was indeed a great achievement for the Modi government, which successfully got the Land Boundary Agreement endorsed by the Indian Parliament on May 7, 2015. The passage of the bill after 41 years was a sign that Modi's 'neighbourhood-first' policy was beginning to work. In a landmark development, India and

---

82 Subir Bowmik, *'The Agartala doctrine'*, BD news, B D news 24.com, July 19,2014

83 Author's interview with Sushma Swaraj, (March, 2015)

Bangladesh activated the LBA on June 6, 2015 when Modi visited Bangladesh. As a result, on August 1 2015 the two countries swapped 161 enclaves between the two countries. "The 111 Indian enclaves are spread over 17,158 acres of land and have a population of 37,369. They are spread across four districts in Bangladesh — Kurigram, Lalmonirhat, Nilphamari and Panchagarh. The 51 Bangladeshi enclaves, all located in Cooch Behar district of West Bengal, are spread over of 7,110 acres of land and have a population of 14,215. The Constitution (One Hundred and Nineteenth) Amendment Bill, 2013, proposes to give effect to this India's land boundaries." [84]

Even in 2014 the Trinamool Congress, the Asom Gana Parishad (AGP) and the Bharatiya Janata Party (BJP) blocked the passage of the Constitution (119th Amendment) Bill, 2013, in the Rajya Sabha that sought to ratify the Land Boundary Agreement. Mamata Banerjee seems to have taken a U-turn on the issue later. With the Modi government eager to approve the agreement before his visit to Dhaka and the Standing Committee on External Affairs, headed by Congress Member of Parliament Shashi Tharoor, endorsing its ratification by parliament, Banerjee's nod for the LBA has given the residents of the enclaves, a new life. **The moral of the story is that both of them now realise that it is to their advantage to cooperate rather than confront each other. This fits in with Modi's pet concept of cooperative federalism. "I am confident that with the support of the State Governments in India, we can reach a fair solution on the Teesta water-sharing agreement and Feni Rivers. We should also work together to renew and clean our rivers", Mr Modi had said.**[85]

This long overdue measure endeavours to harmonize India's land boundaries. Correspondingly, India has 111 enclaves inside Bangladesh that have no connectivity with the Indian mainland. The people of these Indo-Bangla enclaves – numbering around 60,000 – have been rendered Stateless due to a cartographic anomaly. Devoid

---

84 Kalyani Shankar, '*A test for Modi*' The Pioneer, 5, December, 2014

85 Kalyani Shankar, '*Modi and Mamata bond in Bangladesh*', The Pioneer, June 12,2015

of basic services such as electricity, hospitals or schools, the residents are stuck without any relief or identity.

Folklore has it that the islands of enclaves in India and Bangladesh were the result of a series of chess games between the Maharaja of Cooch Behar and the Faujdar of Rangpur. These noblemen used these villages as a wager instead of currency. That was before the British Raj and long before the independence of South Asia's modern republics. Thus, villages in Cooch Behar became the properties of Rangpur while villages within Rangpur came to be owned by the Cooch Behar Maharajas. This informal arrangement between the two rulers allowed collection of revenues and administering of the respective 'enclaves.' But everything changed in 1947. Rangpur became part of East Pakistan (now Bangladesh) while Cooch Behar became part of India when its Maharaja Jitendra Narayan acceded his princely State to India in August 1949. During the Partition, these places have been left as they were found by both India and Bangladesh. "Four agreements had been attempted before. The first was Prime Minister Jawaharlal Nehru's pact with his Pakistani counterpart Feroz Khan Noon in 1958; the second was between Prime Minister Indira Gandhi and her Bangladeshi counterpart Sheikh Mujibur Rahman in 1974; the third was between Prime Minister Rajiv Gandhi and General HM Ershad in 1986; and the fourth between Prime Ministers P.V. Narasimha Rao and Khaleda Zia in 1992."[86] The fifth was to have been between Prime Minister Manmohan Singh and Sheikh Hasina in 2011, but Mamata Banerjee blocked it. The passage of the amendment gave India a huge advantage of a secure boundary and would enable it to curb illegal migration, smuggling and other criminal activities. Those living in Bangladeshi enclaves in India had been granted Indian citizenship under Section 7 of the Indian Citizenship Act, 1955 (as applicable to populations residing in territories incorporated into India). The amendment helped settle border disputes at several points in Tripura, Assam, Mizoram and Meghalaya besides West Bengal.

---

86 Kalyani Shankar. *'Land border solved, bonds strengthened'* The Pioneer, May 8,2015

Gen. Ershad notes that for 68 years or so these people had no State. The moment they get out of the enclave they are caught and sent to jail. "We must do something about it. This should be above politics. They have no identity and no medical treatment. From that point of view Indian government should take a soft stand.[87]" He claims that border issue was always there but it was very difficult to deal with a giant.

Assam objected and said the State was losing more land. "But how much land? You are a big country and we are a small country and a few thousand acres of land is nothing to you. As land we get ten thousand acres of land. This has remained an irritant but it can be resolved.[88]"

Saugata Roy questions how could a country sign the Treaty without ascertaining the views of the people of the affected States just to appease Bangladesh? "In the name of foreign policy objectives we cannot barter away our interests if our concerns are not addressed. It is true that Hasina helped us in the matter of nabbing ULFA militants. But water and land are important issues. This is something that has to be taken into account. "[89]He asserts that in India in future all federal governments have to take care of this point. **In December 2014, Mamata came on board after the Centre agreed to provide a rehabilitation package for the affected persons. External Affairs Minister Sushma Swaraj, Finance Minister Arun Jaitley and a few other confidants of both leaders had prepared the ground. This culminated in the unusual gesture on Ms Banerjee's part when her interests converged with that of the Centre.**

Mamata Banerjee comes on board on LBA

External Affairs Minister Sushma Swaraj points out that this was because the Modi government has addressed her concerns. "When you talk of exchange of enclaves naturally you have to take the Chief Minister of West Bengal on board or Teesta water you have

---

87 Author's interview with Gen Ershad, (3-7, March 2014)

88 Author's interview with Gen. Ershad, (3-7,March 2014)

89 Author's interview with Saugata Roy (17 July 2014)

to take the CM on board. The earlier government also tried that and we are also trying to do that. We took Mamata Banerjee on board and she also expressed that she is ready for the exchange as well as adverse possession. So there is no contradiction in the policy. She was not opposing it and she was expressing her concern. But now after due deliberations she is on board and she is only saying you have to give me a financial package with that. Suppose there is an exchange of population you need that money. Otherwise the agreement says 'as is where is' condition but the option has to be given to the people who are living there. Suppose one tenth of the population want to come back naturally the Chief Minister needs the infrastructure. So she was only saying give me a financial package. That concern has to be addressed.[90] Swaraj is confident that things are moving in the right direction regarding Indo-Bangladesh ties. For example she had talked to Mamata Banerjee before the latter went to Dhaka in February 2015 at the invitation of Bangladesh. A senior official from the Ministry of External Affairs accompanied her to Dhaka. "Without consultation it was not possible. There was a meeting between the Foreign Secretary, Home Secretary and Chief Secretary of West Bengal. We have decided the financial package after consulting the State. They sat and decided the fixed package and interim package. So political leadership is also talking and the executive are also talking.[91]"

But the Centre ignored the protests from Assam. There was lack of consensus in Assam which was also a key player in the exchange of the enclaves though there are no issues posed by Tripura, Meghalaya and Mizoram- the other players involved in the exchange. "Assam stands to lose some territory and hence a divided polity in the State unlike some gain to other States in the 2011 protocol that envisages India to receive 2,777.038 acres of land and hand over 2,267.682 acres. The Assam BJP found itself in an embarrassing position from Modi's declaration to ratify the pact during his Assam visit."[92] **The**

---

90 Author's interview with Sushma Swaraj (March, 2015)

91 Author's interview with Sushma Swaraj, (March 2015)

92 FPJ bureau, *'Mamata key to border deal with Dhaka',* Free press Journal, 9 December, 2014

Modi government did not address Assam's concern because the Centre felt it was advantageous to go ahead with the LBA and exchange of enclaves. It also ignored the local BJP's opposition for the deal. So Assam, including the local unit of the BJP lost out.

Illegal immigration

Most Border States in the Northeastern region suffer from the illegal immigration from Bangladesh. It is raised by the BJP in West Bengal and Assam, the AGP in Assam, in Maharashtra by the Shiv Sena. States like Assam express concern on the continuous pouring in of the immigrants.

The BJP says that only the Muslim immigrants are illegal and not the Hindus as they have no other place to go. Illegal immigration has been a bone of contention between the two countries for decades. The Bangladeshi leaders have been in a denial mode all through. While successive Indian governments have been trying to deport them the sheer number makes it impossible to do so. There is concern about the continuing influx of the undocumented Bangladesh migrants through a 4000 km-long porous international borders. The bulk of illegal Bangladeshi immigrants have migrated to West Bengal, although many others have settled in Assam, Meghalaya, Tripura, Delhi and Mumbai. In fact we don't even have the actual number of illegal Bangladeshi immigrants living in India.

Domestic resistance on illegal immigration in India

Migration from Bangladesh is a highly complex issue. Political parties have often made use of this as an election issue from both sides. Sentiment runs so strong that political parties often exploit the issue to gain popular support. The main question is how to deal with the problem when the government has not been able to assess the exact number of these illegal immigrants living in India? Sealing the borders and efficient patrolling rarely works. Even the US government with its mighty infrastructure and State of the art technological apparatus has not had much success in sealing its borders with Mexico.

By 2006, illegal immigration from Bangladesh became a dominant theme of West Bengal elections. The ruling elite belonging to the Communist government sympathized with illegal immigrants and reportedly even encouraged them but the then Chief Minister Buddha Dev Bhattacharya had opposed it. He told a press conference during his election campaign in 2006 that "It is a very serious issue and we are trying our best to counter it. Actually this problem should be handled by the Central government. For, we are talking about an international border protected by the Border Security Force. I am in constant touch with the Centre about this issue. I make it a point to bring it up during my talks with the Home Minister and the Prime Minister. When I met Dr Manmohan Singh in March, I told him: 'enough is enough. The migrants should be told in no uncertain terms what we want.' But sadly, the problem still exists.[93]"

Added to the woes are the demands from the BJP ally Shiv Sena that insists that these illegal immigrants should be thrown out. Shiv Sena has been against the Bangladeshi immigrants since the mid seventies and eighties. The issue of migration has always raised passions in Mumbai. In November 1995, Balasaheb Thackeray, the late Shiv Sena supremo, said the city had no place for illegal residents who were making the metropolis resemble a slum and who were taking jobs meant for the local people. "There are 20 million Bangladeshi residents in Mumbai and I will have the entire community exterminated," he thundered.[94] In August 2012, when a riot broke out at Azad grounds during a rally held to protest against the killing of Bangladeshi Muslims in Assam, Thackeray again declared that he would not "tolerate Muslims from Pakistan and Bangladesh inside Maharashtra".[95] Like the Shiv Sena, its offspring Maharashtra Navnirman Samithi (MNS) led by Thackeray's nephew Raj Thackeray has often used the migrant issue to further its agenda. There have been several attacks on the North Indians, the minorities, and the Bangladeshi migrants in the city in the recent

93 Indrani Roy Mitra, '*The naxalites only want to kill the police and the CPI-M'* Rediff.com, May 5,2006

94 Anupama Katakam, 'The outsiders' Front line, November 29,2014

95 Anupama Katakam, 'The outsiders.' Front line, November 29, 2013

past. In 2003 November the party had promised to deport all the Bangladeshi migrants from Mumbai besides slapping a blanket ban on cow slaughter in the city. **The Shiv Sena, being a long standing ally of the BJP and a partner in all the NDA governments has provided support to the BJP.** The BJP has also consistently been against illegal immigration. "You can write it down. After May 16, these Bangladeshis better be prepared with their bags packed," Modi thundered in Serampore in West Bengal, which shares a porous border with Bangladesh during the 2014 campaign.[96] Pat came the response from Mamata Banerjee "Touch a single person, we will see. The paper tiger should know there is a Royal Bengal tiger in Sunderbans. First you face that," [97] the Chief Minister, told another election meeting. **But once he took over Prime Minister Modi has not been using this kind of language and is going slow on the issue. Whenever the BJP led NDA comes to power, the BJP is reticent in throwing the illegal migrants out due to the political compulsions.**

Kanwal Sibal points out that the different parties have allowed the Bangladeshi Muslims to come through the border for local politics and they have changed the local demography of certain districts in West Bengal, which means the Muslim votes have become crucial. "The Marxist regime earlier had used these immigrants for their vote bank politics and so does Mamata Banerjee now. Some critics even allege that a spurt of new mosques and the restoration of older ones implied an increase in the Muslim population and also that the Madrasas are given encouragement by the State government although Hindus still remain a majority."[98]

Disputing this, Gen Ershad asks, "Do you think we can create a group that would be a big threat to security? I doubt very much. There is a doubt in the minds of the Indian government and the Indian people, but we don't have that capability unless it comes from

---

96 Edited by Deepshika Ghosh, *'Come May 16, Bangladeshi immigrants must pack up: Narendra Modi'*, NDTV, April 28, 2014

97 Press Trust of India, 'Mamata dares Modi on Bangladeshi Migrants issue,' The Indian Express, May 3, 2014,

98 Author's interview with Kanwal Sibal (13 JULY, 2014)

abroad. Here was some militancy inside but this militancy could go across the border and disturb India, in my opinion it is a far cry."[99]

Assam puts pressure to check illegal immigration

The All Assam Students Union (AASU) in the early 1980s was against these infiltrators and their agitation rattled Assam. West Bengal and Assam bear the major brunt of these infiltrators. They affect their economy and also the livelihood of the ordinary and poor people, thus causing major resentment and leading to severe unrest. The Assam government was under pressure from several quarters over the issue of alleged non-implementation of the historic Accord, which marked the ending of six-year long Assam movement.

There have also been allegations that not much has been done by the subsequent State governments in the last 3 or 4 decades to detect and deport the illegal foreigners, mainly Bangladeshi nationals from the State. The situation in Assam is that the migrants, mostly Muslims had been legitimized over the years and have now become a substantial vote bank. They support the incoming illegal immigrants and the result is that there have been increasing social and communal tensions. Hence, they demand for a sealed border, a repatriation Treaty with Bangladesh, an updated National Register of Citizens (NRC) and only backed by the political will of the Central and the State government, without which the foreigner problem of Assam can be solved. **The Assam Accord was one of the classic instances of the domestic politics having a bearing on India's foreign policy. It was specially meant to satisfy Assam where there was agitation against the illegal immigration creating ethnic tension.**

In order to tackle it the Centre came up with the Illegal Migration (Determination by Tribunals) Act, 1983. It was applicable only to Assam and declared that anybody settled in Assam before 1971 was a legal citizen. Significantly, for the rest of India, the cut off date for acquiring Indian citizenship is July 19, 1948. The IMDT Act therefore failed to effectively identify and deport illegal migrants. Subsequently, in a landmark judgment on July 12, 2005, the Supreme Court, while ordering for the repeal of the controversial

---

99 Author's interview with Gen Ershad, (3-7,March,2014)

Illegal Migrants (Determination by Tribunal) Act in Assam, had made several pertinent observations regarding the infiltrators. The court held that the "influx of Bangladeshi nationals who have illegally migrated into Assam pose a threat to the integrity and security of North-eastern region. Their presence has changed the demographic character of that region and the local people of Assam have been reduced to a status of minority in certain districts,"[100] It also added that the foremost duty of the Union Government was to protect its borders and prevent trespass by foreign nationals. But this too became problematic when Bangladesh refused to accept them. The deportation is becoming extremely difficult due to various factors including commonality of language, culture and religion between the two countries.

Assam Chief Minister Tarun Gogoi is opposed to the idea of more illegal immigrants coming into his State. The main Opposition party the Asom Gana Parishad is also opposed to it. The Chief Minister has asked for facilities like flood lighting on the border. But despite the pressure, the Centre is yet to resolve the issue because Assam does not have enough clout to make the Centre listen to its demands. Gogoi notes "It is the job of Government of India to stop infiltration. My job is from the moment they enter Assam. They (BJP) remember foreigner issue only during election time. The moment elections are over it is forgotten. Vajpayee at one time talked of work permit but I opposed it. If you give them permit they will sit here.[101]"

Bangladesh Minister Noor has a different view. His constituency Nilo Phamari is close to the border near Cooch Bihar where the British cultivated blue Indigo. He claims, that two types of migration happen. One was the rich Hindus who have relatives on the other side slowly they migrate to India. They go illegally because legally it is not possible. "The poorer sections of the Hindus normally don't go because they don't have any other alternative. Possibly they are cultivating somebody's land as farm labourers. They do the same

---

100 Ram Madhav,'*Why Modi is right on the Bangladeshi migrant's issue,*' Rediff. Com, May 13, 2014

101 Author's interview with Tarun Gogoi, (26 November 2013)

thing in India. So this is not very favourable for them to go across. But the poorer people also migrate when there are communal tensions. In the last few months, the Jamaat and the BNP have been attacking the temples, burning their houses and that kind of things. A section of Muslims also migrate to big cities. I am also from a migrated family.[102]"

Former Bangladesh Foreign Secretary Farooq Sobhan argues that a large part of the Bengali community in Assam has been there for over a century. "Whom are we talking about? Are we talking about 1947? Or are we talking about 1971? What is the period we are talking about? Are we talking about the Hindus and Muslims or are we talking about only the Muslims? The BJP does not look upon Hindus as illegal immigrants. So there is a whole range of issues coming to play.[103]" Sobhan claims that they go to India only because there is demand. In Assam they are the major support in agriculture. "We have 500,000 Indians working in Bangladesh and 90 per cent are illegal. They are holding different positions some as teachers some as some other post and they are remitting 5 million US dollars every year. Our economic migrants remit nothing back to Bangladesh. They are for all practical purposes Indians today. The reality is how do these people cross? It is by bribing the BSF on the border.[104]"

Khaleda Zia, during whose regime the immigration figures had gone up, refuses to accept that there is any illegal immigration into India. She claims that the onus of preventing so-called illegal immigration falls on the receiving State. "When did this illegal immigration take place? India is on record in stating that all ten million refugees had returned to Bangladesh in 1972. Over the last few years India has been constructing a fence around Bangladesh as deterrent to illegal immigration. Indian Border Security Force personnel rigorously guard this fence to prevent any unlawful

---

102 Author's interview with Noor (3-7,March, 2014)

103 Author's interview with Farooq Sobhan (3-7,March 2014)

104 Author's interview with Farooq Sobhan, (3-7,March 2014)

crossing of people from Bangladesh," she argues.[105] According to her there are millions of Bangladeshis living and working in a large number of countries in the Middle East, Europe and America, as do Indians. People primarily migrate to foreign countries in search of better employment opportunities as well as for a better quality of life. Under the circumstances, she does not see any logic for Bangladeshi job seekers to migrate to India.

Dipu Moni admits that people migrate for economic reasons. Once the border is settled both the countries can take more concrete steps. Some economic migration would continue to take place as Bangladesh too has this influx from Myanmar. "We exchanged some of the terrorists and there are some bad elements from our side in India too. Indian security forces whenever they apprehend them they hand them over to us. Most of your Northeast they were very happy that there were no safe havens for the insurgents here.[106]"

So what can be the way ahead? **A lasting solution can occur only when the two governments sit down and tackle the problem and find a viable solution and there is need to involve the Border States in this regard.**

The first is to stop future immigration and the second is to find ways of allowing the immigrants with some work permit or some such thing. The free movement between India and Bangladesh is not feasible because the Indian Home Ministry objects to such steps on the ground that once the floodgates are opened there will be no control. Thirdly, the government must work out a comprehensive policy about this issue in consultation with the States and also with the neighbouring governments. There should be some kind of census on the illegal immigrants. There should be compulsory registration of births and deaths so that it could give an indication.

External Affairs Minister Sushma Swaraj is confident that the issue could be resolved amicably. Arguing that when the boundary is decided and once the border is fenced, the illegal immigration automatically goes down, she says, pointing out "Our relations with

105 Author's interview with Khaleda Zia (3-7,March 2014)

106 Author's interview with Dipu Moni,(3-7, March, 2014)

Bangladesh today are at our best. Our relations with Nepal are at our best and also with Sri Lanka. After all these frequent high level visits are the pillars of your strength. So today that anti India feelings are totally gone. They say China promises and delivers. India promises but forgets. We are going to change that perception. I am monitoring all these projects with Bangladesh, Myanmar, Sri Lanka and Nepal. We are going to change this perception. We have been successful in that.[107]"

Drug trafficking

Drug mafia operates from Myanmar and other countries of the golden triangle, to different destinations, and they are increasingly using Bangladesh as a transit point. It has become the prime transit route for trafficking heroin to Europe from Southeast Asia. The routes for smuggling heroin into Bangladesh are by courier from Pakistan, commercial vehicles and trains from India, and via sea or overland by truck or public transport from Myanmar.

Security concerns between India and Bangladesh

The security and strategic issues are yet another major concern. Mutual security concerns play an important role in the bilateral relations. New Delhi had sought Dhaka's cooperation in fighting anti India terrorist elements and insurgent outfits operating from its soil claiming that there was credible evidence of the Pakistan's ISI (Inter services intelligence) agency operating from Bangladesh.

Begum Zia disputes this allegation. "I agree that security related issues are important subjects in the scope of our bilateral relations. Bangladesh has never been, nor will it ever be, a safe haven, neither for terrorists of any form nor for any insurgents. As friendly neighbours, we must be responsive to each other's security concerns and not allow our territories to be used by anyone against the security interest of the other.[108]"

When Hasina came to power things got better but in her first stint in 1996, she had no majority and was therefore unable to do

107 Author's interview with Sushma Swaraj, (March 2015)

108 Author's interview with Khaleda Zia, (3-7, March 2014)

much. The Government of India understood her helplessness and gave her administration a benefit of doubt and said such activities might have been taking place clandestinely. In December 2008, following two years of military-backed caretaker government, Sheikh Hasina's Awami League swept into government with a landslide (263 seats in Parliament out of 300), on the plank of change, employment, law and order, and long-pending war-crimes trials relating to the events of 1971. The decisive Awami League victory allowed Prime Minister Hasina to reach out to New Delhi. The armies of both countries have, in the past, proved their might by fighting the ULFA cadres. Sheikh Hasina has helped India in containing the terrorist activities and chasing their leaders from Bangladesh, which they were using as a safe haven. Tapan Patowary, the leader of the Kamtapur Liberation Organisation (KLO) was caught in Dhaka in October 2009. The chairman of ULFA, Arabinda Rajkhowa, and its Deputy Commander-in-Chief, Raju Baruah, were caught in Cox Bazaar on December 4, 2009 and later arrested by Assam police across the Meghalaya-Bangladesh border. The ULFA had been running some ten camps in the Mymensingh-Chittagong areas and had amassed a huge fortune through the real estate and restaurant businesses in Bangladesh.

It is now established that most of the armed insurgent groups in Assam like the United Liberation Front of Asom (ULFA), the Kamtapur Liberation Organisation (KLO), and the National Democratic Front of Bodoland (NDFB) had established camps in Bangladesh and also procured their weapons from the Cox Bazaar area near the Bangladesh-Myanmar border. The ability to function with impunity within Bangladesh was not only due to help from within Bangladesh but also because of facilitation provided by a network of illegal migrants from within Assam to the ULFA. **The lack of political will of both the Central and the State government to solve the foreigners problem and lack of proper census figures or adequate information about the illegal migrants, the vote bank politics of the political parties – all these are making the foreigners issue more complex. Assam is worried that even in 2011, when the Indo–Bangla land transfer Treaty was signed in Dhaka, the influx** issue was not flagged by the Indian government in their bilateral talks although the Congress party ruled at the Centre and in Assam.

The Teen Bigha corridor

The Teen Bigha corridor is no larger than a football field. The Nehru-Noon accord of September 3, 1958 provided for a straightforward exchange of enclaves between India and East Pakistan. A formal agreement was signed on September 10, 1958. At the time of Berubari agreement, the Bharatiya Jana Sangh, the erstwhile avatar of the BJP, under the leadership of Pandit Deendayal Upadhyaya and Atal Behari Vajpayee had taken a firm stand against the Nehru - Noon Accord. Berubari was to be split horizontally and equally but New Delhi never issued the notification. Under the Indira – Mujib accord, India agreed to lease in perpetuity to Bangladesh an area of approximately 178 meters by 85 meters near Teen Bigha to connect Bangladesh with its enclave Dahagram. The agreement was opposed by many political parties including the Bharatiya Janata Party when the P.V. Narasimha Rao government formally wanted to hand over the leased territory to Bangladesh. The Akhil Bharatiya Vidyarti Parishad (ABVP) gave a call for a march to Teen Bigha on the day of the transfer of the territory - June 26, 1992 but was prevented from proceeding further. "The Teen Bigha corridor was transferred in perpetuity to Bangladesh by Indian government led By Shri P.V. Narasimha Rao in 1992 despite massive popular protests all over the country." [109]

Initially the transfer provided for access to Bangladesh to use this corridor on alternate hours during the day in 1992. But during the 2011 visit of Prime Minister Dr Manmohan Singh to Dhaka, Sheikh Hasina prevailed upon him to provide 24-hour access to their citizens through the corridor. India had agreed to this proposal and a flyover bridge is being built to facilitate this movement

New Moore Islands

For nearly 30 years, India and Bangladesh have argued over the control of a tiny rock island in the Bay of Bengal. India called the

---

109 Ram Madhav, '*Govt Must Renegotiate Pending Issues in Indo- Mujib accord before ratifying* it" Samvada, April, 20,2013

island the New Moore and Bangladesh called it South Talpatty. They lie at the mouth of the Hariabhanga River, which separates the two countries. They are mudflats with no human or animal life. It became an issue in the maritime boundary talks in 1979. A US satellite discovered them in 1974. Bangladesh claims that in May 1979 Prime Minister Morarji Desai agreed to hold a joint survey. However, on April 9, 1980 Indira Gandhi, when she came back, claimed that the islets belonged to India. There were no permanent structures in New Moore, but India sent some paramilitary soldiers to its rocky shores in 1981 to hoist its national flag. Based on a case filed by the Bangladesh government in October 2009 at then Permanent Court of Arbitration, the dispute was settled in July 2014 by a final verdict not open to appeal and in favour of Bangladesh. The UN decision and its acceptance of the ruling by both were seen as a positive step. With that decision, both India and China stand to gain from a settled maritime boundary. "In a landmark judgment, the Hague-based Permanent Court of Attribution (PCA) has awarded Bangladesh an area of 19,467 sq. km, four-fifth of the total area of 25,602 sq. km disputed maritime boundary in the Bay of Bengal with India on July 7. The Tribunal's award has clearly delineated the course of maritime boundary line between India and Bangladesh in the territorial sea, Exclusive Economic Zone (EEZ) and continental shelf within and beyond 200 nautical miles (nm). Now, Bangladesh's maritime boundary has been extended by 118,813 sq. comprising 12 nm of territorial sea and an EEZ extending up to 200 nm into the high seas. In addition, the ruling acknowledged Bangladesh's sovereign rights of undersea resources in the continental shelf extending as far as 345 nm in the high seas, taking Chittagong coast as the base line." [110]

The award has wide security and economic implications not only for India and Bangladesh but also for the entire Bay of Bengal region. The verdict would contribute towards establishing strategic partnerships among the nations sharing borders in the Bay. The award would have positive impact on emerging multilateral forum like the Bay of Bengal Initiative for Multi-Sectorial Technical and

---

[110] Rupak Bhattacharji, *'Delimitation of Indo Bangladesh maritime boundary,'* IDSA, August 9, 2014

Economic Cooperation (BIMSTEC). India has already settled its maritime borders with Sri Lanka, Myanmar and Thailand. Similarly, Bangladesh's maritime issues with Myanmar are also resolved.

The award has huge economic significance for a small country like Bangladesh. Now Dhaka can open up its waters for foreign firms to explore and exploit hydrocarbons in the Bay. Bangladesh's maritime dispute with India had deterred many international petroleum companies to invest in the sea-blocks. The ruling has confirmed Bangladesh's right to exploit the potentially rich waters in the Bay region. New Delhi is also happy with the ruling and considers it as a diplomatic breakthrough for various reasons. Among other gains, the verdict has recognized India's sovereignty over New Moore Island and received nearly 6000 sq. km of the contested zone where the island had once existed.

Hasina's third term

The year 2014 was important for both India and Bangladesh. The 2014 elections in Bangladesh were held amidst controversy as the 18-party Opposition boycotted it. The BNP chief Khaleda Zia was kept under virtual house arrest and the Jamaat was banned. The Jatiya Party was forced to participate. Because of the boycott 154 seats out of 300 seats remained uncontested and about 22% people voted in the election. Sheikh Hasina became the Prime Minister once again raising questions about her political legitimacy. The US, European Union and the Commonwealth had principally blamed Hasina for the failure in conducting a participatory election. They had also refused to send observers to monitor the elections, which were being seen as an indication that they do not intend to recognize the legitimacy of the poll verdict. "India, however, stood by the Hasina government ahead of the polls, which many believe gave her the courage to hold the election. Manmohan Singh more than made up for not signing the Teesta Treaty by strongly supporting Hasina over the January 5, 2014 elections. In backing Hasina, Dr Manmohan Singh appeared as resolute as in going about the Indo – US nuclear deal though he could not get around Mamata Banerjee on the Teesta."[111]New Delhi's open support to the Awami League has led to the other political parties questioning India's commitment to supporting a stable multi-party democracy in Bangladesh.

Almost simultaneously, there was a regime change in India after the 2014 May polls. The BJP led Modi government took over with a massive majority. The BNP-Jamaat combine made no secret that it wanted the Congress out of power and believed that the Modi government would follow Vajpayee's line of not playing favourites in Dhaka. Hasina Wajed, in contrast, wanted Modi to continue the current India's policy of strong support to her regime and break the ice on Teesta and the Land Boundary Agreement.

Despite their apprehensions, Hasina and her rival Khaleda Zia, were both quick to congratulate Prime Minister Modi. Begum Zia wanted to convince Modi that she was ready to go for a fresh beginning with Delhi. Sheikh Hasina wanted to assure the Modi government of Bangladesh's sincerity in sustaining a cooperative framework of relations between the two countries. When Hasina congratulated Modi on assuming office, most of the conversation was focused on Teesta water-sharing agreement. The Bangladesh Speaker Shirin Choudhury followed this up quickly, as she touched upon all the important issues between the two countries in her first meeting with Modi. She came to Delhi to participate in Modi's swearing in ceremony in May 2014.

Sushma Swaraj visits Dhaka

Prime Minister Modi responded warmly by deputing his Foreign Minister Sushma Swaraj to Dhaka within weeks. It was seen as adding substance to the new foreign policy perspectives of the Modi administration. Swaraj assured that India would work with Hasina to further strengthen relations and at the same time by meeting with the BNP Chairperson Khaleda Zia, showed her prudence and sense of pragmatism. Swaraj's visit to Dhaka yielded several significant concessions on the part of New Delhi. Most notably the Indian visa

---

111 Devadeep Purohit and Charu Sudan Kasturi, *'For Hasina, India swims against tide, Delhi stands by ally despite sham polls,'* The Telegraph India, January 7,2014

requirements were relaxed for the Bangladeshi nationals above the age of 65 and below the age of 13. The somewhat surprising move was a stark contrast from Modi's campaign rhetoric. The fact that both countries wanted quick result was shown by the December 2014 visit of the Bangladesh President Abdul Hamid to India. The high level visits are seen as a desire on both sides to improve the relations. This was received well in both the countries.

At his meetings with the Bangladesh Prime Minister on the side-lines of multilateral evens such as the SAARC summit in Kathmandu in November 2014 and the United Nations General Assembly in New York in September 2014, Prime Minister Modi reassured Sheikh Hasina on the Land Boundary Agreement and Teesta. The two issues, he assured her, would be resolved soon. He was able to deliver the Land Boundary Agreement before his June2015 visit to Dhaka while Teesta is still on the table.

Modi was keen to take forward the framework laid down by his predecessor Manmohan Singh both during Hasina's visit to Delhi in 2010 and his own visit to Dhaka in 2011. At the bilateral level, it will be a major challenge to overcome the growing anti-India sentiments in Bangladesh. Sushma Swaraj claims that these were things of the past. "You should speak about this in the past tense. There was an anti India feeling but if you go now you will see a change. It is totally a different thing."[112]

With regard to cross-border security, Modi will have to continue to rely on Bangladesh's cooperation to prevent insurgent groups. This is imperative because the situation in the Northeast improved significantly due to Hasina's action against insurgent groups working against India's interest. Dhaka also expects that Modi would play a catalyst's role in expanding Indian business in Bangladesh given his close connections with the business houses.

Modi and the Northeast Chief Ministers

In the changing political environment, regional stakes are increasingly becoming a factor. While foreign policy may be the Centre's responsibility, New Delhi also needs to involve concerned

112 Author's interview with Sushma Swaraj(March 2015)

States in some of its foreign policy formulations and decision-making processes. Modi's commitment to bring about economic recovery and create jobs can only be executed when peace prevails inside India and in the neighbourhood. Bangladesh is a huge market for India, which could be exploited and vice versa. However everyone knows that disputes between Bangladesh and India directly involve the Indian States of West Bengal, Assam, Tripura, Meghalaya and Mizoram, and the Modi government needs to seek their views, particularly the non-BJP -ruled States.

India's domestic and electoral compulsions, however, have become more complex. Mamata Banerjee and Modi are not on the same page on many issues and developments within West Bengal and the changing dynamics of the Centre – State relationship has also come into play. Mamata's own position has become shaky with scams emerging involving her party leaders. In the face of the persisting Sardha chit fund scam and emerging evidence of Bangladeshi terror networks operating out of West Bengal, Mamata desperately needs some quick deflection.

Also, with Muslims making up over 30% of the West Bengal electorate, the choices were obvious. What better way to strengthen its hold on the Muslims than by extending a hand of friendship towards Bangladesh? Her visit to Dhaka from February 19 -21, 2015 was a significant development. She sent out positive signals to Prime Minister Sheikh Hasina, who was disappointed with her refusal to accompany Manmohan Singh in 2011. The BNP-led Opposition looks uncompromising and the Awami League's popularity is not soaring either. A possible resolution of Teesta would be very welcome for Hasina. While Mamata is in a position to prepare the ground to move positively on this critical outstanding issue Hasina would be grateful for the rescue, and Modi would be indebted to West Bengal for making a deal possible. The visit had gone off well with good atmospherics and good neighbourly gestures. It is clear that when the interests of the State and the Centre converged there were positive results.

Modi visits Bangladesh

Prime Minister Modi's visit to Bangladesh, which followed in June 2015, took the ties to a new height. Modi went to Dhaka armed with the Land Boundary Agreement and secondly he also managed to take Mamata with him while signing the agreement in Dhaka. **On the LBA, Modi has shown his political deftness by neutralising opposition from his own party units in Assam and West Bengal and then bringing Chief Ministers — Tarun Gogoi of Assam and Mamata Banerjee of West Bengal — on board. When the Centre could persuade the regional satrap, the Centre gets it way.** Mamata did show that she followed her independent politics by travelling separately to Dhaka. Sheikh Hasina received her rolling out a red carpet befitting a Head of State.

Modi's intent to improve the ties was reflected in the 22 agreements the two neighbours signed on various issues including connectivity, education, infrastructure, maritime and energy security, and trade, among others. He didn't forget to assure Dhaka that the contentious water-sharing issue would be pursued. "Panchi, Pavan aur pani" (birds, air and water) do not need visas; he said which was hint enough that there would soon be some movement on the Teesta water-sharing issue.

The agreement on establishing a Special Economic Zone (SEZ) near the Bangladesh-India border had also broken new ground. This will help Indian companies for domestic markets in both countries and for export. "The $2 billion new Line of Credit announced by Modi during the visit will help in such capital- intensive projects. The Inland Waterway Trade and Transit Treaty (IWTT) had been renewed as has the omnibus Trade Agreement."[113] In short, by any standard the 36- hour Modi visit to Bangladesh was seen as highly successful

Begum Khaleda Zia has also shown positive signs of having good relations with the Modi government. Begum Zia's optimism

---

113 Pinaki Ranjan Chakrvarti, *'PM Modi's visit has set the tone for future cooperation beteen the two countries even closer'* June 8, 2015. The Economic Times Blogs,

is evident when she says; "I am confident that Indo-Bangladesh relations will see stability and balance when our Party is in office. We believe in bilateral relation that ensures mutuality of benefit in all fields and where our outstanding problems are resolved urgently through dialogue and discussions in a spirit of goodwill. Such an approach will enhance mutual trust and confidence and give our relations a positive boost."[114]

Modi however did not raise the critical issues of infiltration, repatriation, smuggling and illegal trade with his Bangladeshi counterpart.

The credit for leaving such a big impact and raising such high hopes goes to both the leaders, Narendra Modi and Sheikh Hasina. Mamata Banerjee also gets some share of credit as she had ultimately supported the LBA. Regional connectivity will help not only both nations, but also the entire region. Indeed, neither India nor Bangladesh can expect to be part of the Asian Highway without connecting with one another

Indo Bangladesh Economic ties

No doubt economy and trade occupies a special place in the Indo-Bangladesh relations. Bangladesh is one of the most important markets in the SAARC region for the Indian exports. On the other side Bangladesh's exports to India had been consistently declining over the decades. India and Bangladesh need to establish long-term economic linkages in trade, investment and infrastructure for mutual benefit. Diversifying trade and commerce would give a boost to economic relations. The two countries should try to keep contentious issues aside and concentrate and cooperate on issues of common interest, which would help both the countries.

Indeed the full potential of the economic cooperation are yet to be fully exploited. The trade balance of Bangladesh with India has always been in the negative. As Muchkund Dubey notes, "There are various reasons for the trade imbalance between the two countries. These include faster trade liberalization by Bangladesh as compared to that by India and the declining rate of the exchange value of the

114 Author's interview with Khaleda Zia, (3-7 March, 2014)

rupee as compared to that of Bangladesh currency Taka. However, the main reason lies in the structural asymmetry of the economies of the two countries. Whereas the Indian economy is diversified and technologically advanced, the economy of the Bangladesh suffers from a backward industry and inadequate infrastructure, low productivity and a limited export base."[115]

After the first four years of planned process after the Liberation War, there has not been any structured model for trade and economic cooperation. The Treaty of Cooperation, Friendship and Peace signed between Indira Gandhi and Mujibur Rahmanhad the exports and imports identified, trade limited to the two governments and the payment was in rupees. It also provided for border trade between Bangladesh and Indian Border States like Assam, West Bengal, Tripura, and Manipur. But this was suspended in October 1972 after it was found a lot of illegal trade was taking place. Rupee trade also was stopped since 1975. A joint Economic Commission experiment in 1972, 1982 were not a success as they hardly ever met. While the trade between the two countries showed a sharp upward trend in the mid nineties following Bangladesh adopting liberalization measures, New Delhi also made efforts to increase the trade. Under the SAARC Preferential Trading Arrangement (SAPTA) India has offered duty concessions on a large number of items. The trade volume of $6.5 billion between the two countries is impressive Bangladesh's exports to India account for a mere $ 500 million. India needs to narrow the gap. There is a growing feeling in Bangladesh that the growing trade only benefits India.

If India's access to Northeast becomes a political issue in Bangladesh, its access to Nepal, Bhutan and Myanmar could also be treated the same way by India. Trade and transit through waterways between the two countries is regulated by the Protocol on Inland Water Transit and Trade, which was first signed in 1972. The Protocol has been in force continuously since then being renewed regularly for periods of 2 to 3 years. Cargo vessels intending to operate under the Protocol have to obtain voyage permission of the Bangladesh Inland

---

115 Muchkund Dubey, *'India's Foreign policy,'* Pearson Publishers, 2012, P 109

Water Transport Authority and Inland Waterways Authority of India for operating in the waterways of the respective country.

One important thing is that the economic reforms initiated by Bangladesh in 1982 and by India in 1991 have resulted less government control in both the countries. However, the private sector is still not very keen to invest in either country. The major business/investment destinations in the Northeast fall within 20 km perimeter from the Bangladesh capital, Dhaka that gives an exclusive attraction for business between Bangladesh and Northeast India. Since many states in the Northeast suffer from underdevelopment, they have huge demands for the outside products. Bangladesh-Northeast trade is mainly conducted through Assam, Meghalaya and Tripura with ranking Meghalaya number one in terms of trade volume.

Another ticklish issue is the export of natural gas from Bangladesh to India. "Bangladesh Oil reserves are estimated at 56.9 million barrels and the country's proved gas reserves are estimated at 10.6 trillion cubic feet (tcf) although a 2000 study by the USGS places them at 32.1 tcf."[116] While India needs this gas, anti- India elements in Bangladesh oppose it arguing that selling gas to India would make it more powerful. Ambassador Deb Mukharji notes, " The fact that Bangladesh would be able to virtually wipe out the trade deficit with India (assuming it has sufficient reserves) with even moderate gas export and create a State of some dependency of its large neighbour is rarely touched upon. What should be clear and relatively simple economic decision gets bogged down in politics"[117]

Bangladesh is experiencing huge energy shortages. It has for long been keen on sourcing hydropower from Nepal and Bhutan. Both countries have agreed to expedite inter-grid connectivity and showcased their willingness to cooperate in the development and sale of electricity, including generation from renewable sources.

---

116 Centre for energy economics, http://www.beg.utexas.edu/energyecon/ new-era/case_studies/Gas_Monetization_in_Bangladesh.pdf

117 Deb Mukharji, *editor J.N. Dixit, 'External affairs, Cross Border relations.' Bangladesh chapter,* Roli books, 2003, P 208

Lessons Learnt and the Way Forward

New Delhi has to shed this patronising way of dealing with Bangladesh and convince Dhaka that New Delhi is indeed a good friend and not a bully. Indeed, Indian policy towards Bangladesh varied from treating it as a friendly but weak nation to taking it for granted over the decades. India's overt meddling in Bangladeshi politics has led to an anti-Indian sentiment in that country. The Modi government can give a clear message that they are interested in friendly relations with Bangladesh.

The second is to resolve some of the outstanding issues like the Teesta River water sharing. While doing so, New Delhi should give an impression that Bangladesh gets its justified share of water. The third is to continue high level visits and interaction at the highest level so that misunderstandings are removed. The fourth and more important lesson is to keep the Border States including Assam and Tripura on board on any dealings with the neighbour even if the Opposition parties rule them.

The fifth is to improve connectivity, which will help not only the North-eastern States but also Bangladesh to gain more prosperity and access to the neighbourhood. The sixth is facilitating trade and economic cooperation between India and Bangladesh. The on-again off-again relationship has not helped trade. Exchange, though the cultural and people-to-people relationship across the border has remained warm and close. Access to seaport in Chittagong and road transit rights through the country will transform the troubled economies of India's Northeast and integrate them far better to the mainland. Bangladeshi entrepreneurs are cash rich and innovative, and free trade and investment opportunities between the two countries will benefit India as much as it will do to Bangladesh.

The balance of trade is hugely adverse against Bangladesh. This is a matter of great sensitivity even though there is, in most years, an even larger adverse trade balance for Bangladesh with China. In recent years the Government of India has been positive and liberal towards Bangladesh on trade related issues through a number of unilateral concessions, both bilaterally and within the ambit of SAFTA (South Asia Free Trade Agreement).

The Agreement on Bilateral Investment Promotion and Protection signed between India and Bangladesh in February 2009 is one such important facilitator. This should ease the consideration and approval of major investment proposals such as the one made by India's Tata group of companies for a $3 billion investment in Bangladesh.

The seventh is not to give an impression to the Bangladeshis that New Delhi prefers one political party and not the other as it did in the 2014 January elections when the Indian government openly lobbied for Prime Minister Sheikh Hasina. It left a bitter taste.

The eighth is to build the future relationship with the neighbour on a solid foundation of mutual trust. New Delhi should extend generous grants and soft loans to Bangladesh for important projects such as the Ganges Barrage project and the modernization of the Bangladesh railway system. This will go far in bridging misunderstandings and demonstrate India's genuine interest in their prosperity and yield rich dividends.

The ninth is to narrow the list of irritants between the two countries. It ranges from sharing waters of the common rivers and cross-border movement of people (border killings), incidences of abduction of the Bangladeshi citizens from bordering area to balance of trade (reducing deficit), addressing border disputes and many more.

The tenth is that since New Delhi has been given assurance that its security concerns will be addressed; now it is the turn of the Modi government not only to enhance the bilateral relations but also find common ground. Despite political and security impediments and a historical record of mistrust, Bangladesh, India and Myanmar can look beyond. Bangladesh is militarily important and it is in India's interest to ensure military and security cooperation.

It is only after Hasina came back to power in 2008, that corroborative evidence of such activities is coming to light. The Pakistan Army and ISI have successfully retained active links with the Bangladesh Army, its intelligence agencies and with religion-based political parties like the Jamaal e -Islamic. Therefore it is important for the Modi government to keep good relations with not only Bangladesh but also with other neighbours like Bhutan, Nepal and Myanmar. In the affairs of South Asia, it is time New Delhi thought and acted like a big country, and engages the neighbours with sincerity and fairness. India needs Bangladesh as much as Bangladesh needs India.

Chapter 4

India and Nepal

No two neighbours could be as closely linked as Nepal and India. Their destinies have been intertwined for centuries and their geophysical proximity is equally important. They have strong religious, political, social and cultural ties as well as an open border, which binds the two countries. Further, Nepal is located between two giants - India on its South and China on the North and borders on three sides with India while its Northern Frontier lies with Tibet (China). Nepal is India's sole buffer with China, especially after Tibet was absorbed by China during the 1950s. Nepal's foreign policy is also influenced by its internal political dynamics. So it is not surprising that centuries of interaction between Nepal and India have created tremendous religious, ethnic and cultural affinities.

India's relations with Nepal have seen highs and lows over the decades and their relations are at multiple layers. The traditional elites of Nepal- the Ranas and the Shahs- continue to have matrimonial links with the erstwhile princely families of India. At another level, the Madheshis of the Terai region have what they call the 'Roti- Beti ka Rishta' with the people of Bihar, UP and other Himalayan Border States. In yet another level, there are many Nepalese who live and work in India and have family links with Indian citizens of Nepali origin. The chief of Nepal army is an honorary General of Indian army which honour has been reciprocated by Nepal to the Indian chief of army. There is a separate Gorkha regiment in the Indian army. Therefore these ties make the Indo Nepal relations unique. As Prof Muni explains, "at any given point of-time India's Nepal policy was shaped by multiple stakeholders including ministry of external affairs, bureaucracy, the Indian army, business community, members of former princely rulers, political parties, Hindu interest groups and States bordering Nepal like U.P, Bihar, Uttarakhand and Sikkim. There came a time when India led the international community shifting its strategy from supporting the palace against the Maoists to even considering the Maoists as part of a democratic solution. The Maoists used the political instability to achieve their goals."[1]

New Delhi has been an active player in Nepal's domestic politics for decades. "The open border runs across 20 Districts of five Indian States - Bihar, Uttar Pradesh, Sikkim, West Bengal and Uttarakhand. "The legality of the border is enforced through specific border check-posts, including 19 agreed immigration check posts, 22 mutual trade routes and 15 third-country transit routes. There are six transit points for nationals of other countries, who require entry and exit visas to cross the border. One important factor in the Indo – Nepal ties is the role played by the leaders from U.P and Bihar in influencing the Nepal policy right from Jawaharlal Nehru's time."[2]

Ambassador Shyam Saran points out that any government in New Delhi was always pro- Nepali Congress. "It was not as if anybody in the political circle was hostile to Nepal or hostile to any kind of democratic system coming in Nepal. Yes, to that extent Nepal received high level political attention and certainly people like Jayaprakaash Narayan and Chandrashekhar played an important role."[3]

The vital role of UP, Uttarakhand and Bihar in Indo- Nepal ties

One should understand the relationship between Nepal and Indian Border State leaders, particularly Bihar, Uttarakhand and U.P. There had always been some connection between the two during the pro democracy struggle and even later. Their close relationship with Nepal has been age old. Nepali Congress leaders Ganeshnan Singh, Krishna Prasad Bhattarai, Girija Prasad Koirala and B.P Koirala were

---

1   Author's interview with Prof. S.D. Muni (30 January 2014)

2   Ajit Kumar Singh, *'India Nepal subversion without borders'*, http://www. southasianoutlook.com/issues/2006/december/southasia.html

3   Author's interview with Shyam Saran, (6 January 2014)

in close contact with Indian leaders including Jawaharlal Nehru, Dr Ram Manohar Lohia, Jayaprakash Narayan and Samajwadi Janata Party (SJP) leader Chandrashekhar who later became Prime Minister in 1990.

The Nepal democratic parties generally desire to have good relations with the people on the other side. Kathmandu had also understood that the Himalayan Border States were vital for maintaining cordial Indo-Nepal relations and that engagement with them had to be more prominent especially when it came to vital issues like water, land and power.

My Hypothesis

The hypothesis in this chapter is different from Bangladesh and Sri Lanka chapters as in the fifties, sixties and seventies it was the national leaders who had roots in UP and Bihar who played a major role in influencing the Nepal policy. **Though they were of national stature, stalwarts like Jayaprakash Narayan, Dr Lohia and Chandrashekhar, who hail from these States, had deep interest in India's Nepal policy. In short, these leaders of stature are able to influence the Centre's Nepal policy when it converged with the interests of New Delhi.** They were the ones who supported the birth of Nepali Congress and its fight with the Ranas and then the monarchy. This relationship continued through the decades and Indian leaders including the Communist leaders like Surjeet Singh and Sitaram Yechury and NCP leader Devi Prasad Tripathi have played a significant role in the subsequent political developments of Nepal. Even Prime Minister Nehru went along when they supported the removal of the Ranas and helped the return of the King in the fifties. New Delhi had provided sanctuary for the rebels in India. Even in the nineties and after, the Nepali Congress leaders had close links with various political parties in North India who supported the 1990 Jan Andolan 1 and the 2006 Jan Andolan 2. **It was Chandrashekhar's influence with the then National Front government, which helped the emergence of the multi party democracy in 1990. In 2006, Prime Minister Manmohan Singh supported the Jan Andolan 2 and the subsequent peace process and facilitated the return of democracy bowing to the pressure of his alliance partners including**

the Left parties and the Nationalist Congress Party. The 12- point agreement of November 2005, between mainstream political parties and the Maoists was concluded in Delhi with Indian government's blessings and facilitation. The present Modi government is helping the peace process. There are several other such examples of India helping the Nepal rebels. Therefore India is often charged with an intrusive approach in Nepal's internal politics. That is why the Indo-Nepal relations do not fall under the usual paradigm of inter-state relations.

2. The second hypothesis is that when the views of the national leaders hailing from the region or the regional chieftains differ with the views of the Centre, they are unlikely to influence the Centre's Nepal policy. The Bihar Chief Minister Nitish Kumar has often raised the issue of floods and advocated water management to tackle floods and boost hydropower. So does the Uttarakhand chief minister Harish Rawat. Bihar and Uttarakhand demand that there should be big dams on these rivers and water should be released from them in regulated manner, so that the rivers in Bihar do not overflow and their courses do not change. But Bihar or UP has to talk with Nepal via our foreign office, and a communication gap has developed over time. Our External Affairs Ministry too has its own priorities while dealing with Nepal with the result the regional chieftains are unable to influence India's Nepal policy to the extent they desire.

India's Nepal policy has always been crafted by a handful of officials and former princelings, which had connections with the Nepal royal family. Ambassador K.V. Rajan, who served as the Indian envoy to Nepal sums it up succinctly "The past five decades of India – Nepal relations have witnessed many lost opportunities, costly misjudgements and avoidable misunderstandings. It is remarkable that successive governments in both countries have so comprehensively failed to establish a stable mature relationship based on mutual trust and a long term vision of cooperation."[4]

---

4   K.V. Rajan, *Editor J.N. Dixit, 'External Affairs, cross border Relations,' Nepal chapter*, Roli books 2003, P 97

Major concerns of the Border States

What is however lacking by and large is that the Centre consulting or taking the advice of the regional chieftains. In the fifties, sixties, seventies and eighties, the Centre took unilateral decisions on its Nepal policy although Nehru informed Jayaprakash Narayan and Dr Lohia and chief ministers like G.B. Pant, Sri Krishna Sinha. Even later on the Bihar and UP governments did not have much say in the Nepal policy though they express their concerns on water, security and border related issues.

Issues and concerns

What are the major concerns of these Border States regarding Nepal? Ambassador Shyam Saran notes that they raise mainly water related issues like Koshi Barrage and Gomantaka Barrage. There were also issues relating to security, particularly when the Maoist insurgency was at its height in Nepal. There were apprehensions about connections with similar groups on the Indian side of the border. "So the involvement of the State governments was in relation to certain specific issues rather than on a broad based kind of a thing. Essentially it was about these two issues – water and security. In a couple of cases we also had some concern from Sikkim and Uttarakhand–where the issue was about immigration. Because of the economic and security situation in Nepal fairly a large number of Nepalese were migrating to these States. Earlier they used to come as labour during winter months and go back in summer. When the situation in Nepal started deteriorating they did not go back and instead became residents in some of these States. So once in a while that used to come up, particularly with respect to Sikkim and Uttarakhand. Chief Minister at that time in Bihar was Rabri Devi and Pawan Kumar Chamling in Sikkim and in UP it was Mayawati. So there was no overriding involvement in our relations with the neighbours.[5]"

Kanwal Sibal, another former Foreign Secretary notes that there is need for a clear-cut Nepal policy in view of the open border between India and Nepal. There is need for a much larger concern on

5   Author's interview with Shyam Saran, (6,January, 2014)

account of fake currency, counterfeit currency and terrorists coming across open border. But in terms of actually restricting movement on the border, it becomes a huge issue because of the intermingling of populations, which had gone on for centuries. There are areas where the so called border is going through actually inhabited areas on one side of Nepal and the other side of India. Then it is difficult to give them a feeling that India no longer considers them as part of age- old ties because they are also instruments in terms of influencing domestic Nepalese policies. Then the other big issue has been connectivity. "New Delhi has neglected this important aspect of improving connectivity with Nepal."[6]

Nepal is also important for various other reasons. New Delhi feels that Kathmandu has not given due consideration of its security concerns as the open border makes it easier for hostile forces to infiltrate, pushing counterfeit and fake currency, encouragement of fundamentalist religious groups and insurgents to function to the detriment of Indian interests. New Delhi is aware that with Pakistan and China wooing Nepal, India will no longer be of the same importance to Kathmandu.

Another key issue is its economic development. The landlocked Nepal has been mainly depending on India for its economy. If Nepal has to prosper it can only be through mutual economic cooperation between the two countries. Nepal needs energy, connectivity, a new Constitution that is durable, inclusive and democratic, and a political disposition that supports the entrepreneurial talent of its people.

India accounts for nearly two-thirds of Nepal's foreign trade, 70 per cent of Nepal's exports, and almost half of its foreign direct investments. "Around 40 per cent of Nepal's tourists come from India and more than 5 million Nepalese find employment in India. The trade balance between the two countries has been quite skewed. The other big opportunities include Indian partnership in water and environment management for the protection of the Himalayan ecosystem, including soil conservation, re-forestation, and rational land use for horticulture and bio-agriculture.

---

6   Author's interview with Kanwal Sibal(13 July 2014)

On connectivity and infrastructure, India could help by building a road bridge over the Mahakali, extend Exim Bank loans and provide viability gap funding for the Kathmandu-Terai Fast Track road, the international airport at Nijgadh and new cross-border power grids. Nepal could build an East-West railway (prospected by Rail India Technical and Economic Service (RITES),) along the highway built by India. There are many more such opportunities, which could be exploited by both countries.

A major area of concern is the exploitation of water resources for mutual benefit and attracting Indian investment to Nepal by creating a favourable environment for investors. Rivers flowing from Nepal to India have been frequently shifting their course during the monsoons over the decades. As a result, certain parts of the border regions either shifts to Nepal or to India depending on the shifting of the river course. This affects the Border States like UP, Bihar, Uttarakhand and other Himalayan States and farmers from both countries find encroachment upon it for agricultural purposes. Both countries have already (unofficially) agreed that 98 per cent of the border is demarcated except two disputed areas in Kalapani and Susta.

Indo- Nepal historic ties

To understand the Indo-Nepal ties, tensions, problems and positive and negative aspects, one has to trace their age- old ties. Historically, Nepal-India boundary demarcation took place after the Anglo-Nepal War of 1814-1816. As there was no big territorial dispute between Nepal and China both have respected the existing traditional line and have lived in harmony.

The history of Nepal could be traced back to 1769 when King Prithvi Narayan Shah unified some principalities and named it Nepal. Nepali became its common language and Hinduism its religion. The rapid expansion of Nepal was halted in 1816 when the British East India Company defeated the Gorkha army.

Nepal's strategic ties with India date back to the Treaty of Sugauli of 1816 signed between the Nepalese King and the British East India Company. Under the Treaty, Nepal ceded those areas won by the Gorkha army to the British and also withdrew from all the occupied territory in Sikkim, as there was no formal Treaty regarding Nepal-Sikkim boundary. The British annexed large parts of Nepal (including parts of present day Uttarakhand, Himachal Pradesh and Sikkim) and stationed a British Resident in Kathmandu. Nepal regained some of the lost territory when the monarch helped the British during the 1857 uprising. However, Nepal still lays claim to certain parts of Indian Territory, like Kalapani, along the India-Nepal border.

The whole thing changed in 1846 when Jung Bahadur Rana, a military official seized power and installed the Rana autocracy for the next 104 years. The Ranas followed a hereditary system and became Prime Ministers although they kept a powerless monarchy alive.

Paradigm shift after India's independence

The Indo – Nepalese relations underwent a paradigm shift after India's independence in 1947. While India gave shelter to the rebel Nepali leaders during political disturbance in the forties, fifties and sixties, Indian socialist leaders like Ram Manohar Lohia and Jayaprakash Narayan had also been hiding in Nepal. As author Tribhuvan Nath points out even earlier a crucial turn came in 1946 when Jayaprakash Narayan and Dr Lohia, then hiding underground for their role in the 'Quit India' movement found sanctuary in the Nepal Terai region close to Bihar. The Ranas held them hostage in the Hanuman Nagar prison. But the two leaders escaped to the jungles of Terai. **"The genesis of Nepali liberation from the Rana rule was actually laid during this rendezvous between obscure Nepalese workers and two socialist leaders."[7]**

The case for Nepalese freedom became a burning issue in both the countries when Dr Lohia, as chairman of the foreign policy committee of the Congress Socialist Party mentioned it in the party's report. In October 1946, the Nepali Congress was born in Benares in Uttar Pradesh with the backing of the Nepalese students living in that town.

---

7   Tribhuvan Nath, ' *The Nepalese dilemma, 1960-74,*' Sterling Publishers, 1975, P 157

Rebellion against the Rana rule

Eclipsing the royal authority, the Ranas ruled Nepal till 1950. "The system of hereditary Prime Ministers was dealt with a fatal blow by the armed insurrection started by the Nepali Congress Party in the autumn of 1950- 51 with the secret blessings of King Tribhuvan and the connivance of the Government of India."[8] As Rishikesh Shaha notes that apart from allowing the Nepali rebels to use Indian Territory as a base for their activities, the Nehru government continued to recognize and support King Tribhuvan even after he took refuge in Delhi. When the Ranas removed the King, New Delhi sent two planes on November 10, 1950 to bring him and his family to Delhi and accorded all courtesies due to a visiting head of a State.

The Ranas pronounced the three- year old Prince Gyanendra Bir Bikram Shah Dev as the new King on November 7, 1950 declaring that King Tribhuvan had abdicated. When the British wanted to give recognition to the boy King Gyanandra, Nehru successfully prevailed upon the British Prime Minister not to recognize him. However, Gyanendra became the King after the 2001 palace massacre.

Nehru kept the U.P Chief Minister Govind Ballab Pant informed about these decisions. In a letter to Pant on November 20, 1950 Nehru wrote, "I am at present merely taking you into my confidence so that you may keep in touch with developments. The decision that we have already taken in regard to the King is an important one and from that all kinds of consequences flow. It will necessarily mean following it up in some way or other later, if the present Prime Minister refuses to accept our decision."[9]**While taking the decision, Nehru merely kept Pant informed and did not consult him.**

King Tribhuvan returns to Nepal

As mentioned earlier, Prime Minister Nehru played a crucial role in the return of King Tribhuvan to Kathmandu. It was Nehru who

---

8 Rishikesh Shaha, *Editor D.P Tripathi, ' Nepal in transition, Monarchy in Nepal: Where does it go form here,'* Vij Books India Private Ltd, P 166.

9 Avtar Singh Bhasin, *Nepal-India, Nepal-China relations Documents 1947- June 2005*, Geetika publications, P 130

nudged the Ranas to go for political reforms and persuaded them that any solution to the Nepal issue must consist of the King not only returning to Kathmandu with full dignity but also introduction of democratic reforms, including sharing of power with the people's representatives. Pushed to a corner, the Ranas fell in line.

Within weeks, the Ranas, New Delhi and the Nepali Congress signed what is called the "Delhi Samjhota" (Delhi Accord) after which the King returned to Nepal on February 15, 1951. He formed a cabinet three days later and declared democracy ending 104 years of Rana rule on February 18. This restored the King to the position of Constitutional monarch. Nehru advised the King to choose Matrika Prasad Koirala, brother of Bishweshwar Prasad Koirala as Prime Minister. This developed tension between the two brothers and it was Jayaprakash Narayan who later brought them together. The Koirala family has dominated the Nepal politics for decades.

Treaty of Peace and Friendship of 1950

The first important milestone came when India and Nepal signed a Treaty of Peace and Friendship in 1950. This enabled the two countries to respect each other's sovereignty and territorial integrity and granted rights to Nepalese and Indian citizens to reside and work (and even obtain citizenship) in India and Nepal respectively. Further, India allowed transit trade across its territory and the use of Indian ports for importing and exporting commodities free of customs duties. Gorkhas still form a part of the Indian army and there is a Gorkha regiment.

As Ambassador K.V. Rajan puts it, the Treaty which was a straight forward imitation of understandings dating back to British India days, and basically offered economic opportunities in India for Nepalese nationals against Nepalese assurances that India's security concerns would be respected, became an irritant in India-Nepal relations as soon as it was signed on 31 July, 1950. In Nepal's eyes, India's growing sense of insecurity, generated by an apparently aggressive China, had compelled it to yield to expediency, abandon its support for the incipient democratic movement against the autocratic Rana regime, and seek to constrain Nepal's sovereignty so that it was compatible with India's security perceptions. "The Treaty, signed between the Indian Ambassador with Prime Minister Mohun Shumshere Rana (a disrespect for protocol which added insult to Kathmandu's sense of injury) in the last days of his discredited regime, was accompanied by an exchange of letters which was not made public until many years later — in 1959, when they were placed on the table of the Indian Parliament."[10] With the exception of King Tribhuvan (who actually suggested Nepal's merger with India), the monarchy in Nepal was actively engaged for several decades in undermining the Treaty in letter, or spirit or both.

Kathmandu was filled with slogans of "Nehru Ki jai" on June 18, 1951 when the visiting Indian Prime Minister addressed his first public meeting. In an effort to assuage their feelings Nehru assured the Nepalese people, "If some of you feel that India wishes to interfere in your affairs, then that would be a wrong notion. Firstly because this would be contrary to the fundamentals of our national policy, and secondly, it is in our own interests to honour your independent status."[11]

Nehru explains the Treaty to chief ministers

At home, explaining the main points of the Treaty, Nehru told the Chief Ministers in his letter of March 1, 1950: "Of course, it does not mean that we approve of the political or social structure of Nepal at the present moment. Unfortunately this structure is completely feudal and backward and we have been laying the greatest stress during the past two or three years on substantial reforms being introduced. I regret to say that practically no results have been reached thus far in spite of this pressure."[12]

After India became independent, relationship with Nepal changed due to two main reasons – the rise of communism in China and the increasing Chinese involvement in Nepal. Even today the

---

10 K.V. Rajan, '*should the 1950 Treaty be scrapped?*' The Hindu, May 3, 2008

11 A.S.Bhasin, *Nepal- India, Nepal-China relations Documents 1947- June 2005*, Geetika publications, 2005, page 50, Volume 1

12 A.S. Bhasin, *Nepal- India, Nepal -China relations Documents 1947- June 2005*, Geetika publications, 2005,P no xx1x

Chinese influence in the neighbourhood is a concern for India. Moreover, New Delhi worked with the Nepali Congress because it was closely associated with India's independent struggle and Indian leaders from UP and Bihar.

Nehru pointed out later "In the past, before India became independent, Nepal was not really independent. It was very much under the British government, in regard to external matters. When we became independent we went much further in recognizing the independence of Nepal than the British government had done – and this was before the changes when the Rana regime was there. India's special position with regard to foreign affairs was recognized and that was an admitted fact. As far diplomatic relations between Nepal and China, that is a matter which the Nepalese government will deal with in its own way."[13]

Even after independence, India did not free itself from the British mind-set. As K.V. Rajan puts it, "India's security perspective was essentially a hand -me -down from British India. India expected that, given an age old ties of history, culture and religion and the sheer facts of geography, Nepal's own self interest would compel acceptance inextricable inter linkages between the security interests of the two countries."[14] Nepal challenged this thinking. The imminent takeover of Tibet by China left India with no option but to formalize common security arrangements with Nepal as quickly as possible.

Nehru's patronizing attitude

Nehru adopted a patronising attitude towards Nepal. There was complete understanding between the Indian and Nepali Congress leaders but Nehru had a larger vision for Nepal. In a letter to Jayaprakash Narayan expressing his dismay at the behaviour of the Nepali Congress leaders Nehru predicted, "Nothing can stop a revolution in Nepal, except the folly of those who are supporting it. The revolution is, I believe, an indigenous one and a large number

---

13 Avtar Singh Bhasin, *Nepal- India, Nepal -China relations Documents 1947- June 2005*, Geetika Publications, 2005, P no 59

14 K.V. Rajan, *editor J.N. Dixit, 'External Affairs :India's cross Border relations'*. Roli books, 2003, P 105

of the people of Nepal sympathize with it. Most people in India also sympathize with it. Your opponents abroad to show that this is just an example of Indian imperialism and that we have engineered all this are carrying on widespread propaganda. This obviously can do a great deal of harm to the whole movement. We cannot ignore external forces at work against us. What Koirala suggested would have put an end to the idea of an indigenous movement and made it just an adventure of the Indian government. That is just what I am afraid of. Adventurist tactics in politics or warfare seldom succeed. Daring does succeed and risk may be taken, but adventurism is infantile"[15]

Nepali Congress involvement in freedom struggle

Viewing it from the other side, B.P. Koirala recalls how the Nepali Congress leaders got involved with the Indian freedom movement. "One was we were exiled from Nepal. When it became too hot for us to be in Nepal we had come to India. We came in contact with the people of revolutionary movement in Benares (Uttar Pradesh) and Bihar. That is how we started. Then ultimately we came to the conclusion that the liberation of Nepal or the democratization of Nepalese system was not possible unless India got her freedom.[16]"

Koirala recalls his meetings with Mahatma Gandhi. He also recalls the Kanpur All India Congress Committee (AICC) session of 1925, which he attended when Sarojini Naidu was the President. "I remember this because I did not understand a word of her speech. She spoke in English and that too very fast."[17] He first met Jawaharlal Nehru at the Meerut Congress session in 1946. He was sympathetic to the Nepal's problems. But at that time Nehru was the vice president of the Executive Council of the Viceroy and so he could not help much.

---

15 Avtar Singh Bhasin, *Nepal- India, Nepal -China relations Documents 1947- June 2005*, Geetika publications, 2005, P 133-134

16 D.P. Tripathi, *Editor, D.P. Tripathi, 'Nepal in transition,' Koirala interview*, Vij Books India PVT Ltd, P 47

17 Ibid P 45-46

Koirala got interested in Indian politics because he had some association with the people of the revolutionary movements in Bihar and UP. He first came into contact in Benares with Jayaprakash Narayan's brother Rajeshwar Prasad who was his class fellow. Jayaprakash came to visit his brother in 1933. Lohia stayed with Koirala's another class fellow but he was not very intimate with Lohia. Explaining how they jumped into the Indian freedom struggle he recalls "Ultimately we came to the conclusion that the liberation of Nepal or the democratization of Nepal was not possible unless India got its freedom. In 1946 when we started Nepali Congress one of our slogans was that unless India became independent there would be no democratic movement in Nepal, because ultimately it was the same power, which was holding India to subjugation and was preventing the liberalization or democracy in Nepal. So our struggle for democracy in Nepal and the Indian people's struggle for independence became a joint venture in our eyes."[18]

B.P. Koirala acknowledges the contribution made by Ram Manohar Lohia in shaping the Nepali Congress. "Then Lohia got Gandhiji also interested in our movement. On the 28th January, two days before Gandhiji was killed I went with Lohia to meet him. It was he who introduced me to Gandhi and I spent the whole day with him."[19] Koirala was disappointed when Gandhi said "he could not be of any help to them. The Mahatma bluntly told him 'When my own people do not listen to me, how can I expect the Ranas to concede; I cannot be of any help.' These were his words. He was in a very frustrated mood."[20] Koirala has fond memories of Nehru but had disagreements with him on his China policy. They also differed on the economic policies.

---

18 D.P. Tripathi, *editor D.P. Tripathi 'Nepal in transition,'* Koirala interview, Vij books India Pvt. Ltd, P 47

19 Haridev Sharma, *Editor D.P.Tripathi, 'Nepal in transition, '* Koirala interview chapter, Vij Books India Pvt.Ltd, P49

20 Haridev Sharma, *Editor D.P.Tripathi, 'Nepal in transition,'* Koirala interview chapter, Vij Books India Pvt.Ltd, P49

Lohia and Jayaprakash Narayan influence India's Nepal policy

As a liberal and an ardent admirer of democracy, Jayaprakash Narayan advocated the end of monarchy. When B.P Koirala formed the Nepali Congress he became the foremost leader of the democratic Movement in Nepal. Jayaprakash Narayan openly supported the anti – Rana movement that also involved the use of arms. The Nationalist Congress Party (NCP) leader D.P. Tripathi recalls that the Nepali Congress leaders had very good relations with the Indian National Congress (INC) leadership. They decided to form the Nepali Congress on the lines of Indian National Congress. Since they were closer to the socialist leadership there was far more socialist content in their programmes. As Ambassador Bimal Prasad, who was India's envoy to Nepal in the nineties points out "He was so keenly interested in the end of Rana regime that he arranged supply of arms through Burma (Myanmar)."[21]**When Delhi also decided that the moment was ripe, it supported the Nepali Congress and the King in overthrowing the Ranas. Leaders like Jayaprakash Narayan and Dr Lohia carried a lot of weight.**

It is interesting to note that former West Bengal Chief Minister Jyoti Basu inaugurated the foundation of the Communist Party of Nepal. Then this party split into various factions but they had a very important role to play. D.P. Tripathi notes, "I remember Comrade Surjeet Singh telling me that the unity of these two- the Nepali Congress and the Nepali communists -would be good. We used to keep the rebels in the Jawaharlal Nehru University (JNU) hostel. Even when the hijackers came in 1974 – Durga Subedi and others had no place to go. So we kept them in the JNU. Nepali congress hijacked the plane, which was carrying money and gave it to B.P Koirala who was in Delhi. Before that many of them lived in Benares. Even B.P. lived in Benares for a long time. Then he came to Delhi and was living in H block in Green Park.[22]"

---

21 Bimal Prasad, *Editor D.P. Tripahti, 'Nepal in Transition,' Jayaprakash Narayan and Nepal*, Vij Books India Pvt.Ltd, P 134

22 Author's interview with D. P. Tripathi (7 January 2014)

Nehru's dominance over Nepal

There was impression that New Delhi treated Nepal as India's backyard since the time of Nehru and this mind-set continues even today in the Indian establishment both at the political as well as bureaucratic levels. In all matters relating to the conduct of foreign relations Nehru wanted Kathmandu to consult New Delhi. He told the Nepalese leaders "It is clearly understood that the foreign policy of Nepal and India is to be coordinated. This means that in any matter which affects Nepal, directly or indirectly India should consult the Nepalese government, and in any foreign policy matter which comes before the Nepalese government, they will consult the Government of India and coordinate their policy with that of India."[23]

How much Nehru influenced the leaders of Nepali Congress was evident when he wrote a letter on August 15, 1953 to the Nepalese Prime Minister M. P. Koirala. Nehru conceded Nepal's full independence yet expressed his reservations. "In another official Minute dated October 24, 1953 Nehru again asked the Ministry of External Affairs to draw the attention of the American Ambassador in Delhi to the activities of the Americans in Nepal and tell the Ambassador that, by Treaty and understanding, Nepal's foreign policy is conducted in consultation and in association with India's. Therefore, we expect other friendly countries to appreciate this position."[24]

King Mahendra brings uneasiness in Indo – Nepal ties

Meanwhile, when Mahendra, son of Tribhuvan Shah became the King on March 13, 1955, he took back all powers of the Ranas. He managed to dismantle Nepal's short-lived democracy and brought back absolute monarchy altering the course of Nepal politics. One by one almost all the political leaders were discredited and political power became centralized in the Royal palace. His regime ushered in a period of uneasiness between India and Nepal and also uncertainty

---

23 Avtar Singh Bhasin, *Nepal- India, Nepal -China relations Documents 1947- June 2005*, Geetika Publications, 2005, P xxxviii

24 Avtar Singh Bhasin, *Nepal-India, Nepal-China relations Documents 1947- June 2005*, Geetika Publications, 2005, P xxx

about the democratic process. He had a mind of his own and kept his own counsel. **Naturally, leaders like Jayaprakash Narayan and Dr Lohia viewed him with suspicion as he was against the Nepali democratic forces they supported.** Knowing that Nehru would not bless his actions, King Mahendra went ahead in a calculated manner.

King Mahendra moves closer to China

Almost at this point of time, in 1955 at the first large-scale Asian–African or the Afro Asian conference, also known as the Bandung Conference Nepal and China came closer. The two countries established formal diplomatic relations in the same year. By then Nepal was also admitted to the United Nations Organisation as a full- fledged member with the help of India. Within weeks of assuming power King Mahendra felt that the question of relations with China could not be postponed any longer. He chose Tanka Prasad Acharya, a votary of Marxism as his Prime Minister thinking Beijing would be pleased but Acharya soon realized that sharing power with the King was not workable. He resigned on July 13, 1957 and Kunwar Inderjeet Singh succeeded him. Significantly, China did not disturb India's moves in Nepal but there were gradual efforts on the part of Beijing to change the ' special position' held by New Delhi. The King began to talk of a 'balance of power policy' in relation to the neighbouring countries. Nepal and China opened negotiations for comprehensive relationship particularly relating to Tibet without taking India into confidence in the next year. The talks were held in Kathmandu contrary to the Indian advice to hold them in New Delhi. Nehru was annoyed when the new King did not consult the South Block. In fact it was the Chinese Premier Chou En-Lai who informed Nehru on August 18, 1956 that the Nepalese in their talks insisted on a Consulate General in Kathmandu and Lhasa on a reciprocal basis. Nehru reacted to these developments sharply and felt betrayed. In a letter to Bhagwan Sahay, the Indian envoy in Nepal on September 2, 1956 a miffed Nehru wrote "I wish to emphasize that, as I once pointed out to you previously, we must reconsider our attitude towards Nepal.... They have not only by passed us and practically ignored us, but have also done so with discourtesy. This is obviously a deliberate attitude to emphasize their complete independence from us. According to Chou En-Lai the

Nepalese government have stated to him that they have exchanged notes with USA concerning such matters as Consular representation, treatment of nationals, etc. All this is news to us. We seem to know less about Nepalese foreign relations than foreign countries."[25]

Nehru was in for more surprises when Nepal tried to expand its relations with other countries. On July 27 Moscow conveyed to New Delhi that the Soviet Union and Nepal had agreed to establish diplomatic relations and a resident mission was set up in Kathmandu for this purpose. Nehru was further surprised to learn that the two countries would be signing a Treaty of friendship. "The 'special relationship' that New Delhi perceived it enjoyed with Kathmandu, in fact never existed in so far as Nepal was concerned. The Nepalese political leaders, as pointed out above, had utilized every opportunity to undercut New Delhi. They listened to the homilies of New Delhi when visiting India, but had no compunction acting otherwise on return home. That King Tribhuvan was deferential to the Indian advice did not matter."[26]

President Rajendra Prasad visits Nepal

Another prominent Congress leader and India's first President Rajendra Prasad too had special interest in Nepal as he hailed from the bordering Indian State of Bihar. He was friendly and reiterated the warm ties between the two countries when he visited Kathmandu in 1956. He had also suggested a few things on Indo-Nepal relations in his letters to Nehru. In his banquet speech on October 22, the President said, "Your country and mine follow a policy of peace and friendship towards all. Therefore your friends are our friends and our friends are your friends. Any threat to the peace and security of Nepal is as much a threat to peace and security of India."[27] He

---

25 Avtar Singh Bhasin, *Nepal-India, Nepal-China relations Documents 1947- June 2005*, Geetika publications, 2005, P xxxv

26 Avtar Singh Bhasin, *Nepal-India, Nepal-China relations,Documents 1947- June 2005*, Geetika Publications, 2005, P xxxvii

27 Avtar Singh Bhasin, *Nepal-India, Nepal-China relations,Documents 1947- June 2005*, Geetika Publications, 2005, P 60 volume 1

reiterated once again the India would not interfere with the affairs of Nepal.

Nepali Congress wins democratic elections

In 1959 the multi- party Constitution was adopted. King Mahendra called for the first ever general elections in Nepal after much turmoil and a succession of short- lived governments. The Nepali Congress won as many as 74 of the 109 seats. However, when B.P Koirala took over as the Prime Minister of Nepal, there was tension between the King and newly elected Prime Minister.

Koirala maintains a balance between India and China

The Indo- Nepal relations became strained during Koirala's 18-month rule. New Delhi did not appreciate his attempts to maintain a balance between India and China. The duality of Nepal's policy towards her two big neighbours became more pronounced since the 1960 coup. As author Lok Raj Baral points out, "On the one hand King Mahendra was using China as a countervailing force against India until India and Nepal improved their strained relations. The hit and run activities carried out by the Nepali Congressmen from the Indian base had also made Mahendra and his lieutenants paranoid with the alleged support to the anti regime elements then considered as 'anti nationals'. Eventually both the King and China used each other for enhancing their interests.

King Mahendra took a bold decision, obviously to the chagrin of India by opening up the Himalayan route allowing the Chinese to construct a road linking Tibet with Kathmandu. Ridiculing Indian criticism, the King said that if communism didn't travel on a mule how it could come on a taxi!"[28] The King exploited Nepal's strategic location to a tremendous advantage. Secondly, he had successfully made sure that the Nepali Congress was fragmented. **India did not continue to support the ousted Nepali Congress leaders for political reasons despite local pressure.** King Mahendra's imposing monarchy lasted for the next 30 years.

---

28 Lok Raj Baral, *editor D.P. Tripathi, 'Nepal in Transition,' Monarchy in Nepal: where does it go from here,* Vij Books Pvt Ltd, P 161

Nepali Congress reaction against King Mahendra

Nehru was not happy when King Mahendra dismissed B.P Koirala on December 15, 1960 and took back full control with the help of the army. That year also marked the growing strain between India and China. The King justified his action by arguing that the Parliamentary democracy was not suited to Nepal and that he was going to introduce a democratic Panchayat system. Koirala's dismissal on December 15 had far reaching impact on the Indo – Nepal relations. For Nehru it came as a shock. Several members from the erstwhile ruling party crossed over to India and began operating from the Indian soil. New Delhi's reaction against the King's unexpected coup acted as a morale- booster for the Nepali Congress and other pro – democracy elements.

Blaming the political parties the King instituted a party-less Panchayat system two years later, which continued until 1990. Although for some months he knew that the King was not satisfied with the way things were and he was going to take some action Nehru did not know what action it would be. Speaking on the issue in the Indian Parliament on December 16, 1960, Nehru said, "A democratic experiment or practice that was going on has suffered a setback. That is all I can say about it."[29]

Former Foreign Secretary Shyam Saran recalls that the strained relations between the two countries were due to various reasons. It was there because for any Nepalese government whether it was monarchy or democracy, the best way to try and consolidate their political position was by playing the nationalist card. "Whom do you play the nationalist card against? The only country, which you can play this card against, is India because it has a very visible presence in Nepal. That aspect has been a kind of running theme in Nepal since King Mahendra's time. In 1960 when he dispensed with the old system with the multi-party system with the King exercising all political powers he did it by playing nationalist card by appearing to be the champion of Nepali rights vis- a -vis India. Also there was an opportunity because the year 1960 also marked the time when India - China relations began to sour. That also gave him space to play off

29 ibid. Page no 71

India against China".[30]So it was from 1960 onwards Nepal began to project India as the main threat to Nepali independence and Nepali sovereignty despite the fact that on the ground India continued to have great presence in Nepal whether in the economic or cultural side. The monarchy had actively promoted this sentiment with the result you have Nepali elite, which is psychologically conditioned to think in terms of this relationship with India. This was something India has to live with.

New Delhi irked by the China card

As mentioned above, Peking was courting Kathmandu in every possible way while repeatedly claiming that Maoist China had nothing to do with the Maoists in Nepal. The first Nepali Ambassador to China was posted in July 1961. Two months later the two countries also signed an agreement for fresh economic aid to Nepal. When the King paid his first visit to Peking, the Chinese rolled out a red carpet welcome sending signals of warm friendship. This followed the Boundary Treaty between the two on October 5, 1961. Armed with these, the King felt he was in a position to deal firmly with his southern neighbour India. The rift continued as Nepal felt India had done nothing to stop the activities of the Nepali Congress leaders based in India.

As relations began to strain further, King Mahendra began to cultivate not only China but also Pakistan, which irritated New Delhi further. In 1962 he brought in a new Constitution providing for non- party Panchayats under which the King became the sole power. He paid a State visit to India in April that same year. Speaking at the banquet hosted for the King, President Rajendra Prasad concluded his speech saying " Let us all make it a habit of being blind to one another's shortcomings and kind to one another's excellences because this is the key to the of international peace and cooperation.[31] "

---

30 Author's interview with Shyam Saram (6 January, 2014)

31 Avtar Singh Bhasin, *Nepal-India, Nepal-China relations Documents 1947- June 2005*, Geetika Publications, 2005, P 102

Nepal turns neutral during Chinese aggression

Kathmandu decided to remain neutral when the Chinese aggression took place in 1962. Prime Minister Nehru was shocked when the Indian army was humiliated, as India was not prepared for war. This was the time when King Mahendra began to create an independent role for Nepal, as Kathmandu, till then a steadfast friend of India turned neutral. He was annoyed by the role played by the Indian government who had never hidden their sympathies for the Nepali Congress and the Koirala brothers. The King's visit in March 1962 had not fully ironed out the differences between the two countries although it smoothened the relations to a limited extent. The King in a press interview on November 10, 1963 made Nepal's stand clear that "This being a dispute between India and China, Nepal deems it most appropriate they should resolve it through mutual understanding. Hence judging from the developments in the present crisis, Nepal sees no reason why she should not become a victim of the struggle between her two big neighbours nor in fact does she want to be in that position."[32] Nehru was disappointed when Nepal was not supportive of India in its hour of crisis. "He (King) expressed similar sentiments refusing to take a formal position on the Indo-Pak war on November 25, 1965 while speaking in the banquet in New Delhi."[33]

Nepal benefitted by this neutral approach. "It created the impression that in the event of any pressure from the south, there will immediately arrive matching forces from the north to protect Nepal's sovereignty. This was a message, which restrained both the Nepali Congress and India. As further developments showed, it acquired a lasting validity."[34]

---

32 Avatar Singh Bhasin, 'Press interview of King Mahendra to the Representative of the Rashtriya samvad samithi, November 10, 1962, *Nepal-India, Nepal-China relations Documents 1947- June 2005*, Geetika Publications, 2005, P 124

33 Ibid, P lxvi

34 Tribhuvan Nath, *'The Nepalese dilemma,'* Sterling Publishers Pvt Ltd, 1975, P 376

Lal Bahadur Shastri humours the King

Despite all these, both countries initiated a move to normalise the relations in 1962 when the then Home Minister Lal Bahadur Shastri paid a visit to Kathmandu in the spring of 1963. Being a leader from Uttar Pradesh he understood Nepal politics and his visit opened up a new phase in the Indo – Nepal ties. He recognized the need for cultivating a neighbour sitting next door to hostile forces. "He was willing to pay any price to maintain friendship with Nepal provided he did not have to compromise on the principles held by Nehru. He promised that the completion of India – aided projects will be speeded up but he turned down the demand for the surrender of the Nepalese Congress leaders living in India."[35] This paid dividend as King Mahendra observed on June 11, 1963, eight weeks after Shastri's visit, "Today friendly India too has shown a proper understanding of our strain, objectives and a concordant change in the direction of friendship and cordiality towards us.[36]" Nehru had his last contact with the King just three weeks before his death on May 27, 1964 when he went to inaugurate the construction work at Gandak project despite his illness. In fact it was one of Nehru's last engagements before he died.

Having arrested the deterioration, Shastri wanted to consolidate the gains by taking steps to remove further irritants. As a first step, on the advice of Shriman Narayan Indian, envoy to Nepal, he took measures to curtail the activities of Nepali Congress in the Indian soil. **Shastri, by now had come to the conclusion that India should not do anything to displease the King or interfere in their internal affairs. This was against the wishes of the leaders like Jayaprakash Narayan and Dr Lohia who wanted to support the Nepali Congress in their fight against the King.** Unfortunately Shastri's regime was too short to make further progress. Had he lived longer, he would have played a more significant role with his common sense approach.

---

35 ibid, Tribhuvan Nath, *'The Nepalese dilemma,'* Sterling Publishers Pvt Ltd, 1975, P 371

36 Ibid, Tribhbuvan Nath *The Nepalese dilemma,'* Sterling Publishers Pvt Ltd, 1975, P 371

Indira Gandhi discourages Nepali Congress

When Indira Gandhi succeeded Shastri in January 1966, she too did not encourage the rebel Nepali Congress leaders functioning from India. In return, New Delhi sought Kathmandu's support for India's candidature for the UN non-permanent representative of the Asian group in the UN Security Council and promised to support Nepal when India vacated the seat.

But to the disappointment of New Delhi, Nepal soon began to unofficially speak for Rawalpindi and Peking, which naturally upset India. But the conclusion of the Indo - Soviet Friendship Treaty in August 1971 made Kathmandu sit up and look at India with a new light. The Indian role in the liberation of Bangladesh added to it as Kathmandu clearly saw the changing balance of power in the region with the Soviet interest growing in the subcontinent.

Nepali population of Indian origin becomes contentious issue

Meanwhile the Nepali population of Indian origin became another contentious issue. They became sudden suspects in the post- 1960 period. They had substantial presence in Bihar, U.P, West Bengal, Assam, in some parts of now Uttarakhand and Northeast also. So New Delhi put pressure on resolving their citizenship issue. Many Nepalese who work in India are also voters in India. During her brief visit to Nepal Prime Minister Indira Gandhi took up this issue in 1966. The King promulgated an ordinance replaced by an act called Nepal Citizenship (amendment) Act, 1967. This law vested absolute powers in the local Anchaladish to decide the claims. The large- scale eviction of people of Indian origin continued in 1969-70.

Secondly, terrorism and the Pakistani ISI involvement also caused concern. Pakistan was using the border especially in UP and Bihar to infiltrate and destabilize India. China was not supporting terrorist activities but was trying to improve its effective presence in Nepal in economic, social and political areas and every way. Another State where the Nepalese are in large number is Sikkim. "The population of Sikkim is 5 lakh 40 thousand, mainly consisting of the Nepalese, the Lepchas and the Bhutias. Of these, the Nepalese are the largest in number followed by the Bhutia and Lepcha communities.

Despite such an ethnic diversity, a remarkable feature of Sikkim's society is the tolerance and acceptance of different cultures and their harmonious co-existence." [37]

Indira Gandhi assures non-interference

When King Mahendra died on January 31, 1972 and his son Birendra Shah succeeded him, he faced political insecurity in view of the rebel activities of the Nepali Congress leaders still living in India. Indira Gandhi assured non- interference in Nepal's activities and during Emergency even asked the Nepali Congress leader B.P Koirala to go back to Nepal. This was also due to the fact that Jayaprakash Narayan had turned against her and was leading an agitation against her perceived corrupt rule. Since he was supporting the Nepali Congress leaders functioning on the Indian soil Gandhi decided not to encourage them. This was an instance when the Centre and the interests of UP- Bihar leaders did not converge and the latter could not win their case.

Altered regional equation after the birth of Bangladesh

Meanwhile the birth of Bangladesh and India's military support to the East Pakistan liberation movement in 1971 had altered the regional equation. Kathmandu began to view it as India's efforts to dominate the smaller countries of the region and was apprehensive of what it considered Indian hegemony. Although New Delhi assured non-interference in Nepal's internal affairs the King's apprehensions were not removed resulting in expressions of anti – India orchestrations. Added to that was the annexation of Sikkim, which created further apprehensions and the palace, reacted sharply. Bilateral relations came under further strain with continued misconceptions on both sides. Nepal felt that they were being cheated in slow implementation of Koshi and Gandak. All these resulted in the growth of anti Indian sentiments, which also encouraged Nepali nationalism.

Moreover the Cold War politics also affected the Indo-Nepal relations. The impact of the Sino-Soviet differences and the growing Sino-US rapprochement in the international politics percolated

<hr>

37 C.K. Dorjee, '*The ethnic people of Sikkim*', http://pib.nic.in/feature/feyr2003/fdec2003/f051220031.html

down to South Asia. By this time US President Nixon made his normalisation efforts with China and went on a week's visit. Nepal soon followed the policy of distancing from India to reap advantages from the global and regional actors. But things changed once the cold war ended.

Morarji Desai government boosts Nepali Congress

When the Janata government headed by Morarji Desai took over in 1977, the democratic forces inside and outside Nepal got a further boost with the Janata Party President Chandrashekhar playing an important role publicly supporting the pro democracy movement. He was a close friend of the Koirala family and they often used him to convey their messages to the Indian government. It was also because the earlier generation of leaders had very close personal relationship with the Nepali Congress.

The Nepali Congress and other political parties were agitating for multi- party system. Coming under pressure King Birendra called for a referendum whether the people wanted a multi party democracy or reformed Panchayat system in 1980 and managed to persuade the people to opt for the Panchayat system and got a new lease of life to his regime but it lasted just for about a decade. The fall of Berlin wall and collapse of the Soviet Union later encouraged the movement further.

Trade embargo and Rajiv Gandhi

After Indira Gandhi's assassination in October 1984 her son Rajiv Gandhi took over. Initially the Indo – Nepal ties were comfortable but soon it soured because of the bad chemistry between Rajiv Gandhi and the King. Several factors led to this. One of them was the King moving closer to China. In 1988, King Birendra concluded a secret arms purchase deal with China, at bargain prices. New Delhi protested promptly pointing out this was in violation of the 1950 Treaty. India naturally interpreted the deal as a dangerous precedent and challenged it. As bilateral tensions mounted, the King insisted that Nepal had the sovereign right to determine its own defence requirements, which further put off New Delhi. When the Indo – Nepal trade and transit agreement came up for renewal in March

1989, Rajiv Gandhi refused to extend it unless Nepal agreed to meet India's commercial, defence and security concerns. As a result only two of the 15 border check posts remained open cutting off Nepal's trade to the outside world. The blockade choked Nepal. The King's efforts to mobilize support form the Western powers did not succeed as they distanced themselves asking the two countries to resolve their differences. As Ambassador Rajan observes "it was the comprehensive failure of domestic and foreign policies that united political parties of the left and right in the successful mass movement for restoration of democracy of 1989-90."[38]

After about fifteen months of trade embargo finally both sides reaffirmed the 1950 Treaty, and Kathmandu climbed down and agreed not to purchase defence items without consulting New Delhi. King Birendra was forced to stop delivery of a final shipment of air defence equipment from Beijing. Relations gradually returned to normal and even improved significantly after Nepal's democratically elected government assumed office in May 1991. The trade restrictions were lifted from July 1, 1990 after both countries had new governments.

Multi party democracy and Indian involvement

The nineties saw systemic political changes in Nepal. Instead of adhering to the principle of non- interference in Nepal affairs, Indian political parties openly joined hands with the Jan Andolan I (people's movement) when the Panchayat system collapsed in 1990. Chandrashekhar supported the Koiralas in exile and the Nepali Congress in whatever form of struggle they decided. This author was present when a galaxy of Indian leaders from various parties including Chandrashekhar, D.P. Tripathi and Dr Subramanyam Swamy shared the platform in Kathmandu in January 1990 with the leaders of the underground movement like Ganeshman Singh and Girija Prasad Koirala. Other major political parties except the BJP also helped the Nepali Congress leaders.

The NCP leader D.P. Tripathi recalls how they- the Congress, Left and others- had come together to help the pro democracy forces

38 K.V. Rajan, *Editor J.N. Dixit, 'External affairs – Cross Border relations,'* *Nepal chapter,* Roli Books, 2003. P 105

because their interests converged. He took initiative and went to Janata Dal leader Chandrashekhar in late 1989 and requested him to lead a delegation to Kathmandu to support them. Chandrashekhar also wanted to settle scores with V.P. Singh, whose choice as the Prime Minister was against his wishes. "Chandrashekharji asked me whether the Leader of Opposition Rajiv Gandhi would support such a move and I said yes. I made him talk to Rajiv Gandhi, who wanted to embarrass Prime Minister V.P Singh, promptly agreed. Communist Party leaders including Mahmood Farooqui were also part of the delegation. That created an impact and Chandrashekhar and others spoke effectively at the Nepali Congress meeting in January 1990."[39] For this author who was present at the meeting it was evident that the movement would succeed and so it did within weeks. The palace and the people accepted the concept for popular sovereignty. The time was ripe for such a step because of the overall failure of the domestic and foreign policies, which united the political parties against the monarchy. V.P. Singh, as expected was embarrassed. He appointed Srinivas Kumar Sinha as the new ambassador. He was told to cultivate the palace without offending the Nepali Congress leaders. However, the unprecedented success of the multiparty democracy movement resolved the South Block dilemma. Within 60 days the movement succeeded and Krishna Prasad Bhattarai was sworn in as Prime Minister and an interim government came in to being. **This was an instance of the powerful national leaders with regional roots like Chandrashekhar and national leaders like Rajiv Gandhi putting pressure on Delhi and they succeeded in their efforts despite Prime Minister V.P Singh not in favour of it. Chandrashekhar was too important a leader in the party that V.P. Singh could not go against his wishes.**

Nepal resolves Crown versus people

Internally Nepal resolved the age-old conflict of crown versus people in favour of the latter. A new Constitution was promulgated in November 1990, which confirmed Nepal as a Hindu State and accepted the King as the supreme commander of the Nepal army. The elections were held in 1991 and Nepal Prime Minister Krishna

---

39 Author's interview with D.P. Tripathi (7 January 2014)

Prasad Bhattarai and his successor Grirja Prasad Koirala maintained good relations with New Delhi for the next two years.

Nepal underwent a change both internally and externally after the elections. The absolute monarchy became the Constitutional Monarchy giving up its executive powers to the democratically elected government. Externally the imbalance in Nepal's relations with its neighbours in the pre-1990 period was corrected. The signing of the new India – Nepal trade and transit treaties mended fences to a large extent between the two countries. But after a while the successive Nepal regimes restored the old policy of balancing the two big neighbours India and China.

Prime Minister Chandrashekhar helps Nepal

The Indo- Nepal relations reached a new high when Chandrashekhar became the Prime Minister after dethroning V.P. Singh on 10, November 1990 for a brief period supported by the Congress Party. He visited Nepal on February 13-15, 1991, his only foreign trip during his brief term apart from going to Maldives for a multilateral visit. He raised a lot of expectations in Nepal. He accepted the Joint Communiqué signed in 1990 as the basis for India's relations with Nepal. It was decided that India would restore the Jayanagar-Janakpuri-Bizalur railway line and also agreed to open three more entry points at Nepalganj, Gauriphaula and Banbasa for third country nationals on the Indo-Nepal border. He held discussions on harnessing of water resources, restoration of registration facilities for vehicles owned by Indian residents, removal of impediments to ensure free movement of Indian currency from Nepal to India and removal of discriminations against the Indian teachers working in Nepal. As for the 1950 Treaty, Chandrashekhar asked Nepal to spell out what Nepal wanted and was willing to go an extra mile. Unfortunately, the decisions taken were not implemented as his government fell soon afterwards.

P.V. Narasimha Rao for improved Indo- Nepal relations

After the Congress withdrew its support to the short- lived Chandrashekhar government on March 6, 1991 elections were held after which the Congress led P.V. Narasimha Rao government came to power on June 21, 1991. Rajiv Gandhi was assassinated in the midst of the campaign. Rao was an experienced politician, who had dealt with Nepal, as external affairs minister of both Indira Gandhi and Rajiv Gandhi and was keen to improve relations. So New Delhi agreed to improve and simplify the rules for export of goods from Nepal during Rao's visit to Kathmandu in October 1992. "India also agreed to extend stand- by credit facility to Nepal from Rs. 35 to Rs. 50 crores. The term of the agreement was extended from one to three years during which period the interest rate of 7 per cent per annum was levied."[40] Nepal's private vehicles were allowed to move from its border to Calcutta and Haldia ports and back to facilitate Nepal's exports to India. Nepal was also allowed to import goods from India in convertible currency. All these resulted in improving the economic ties to a certain extent.

Nepal's Multi party democracy fails

However, hopes that Nepal would emerge as a functional democracy were dashed soon as the democratic political parties were unable to meet the expectations and gradually surrendered their powers to the monarchy to the delight of the palace and the disappointment of India. The multi -party democracy could not deliver socio -economic development while the King was waiting to take over the reins again. Another disturbing factor was the rise of Maoist insurgency since 1996. This was again due to the failure of the democratic forces leading the government. But the Communist Party of Nepal Unified Marxist – Leninists tried to whip up anti- India sentiments against Prime Minister Koirala's pro- India sentiments and even demanded the abrogation of the 1950 Treaty. Ultimately when midterm elections were held in 1994, it resulted in a hung Parliament. The UML (Unified Marxist – Leninist) government headed by Manmohan Adhikari took over but this government was short- lived and fell within nine months in office. Although the UML Government had conveyed its intentions to improve relations with New Delhi even in that short period but stability evaded Nepal. Ambassador Rajan points out, "In September 1995,

---

40 Sangeeta Thapliyal,' *Changing trends in India Nepal relations*,' IDSA, www.idsa-india.org/an-dec-5.html

Sher Bahadur Deuba succeeded Man Mohan Adhikari as the head of a three party coalition of Nepali Congress, Rashtriya Praja Tantra Party and National Sadhbhavana Party. Lokendra Bahadur, leading a coalition of dissident group of RFP, the UML and NSP replaced him in February 1997."[41] One important measure during this period was the signing of the Mahakali Treaty between Prime Minister Rao and Nepal Prime Minister Deuba in April 1996. This was appreciated in both the countries.

United Front government takes over in India

Meanwhile there had been regime changes in India too. When the Rao government lost the elections in 1996, Vajpayee took over for 13 days but his government fell giving place to the two successive United Front governments led by Deve Gowda followed by Gujral from 1996 to 1998. By the time the Treaty was placed before Nepal Parliament the Gujral government had taken over in India. Soon Deuba government fell and was succeeded by a coalition government led by the anti- Mahakali dissidents in the Rashtriya Prajatantra Party (RPP) and Communist Party of Nepal (UML) but it decided to honour the international commitment made by its predecessor. "The Mahakali Treaty attracted attention in a number of countries as an important indication of the ability of two multi party democracies to reach an agreement on cooperation in water resources on the basis of equality, transparency and equitable sharing of costs and benefits."[42] The Vajpayee led coalition government, which succeeded in 1998, fell within 13 months but it came back in 1999 with more seats.

Vajpayee invites King Birendra as India's Republic Day guest

There was a predictable change in the palace politics during the Vajpayee regime. The BJP always had good relations with the palace. King Birendra also changed his attitude towards New Delhi and sent a signal that he was for a strengthened relationship with India. Vajpayee reciprocated promptly by inviting the King to be the chief

---

41 K. V. Rajan, Editor, J. N. Dixit, *'External Affairs- Cross Border Relations'*, *Nepal chapter,* Roli Books, 2003, P 107-108

42 K.V. Rajan, Editor, J. N. Dixit, *'External Affairs- Cross Border Relations,'* Nepal chapter, Roli Books, 2003, P 107-109

guest of the Republic Day celebrations in 1999, the first time a Nepal King was ever invited for such a function. For the BJP the fact that Nepal is the only Hindu Kingdom in the world also was a factor. But then came the Indian Airlines plane- hijacking incident, which brought some strain in the relationship. The IC 814 Indian Airlines plane was hijacked from Tribhuvan international airport in Nepal on its way to New Delhi on 24 December 1999. Harkat-ul-Mujahideen, a Pakistan based Islamic extremist group was accused of hijacking. India suspected that the ISI was getting a foothold in Nepal. By the end of the Nepal government's decade-long struggle against the rebels, the parliament was dissolved and the King assumed absolute power once again.

Maoist movement picks up in Nepal

The role of the Maoists in Nepal's struggle for democracy and also that of the Indian political leaders need a special mention here. The movement, which began in 1996, was a significant development in Nepal's democratic history. There were several reasons for the sudden surge of Maoist insurgency. The first was the squandering of the promise of the immediate post- 1990 period manifested by its gradual transformation into politics of power. The second was the continued neglect of the aspirations of the people, which gave the Maoists a pretext to launch an armed struggle for their liberation. Without the constitutionally guaranteed freedom to organise politically, the Maoists would not have been able to build up their strength so quickly for armed action. The third was the splintering of the polity further. The factional politics led to mushrooming of political parties that only resulted in further instability and a more fractured polity. The fourth was the internal squabbles among the ruling coalition and their political rivalry.

Pushpa Kamal Dahal, known as 'Prachanda' became the General Secretary of the Maoists in 1995, and in 2000 the Chairman of the Communist Party of Nepal (Maoist). The King deployed the Royal Nepal army to crush the Maoists but it was unable to tackle the insurgency. Nepal faced an emergency, escalating political turbulence and insecurity. On February 13, 1996, the Maoist insurgency intensified its attacks on the police posts in six districts.

Using guerrilla tactics the insurgency grew in the next four or five years when the Maoists took control of almost 80 per cent of Nepal. They attacked the Royal Nepal army barracks on November 23, 2001 in Dang district signalling the escalation of the Maoist violence. At that time they were operating from India. Several underground communist parties combined together to launch the People's War movement.

Transition from Insurgency to democratic movement

The transition from Maoist insurgency to peaceful democratic movement was indeed the most fascinating aspect of the Nepal story. The long time Nepal watcher and author Prof S.D. Muni points out that there were four main players in Nepal's political transition – the Maoists, the mainstream political parties, the King and the international community. The Maoists were obviously the game changers. "They set the agenda for transition- a People's Republic through an elected Constituent Assembly- through their decade long struggle, the People's War. The Maoists had sought to forge an alliance with the other parties with the objective of eliminating monarchy even before the palace massacre of June 2001, at a time when they still enjoyed support and some patronage from the palace.[43]"

From 2000 to 2006, the Maoists controlled a large part of Nepal rendering the army and the police helpless. Prof Muni points out that King Birendra had encouraged covert links with the Maoists through his younger brother Dhirendra Shah and other trusted interlocutors. This was to resolve the insurgency as well as marginalize the other political parties. A section within the Maoists was not averse to having a deal directly with the King. What ultimately prevailed was the strong faction, which wanted a Republican Nepal while the King was not ready to abdicate even though the Maoists were willing to make him the first president of the Nepal Republic. Quoting Prachanda, Prof Muni notes "Birendra's youngest brother Dhirendra was in touch with us and we were to start direct talks with him

---

43 Prof. S.D. Muni, Editor Sebastian Vo Einsiedel; David Malone, Suman Pradhan, 'Nepal in Transition – From people's was or fragile peace, Cambridge University Press, 2012, p316

within a month with the request to abdicate his throne and become the country's first President. He was killed in this backdrop."[44]

Palace massacre in Nepal

The massacre of the royal family at the palace by the demented prince was a crucial turning point in the history of Nepal. In 2001, the crown prince Dipendra Bir Bikram Shah Dev massacred ten members of the Nepal royal family, including King Birendra and queen Aishwarya and then committed suicide. Monarchy underwent a drastic change after the palace massacre. Nepal entered a five –year period of instability of violence, political instability and social chaos. The Maoist violence spread all over. The King's inherent contempt for the political class and his inflated ego about his own powers of manipulation led to further chaos in Nepal.

Maoists seek help from India

By this time the Maoists sought contacts with Indian and other international community. Alarmed by the growing international support for the Royal Nepal Army the Maoists wanted to reach out to India. They pursued contacts with the mainstream political parties by sending the Maoist leader Baburam Bhattarai to New Delhi to establish political contacts. New Delhi initially did not take the Maoists seriously and saw the violence as Nepal's domestic law and order problem.

Prof Muni recalls that Bhattarai contacted him in early 2002. Initially neither Bhattarai's old Jawaharlal Nehru University (JNU) contacts like Sitaram Yechury (CPI-M), D.P Tripathi (NCP) and the late Digvijay Singh of the Janata Dal (U) showed any interest. The Indian establishment was wary of dealing with the Maoists but when he approached Brajesh Mishra the then principal secretary to Prime Minister Vajpayee who was also the National Security Adviser, Prof Muni found that Mishra was willing to keep the door open asking the Maoists to put in writing what they wanted. "Packaged in radical rhetoric the letter written by the Maoist duo – Prachanda and

---

44 Prof. S. D. Muni, Editor Sebastian Vo Einsiedel; David Malone, Suman Pradhan, 'Nepal in Transition – From people's was or fragile peace, Cambridge University Press, 2012 P314

Bhattarai assured the Indian leaders they wanted the best relations with India and would not do anything to harm its interests."[45]. This satisfied the Indian establishment. As a result the intelligence surveillance against the Maoists in India was relaxed.

Meanwhile the Vajpayee government's comfort level with the Nepali Congress came down. Nepal started buying its arms from other countries also. New Delhi perceived that not only the palace but also Prime Minister Deuba and the Royal Nepal army were getting closer to the US and resented this. There was also an internal power struggle among the Maoists as Prachanda and Bhattarai fell out and the latter was suspended and kept under the Maoist army control.

King Gyanendra's successful coup

In 2004, there was a change of government in India, The Vajpayee government was defeated and the Manmohan Singh government took over. Meanwhile, King Gyanendra was engaged in his efforts to take over power, which culminated in his military coup of February 1, 2005. The King under the pretext of fighting the Maoists dismissed the democratically elected government and took complete control. The King obviously underestimated his vulnerability and did not expect such sharp reaction from various quarters including New Delhi on this coup. It exploded an internal political upheaval, which he could not control to his dismay. Soon political leaders who were put behind bars by the King joined hands to force the palace to roll back the takeover. The students came out on the streets while the media also turned hostile. The palace found no support from the public. The palace massacre had left behind many doubts about the alleged dubious role of the new King and his son. The mistake King Gyanandra committed was that instead of being benign, he chose to confront them. New Delhi expressed grave concern to the serious setback to democracy. The King misread the situation and believed that things would work out in the South Asian Association for Regional Cooperation (SAARC) meeting scheduled for February 6

---

45 Prof. S. D. Muni, Editor Sebastian Vo Einsiedel; David Malone, Suman Pradhan, 'Nepal in Transition – From people's was or fragile peace, Cambridge University Press, 2012, P321

in Dhaka where he could explain the reasons for his action personally to Prime Minister Manmohan Singh. King Gyanendra also mistakenly expected that the fear of Maoist insurgency spilling over into India would compel New Delhi to support him. Contrary to his expectations, Prime Minister Manmohan Singh backed off from the summit citing 'the recent developments in the neighbourhood 'with the result it was cancelled. South Block clearly conveyed to the King, 'the two pillars of political stability in Nepal, the Constitutional Monarchy and Multi-Party Democracy' must work in tandem and provide the equilibrium so essential for political stability in the country."[46]

The developments in Nepal caught India in a dilemma. New Delhi was concerned about the instability all around India's neighbourhood and feared that violence would soon spread to other areas. Already almost the entire Northeastern region of India was in turmoil. The Left-wing extremists had expanded influence at least in a dozen Indian States.

The King felt relieved when the Defence Minister Pranab Mukherji stated on February 9, that the developments in Nepal were an internal matter of that country. In April during the Afro – Asian Summit in Jakarta both the External Affairs Minister Natwar Singh and Prime Minister Manmohan Singh met with the King and assured him of some military supplies in return for setting out a road-map for restarting the political process in Nepal. New Delhi, while allowing some military supplies to move also exerted political pressure on the King to roll back the measures taken by him. But coalition compulsions forced the UPA government to stick to the initial policy of supporting the pro -democratic forces. In this case, it was the not the regional but the national leaders who put pressure on the centre and won their case. **There was strong opposition to the resumption of military supplies from the UPA coalition partners like the Nationalist Congress Party and the Left parties. Singh could not ignore the Left parties, which had a strong contingent of 64 members supporting the UPA coalition.**

---

46 Avtar Singh Bhasin, *Nepal-India, Nepal-China relations Documents 1947- June 2005*, Geetika Publications, 2005, P x111

The options for the King slowly narrowed down. The international community too was losing faith in his protestations for democracy. So the King felt it was high time to regain the initiative and win the confidence of his people and the international community by reverting to status quo ante that existed not on February 1, 2005 but in October 2002. He had already promised local and parliamentary elections and set a time- table too. The need was for removal of restrictions on the media, restoration of fundamental rights and political activity.

Karan Singh visits Kathmandu as PM's envoy

Ambassador Shyam Saran recalls the visit of senior Congress leader Dr Karan Singh to Kathmandu on April 19 to persuade the King to see reason. The then Foreign Secretary, Saran had accompanied him. Karan Singh was the former Maharaja of Jammu and Kashmir and has family relations with the Nepal royal family. The senior Congress leader had a one- to -one meeting with the King when he handed over Prime Minister Singh's letter to King Gyanendra. Prime Minister wanted to persuade the King to see reason and had also assured the King of his safety. Dr Karan Singh conveyed to the defiant King India's readiness to support all efforts to overcome the crisis. He emphasized the fact that a lasting solution could only be found by the people of Nepal through a peaceful political process. He provided the King with a face saving formula to roll back the autocracy that he had established after sacking the then Prime Minister Sher Bahadur Deuba on February 1, 2005. "The visit was basically to persuade the King to step down and allow an all party government to take over. To my mind the best position for India was not to try and play favourites - pro one party or anti other party. If we had accepted that there should be democracy in Nepal whichever leadership is thrown up in the elections India should be ready to deal with that.[47]"

At the government level the South Block made efforts to preserve the monarchy as one of the "two pillars" of Nepal's politics, a policy that it had been following for long but did not succeed. It was Shyam Saran who later tried to do some damage control by

---

47 Author's interview with Shyam Saran, (6,January, 2014)

stating that it was up to the people of Nepal to decide on how to take the process of democratisation forward. India, he emphasised, had all along supported multi-party democracy in Nepal and recalled that India had condemned the King's dismissal of the civilian government in February 2005.

Seven Party Alliance

As the Maoist violence increased, the international concerns also began to grow. While China supported the palace throughout, the US put the Maoist Organisation under its banned terrorist organizations list. The British and the Americans maintained their ban on military supplies to Nepal.

The King's ruthless action in 2005 united the democratic parties in to a Seven Party Alliance, which sought peace negotiations with the Maoists while New Delhi facilitated this 12- point peace understanding. In 2006, it further led to a ceasefire and Comprehensive Peace Agreement. Thus the Jan Anndolan 11 brought back not only the political parties but also the Maoists into the democratic stream and the establishment of Republic in Nepal in 2007.

By this time things were changing in India too. The Maoists had made contact with some Indian leaders, particularly from the Nationalist Congress Party (NCP) and the Left. The NCP leader D.P. Tripathi recalls how he took initiative to coordinate with major political parties of India to form the Nepal Democracy Solidarity Committee. They agreed to work on a common platform. The Left parties, the Congress and in fact almost all political parties except the BJP became its members. The late Comrade Harkishen Singh Surjeet of the CPI- M became its chairman while Tripathi became its Secretary General. The job of this committee was to support the democratic struggle of Nepal people. According to CPI-M leader Sitaram Yechury, Prime Minister Manmohan Singh requested him in 2004 whether he could make use of his contacts with the Maoists and try to bring them to the mainstream. Soon with Prof Muni's help Yechury met the Maoists leaders.

New Delhi was initially concerned about linkages between the naxalites operating in India and the Maoists. South Block was also worried about the increasing Chinese and Pakistani interests in its backyard. **This was achieved because of the efforts of the non -BJP political parties, well - intentioned people like Prof Muni and others. The Centre went along with their sentiments,**

Nepal Democratic forces unite

When the Maoists and political parties joined hands to fight the palace, with the help of some Indian political parties, naturally the palace was defeated. D. P. Tripathi, who played a significant role in their unification, recalls how the 12- point understanding was reached in Delhi. He recalls, "Sitaram Yechury met Prachanda for the first time at my flat in Vasantkunj in New Delhi when he surfaced from underground in March 2006. Prachanda came sitting behind on a bicycle. We had long discussions and ultimately finalized their support. The first task before us was the formation of the Seven Party Alliance (SPA) in Nepal. The other major challenge was to facilitate the 12-point understanding of November 2005. This became the basis for all future developments. Unfortunately the Nepal leaders were not able to implement it."[48]

Tripathi initially found it difficult to convince the Indian government that the Maoists wanted to be part of the Nepal freedom struggle. There were also apprehensions that they may not give up arms. Initially, Chandrashekhar and Surjeet Singh were the only two leaders who agreed to talk to the Maoists according to Tripathi. Then Prime Minister Dr Manmohan Singh agreed to support the Nepal democracy movement. In March 2006 when the movement was just beginning in Nepal Tripathi discussed the issue with him. "I assured the Prime Minister that it would not take more than ten days for them to declare peace and go for multi party democracy. I was in direct touch with PM and I convinced him that the Government of India should not create any problems. I requested him that the Maoist leaders should not be arrested in India. I suggested that it was for him to use RAW or IB or any other agency to deal with them.[49]"

48 Author's interview with D.P. Tripathi,(7 January 2014)

49 Author's interview with D.P. Tripathi

The CPI-M leader Sitaram Yechury was instrumental in convincing the Maoists to open dialogue with the Opposition parties. After meeting Prachanda, he became one of the primary channels between the Maoists and the Indian political leaders. Prof Muni organised Prachanda's meeting with CPI-M leader Prakash Karat in May 2005, which opened the doors further. Back-channel contacts between the Indian government and the Maoists were opened largely due to Yechuri's efforts. It was during his visit to Kathmandu in January that the plans for nationwide pro-democracy demonstrations and strikes were first made in consultation with the Seven Party Alliance and the Maoists. Sitaram Yechury had kept the Indian government informed about their plans to take on the monarchy jointly in April.

Yechury formula to defuse the situation

By accepting the proposals of Yechury, all parties involved in the standoff played a key role in defusing the situation. "The four-point 'Yechury formula' called for the recall of Parliament on the understanding that it would announce elections to a Constituent Assembly. The other points related to implementing the 12-point Agreement with the Maoists, inviting them for talks and Parliament taking legislative measures to undo the steps taken by the King." [50]

With the signing of the agreement on 21, November 2006 in New Delhi, the Nepal political parties stood on a new ground as the mainstream parties had decided to do away with monarchy and go for a new Constitution. It ended the civil war and created a road map for elections to the Constituent Assembly. Realizing the anti-King sentiments in the country, New Delhi recognized the Nepal Republic. On April 1, 2007 an interim government was constituted.

From monarchy to democracy again, Prachanda becomes PM

The credit goes to the people of Nepal who chose democracy in place of monarchy. There were several reasons for this. First of all, the Maoists had decided to come in to the mainstream giving up their armed struggle. Secondly, people were fed up of the ill- timed

---

50 John Cherian,'Indian flip-flop' The Frontline, Volume 23 - Issue 09: May 06 - 19, 2006

actions of King Gyanendra. Thirdly, the democratic political parties in Nepal became more effective in their revolt. Fourthly, people were encouraged to choose a multi party democracy because of the success of Jan Andolan 1.

The 2008 elections legitimized the Maoist party and the Maoist movement when they won a landslide victory much to their own surprise and also to that of the international community but still they lacked the majority. The Maoists emerged as the single largest party with 240 seats and achieved their main goal of ending the 239 years of Hindu monarchy. The Constituent Assembly elections on April 10, 2008 showed that except the crash of the monarchy other pillars like the military, police and the bureaucracy continued unaffected. But the results made the Maoists complacent while the two other major political parties – the Nepali Congress and the UML became insecure. At its first session, in May 28, 2008 Nepal was declared a federal republic. Prachanda was elected Prime Minister on August 18, 2008. King Gyanendra, the world's last Hindu monarch vacated the palace to live as a commoner.

New Delhi frowned when Prachanda accepted Beijing's invitation to participate in the 2008 Beijing Olympics inauguration. It was the practice of Nepal Prime Ministers to visit Delhi first before undertaking any other foreign tour. Ambassador Shyam Saran points out that when Prachanda became the Prime Minister, India accepted it and accorded him a red carpet welcome during his first political visit to New Delhi on September 15, 2008. A highly visible Prachanda created an interest even among the Indian public during his brief visit. The South Block conveyed to him that New Delhi expected him to complete the peace process and restore stability. "Whatever he asked for by way of support and assistance we gave them. He then thought that if he had an opportunity, he should make his party the single dominant party. That was when we said we would not offer support because it would have meant that the Nepali army would have been transformed. He wanted to kick out the army chief. We insisted that no change should be made in the army without a political consensus because this was a sensitive issue. When he unilaterally tried to change this, the other mainstream parties got frightened. Only then did we make our position clear that we cannot accept what he was trying to do. So I don't think that in terms of policy we made any major mistake in dealing with the Maoists. We saw the political reality. After all, the role India played in bringing about an understanding between the Maoists and the other political parties was what enabled the monarchy to be side lined. Otherwise in 2005 there was a bid that they would go back to the old monarchical system where the King was an absolute ruler.[51]"

For all purposes the monarchy in Nepal is dead. Maoist leader Prachanda was categorical in saying that "In Nepal majority are Hindus. I think the State should be secular. There should be many religions in the State. The religion will be there and we respect their sentiments but the State should be secular." [52]

Prime Minister Prachanda resigns

Prachanda's rule did not last long. He resigned on May 4, 2009, after nine months following a confrontation with the Nepal President Ram Baran Yadav over the dismissal of the army chief. The Prime Minister announced his resignation in a televised address on May 4, 2009. The crisis started a day earlier when Prachanda sacked the Nepal army chief Rookmangud Katawal for disobeying instructions about the enlistment of former Maoists into army ranks. However President Yadav overruled this decision with the tacit support of New Delhi. The Maoists decided to intensify struggle in Parliament and outside until the President withdrew what they described as an "unconstitutional" move. Dahal's position had also become untenable after two key alliance partners deserted the government, reducing the ruling coalition led by the Communist party to a minority in the constituent assembly.

Why did the Maoists fail?

There were several reasons for this crisis. The Maoists were feeling uncomfortable and refused to transform into a democratic party accountable to Parliament and implement the internal peace accord. It takes a lot of courage for a Maoist leader to admit his mistakes.

---

51 Author's interview with Shyam Saran, (6 January, 2014)

52 Author's interview with Prachanda, (18 July 2015)

Prachanda told this author later in 2015, "I think one of the basic things was that we were having very little experience as to how to handle this competitive politics. In government we were having very little experience. We came here in the transition with compromise with other parties. G.P. Koirala and I were the signatories of the CPA. After I became the leader of the largest party I should have given the presidency to G.P Koirala but we did not do so. There was this sort of subjectivism we were having and it was a mistake. Then I took action against the chief of army at that time. After three months, the chief would have retired. But I was in a hurry and that action boomeranged on me. I had to resign and that kinds of mistakes were there. I am trying; I am trying to take the synthesis of all the positive and negative things now." [53] The most important change was that he was clear that he would not commit such mistakes if he came back to power.

Secondly, the Maoists faced an uphill task of rebuilding the infrastructure that had been destroyed in their decade-old civil war. Moreover, they faced severe problems with the Nepalese army and did not know how to integrate their cadre into the society. Despite all these Prachanda believes that Maoists will continue to be relevant even in a democratic setup. "Whenever we try to address the issue of oppressed and depressed communities the relevance of Maoist movement will remain. It is because we are trying to address every issue and concerns of the oppressed and depressed classes in the new constitution. When the draft process was going on women from different parties congratulated me. They congratulate me that due to my initiative women have got 33 per cent in legislature. Therefore the validity of the Maoist movement will continue to remain."[54]

Thirdly, their insistence on federalism on ethnic lines with a right to self-determination also injected uncertainty about Nepal's status as an integrated State. Fourthly, the change in regime caused more political instability – five Prime Ministers in as many years. So the hopes generated in 2006 evaporated soon and turned into frustration. After the withdrawal of the Maoists everything collapsed

---

53 Author's interview with Prachanda (18 July 2015)

54 Author's interview with Prachanda, (18 July 2015)

while the main task of rewriting of the Constitution got stuck in the middle.

Does Prachanda regret that the Maoists have left their path of violence to join the mainstream politics? "Marxism and Leninism taught us to think in philosophical terms. The whole international situation, regional situation and our national situation will not permit us to do so and will have to judge all the changes that had occurred all over the world. The basic motto is to serve the people. We have to understand the reality,"[55] he says.

After Prachanda's resignation, despite being the biggest party, the Maoists had to sit in the Opposition when 22 of the 24 parties got together to oust them. Another coalition government, comprising of all the political parties took over. Madhav Kumar Nepal of the Communist Party of Nepal (Unified Marxist-Leninist) became the Prime Minister. Prachanda announced the launch of a national independence awareness campaign in May 2010 and took to the streets with thousands of his supporters demanding ouster of the government. But Prime Minister Madhav Nepal, backed fully by New Delhi, held on. Within a week Prachanda announced withdrawal of his protests. Madhav Nepal's government lasted till February 2011.

Term of Constituent Assembly extended

Meanwhile the term of the Constituent Assembly had to be extended, because it had not completed its task. The Maoists insisted that Prime Minister Nepal should resign first if they had to cooperate. Ultimately a compromise formula was worked out which stipulated that Prime Minister Nepal would resign in June and the Maoists would cooperate in the meantime.

New Delhi believed in propping up a broad Democratic alliance. Prachanda tried to bid for power but New Delhi blocked him and Madhav Nepal continued through 2010 as caretaker Prime Minister. Only in early 2011 UML Chairman Jhalanath Khamal, with the support of Prachanda took over. The relationship between the new Prime Minister and New Delhi was not good, as neither

---

55 Author's interview with Prachanda, (18 July 2015)

trusted the other. He was not even invited to India as every other Nepal Prime Minister was. When 27ᵗʰMay, 2011 came still there was no progress in the peace process, which weakened the Khamal government. The Maoists were busy fighting amongst themselves. The Nepali Congress and the Madheshi parties, with the backing of New Delhi took to the streets demanding Khamal's resignation. A formula was hammered out and he resigned paving the way for National Unity government and the Constituent Assembly's term was extended for three months. On May 6, Baburam Bhattarai formed the National Unity government. His government completed the integration and rehabilitation of Maoist combatants, which was one of primary sticking points of the peace process. But it did not make any progress on statute drafting. The Nepali Congress and UML cooperated with the Bhattarai-led Government in army integration, as they understood that this process could not be completed under their leadership.

After the first Constituent Assembly (CA) failed to frame a Constitution in May 2012 the Bhattarai government insisted on second CA elections. But the other parties refused to accept this. Brokered by Prachanda, an interim government took over in March 2013 to hold elections by the end of that year. The 2013 polls turned out to be different from the 2008 elections. The Maoists lost out in that election as the other parties made it a referendum of the Maoist performance. The Nepali Congress, the country's oldest political party won 196   seats. The Communist Party of Nepal (Unified Marxist-Leninist) came in second with 175 seats. Despite their party's name, the Marxist-Leninists are considered centrists in Nepal. The Unified Communist Party of Nepal (Maoist), the dominant Communist party, secured only 80 seats, a small fraction of the total it earned in the 2008 elections. Because a two-thirds majority in the Constituent Assembly is required for a Constitution to be adopted, the Maoists played a critical though reduced role. Prachanda and his deputy Bhattarai were pointing a finger at each other for the rout in the elections. There were also charges of corruption.

Sushil Koirala becomes PM

In February 2014 Nepal political parties decided to share power and Sushil Koirala of the Nepali Congress was elected as the Prime Minister. Nepal has made a transition several times over and has been exploring ways to become a federal state from a unitary state. There is still political uncertainty and the economic situation has not improved but at least the kind of civil war situation of the 2001 is not there today.

Major earthquake hits Nepal, India helps.

Meanwhile, the Modi led National Democratic Alliance government replaced the Manmohan Singh government in May 2014. Prime Minister Modi wanted to pursue a 'Neighbours first" policy making all the right gestures, which encouraged Kathmandu.

The major earthquake in April 2015 in Nepal had added to the political crisis, as the government was not prepared to tackle the natural calamity. "On 25 April, a powerful 7.9-magnitude earthquake, with its epicentre located at about 80 km north-west of Kathmandu, hit the country and left a trail of death and devastation, killing over 7,000 and injuring 14,123 others."[56]It had to tide over the situation with the help of international community and India was in the forefront on rescue operations.

Soon after the top political parties decided to form a National Unity government in order to handle the crisis and also draft the Constitution. Prachanda told this author "We are having four basic issues in the new Constitution – One is federalism to transform the unitary society and unitary system into a federal system, which is a qualitative leap and big jump. Therefore it is a very challenging job. The second thing is the republicanism; I think we should institutionalize the republicanism in the new Constitution. The third is inclusiveness. It means proportional representation in all the State -organs, as even in the representative institutions there should be proportional representation. This is also an important feature of the new Constitution. We have already decided that 33 per cent

---

56 Press Trust of India, 'More than More than 3,00,000 houses damaged, says UN report,First post, May 3, 2015

of women will be in the legislature and that will be the necessary provision. Without that it will not be legal. This is also a major achievement. We are trying to ensure inclusiveness for the oppressed community. The fourth is the social justice. Only development will not satisfy the whole necessity of society. There should be a social justice and development. There should be a balance between these two."[57]

The delay in the Constitution drafting had frustrated everyone including New Delhi. This was because the process has been stalled by the power games of these players. As Aditya Adhikari notes, "the older parliamentary parties fear that the Maoists have become too powerful and they are intent on establishing permanent control over the State apparatus. The Maoists in turn feel that the parliamentary parties are intent on marginalising them and their agenda. The struggle for power is manifested through conflicts on issues such as power sharing and government formation and the future of Maoist combatants. Much of the energy of leaders of all parties is being spent on such issues, and as such inadequate attention is being paid to the constitution drafting process.[58]"India was and is keen that the Constitution should have a maximum consensus.

Koshi River water dispute

Water is as critical an issue for India as it is for Nepal or in fact any other country in the world. It is often predicted that if there will be a Third World War it will be on water. The magnitude of the annual flood problem caused by the Nepalese rivers in Bihar and Uttar Pradesh is enormous. The most important feature of the floods in North Bihar is that except Burhi Gandak all rivers originate in Nepal. More than two-thirds of farmland in Bihar is vulnerable to floods in Koshi, Budi Gandaki and Baghmati rivers. During the devastating 2008 Koshi flooding, several villages on both sides of the border were wiped out. While UP and Bihar leaders blame Nepal for the flooding in the region the Nepalese blame India for the severe floods,

---

57 Author's interview with Prachanda, (18,July 2015)

58 Aditya Adhikari, Editor D.P. Tripathi, '*Nepal in Transition, Nepal's Constituent Assembly,*' P 214

which they think is largely due to the construction of embankments in Nepal's border by India. This 'blame game' goes on during every rainy season, but subsides thereafter.

It should be noted that in the 1950s, the Nepalese and Indian governments had successfully tamed the same Koshi River by constructing barrage and embankment over it. With the completion of the Koshi project, the two countries tried to solve the problem of inundation of their land. The barrage facilitated the transportation system and connected Nepal's Eastern part with the Western side.

The embankment system in Bihar needs to ensure that the riverbed is cleared of silts and sands in the off-season. Secondly, blanketing of the total embankment should be done every year as in the coalmines. As far as possible, rivers must be allowed to have a natural way. Various governments had ignored this aspect and did not provide funds in their budgets. "There are two principal points of contention between India and Nepal over the Koshi Treaty -- the issue of water rights and that of the management, control and operation of the Barrage." [59] In Nepal, the Maoist party had opposed the Koshi Treaty since 1996 calling it anti -national and discriminatory.

Importantly, flood protection is a State subject under the Indian Constitution while the floods caused by the rivers flowing from a neighbouring country is a Central subject. Therefore it creates a complex problem as both the Centre and the State governments are responsible for this deluge.

Mahakali Treaty

The Mahakali Treaty, signed with great expectations in 1996 February, has made little progress in implementation. Essentially, Nepal feels that the earlier agreements were detrimental to Nepal's interests. Equally, much more is required on India's ability to communicate adequately in the vital question of water management, be it with Nepal or Bangladesh. In the case of storage dams, Nepal would be justified in seeking remuneration for flood control or augmentation benefits that might accrue to India or Bangladesh.

---

59 Akanshya Shah, *'Need for stronger role of States in ties with neighbours'* Observer research foundation, 28 February 2012

A multitude of political issues, particularly failure of water talks with Nepal is due to lack of effective participation by the States concerned. The Central government needs to consult the concerned States before its bilateral dealings because they are affected.

Nepal is faced with an acute power shortage. "The northern grid of India is faced with a whooping energy shortage of 18,000 MW. The current demand in Bihar is 3000 MW in peak hour, but it has an installed capacity only 600 MW at present. Moreover, managing these rivers is also vital for the agricultural growth of Bihar, which is a priority sector in Kumar's administration. So effective water management will provide relief to both Nepal and Bihar."[60]

Nepal leaders cultivate Bihar

In such circumstances, Nepal as well as the Border States should evolve some out of box thinking. Kathmandu should develop partnership with not only Delhi and Beijing but also with Patna, Dehradun and Lucknow. Bihar could not only be a model for Kathmandu but also become its natural economic partner on the other side of the border. This is why some Nepali leaders have taken up the issue not only with New Delhi but also with Bihar Government at times. During his visit to India Nepal Prime Minister Prachanda suggested a high dam on the river. He also discussed this issue with Prime Minister Manmohan Singh. By harnessing rivers originating from Nepal, Bihar could expect to rid itself of perennial devastation, while hoping to solve the power problem.

Nepal Prime Minister Baburam Bhattarai also visited Patna, on February 18, 2012 to inaugurate 'Global Summit on Changing Bihar: Forging Partnership for Development". He wanted to learn how Bihar changed its face within five years of the Nitish Kumar led government. During his visit to Patna, Bhattarai discussed a range of issues including the border dispute between Bihar and Nepal, development and bilateral cooperation. Also, the prospect of exploring cross-border water utilization, cross-border inundation

---

60 Akanshya Shah, *'Need for stronger role of States in ties with neighbours'* Observer Research foundation, 28 February 2012

and implementation of the Koshi Multi Purpose Project were on the agenda.

Bihar leaders assert to influence Nepal policy

The leaders from Bihar belonging to different parties too had made efforts to influence the South Block. The then Railway minister Lalu Prasad Yadav wanted to play a role in resolving the Koshi flood havoc and he wanted to visit Kathmandu to take it up with Prime Minister Prachanda in the first week of September 2008. However, Ministry of External Affairs persuaded him to drop the idea, as he had no Locus Standi to deal with Nepal. New Delhi frustrated **Lalu's efforts to directly talk to Nepal, as the State could not directly deal with the issue. In 2015, after Nepal adopted the new Constitution, when the Madeshis were protesting against it, Lalu and other Bihar leaders gave them vocal support.**

The Bihar Chief Minister Nitish Kumar has been putting pressure on the Centre to check the flow of the rivers from Nepal and bring the streams of Koshi River back to the previous level. He also seems to be doing his best to woo all sections of Nepali political opinion. He welcomed the Nepali Congress leader Pradip Giri in 2012 to Patna. The then Nepal Prime Minister Madhav Kumar Nepal and Chief Minister Nitish Kumar met on July 28,2013 and held detailed discussions on an extended Buddhist circuit involving Lumbini in Nepal and Bihar's Bodh Gaya, Rajgir and Vaishali. Nepali Congress President Sushil Koirala soon after taking over travelled to India on August 5, 2013 for five days and met the Prime Minister, foreign minister and also the Chief Ministers of U.P and Bihar. Even during Prime Minister Modi's visit to Kathmandu in 2014, tourism was a major topic of discussion.

Need to resolve the flood havoc caused by rivers from Nepal

Now the time has come for Nepal and India to work seriously to resolve the floods caused by the Nepalese rivers within the country and also across the border. The Border States are also looking for other forms of cooperation. Uttarakhand, which had been carved out of U.P in 2000, is also demanding its share of electricity. "The Uttarakhand government has asked the Centre to provide 13 per cent of power free of cost to the State as compensation for the Pancheswhar Multipurpose (PMP) project in Champawat district which will submerge an area spread over 120 square km and displace a substantial population. In a letter to Union Water Resources Minister Uma Bharti, Chief Minister Harish Rawat said an area spread over 120 km will be submerged by the proposed project affecting 19,700 people in 60 villages. Hence, the Centre should provide 13 per cent of power from the project to the State for free, besides giving it the first rights to purchase 50 per cent of the remaining amount of power from the project" [61]However, despite pressure, **the State leaders have not been able to make much headway so far because the Centre is not paying heed to their demands.**

Modi's overtures to Kathmandu

After Prime Minister Modi took over in May 2014, the relationship with Nepal began to change. Within days, he deputed his Foreign Minister Sushma Swaraj to Kathmandu. This came at a time when Nepal was struggling with the making of the Constitution and at a critical phase of political transition. Modi himself had visited Nepal twice. His bilateral visit in August 2014, one by an Indian Prime Minister after 17 years, had raised hope and tremendous goodwill in Nepal. He charmed the Nepalese with a rousing address in the Parliament of Nepal - the first by a foreign leader. He announced a soft loan of $1 billion and promised several infrastructure development projects. Prime ministers of India and Nepal agreed to review the Treaty of Peace and Friendship of 1950 and other bilateral agreements. Similarly, the Joint Commission which was formed in 1987 at the Foreign Ministers' level with a view to strengthening understanding and promoting cooperation between the two countries for mutual benefits in the economic, trade, transit and the multiple uses of water resources was reactivated after a gap of 23 years during the Nepal visit of External Affairs Minister Sushma Swaraj in July 2014.

Seeking to alley fears of Indian interference in Nepal's affairs, Prime Minister Modi had assured that India had no intent to "dictate" and it should choose its own course in its efforts to build a stable and

61 Press trust of India, '*Uttarakhand demands 13 per cent power from PMP project for free.*' The Hindu, August 3, 2014.

prosperous democratic republic. His second visit in November 2014 was for the SAARC summit, which also went off well.

Constitution making of Nepal

India and the Border States had their concern about the new Constitution. The Madhehsis, who have relations in UP and Bihar wanted a stake in the new Parliament. Naturally their cousins in Bihar and UP supported this claim. Nepal had been without a Constitution since 2008. Since 1950; Nepal has experimented with various Constitutions. It had two interim Constitutions (1951 and 2007) and three formal Constitutions (1951, 1962 and 1990.) The 2015 Constitution was the latest.

The Constitution writing was stuck on divisive issues like whether the government should be unitary or federal, the geographies of the federal units and the extent of devolution of authority to them. The two parties - the Nepali Congress and the Communist Party of Nepal (Unified Marxist Leninist), which hold together more than two thirds of the seats in the Assembly, wanted Nepal to be a unitary State. As this would concentrate power in the hand of the upper caste Nepalese, Madheshis, Tharus and others who form more than half the population opposed it. The Maoists and the regional parties had mooted an alternative proposal for a federal state and wanted the Constitution formed on the basis of consensus and not on the majority.

Nepal has different views on New Delhi's present role. One view was that since India facilitated the peace process in November 2005, it has a moral responsibility to ensure the successful conclusion of the process. The contrary view was that India should not interfere in the internal affairs of Nepal as it has been doing all along. In contrast, Beijing has kept away expressing that the Nepalese are capable of drafting their own Constitution. Chinese Premier Wen Jiabao during a visit to Nepal in January 2012 made it clear that it was entirely for the Nepalese people to prepare their Constitution without outside involvement. China has been investing heavily in Nepal's infrastructure, roads, rail and hydro -power projects. Even during the 2015 economic blockade Beijing came to the rescue and signed an agreement with Nepal to tide over the fuel and supply of essential commodities crisis.

Nepal is now going through its worst political crisis. The political parties had not been able to agree on a model of federalism and 118 other issues that are related to drafting the constitution. The Madheshi parties represent the entire plains area comprising 18% of the total geography of Nepal with 48% of the population. Anon-partisan approach was lacking among the stakeholders. Moreover, the unstable nature of Nepal's political system with 20 Prime Ministers in as many years keeps parties focused on remaining in power rather than delivering on a policy agenda.

As former Indian envoy to Nepal Shiv Shankar Mukherjee notes it happened "nine years after the people power ousted an entrenched monarchy and brought an armed insurgency into mainstream politics, eight years after an interim Constitution, two elections to a Constituent Assembly, followed by seven years of frustrating debates where politicians reverted to their addiction to squabbling. It took a devastating earthquake to force a sense of urgency to complete the exercise, which would form bedrock of Nepal's democracy." [62]

While it should have been a joyous occasion Nepal witnessed violence and discontent after the declaration of the new Constitution on September 20, 2015. The blame should certainly go to the mainstream parties like the Nepali Congress, the CPN (UML) and the Maoists as they were united in marginalizing the Madheshis, Janjatis and Dalits who have been denied adequate representation. As expected there was revolt in the Terai region and army was sent to quell the dissidence.

Oli takes over as Nepal Prime Minister

After the declaration of the Constitution on September 20, 2015, Prime Minister Sushil Koirala stepped down as required by the new Constitution and Nepal's Parliament has chosen Khadga Prasad Sharma Oli of the Communist Party of Nepal (Unified Marxist-Leninist) as the new Prime Minister, challenging him with rebuilding

---

62 Shiv Shankar Mukherjee, *India should ignore criticism of its Nepal policy and continue what it is doing*, Times of India, September 25, 2015.

recently earthquake-hit areas and calming street protests, to soothing tensions with neighbouring India.

The declaration of the new Constitution has not brought peace and stability to Nepal. The much-trumpeted "consensus", since 2006, only meant power sharing among the eight parties that came together under the 12-point agreement to form basically an anti-monarchy front. It has created a crisis with the Madehsis revolting. They had blocked the entry point at Raxaul – Birgnaj border, which feeds more than half the supplies to Nepal, which has resulted in long queues in front of gas stations, phenomenal price rise and looming scarcity of essential commodities since the promulgation of the Constitution on September 20. Madhesi leaders had specified their demand that at least 83 of 165 seats in the House of Representatives should be from Madhesh because they form the 51 per cent of the population, which means the rest will have less than 50 per cent of the seats. Kathmandu alleged that it was an undeclared official blockade supported by India backing the Madheshis. **As the Madeshi agitation affects the neighbouring Bihar, the Rashtriya Janata Dal of Lalu Prasad Yadav and JD (U) of the Nitish Kumar have expressed support to the Madheshis for their agitation while Delhi has been cautious. Even the leaders from UP like some BJP M.P.s have supported the Terai people. The Modi government felt that the Madheshi agitation might have an impact on the November 2015 Bihar elections because of their 'Roti-Beti ka Rishta' and went soft on the issue.**

In Nepal, the State- sponsored celebrations to welcome the Constitution were cut short and anti-India rhetoric and protests became routine even as the new regime of Prime Minister Oli was seen unstable. Both the Prime Minister and the new President Bidya Devi Bhandari are from the UML. Prachanda was more inclined to China and has openly said Nepal cannot be a 'yes man 'to India in his press statements.

Strained Indo- Nepal ties again

All the efforts of Prime Minister Narendra Modi to improve the ties with Nepal have more or less gone astray, as New Delhi is being blamed for the post- Constitution declaration crisis and Modi is being seen not as the hero that he was perceived earlier.

Nepal is being pushed into the arms of China once again as Beijing had come to its rescue by helping Kathmandu in its hour of need when the blockade continued. It had signed a Memorandum of Understanding with Kathmandu for supply of fuel to tide over the Blockade crisis. This is despite the fact that neither Kathmandu nor the Nepali citizens feel that China could become a substitute for India. However, there is no doubt that Beijing with its deep pocket can do much more than India to help Nepal financially.

Indo- Nepal economic relations

Geographical location of the land- locked Nepal has made the Nepalese economy dependent on India for decades. Kathmandu embraced economic diplomacy as a vital aspect of its foreign policy, particularly after the restoration of the multi party democracy in 1990. Since then, it is grappling with finding a way towards economic prosperity by liberalising its economy. "Nepal's remittances stand at $400 - $450 million accounting for nearly 25% of the country's GDP. According to the recent Asian Development Bank, Nepal's per-capita remittance income is one of the highest in world. Yet, a closer study of Nepal's remittance economy reveals that it has had little impact in altering the basic economic structures in Nepal." [63]

At a bilateral level, Nepal deals with other countries in trade, investment, and avoidance of double taxation. The Treaty of 1950 was the basis for political and economic relationship between India and Nepal. It established the framework for the unique relationship between the two countries. India has contributed significantly to the socio-economic development of Nepal including basic infrastructure such as airports, irrigation, agriculture, roads, bridges, power projects, industrial estates, communication, forestry, buildings along with some vital social sector areas like health, education, human resource development etc. A number of projects are underway. The Raxaul-Birgunj Broad Gauge Rail Link Project has eased the trade of both

63 Ruminations, '*Nepal's economy and future challenges,*'http://wordoutput. tumblr.com/, August 3,2014

countries. Setting up of an Emergency and Trauma Centre at the Bir hospital and the Mahendranagar-Tanakpur Link Road Project are some of India's other commitments.

Since the early 1950s, Nepal has been receiving much foreign aid for the development of agriculture, electricity, communications, education transportation, and the health sector. The globalisation and growing integration of Nepal's economy with the outside world has added new dimensions to its foreign policy. Nepal is not only a member of regional economic forums likes the South Asian Free Trade Area (SAFTA) and The Bay of Bengal Initiative for Multi-Sectorial Technical and Economic Cooperation (BIMSTEC) but also associated with the multilateral institutions like the World Trade Organisation (WTO), International Monetary Fund (IMF) and the World Bank.

Unfortunately, the successive Nepalese governments had not been able to improve its economy, due to political instability and also lack of vision. "India continues to be in the forefront of Nepal's all-round development as it shares an 1850-km-long open border. India has thus far funnelled in over Rs 3,600 crore as assistance to Nepal and is currently engaged in more than 370 developmental projects across Nepal with a total outlay of Rs 402 crores."[64]

New Delhi is proactively involved in upgrading Nepal's infrastructure and improving Indo-Nepal road and rail connectivity and has been a part of Nepal's growth story in such diverse areas as water resources, human resource development, health, power, civil aviation, tourism, and agriculture. India's upcoming high-priority connectivity projects in Nepal include construction of over 600 km of roads in the Terai region, setting up two integrated check-posts and two cross-border railway links over the next three years. In the second phase, additional 800 kms of roads, three cross-border railway links and two integrated check-posts would be constructed which would provide big boost to trade, investments and people-to-people

---

64 Rajeev Sharma, '*Why Nepal cant ignore India despite cosying up to China,*' First Post, July 9,2013

contacts between the two countries."[65]India is already engaged in building massive cross-border connectivity and infrastructure projects, which include 1450 kms of Terai roads and cross-border rail links at five locations.

Issues relating to trade and transit remain irritants even today. Many of Nepal's agricultural and industrial Centres are concentrated in the Terai region bordering UP and Bihar. This is mainly because Nepal's trade with other countries involves the transit of goods through Indian Territory. Nepal's nearest port facilities are at Haldia port, Kolkata and Chittagong, Mangola port in Bangladesh. Government of India has provided financial assistance to Nepal for the development of cross border trade infrastructure, including the up gradation of four major custom check points at Birgunj – Raxau, Biratnagar - Jogbani, Bhairahawa - Sunau and Nepalgunj - Rupediya to global standards.

Kathmandu insisted on separate treaties for the trade and transit and succeeded during the Morarji Desai regime in 1978. In March 1983, this Treaty was renewed, which subsequently expired in March 1988. It reached the climax in the late eighties when the chemistry between Rajiv Gandhi and King Birendra became worse. The 1989 stalemate in trade negotiations and the subsequent economic blockade choked the Nepalese economy

Although economic issues were a major factor in the confrontation, there were other factors for the souring of relationship. China and Pakistan spoke against the economic blockade. The United States came very close to faulting India for the impasse.

Eventually, the trade and transit dispute was finally resolved in June 1990 when there was a regime change in Nepal and also India. Kathmandu had realized that to resolve any difficulties in the economic sphere, it was important to maintain friendly relations with India. In June 1990 the two countries established a special security relationship when the new Nepal Prime Minister Krishna Prasad Bhattarai visited New Delhi. The next step was when Nepal

---

65 Rajeev Sharma, '*Why Nepal cant ignore India despite cosying up to China,*' First Post, July 9,2013

Prime Minister G.P. Koirala visited New Delhi the two countries signed new separate trade and transit treaties and new economic agreements benefitting Nepal.

During the Narasimha Rao regime from 1991 to 96, Nepal Prime Minister Manmohan Adhikari insisted on a re-look at the 1950 Treaty seeking greater economic independence for his country. A far-reaching trade Treaty was signed in December 1996, which provided duty free access to Nepalese goods in Indian market.

The Sher Bahadur Deuba government adopted a consensus approach in signing a Treaty on Integrated Development of the Mahakali Basin in February 1997 in New Delhi when the Treaty came into effect. By this time there was a regime change in India led by Deve Gowda and succeeded by Inder Kumar Gujral. It was Gujral who agreed to the long time request of Nepal for alternative transit route to and through Bangladesh. During Gujral's visit to Nepal in June 1997, a power agreement was also signed to encourage private and semi-government investment in Nepal. After the Mahakali Agreement this was a significant development. Also, both the countries had the freedom to enter into an agreement with a third party to generate resources for exploiting power. A Memorandum of Understanding was signed on civil aviation, which allowed private airlines to operate between the two countries in the light of growing business and tourism; Bangalore and Lucknow airports were opened up for the flights arriving from Nepal. It was indeed a huge step forward when Vajpayee agreed to automatically renew the Treaty every seven years unless either party gave a notice to end it.

Bilateral trade between India and Nepal has received further impetus after the signing of the revised Trade Treaty in 2009, which allows Nepal greater access to the Indian market. It was aimed at greater trade promotion. There has been an effort to simplify, standardize, and harmonize all customs, transport, and other trade-related procedures and has tried to help in the development of border infrastructure.

"India is Nepal's largest trade partner as nearly 67 per cent of Nepal's foreign trade is with India. Nepal's trade deficit reached nearly Rs 400 billion during the last fiscal year, and almost 68 per cent of the imbalance was with India. To meet the trade deficit, Nepal has been selling US dollars to India, amounting to 4.8 per cent of India's total external sector accounts, as suggested by the Reserve Bank of India (RBI). Nepali traders and economists have accused India of creating tariff and non-tariff barriers."[66]The Transit Treaty was renewed on 5 January 2013 for 7 years.

"India also remains Nepal's largest source of foreign investment and Indian investments in Nepal amount to Rs2175.5 crores with 525 FDI projects. India accounts for 46% of the total foreign investments in Nepal. In October-November 2011 the two countries have also concluded the Bilateral Investment Protection and Promotion Agreement (BIPPA) and the Double Taxation Avoidance Agreement (DTAA), which provide legal framework for enhancing Indian investment into Nepal." [67]

Need for better Indo- Nepal ties

The future of Indo-Nepal relations is important for India's security concerns and good neighbourly relations. While stability continues to elude the Nepal political establishment India had supported the peace process. The inability of the Koirala government to deal with the massive earthquake that affected Nepal in April 2015 was seen as another example for the weakness of this government. Oli was faced with a first class crisis on his hand with the blockade with the tacit support of India and also the bordering Indian states of Bihar and UP.

In conclusion, Nepal may be looking to other countries like China for its development, but no country can replace India. Nepal being a small country between the two big powers wants to keep China happy. The Chinese have built good roads. Beijing has been openly demanding equal treatment with India and the same kind of treaties with Nepal. With all the projects in Tibet and all that buildings and rails with Nepal border gives them greater accessibility

---

66 Bhim Prasad Burtel, *"Long time, no see"* Kathmandu Times, 3 August 2014.

67 *India – Nepal relations*, http://mea.gov.in/Portal/ForeignRelation/India-Nepal_Relations.pdf

to make their presence felt in Nepal unlike in the past. For instance, China has entered the hydro- electric sector, trying to push Indian and other companies out of Nepal. Beijing also wants to control Nepal in order to ensure there are no activities from the Tibetans across which can be problematic to them. The Nepalese are very sensitive about this and they cooperate. So when there is a powerful neighbour like China with huge financial resources at its command if New Delhi wants to create a friendly image and sink that impression in Nepal that India is a rising power, a big power, economically prosperous then it is in Nepal's interest to join India, take advantage of the Indian market. This is the big task ahead if New Delhi wants better relations with Nepal. "When it comes to Nepal the role of the States in being an integral part of a coherent national level policy is also very important but New Delhi has not developed a system in which such coordination takes place. So there is a big lacuna. It is neither the State's failure nor the Centre's failure but systemic failure.[68]"

External Affairs Minister Sushma Swaraj was candid in what New Delhi expects from Kathmandu. "You can't say that Bihar and UP are hijacking our Nepal policy. Our stand on Nepal is that their Constitution should be made by consensus because only the formulation of the Constitution is not material but that all parties have to own the constituting which is material. All parties will own the Constitution only when it is made by consensus. So we are only telling them again and again that 'you are a sovereign country and we cannot interfere but as a friend we can suggest these things. Please don't go by numbers because we know you have numbers. But the peace process, which was started here, we want that to reach its logical conclusion.' So we wish them well. We are telling them again and again go by consensus and not by majority.[69]"

But the silver lining is that monarchy is dead and there is broad agreement across the political spectrum, excluding the extreme right and left, that Nepal will be a federal democratic republic, and that the new Constitution will reflect the progressive changes in Nepal's

68 Author's interview with Kanwal Sibal, (13 July 2014)

69 Author's interview with Sushma Swaraj, (March 2015)

polity. As Ambassador Jayant Prasad notes, "The inclusive nature of Nepalese society gives reasons for hope that the unfinished tasks of the peace process will be completed. In spite of per capita income levels declining towards close to half of India's average, Nepal has done better than India on several Millennium Development Goals (MDG), including infant mortality, maternal health, child malnutrition and poverty reduction rates."[70]

The mistakes committed and the way forward for Indo Nepal ties

As mentioned above, no other country is so directly affected by internal political developments in Nepal, as India. It is New Delhi, which had supported the successive Nepali generations who fought against undemocratic regimes. Therefore it is important to have a stable and peaceful Nepal in the neighbourhood.

Looking back many mistakes had been committed from both sides. There is tremendous scope for improving the bilateral ties between India and Nepal. New Delhi as well as Kathmandu should look back and rectify the mistakes committed in these seven decades. Both can take their ties to a new level with dynamism and pragmatism if they trust each other. This is what is lacking still. In the past 10-years the political and bureaucratic establishments in Kathmandu and New Delhi have failed to ensure smooth ties. Nepal must also put its house in order and seize the moment of opportunity. Any policies that India may pursue towards Nepal must first attempt an appreciation of Nepali concerns Vis-a-Vis India as they need to be taken note of for future,

For instance, if Nepal resents its dependence on India, the patronising attitude of New Delhi will be of no help as it only breeds resentment. While Nepal appreciates its cultural affinity with India, it also has apprehension when it talks of the Hindu Kingdom. Kathmandu also feels that most treaties and agreements are unequal and not conducive to Nepal's interests. Rightly or wrongly Kathmandu believes that India influences political developments in

---

70 Jayant Prasad, *A new template for Indo – Nepal ties,* The Hindu, August 2,2014

Nepal. The 12- point agreement of the peace accord is cited as a classic example. But New Delhi's defence is that it only does so following requests from Nepal. The desire for change in Nepal provides India an opportunity of recasting the substance of Indo-Nepal relations in a fresh mould.

Prime Minister Modi has been talking of 'neighbours first' policy and has taken the first step forward when he took over in May 2014 by inviting the heads of neighbouring countries for his swearing in ceremony. He had been making the right noises, assuring Nepal of going the extra mile. For Modi, the challenge is to maintain the leverage through social, political and economic means and yet not get too deeply involved in Nepal's domestic politics. New Delhi, on its part, needs to come out with a clear Nepal policy and forget its old mind-set of looking at Nepal as its backyard. South Block should realize that the monarchy is dead and that new forces have emerged in Nepal. While Kathmandu plays the China card New Delhi should not over react and realize that China is its other big neighbour and naturally Nepal would use it for its own benefit.

Hydro-projects and dams situated on the Indo-Nepal border should be maintained and managed by the Indian government. Border crossing should be mechanized to avoid delay and corruption. New Delhi should enhance and upgrade co-operation with Nepalese agencies to patrol and manage the border. Nepalese authorities have aided their Indian counterparts to check the activities of terrorists who have often sheltered in Nepal. Differences between the two countries have prevented the effective exploitation of the Ganga river basin, either for irrigation, flood control or for hydropower. But in recent years, both sides have not only learnt to respect each other's red lines but also their respective limitations. As far as India is concerned, there should be no reservations if Nepal chooses to enter into arrangements with third countries or parties for the development of its most significant resource.

As Ambassador A.N. Ram notes, "essential commodities like cooking gas, salt and sugar etc. go from India at a subsidized rate. Most importantly they were getting oil at subsidized domestic prices. Now we have stopped giving them at domestic prices and are selling them at international prices. The Nepalese who have got used to cheaper goods do not like this. Likewise every Nepalese child who studies in Indian schools used to pay domestic rate of fees but now we are saying they should be charged international fee. This too is resented. Bihar politicians take this up with the Central government and ask why you are changing the status quo. But who is going to pay for it? It is not Bihar but the Centre, particularly if we are not going to get anything in return."[71]

Despite the revival of the Joint Commission during visit of Sushma Swaraj, trust deficit between the two countries continue to exist. There are apprehensions that many issues agreed upon during the meeting would either be delayed, or might not materialize at all. Given the lack of consensus among the Nepalese political parties on India's role in the water and infrastructure projects in Nepal, New Delhi has a difficult task ahead to translate its promises in the joint Statement into reality. Existing treaties, border disputes, security concerns and India's alleged support to certain groups in the Terai region and personal level support to Nepali Congress leaders are major irritants in India-Nepal relations. These issues have been generating anti-India feelings and thus needed immediate attention

As Shyam Saran observes "Nepal policy has failed to keep pace with the multiple and far reaching transitions that have been taking place in the country over the past two decades and more."[72] This aspect has to be addressed by both countries.

Secondly, Kathmandu and New Delhi should ensure that the high level visits continue and all misunderstandings between the two are removed by dialogue at the highest level and through high level visits from both sides. Thirdly, the future of federalism and the aspirations of the Madheshis need to be addressed. This is what New Delhi has been stressing to the Nepal leaders after the declaration of the new Constitution. For this all the political parties including the Maoists must work together putting the interest of Nepal above all

---

71 Author's interview with A.N. Ram (28, September 2014)

72 Shyam Saran, *'Constitutional error,'* *The Indian Express,* September 26, 2015

else. Right now the new Constitution has created more problems than finding a solution.

India is naturally worried that violence in the aftermath of the declaration of Constitution might spill over to Indian Border States; As Shyam Saran notes," But the current crisis also exposes a continuing weakness in India's neighbourhood policy, an attention-deficit that is only episodically shaken when a crisis erupts. It also appears that there may have been mixed political message conveyed to the Nepal side, which may have underestimated India's reaction. Both these aspects need to be addressed in order to avoid similar crisis in the future."[73]

New Delhi has to dispel the feeling in Nepal that the blockade had the blessings of India. Any action that affects the common man in Nepal is not good for India. Neither is a feeling that New Delhi is mounting such pressure on Kathmandu. While there is nothing wrong in India taking up the cause of the Madheshis, it should be subtle. It should rather encourage the two warring sides to sit down and talk to each other. In fact, the challenge before the Modi government is how to address the bitterness that has grown and has turned into anti – India rhetoric.

If Nepal's political system has changed from monarchy to multi- party democracy in the past six decades India too has changed from Congress dominated single party rule in the fifties and sixties to a multi party system, dominated by the regional parties since the eighties.

Thirdly, Nepal needs foreign investments to boost its economy, improve infrastructure and provide jobs to new generation of modern youth. India accounts for the biggest chunk of Foreign Direct Investment coming to Nepal. Nepal government and political parties need to assure the Indian investors that it is safe to invest and also provide a proper business environment. The political leadership should try to utilize the abundant natural resources as well as its human resources to the advantage of Nepal. Kathmandu should

---

73 Shyam Saran, *'Constitutional error,'* The Indian Express, September 26, 2015

also take advantage of its geo-strategic location between two largest markets and strive for greater market access, mobilization of aid for trade, and reducing transit related costs. Given the importance of Nepal to India's security, in both conventional and non-conventional terms, it is time to consider increasing the quantum of assistance.

'China as an option to India' has been a running theme in Nepal's strategic thinking, even if never fully developed. China may be willing to play low cost games in Nepal to frustrate India, but India is not the primary focus of their attention. The primary Chinese concern in Nepal is the establishment of a strong central authority, who can deliver on Chinese security interests in Tibet. That was why Beijing supported the palace, and was wooing the Maoists after their success in elections.

India and China have one common interest in Nepal. Both would like a politically stable Nepal in their backyards. For India, on the other hand, both democracy and the welfare of the Nepali people are of direct and abiding interest. Ambassador A.N. Ram observes, "I think we should restructure our relations with Nepal and make it normal. You do away with some of the aberrations. Nepalese are allowed to work in India. They get citizenship sometimes. They can settle down here. They join the administrative services and they join the army. I am not saying do away with all these but regulate it." [74]

New Delhi wants to focus more on economic engagements with Nepal, which can provide stability and rightly so. Major decisions regarding Nepal should be taken at a senior political level rather than entrusting middle and junior level diplomats or intelligence agencies to dabble in the Nepal policy. Secondly, New Delhi should not meddle in Nepal's internal matters unless it concerns India's interests. Nepal, on the other hand should stop anti- India rhetoric and keep India engaged in fruitful dialogue. After all, Nepal's interests are closely linked with India. The agenda for Indo-Nepal relations is a vast one covering various areas.

Ambassador Jayant Prasad suggests that having developed the confidence over the past decade to work with any democratic

---

74 Author's interview with A.N. Ram (9 November 2014)

electoral outcome in Nepal, India should keep the day-to-day bilateral institutional mechanisms in play. "Many of these need a strong push from the two governments to speed up their implementation. There exists excellent two-way cooperation between the respective security agencies to deal with difficult cross-border issues such as terrorism, smuggling (including of fake Indian currency notes), and trafficking."[75] One thing is certain. There is a running thread of permanence in India's interests and concerns vis-à-vis Nepal and what is valid today will be so for the future.

75 Author's interview with Jayant Prasad, (26February, 2015)

Chapter 5

Conclusions

Do the regional chieftains have an increasing role in influencing India's foreign policy? The answer is yes. Is this a move in the right direction? Some might say 'yes' and others 'no.' In case of conflict of interests between the Centre and the States who should prevail? Undoubtedly the Union Government, as that is what the Constitution says. Has federalism worked well in India? The Emphatic answer is yes. Is there a need for a re-look at the formulation of India's foreign policy in view of the assertion of the regional satraps? Indeed there is every need to take the powerful regional chieftains on board for a smooth, sharper and effective neighbourhood foreign policy. In an era of global politics and interdependence, foreign policy is certainly closer home than ever before. Therefore the domestic politics leaves a stamp in foreign policy, which is increasingly becoming evident in the past three decades. After all, the domestic and foreign policy are the two sides of the same coin.

The coalition era, which began in 1989, has given an indication that the regional players have come to dominate Indian politics because of weak national parties. The Congress has lost its dominance and the BJP has just become an alternative. The Left parties are sliding. The regional parties have limited influence in their pockets. The Centre has become weaker due to the fracturing of the polity. Also in recent times it has been depending on the regional parties for the survival of the government in Parliament. But the 2014 election results have given an interesting scenario with the Prime Minister Modi heading a stable single party government

Coalition and single party rule

Several conclusions can be reached on the basis of the study by this author on the growing clout of the regional satraps in all spheres including the formulation of the foreign policy. This is more so regarding the Border States particularly Nepal, Bangladesh and Sri Lanka, which the author had taken up for study. The one glaring conclusion is that do not take the Indian electorate for granted as they can change the political scenario whenever they want. India is a mature democracy and the voters have a will to change the government ruthlessly when they are dissatisfied. They did so after Indira Gandhi imposed emergency in 1975. They did so when the successor Janata government failed. They threw out the Rajiv Gandhi government after the Bofors scam. They replaced the V.P. Singh government following the 'Mandal and Kamandal' fiasco. When they were not happy with the Vajpayee government despite the "India shining" propaganda, they brought in the UPA 1 and 11 and now the electorate has given Narendra Modi a chance in 2014. They had shown their power more than once that the masses even if some of the voters were illiterate couldn't be taken for granted. The same is the case with regard to the provincial governments.

From the late eighties till 2014, the emerging trend had been that India might be stuck with coalition politics for many more years and the regional players might control the Centre. The question still remains whether the return of the BJP led National Democratic Alliance (NDA) headed by Modi means declining clout of the regional satraps or the country may go back to the coalition era if Modi is not able to deliver his promises. This will be known only in 2019 when the next elections take place.

Two major factors make it imperative that the status quo in making foreign policy is not likely to continue. The first is the rise of the strong regional parties in the context of the coalition governments and why the Union Government cannot ignore them. The other is that some regional satraps have emerged as excellent administrators and have facilitated economic growth in their respective States, which get them votes. In fact the credit for India's success story goes to the States more than the Centre, because chief ministers like Narendra

Modi, Chandrababu Naidu, Jayalalaithaa and S.M. Krishna, played a pivotal role in the growth of economy. Many other States such as Bihar, Madhya Pradesh, Odisha and Rajasthan were lagging behind until good administrators such as Nitish Kumar, Shivraj Singh Chauhan, Naveen Patnaik and Vasundhara Raje took over. Even Tamil Nadu got a boost during Jayalalaithaa's regimes.

As seen in the previous chapters, the foreign policy making is the domain of the Union Government and the States have no role under the Indian Constitution. While they may not have any direct control on foreign policy issues, they have their jurisdiction on three important subjects like land, water and law and order. With a more than comfortable majority it may be tempting for Prime Minister Modi to ignore the provincial chieftains as partners in foreign policy execution. Out of necessity, he might adopt a reconciliatory attitude even with the non – BJP ruled States and appear to be non- partisan, particularly on issues pertaining to the States, if he wants to succeed. He has shown this flexibility when dealing with Mamata Banerjee on the Land Boundary Agreement and persuaded her to come on board. The consultative door with regional leaders needs to be kept open for smooth functioning. **After all, on the economic side many States are courting foreign investment and therefore the cooperation between the Centre and the States should be a regular feature. If they acquire economic clout it would only strengthen the power of India in the world. Strong States and strong Centre is what India needs. Moreover the implementation is in the hands of the States and only a cordial relationship with the Chief Ministers can achieve this.**

If one analyses the 2014 election results, it was the personalities who dominated the poll scene and not the individual regional or national political parties. This is because powerful national and regional personalities dominated the elections. Although the BJP had emerged successful in getting 282 seats, more than the required majority of 272, the 2014 elections have also proved that regional satraps are no less relevant in their respective States be it Mamata Banerjee, (West Bengal) Naveen Patnaik (Odisha), Jayalalithaa, (Tamil Nadu), Prakash Singh Badal (Punjab), Chandrababu Naidu (Andhra Pradesh), and K.Chandrashekhar Rao (Telengana). In fact, even the

BJP's regional chieftains like Vasundhara Raje (Rajasthan), Shiv Raj Singh Chouhan (Madhya Pradesh), Raman Singh (Chattisgarh) to name a few have delivered their States for the BJP. Each one of them has come out with flying colours in the elections and continues to have their sway over the electorate. The latest to join this elite club is the Delhi Chief Minister Arvind Kejriwal whose party won 67 of the 70 Assembly seats in 2015. Bihar has seen the return of Nitish Kumar with a massive majority in November 2015. The exceptions were Mulayam Singh Yadav (SP) and Mayawati (BSP) in Uttar Pradesh. But even earlier the SP and the BSP were not crucial though they supported the Manmohan Singh government for their own self- interest. Both these parties were routed in the 2014 Lok Sabha polls. The BJP has won at the cost of the Congress and the Left parties. Therefore it is clear that when there was a personality clash and the regional chieftains were more appealing than Modi, the voters preferred the regional satraps. **The Union Government is not in a position to bulldoze its views on States when they have strong chieftains. This is why Prime Minister Modi has been talking of teamwork with the Chief Ministers and cooperative federalism.**

Should Centre take note of concerns of States?

The second conclusion is an emerging need for the Union Government to address the concerns of the States. **A time has come when the Nehruvian practice of just informing the States will not work any more, as the State chieftains want to be consulted before and not after the decisions are taken.** Prime Minister Modi is right when he talks of the need to trust Chief Ministers, of allowing them with greater authority and flexibility to decide what is best for the States they represent. He wants the States to take decision on how to spend the Central funds and also of involving them in the formulation of foreign policy that directly impacts their interests. He told the Rajya Sabha on June 11, 2014, "I have experienced how the requests of the States have not been approved for personal reasons," referring to his past experience as Gujarat Chief Minister. He has declared, "I believe in cooperative federalism. We need to work with the States."[1]But this may not happen tomorrow. With the polity

---

1   Hartosh Singh Bal, *'Gaining the upper hand'*, The Caravan, July 1,2014

sharply divided on ideologies, caste and identity politics it may take some time to overcome the differences.

One cannot expect either Prime Minister Modi or the non – BJP ruled States to publicly appreciate each other because of party politics, which directly concerns their vote banks. As Minister of State for External Affairs Gen. V.K. Singh notes "the Chief Ministers come to Delhi and agree on certain things but when they go back, they often change their stand for their vote bank politics." [2] Moreover, Chief Ministers also take often a stand not on the merit of the issue. **To the extent possible the Prime Minister and the Chief Ministers could be on the same page but it needs two hands to clap.** The classic example was the Iraq nurse crisis in 2014. New Delhi and Kerala had worked together to get the Indian nurses stranded in Iraq released putting aside their political differences. The Congress led Ommen Chandy government in Kerala had supported the Centre's move in getting them released and had used its own influence with the church. The States should note that in a situation like this the people want the safety and welfare of their kith and kin and are not concerned whether the same party or different parties rule the Centre and the States.

Growth of Regional Satraps

The third is that **there are indications that the emergence of the regional chieftains may not only continue but also grow in the coming days, if the party ruling at the Centre is not able to fulfil the aspirations of the people.** New States like Telengana and Delhi are adding to the elite club of regional satraps. Even the Telugu Desam Supremo Chandrababu Naidu, who had been out of power for the past 15 years had bounced back in the new bifurcated State of Andhra Pradesh. Going by their personalities and political views they may not have much knowledge about foreign affairs but they could still jump into the foreign policy debate.

The Centre must guard against one danger. Sometimes regional leaders do not have the capacity to comprehend hostile forces, which are at work and shape the power equations at the global, regional and

---

2   Author's interview with Gen V.K. Singh

bilateral levels among nation-States. Therefore it would be wise on the part of the Union Government to not only brief them fully but also seek their suggestions and act on them wherever possible. The situation on this critical issue is becoming increasingly glaring with the result foreign policy has become a foot ball game

Need to Involve all Stakeholders

The fourth is the need to involve all stakeholders. Every country's foreign policy generally has elements of 'continuity and change' when a new government takes over. India's foreign policy under Prime Minister Modi is no different. It is increasingly becoming evident that a sound foreign policy has also to be rooted in the domestic policy.

Some experts feel that the regional parties influencing foreign policy is just another part of how democracy works as these are the new dimensions of democracy and consensus building is part of the policy formation. Modi's foreign policy is still evolving and it should take note of this important aspect. Modi, as Gujarat Chief Minister, did not question the constitutional position on foreign policy, which is that States cannot make independent foreign policy. The policy formulation is within the exclusive jurisdiction of the Centre and there is no mechanism to consult the States and he had accepted that. **Therefore, there is a greater recognition among the foreign policy makers and strategists on the need of reaching out to various domestic interests.**

Assertion by Regional Satraps

The fifth is that the level of assertion by the regional satraps has been on the increase in all aspects including the foreign policy arena. Earlier it used to be just about half a dozen States, but today with the globalisation and the number of Indians migrating to other countries for jobs the stakes have increased. The Diaspora is also putting pressure on the Chief Ministers of their respective States to resolve problems concerning their welfare abroad. Those, which have special links with certain countries, demand that they should be consulted in framing policies towards those countries. For example Gujarat had special relations with the UK, the USA, Africa, West Asia, China and

Japan, Odisha with Indonesia, Goa with Portugal, Puducherry with France, Tamil Nadu with Sri Lanka, Singapore and Malaysia. Bihar, UP, Uttarakhand, Sikkim and Bihar have special ties with Nepal and Buddhist countries. Kerala has economic connection with the Gulf countries and the Keralites have fanned out in various other parts of the world. Similarly Punjab, U.P, Bihar, Uttarakhand, West Bengal, Tripura and the other Northeastern States have strong bonds with Pakistan, Bangladesh, Myanmar, Bhutan and Nepal. Many Punjabis have moved to the U.K, Canada, Australia and the US. Therefore the regional satraps legitimately expect that their interests should be safeguarded, coming under the pressure of the Diaspora.

In some cases even the State units of the national parties take a different line on issues pertaining to their States. For instance the then Punjab Chief Minister Captain Amarinder Singh on July 12, 2014 convened a special session of Punjab Assembly and charted a new course by enacting a legislation to annul all past pacts entered into by the State on sharing of the Ravi and Beas waters, including the 1981 agreement with the neighbouring Haryana and Rajasthan, without the consent of the Congress ruled Manmohan Singh government at the Centre. Tamil Nadu unit of the Congress Party was a party to the resolution in the State Assembly against Sri Lankan government recently. This fact that State units of the national party take different views shows that even for the national parties local interests come first.

Centre giving in to Pressure from States

The sixth is that **there is clear evidence that the Centre has given in to accommodate the demands of the State chieftains, particularly in the last decade or so.** While the Union Government did not pay heed to the discordant voices from Tamil Nadu on the Shastri – Sirimavo pact or Indira Gandhi- Bandaranaike pact earlier, the same Centre has given in to the demands of Tamil Nadu by voting against Sri Lanka in the United Nations Human Rights Commission resolution in 2012 and abstained from voting the next year again bowing to the pressure from the Dravidian parties. Manmohan Singh had even skipped the Commonwealth Heads of State meeting held in Colombo in November 2013 due to the pressure from Tamil Nadu political parties including the UPA ally DMK.

Do the provincial leaders have a larger vision on foreign policy or a worldview? It is quite doubtful because they obviously do not have a full picture. No doubt that there is need for developing a 'vision' for the region and develop a consistent foreign policy line. Prime Minister Manmohan Singh had learnt the lesson the hard way as to how the best of his plans and pet projects had been completely stymied when the States did not cooperate. While he went all out in getting the other parties on board on the Indo – US nuclear deal, the UPA's inability in getting the States' cooperation on counter-terrorism, Foreign Direct Investment in retail, and Land Acquisition Bill were all failed initiatives so far. The Modi government too is now struggling to get these measures passed.

Importance of Border States

The seventh is that **the strategic community as well as the External Affairs Ministry and the Prime Minister's Office have come to recognize the importance of the Border States for security and greater connectivity with the neighbouring countries. There is a growing realisation in New Delhi that Northeast should be given due importance for both economic and strategic connectivity.** There is even a new ministry created for the region. The 'Look East policy' envisaged by Prime Minister P.V. Narasimha Rao in early nineties was a step in this direction and almost all the successive Prime Ministers have given some importance to the development of Northeast but despite that the region is crying for connectivity and development. Now Prime Minister Modi is talking of "Act East" policy, an improvement of the 'Look East 'policy. During the Manmohan Singh regime from 2004 -2014, New Delhi had adopted an open approach in both the Western and the Eastern sides. In the East there were efforts for enhanced connectivity between the Northeast and Bangladesh. In the Western side, Jammu and Kashmir and Punjab demand more trade with Pakistan. Connectivity between the Northeast and Myanmar also has opened up as also between the Northeast and Bhutan, Bangladesh and Nepal by way of improved rail and road links. However, much more needs to be done as the people of the region feel neglected and cut off from the mainstream.

The 'Seven Sisters' would be the gateway to the success of the 'Act East 'policy. **As India's Border States continue to grow with domestic and foreign investment, their influence on the Centre is also likely to grow.**

The ministry for Development of North-eastern region and the External Affairs Ministry want a bigger role for the Border States. Similarly the concerns of Punjab, Jammu and Kashmir, Tamil Nadu, Kerala and Rajasthan should be addressed if the Centre wants to avoid any friction.

External Affairs Minister Sushma Swaraj talks about the Modi government's plans for the connectivity with the Northeast."India, Myanmar, Thailand, Nepal, Bhutan and Bangladesh- all these projects of road and sea connectivity we are doing them. Actually these were not on the agenda of the previous government. Now our connectivity of Northeast with Bangladesh, with Bhutan and with Myanmar all these things are on our agenda and on the top of it.[3]"

Positive and Negative Pressures from the States

The eighth is that there is a consensus over the fact that Chief Ministers have strived to influence both in a positive and negative way. On the positive side, Assam, Tripura, Meghalaya, Arunachal Pradesh, Mizoram, Manipur and Nagaland in the East, which share borders with Bangladesh and Myanmar respectively, have been pitching for closer ties for economic and trade benefits. Others such as West Bengal and Tamil Nadu have been more belligerent at times and get bogged down by local political constraints and their petty vote bank politics. Tamil Nadu could benefit by more trade and investment with Sri Lanka. So it is clear that there is pressure from the States for positive relations and there is also negative pressure for confrontation.

---

3   Author's interview with Sushma Swaraj, (March,2015)

Positive and negative influences on economic side

Even on the economic side, there are positive and negative influences from the provincial leaders. In the context of Pakistan, the Centre will find it difficult to ignore States such as Jammu and Kashmir, Rajasthan and Punjab who want better trade and commercial ties with their neighbours. Business lobbies and the Chamber of Commerce and Industry in Gujarat have also been lobbying for an overland trade route and closer ties with Karachi. Some other States like Odisha, which have more trade with Sri Lanka, press for better relations and this is one of the reasons why the Centre did not want to take a harsh stand on confrontation with Sri Lanka on the Tamil issue.

While there are limitations on the part of the States in dealing with the foreign policy there have been differences on some larger issues like the World Trade Organization, Goods and Services Tax and Foreign Direct Investment in retail. Most State governments want a say in the Treaties. Moreover, there are criticisms that the bureaucracy in New Delhi is unwilling to share the turf with the States. By and large, the Prime Minister's Office, National Security Adviser who reports to the Prime Minister and the foreign ministry continue to play a key role in the policy- making.

Is a special mechanism needed for coordination?

The ninth is the question whether any special mechanism is needed for coordination between New Delhi and the States on foreign policy formulation. Most former Foreign Secretaries this author interviewed agree that there is need for more consultation. Major drawbacks, which have developed in the system in the past decade or so, have emerged partly because of the lack of engagement on the part of the Centre.

It is gladdening to note that the Modi government has already setup a separate division in the External Affairs Ministry headed by a joint secretary to facilitate the requirements of the States in November 2014. Sushma Swaraj points out "Prime Minister Modi wanted to adopt cooperative federalism and when we say 'Make in India' the FDI will come but not to Delhi as it will go to the States. So

States have to be on board. It is the job of the new division to put all State governments in touch with other countries. The joint secretary in charge has become the nodal officer for States coordination with foreign countries. It is absolutely a new post and it will increase the coordination with States and other countries."[4]

Setting up of this new division is indeed a novel idea. This is expected to be a link between India's missions abroad and the States to fulfil their requirements relating to their investment and trade. It is also expected to help the States in investment promotion, tourism, hosting of trade exhibition and education. The division coordinates the visits of foreign dignitaries to tier 2 cities. It facilitates foreign visits by the State delegations, speed up passport processing and issuance and act as a facilitating agent between the States seeking investment promotion and foreign countries. It also ensures coordination between the Centre and States for setting up projects by facilitating political clearances and protocol matters.

However, this is only at the official level. **What is needed is more interaction at the political level between the Prime Minister and the Chief Ministers. Leaders like Nagaland's Rio, Mizoram's Lalthanhawla, Assam's Tarun Gogoi, Sikkim's Pawan Chamling, Tripura's Manik Sarkar and Arunachal Pradesh's Nabum Tuki are far better equipped and knowledgeable to drive foreign policy that benefit the Northeast and India than the mandarins in Delhi.**

The Chief Ministers are not going to listen to the officials and therefore the existing mechanism like the Niti Ayog, National Integration Council or National Development Council and National Integration Council should be utilized for more interaction. The Prime Minister could even form a group of Chief Ministers of Border States and periodically interact with them on neighbourhood policies. This two- way communication could help resolve many knotty problems. Unless the political aspect is addressed there can be no hope for the Union Government and the States walking hand in hand.

---

4   Author's interview with Sushma Swaraj, (March 2015)

Sushma Swaraj, however, is of the view that there is no need for special Border State Chief Ministers Council. "If you call the Chief Ministers of the Border States for a conference for one day you cannot achieve anything. They may come, read their speeches and go. We have developed a new mechanism, which is better because you talk to one by one. This separate mechanism for each State is much deeper and effective than calling all the Chief Ministers of Border States for a meeting. They have different issues."[5]

Greater autonomy for Border States

The tenth is **that Border States should be given greater autonomy when it comes to economic investment and infrastructure projects. Prime Minister Modi has been speaking about the need to grant a more meaningful role to States in foreign policy.** Other States could emulate 'Vibrant Gujarat' shows to attract investment. Bihar has already done it. The participation of Finance Minister Arun Jaitley in the West Bengal Global Summit in February 2015 was an encouraging sign in this regard. Tamil Nadu also hosted a global investor's meet in Chennai in September 2015. While different States have different strengths, they can learn from each other's experience with regard to the organisation of these summits, and understand what makes some more effective than others. The Commerce ministry could have a separate wing to coordinate with the States so that trade and infrastructure cooperation with the neighbours could be promoted further.

First move towards greater autonomy for the States

Looking back, the first move towards greater autonomy to States began during the United Front regime in 1996-98 when a number of centrally sponsored schemes were transferred to them due to the pressure from the regional partners. The National Conference actually passed a resolution for greater autonomy in June 26, 2000. This demand has not disappeared even today.

How will Prime Minister Modi facilitate the participation of Border States in foreign policy making? Will he encourage independence in trade and economic activities or will the security angle

---

5 . Author's interview with Sushma Swaraj (March, 2015)

overshadow everything else? Modi has begun well by emphasising his "neighbourhood first" policy by concentrating on the neighbours. Apart from high- level visits from both sides he should take steps to ensure closer trade relations and increased connectivity.

There will be some interest as to how Modi deals with his new coalition partner the PDP. With the demise of Mufti Mohammed Sayeed in December 2015, things have changed. The People's Democratic Party's (PDP) vision is articulated in the party's Self-Rule document. The document suggests a slew of political measures advocating a sub-regional trade arrangement with a Free Trade Zone in Jammu and Kashmir to be implemented under SAFTA or under a separate arrangement between New Delhi and Islamabad. The PDP also believes that facilitating free movement of goods and people through the traditional cross-LOC routes would help the policy makers on the two sides of the divide to facilitate the political changes in Jammu and Kashmir. It also says that opening up of Srinagar-Muzaffarabad and Poonch-Rawalakote roads along the LOC is a stepping- stone towards forging a new economic alliance in the region.

Trust deficit between the Centre and the States

The eleventh is the trust deficit between the Prime Minister and the Chief Ministers. Often there had been complaints and confrontations between the Prime Minister and the Chief Ministers on some sensitive issues. It was a common occurrence in the National Development Council meetings and the Inter State Council meetings when Chief Ministers like N.T. Rama Rao, Farooq Abdullah and Jayalalithaa had walked out during various regimes protesting against the way they were treated by the Centre. **The 'Team India' concept propagated by Prime Minister Modi will be his litmus test in the coming years, particularly on foreign policy.**

His election campaign and the BJP's manifesto have spoken of a muscular foreign policy, a tougher line on Pakistan, review of India's nuclear doctrine, and also a bigger role for States in foreign policy-making. His campaign speeches, the BJP manifesto, his public statements and interviews to the media have all indicated his intention to radically repair, reform and restructure the Centre – State relations. Will he be able to do it?

The Congress as well as the BJP manifestoes recognized the need to maintain cordial relations with neighbouring countries, but neither had any specific solutions. Nor did the manifestos come up with suggestions on managing relationship with key countries such as China or the U.S. The rather general outlook captured in the manifestos reflects that they are reluctant to commit on complex foreign policy issues.

Modi's priority should be to bridge the trust deficit between the Centre and the States, specifically between the Prime Minister and Chief Ministers. He had often talked about how the policies must factor in regional aspirations. As Chief Minister of Gujarat, Modi had advocated that States should take a more significant role in shaping and directing foreign policy, particularly on economic matters. He had not visualized a formal body, as he would like to work within the exclusive jurisdiction of the Centre. This brings us to the question how he might deal with the States ruled by the Opposition parties? He has no choice but to befriend them if he wants smooth functioning. If he were able to introduce federalism in both letter and spirit, then he would have succeeded in his mission.

There is a huge communication gap between the Prime Minister and the Chief Ministers of the Opposition ruled States. Former Foreign Secretary Shyam Saran notes that Pandit Nehru was in constant touch with the Chief Ministers and informed them regularly of what was happening not only in foreign policy but also in other spheres. This continued and even Narasimha Rao had good rapport with State leaders who were from different parties. Vajpayee also used to be in touch. "This seems to have diminished in the past decade. That is not a good thing. In a federal setup like India that is very critical".[6]

While there is nothing wrong in the system as such what was wrong was that those who were running the system were not running it in the spirit it was envisaged by the framers of the constitution. The

6   Author's interview with Shyam Saran, (6,January, 2014)

first generation leaders or even the second-generation leaders like Narasimha Rao had practiced that consultation process. "It is such a diverse country which required whatever may be your differences politically you needed to have that easy personal relationship with leaders of other parties and State leaders so that on important issues of national interest you are able to get a national consensus.[7] " For instance Rao sent Leader of Opposition Vajpayee to the UN meeting in Geneva demonstrating to the rest of the world that on matters of importance and foreign policy the nation was one. "I think the system that has been put in place is quite all right. You need also people who understand how to work that system and how to take the best in that system.[8] "

Keeping the national interests foremost while taking a decision on foreign policy is also vital. Former Foreign Secretary Muchkund Dubey observes that one of the most difficult issues before the country is that national purpose is getting lost in the preferential priority given to regional considerations. The federal character was distorted to the extent that the States have started interfering in foreign policy of the government. Instead of taking national perspective it is on the narrow perspective of the people of that area. The party in power should not make concessions in policies for opportunistic considerations or domestic considerations. "I am all for India becoming truly federal. But does Mamata Banerjee feel this way or Jayalalithaa feels this way? For them federal means some more money should be given to them. Nitish Kumar wants a special status for Bihar. The country's overall integrity and unity is struck by this kind of behaviour."[9]

Ambassador Kanwal Sibal notes, "too much power has shifted from the Centre to the States. Number two; it has become so important to maintain your popular share of the votes that you are devising all kinds of things to corner those votes. [10]"Consultation

---

7   Author's interview with Shyam Saran, (6,January, 2014)

8   Author's interview with Shyam Saran, (6,January, 2014)

9   Author's interview with Muchkund Dubey (10, July 2014)

10 Author's interview with Kanwal Sibal, (13 July 2014)

with States on mutually beneficial and tricky issues could even prevent ugly diplomatic rows. States have concerns about some contentious issues including Siachen Glacier, Sir Creek, the Rann of Kutch, and Katchateevu. After all, in case of the likely use of missiles, chemical, biological, and nuclear weapons in the eventuality of a war, the border and coastal States would bear the major brunt notes Sibal. This could be done through a consultative committee headed by the External Affairs Minister and including the Chief Ministers of the Border States as its members.

There are others who believe that there is need for a mechanism to evolve and build a consensus with the stakeholders. Holding annual consultation meetings on foreign policy and also bi annual regional consultations on specific issues would go a long way in this regard.

The Prime Minister should also include some Chief Ministers in his delegation when he embarks on his foreign visits. The classic example was when Manmohan Singh took Chief Ministers of the North-eastern States during his visit to Dhaka in September 2011 there was all round appreciation. These are necessary in view of the trend in accepting involvement of State leaders as a matter of policy and necessity. The Centre should also ensure that foreign policy should not be overtaken by domestic politics and regional interests should merge with national interests.

Lessons Learnt

While dealing with the neighbours, the lessons learnt from the past mistakes should also be kept in mind. Being a bigger neighbour, India has had some bitter and some good experiences in its ties with them. A positive lesson is that economic interests overtake other interests in dealing with the neighbours. If you look at the neighbouring countries, the economic ties are getting stronger with the Northeast in the past two decades due to liberalization and the "Look East " policy. This is true of even Pakistan and China where the two countries have decided to keep aside the contentious issues and move forward in trade and commerce. Even in Sri Lanka, Bangladesh and Pakistan, New Delhi began to concentrate on the trade and investment coinciding with the liberalization measures.

The Free Trade Agreement signed in 1998 with Sri Lanka was a laudable measure to boost these ties.

India assumed that after the departure of the British, she would emerge as the regional leader and adopted a big brother attitude towards all the smaller neighbours. The running theme in India's neighbourly relations was that the neighbours, most of them small, feel that India is a big bully and trying to dominate them. Whether it is right or wrong, New Delhi should try to remove this perception. They have good reason to complain because India has interfered in their internal be it Nepal, Bangladesh or Sri Lanka.

A lot has happened in India-Nepal relations as suspicion and mistrust had replaced friendliness and mutual understanding despite the two nations sharing cultural, historic, religious and social traditions. New Delhi had many missed opportunities as Ambassador K.S. Rajan notes. "It is remarkable that successive governments in both the countries have so comprehensively failed to establish a stable, mature relationship based on mutual trust and a long term vision of cooperation."[11] While Modi's visits had inspired confidence of the Nepalese that things would improve, unfortunately after the declaration of the new Nepal Constitution on September 20 upsetting the Madheshis and the subsequent blockade at the open border check points has worsened the situation. Nepal political parties continue to accuse New Delhi of interfering in their domestic politics and destabilising the governments.

Bangladesh thinks that New Delhi was trying to exploit Dhaka in water related and trade and transit issues. India should also learn the lesson that expediting trade and transit facilities with Bangladesh would go long a way in improving the economic situation in both the countries. Things have improved after Modi took over, particularly after the LBA agreement but problems still remain on illegal immigration, water sharing and other contentious issues. Both sides have tried to move forward to bridge deficit and the high level contacts need to be continued. Connectivity schemes and water problems should be taken up on priority basis. For instance, when

11 K.V. Rajan, *Editor, J.N. Dixit, 'External Affairs- Cross Border Relations,'* Roli Books, 2003, P 97

Gen. V.K. Singh, then Minister for Northeast went to Bangladesh in 2014, he had talked to Sheikh Hasina on the up gradation of Chittagong port, which would make transport cheaper and quicker.

The mistakes committed in India's Sri Lankan policy needs a special mention. As Bhasin notes "The story of the ethnic conflict in Sri Lanka is one of false hopes, raised emotions, disappointments turning into bitterness and bitterness into frustration and finally frustration into conflict. With each Indian intervention new illusions were created and entertained, new hopes raised and new bitterness, frustration and conflict followed." [12]

New Delhi got so involved in the Sri Lankan Tamil issue that it burnt its fingers by interfering in the affairs of the island nation. The Sri Lankan policy was inconsistent throughout. Some experts feel that Indira Gandhi's idea of giving training and arms to the LTTE was wrong. By giving training to the militant groups India did not cover herself in glory. They consider Rajiv Gandhi's meddling with the Sri Lankan affairs was a misadventure. Sending the Indian Peace Keeping Force was yet another mistake. The basic fault was that New Delhi took upon the role of the mediator without the corresponding influence with the Tamil groups for a negotiated settlement. The IPKF blunder was yet another lesson India should learn. As A.S. Bhasin notes, "if the aim of Indian intervention was to stop any outside elements a toe-hold in the region, it ended up in achieving just the opposite of it. Politically India stood marginalized from any role in Sri Lanka while elements outside the region ruled the roost. [13]"

It is clear that the Manmohan Singh government not only knew what was going on in Sri Lanka but also cooperated with Rajapakse in wiping out the LTTE. This aspect has come out clearly in the author's interviews with the Sri Lankan and Indian leaders. It bowed down to the pressure of the Tamil Nadu political parties.

---

12 Avtar Singh Bhasin, Avtar Singh Bhasin,' *India and Sri Lanka, Between the Lion and the Tigers,* 'Manas publications, 2004, P326

13 Avtar Singh Bhasin, '*India and Sri Lanka, Between the Lion and the Tigers,*' Manas publications, 2004, P 321.

The mistake of Singh was bowing to the pressure of the State when he could not persuade the West Bengal Chief Minister Mamata Banerjee to agree for the Teesta Treaty. He should have personally intervened to take her on board.

The third was that Manmohan Singh did not bother to undertake any bilateral visit to the neighbouring countries although he did visit them for SAARC summits. This sent a signal that he did not care for good neighbourly relations. His entire first term went concentrating on the Indo -US nuclear deal and the second term in the damage control on the series of scams. To that extent Modi had already visited Bhutan, Nepal and Sri Lanka and Bangladesh.

The fourth mistake was that New Delhi is yet to shed the image of 'the big bully' to its neighbours and make them believe that India genuinely wants the stability and economic prosperity in the neighbourhood. Modi's slogan "B to B" (Bharat to Bhutan) was a good initiative. For the past ten years New Delhi has done little to correct this perception. Even as recently as 2015 May when Nepal faced a massive earthquake, the Nepalese felt that India was trying to boast of its help to deal with the disaster and was upset at the way Indian media showed it in the television with the result the media was asked to leave. Nepal has gone back to the anti- India mode and holds New Delhi responsible for its political instability.

Prime Minister Modi aims to revitalise regional integration and has made it clear that India wants to improve its relationship with all its neighbours at a bilateral level even as efforts to boost regional cooperation will go on a parallel track. In a significant move the Joint Working group consisting of Banglh, Bhutan, Indian and Nepal, held their second meeting in January 2015. Foreign Secretary Jaishankar's SAARC Yatra in February – March 2015 is notable in this direction. Pakistan poses a critical challenge in Modi's policy of proactive engagement with India's neighbours.

In conclusion, when you look at the neighbourhood, India has no real friends. As Prof S.D. Muni points out "During any crisis, there are very few and feeble voices of sympathy and support from the neighbouring countries. Even those who stand by us do not feel confident about whether we would go to their help in the hour of need. We have no political or economic constituencies in the neighbouring countries because we never thought of cultivating such constituencies. Many of India's security challenges, including those related to internal insurgency and terrorism are enhanced and complicated by the neighbours to score bargaining points." [14]

To overcome all these, the Modi government should make efforts to see that the neighbours perceive India to be warm, considerate and friendly to the neighbours. The biggest challenge for India's neighbourhood policy should be to convince neighbours that India is an opportunity, not a threat.

There is need for heavy political initiatives in this regard. As for the growing assertion of the regional satraps Sushma Swaraj says, "All these States have always expressed their concerns, which are their legitimate right, and it is their duty to tell us and we try to address those concerns but the foreign policy is the domain of the Central Government. We will take them on board and try to address their concern as far as possible." [15]

Modi has another three years to complete his term. Only time will tell whether his 'neighbours first' and his 'cooperative federalism' concept will work well on the ground or the "States first" assertion of the regional chieftains will derail it. His intentions are good but it is the implementation, which matters.

---

14 S.D.Muni,' *Win their awe and affection'*, The Tribune special supplement, September 24,2005

15 Author's interview with Sushma Swaraj, (March 2015)

Index

A

Aam Admi Party 4, 28, 29, 30

Akhil Bharatiya Vidyarti Parishad (ABVP) 232

All Assam Students Union (AASU) 186, 226

All India Dravida Munnetra Kazhagam (AIADMK) 20, 44, 47, 49, 64, 66, 82, 86, 93, 94, 106, 108, 111, 114, 117, 118, 119, 121, 126, 134, 135, 137, 140, 142, 144, 146, 147, 148, 149, 150, 151, 159

Amarinder Singh 51, 317

Asom Gana Parishad (AGP) 31, 186, 219

Association of Southeast Asian Nations (ASEAN) 6, 36, 37

Awami League 57, 161, 167, 168, 169, 170, 171, 172, 179, 182, 183, 185, 187, 188, 193, 195, 196, 197, 202, 231, 235, 237

B

Babri Masjid 188

Baburam Bhattarai 53, 278, 289, 293

Bahujan Samaj Party 27, 28, 30, 48, 58

Balasaheb Thackeray 224

Bangladesh, China, India and Myanmar Economic Corridor (BCIM) 215

Bangladesh Nationalist Party (BNP) 183

Bharatiya Janata Party 4, 156, 219, 232

Biju Patnaik 28

B.P Koirala 246, 259, 263, 264, 269

C

Centre for National Security and Strategic Centre 5

Ceylon Workers Congress (CWC) 74, 124